the Unofficial Guide® to San Francisco

1st Edition

Also available from Macmillan Travel:

the Unofficial Guide® to San Francisco

1st Edition

Joe Surkiewicz and
Bob Sehlinger
with
Richard Sterling

Macmillan • USA

Macmillan Travel
A Simon & Schuster Macmillan Company
1633 Broadway
New York, New York 10019-6785

Produced by Menasha Ridge Press
Design by Barbara E. Williams

MACMILLAN is a registered trademark of Macmillan, Inc.
UNOFFICIAL GUIDE is a registered trademark of Simon & Schuster, Inc.

ISBN 0-02-862249-9

ISSN 1096-522X

Manufactured in the United States of America

10 9 8 7 6 5 4 3 2 1
First edition

CONTENTS

LIST OF MAPS

ACKNOWLEDGMENTS

San Francisco, while compact, is an amazingly diverse city—not to mention hectic and intense. We'd like to thank the folks who shared their knowledge of the city and helped us as we researched and wrote this book.

Kudos to Kristin Rhyan Brown of the San Francisco Convention and Visitors Bureau, who always pulled the rabbit out of the hat—from finding us affordable hotel rooms with minimal warning to locating tickets for Beach Blanket Babylon. Renee Wong of the Moscone Convention Center found time in her busy schedule to give us a tour of that huge facility.

Darlene DuCharme of the Sonoma Valley Visitors Bureau provided insight for daytrippers to her neck of the wine country, while Jan Austerman at the Napa Valley Convention and Visitors Bureau flooded us with information—and almost talked us into taking a Calistoga mud bath (maybe next year).

Richard Sterling, author of *The Eclectic Gourmet Guide to San Francisco* (Menasha Ridge Press) wrote our sections on dining and night life. Former *Washington Post* reporter Joe Brown (now a happily transplanted San Franciscan) contributed to our section on shopping. He's also the author of *Frommer's San Francisco by Night* and *Travel and Leisure Washington, D.C.* (Macmillan). Rob Delamater, marketing director of Joie de Vivre Hotels, provided all kinds of insider tips, from great views to some hidden places most visitors miss.

Thanks to Ann Lembo for coming to the city and acting as driver and research assistant for Joe, temporarily hobbled by a broken left wrist. And double thanks to hand therapists Heidi Miranda-Walsh and Mary Formby (in Baltimore) and Nancy Chee (in San Francisco) for working their magic on his left forearm throughout the book-writing process (making it possible for him to type).

Cindy France, Sherry Burns, and Greg Dohler provided invaluable touring insights based on their excursions in the Bay Area. Dewayne Tully of the San Francisco Police Department and Pam Matsuda of SAFE gave us insights into crime pre-vention in the city. Mary Jane Schramm at the Oceanic Society Expeditions provided the lowdown on whale-watching excursions from San Francisco.

To fulfill their task, the hotel inspection team of Holly Brown and Grace Walton braved downtown traffic, brazen panhandlers, and spectacular Marin scenery as they zipped around the Bay Area.

—Joe Surkiewicz

The City by the Bay

America's favorite city sits on the edge of the Pacific Rim, a location that lends romance to its image of sophistication and enchantment. At the place where the edge of the continent plunges into the Pacific, San Francisco is awash with multiple dimensions. Honeymooners are lured by its romantic charm, seasoned travelers like the civilized pace and dramatic views, families appreciate the many attractions for children, and business executives are thrilled to have their conventions here year after year.

Situated on a peninsula that covers only 47 square miles (and 43 steep hills), San Francisco is a steel-and-glass metropolis with a population of 750,000. Mediterranean in mood, it's a city of foghorns and bridges, cable cars and ferries, North Beach and Chinatown. Comfortable with its contradictions, the city jealously preserves its past while always riding the latest wave of fashion, whether in haute cuisine, gay and lesbian politics, or social movements.

The gateway to Asia, San Francisco supports a multicultural population of Chinese, Japanese, Hispanics, Filipinos, Italians, and African Americans. Adding to this cosmopolitan bouillabaisse is a gay population that may constitute as much as 25% of its total population. So it's no surprise that San Francisco is a town with a strong sense of neighborhood; the neighborhoods overlap and interrelate, but they maintain distinct identities.

Most importantly for visitors, San Francisco is an enchantingly beautiful city, offering stunning panoramas, wooden Victorian houses, pocket parks and open green spaces, and the shimmering bay and ocean. Even the town's moody weather patterns contribute to its charm, alternately drenching the city in sunlight and bathing it in swirling fog.

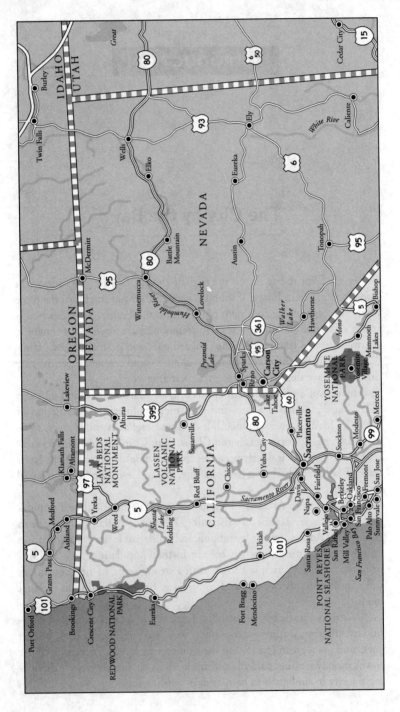

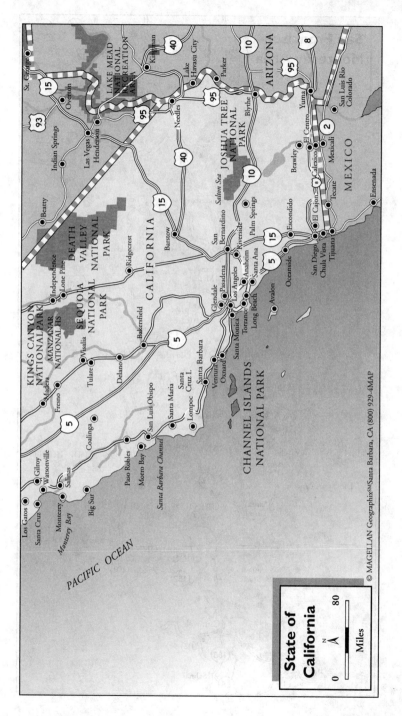

State of
California

© MAGELLAN Geographix℠Santa Barbara, CA (800) 929-4MAP

3

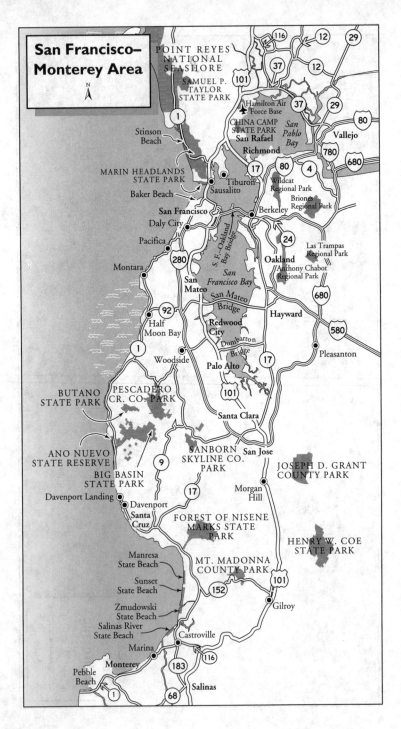

San Francisco–Monterey Area

N

POINT REYES
NATIONAL
SEASHORE

SAMUEL P.
TAYLOR
STATE PARK

Hamilton Air
Force Base

CHINA CAMP
STATE PARK
San Rafael

Richmond

*San
Pablo
Bay*

Vallejo

Stinson
Beach

MARIN HEADLANDS
STATE PARK

Tiburon
Sausalito

Wildcat
Regional Park

Briones
Regional Park

Baker Beach

San Francisco

Daly City

Berkeley

Pacifica

S. F.–Oakland
Bay Bridge

Oakland

24

Las Trampas
Regional Park

Montara

280

*San
Francisco Bay*

Anthony Chabot
Regional Park

**San
Mateo**

San Mateo
Bridge

Hayward

680

92

Half
Moon Bay

**Redwood
City**

Dumbarton
Bridge

580

Pleasanton

Woodside

Palo Alto

17

1

101

BUTANO
STATE PARK

PESCADERO
CR. CO. PARK

Santa Clara

ANO NUEVO
STATE RESERVE

9

SANBORN
SKYLINE CO.
PARK

San Jose

JOSEPH D. GRANT
COUNTY PARK

BIG BASIN
STATE PARK

Davenport Landing

17

Morgan
Hill

Davenport
**Santa
Cruz**

FOREST OF NISENE
MARKS STATE
PARK

HENRY W. COE
STATE PARK

Manresa
State Beach

MT. MADONNA
COUNTY PARK

Sunset
State Beach

152

101

Zmudowski
State Beach

Salinas River
State Beach

Gilroy

Marina

Castroville

116

Monterey

183

Pebble
Beach

68

Salinas

San Francisco's romance factor is high. Visitors climb a hill, turn a corner, and stumble upon breathtaking vistas. It's an easy city to navigate, with a European-style public transportation system that whisks people to its wide array of appealing neighborhoods. This is one of the few cities in the country where you don't need a car to get around.

San Francisco also ranks in the front lines of culture, with a world-class opera house, symphony, and ballet company and several excellent art museums, including the best collection of Asian art in the West. Europeans love San Francisco because it's the most European of American cities, and Hispanics gravitate to its Spanish-speaking community. It's home to one of the largest Chinese populations in the United States. Even New Yorkers like San Francisco, comparing it favorably with the Big Apple.

Yet for all its charms, the city has real problems. Drug use and street crime are a fact of life. As the de facto gay capital of the world, the city continues to grapple with a massive AIDS crisis. The level of homelessness on the streets is a disgrace. Traffic congestion is as bad as anywhere in the country, with no long-term solutions in sight.

Nor is everyone in agreement that San Francisco is, culturally speaking, the Athens of the West. Lewis H. Lapham, whose grandfather was mayor of San Francisco, swore off the city and moved east, where he became editor of Harper's magazine. "Although in the past eighteen years I often have thought of the city with feelings of sadness, as if in mourning for the beauty of the hills and the clarity of the light in September when the wind blows from the north, I have no wish to return," he writes. "The San Francisco school of painting consisted of watercolor views of Sausalito and Fisherman's Wharf; there was no theater, and the opera was a means of setting wealth to music. The lack of art or energy in the city reflected the lassitude of a citizenry content to believe its own press notices."

Lapham continues: "The wandering bedouin of the American desert traditionally migrate to California in hope of satisfying their hearts' desire under the palm tree of the national oasis. . . . Thus their unhappiness and despair when their journey proves to have been in vain. The miracle fails to take place, and things remain pretty much as they were in Buffalo or Indianapolis. Perhaps this explains the high rate of divorce, alcoholism , and suicide."

First-time visitors on vacation also face real difficulties. The city has no distinctive center, such as, say, New York's Times Square or Washington's National Mall. While comprehensive, the public transportation system can be confusing and overcrowded, while some of the best-known neighborhoods (such as North Beach and Nob Hill) lack major attractions for visitors to focus on. Exploring San Francisco for the first time might be likened to plunging into icy waters.

The *Unofficial Guide* can help. This book is designed for folks planning a family trip to see San Francisco's famous vistas, distinct neighborhoods, excellent museums and theater companies, and fabled night life; and for business travelers who want to avoid its worst hassles. We show you the best times to visit the city's best-known sights, how to get off the beaten path, and when to avoid the worst crowds and traffic. We suggest the best seasons to visit and offer detailed itineraries and touring strategies for seeing some spectacular destinations beyond the city limits.

In spite of the city's problems and the challenges it presents to first-time visitors, San Francisco never fails to charm. Like the joke says, San Francisco is everyone's favorite city—even people who have never been there. Although locals have been accused of being smug about the Bay Area, most enjoy sharing its attractions. With their help, and armed with this book, you're ready to discover the incomparable City by the Bay.

About This Guide

▪ How Come "Unofficial"? ▪

Most "official" guides to San Francisco tout the well-known sights, promote the local restaurants and hotels indiscriminately, and leave out a lot of good stuff. This one is different.

Instead of pandering to the tourist industry, we'll tell you if it's not worth the wait for the mediocre food served a well-known restaurant, we'll complain loudly about overpriced hotel rooms that aren't convenient to downtown or the Moscone Convention Center, and we'll guide you away from the crowds and congestion for a break now and then.

Without a well-defined city center such as Chicago's Loop or New York's Times Square, San Francisco can confuse first-time visitors. We sent in a team of evaluators who toured downtown, its outlying neighborhoods and popular attractions, ate in the Bay Area's best restaurants, performed critical evaluations of its hotels, and visited San Francisco's best nightclubs. If a museum is boring or a major attraction is overrated, we say so—and, in the process, hopefully make your visit more fun, efficient, and economical.

We got into the guidebook business because we were unhappy with the way travel guides make the reader work to get any usable information. Wouldn't it be nice, we thought, if we made guides that were easy to use?

▪ Other Guide Books ▪

Most guidebooks are compilations of lists. This is true regardless of whether the information is presented in list form or artfully distributed through pages of prose. There is insufficient detail in a list, and with prose the presentation can be tedious and contain large helpings of nonessential or marginally useful information. Not enough wheat, so to speak, for nourishment in one instance, and too much chaff in the other. Either way, these guides provide little more than departure points from which readers initiate their own quests.

Many guides are readable and well researched, but they tend to be difficult to use. To select a hotel, for example, a reader must study several pages of descriptions with only the names of the hotels in bold type breaking up the text. Because each description essentially deals with the same variables, it is difficult to recall what was said concerning a particular hotel. Readers generally have no alternative but to work through all the write-ups before beginning to narrow their choices. The presentation of restaurants, clubs, and attractions is similar except that even more reading is usually required. To use such a guide is to undertake an exhaustive research process that requires examining nearly as many options and possibilities as starting from scratch. Recommendations, if any, lack depth and conviction. These guides compound rather than solve problems by failing to narrow travelers' choices down to a thoughtfully considered, well-distilled, and manageable few.

■ How *Unofficial Guides* Are Different ■

Readers care about the author's opinion. The author, after all, is supposed to know what he is talking about. This, coupled with the fact that the traveler wants quick answers (as opposed to endless alternatives), dictates that authors should be explicit, prescriptive, and, above all, direct. The *Unofficial Guide* tries to do just that. It spells out alternatives and recommends specific courses of action. It simplifies complicated destinations and attractions and allows the traveler to feel in control in the most unfamiliar environments. The objective of the *Unofficial Guide* is not to have the most information or all of the information; it aims to have the most accessible, useful information, unbiased by affiliation with any organization or industry.

An *Unofficial Guide* is a critical reference work that focuses on a travel destination that appears especially complex. Our authors and research team are completely independent from the attractions, restaurants, and hotels we describe. The *Unofficial Guide to San Francisco* is designed for individuals and families traveling for fun, as well as for business travelers and convention-goers, especially those visiting the city for the first time. The guide is directed at value-conscious, consumer-oriented adults who seek a cost-effective, though not Spartan, travel style.

■ Special Features ■

The *Unofficial Guide* incorporates the following special features:

- Friendly introductions to San Francisco's vast array of fascinating neighborhoods.
- "Best of" listings giving our well-qualified opinions on things ranging from bagels to baguettes, four-star hotels to the best views of San Francisco and the Bay Area by night.

- Listings keyed to your interests, so you can pick and choose.
- Advice to sight-seers on how to avoid crowds; advice to business travelers on how to avoid traffic and excessive cost.
- A zone system and maps to make it easy to find places you want to go to and avoid places you don't.
- Expert advice on avoiding San Francisco's street and highway crime.
- A hotel chart that helps narrow your choices fast, according to your needs.
- Shorter listings that include only those restaurants, clubs, and hotels we think are worth considering.
- A detailed index and table of contents to help you find things quickly.

■ How This Guide Was Researched and Written ■

While a lot of guidebooks have been written about San Francisco, very little has been evaluative. Some guides come close to regurgitating the hotels' and tourist offices' own promotional material. In preparing this work, nothing was taken for granted. Each museum, monument, art gallery, hotel, restaurant, shop, and attraction was visited by a team of trained observers who conducted detailed evaluations and rated each according to formal criteria. Interviews were conducted to determine what tourists of all ages enjoyed most and least during their San Francisco visit.

While our observers are independent and impartial, we do not claim to have special expertise. Like you, they visited San Francisco as tourists or business travelers, noting their satisfaction or dissatisfaction.

The primary difference between the average tourist and the trained evaluator is the evaluator's skills in organization, preparation, and observation. The trained evaluator is responsible for much more than simply observing and cataloging. While the average tourist is engrossed when touring Alcatraz, for instance, the professional is rating the attraction in terms of pace, how quickly crowds move, the location of rest rooms, and how well children can see through the cellhouse windows to the San Francisco skyline across the bay. The evaluator also checks out other nearby attractions, alternatives places to go if the line at a main attraction is too long, and the best local lunch options. Observer teams used detailed checklists to analyze hotel rooms, restaurants, nightclubs, and attractions. Finally, evaluator ratings and observations were integrated with tourist reactions and the opinions of patrons for a comprehensive, quality profile of each feature and service.

In compiling this guide, we recognize that tourists' age, background, and interests will strongly influence their taste in San Francisco's wide array of activities and attractions and will account for a preference of one over another. Our sole objective is to provide the reader with sufficient description, critical evaluation, and pertinent data to make knowledgeable decisions according to individual tastes.

■ **Letters, Comments, and Questions from Readers** ■

We expect to learn from our mistakes, as well as from the input of our readers, and to improve with each book and edition. Many of those who use the *Unofficial Guides* write to us asking questions, making comments, or sharing their own discoveries and lessons learned in San Francisco. We appreciate all such input, both positive and critical, and encourage our readers to continue writing. Readers' comments and observations will be frequently incorporated in revised editions of the *Unofficial Guide* and will contribute immeasurably to its improvement.

How to Write the Authors:

Joe and Bob
The Unofficial Guide to San Francisco
P.O. Box 43059
Birmingham, AL 35243

When you write, be sure to put your return address on your letter as well as on the envelope—sometimes envelopes and letters get separated. And remember, our work takes us out of the office for long periods of time, so forgive us if our response is delayed.

Reader Survey

At the back of the guide you will find a short questionnaire that you can use to express opinions concerning your San Francisco visit. Clip the questionnaire along the dotted line and mail it to the above address.

■ **How Information Is Organized: By Subject** ■
and by Geographic Zones

To give you fast access to information about the best of San Francisco, we've organized material in several formats.

Hotels Because most people visiting San Francisco stay in one hotel for the duration for their trip, we have summarized our coverage of hotels in charts, maps, ratings, and rankings that allow you to quickly focus your decision-making process. We do not go on for page after page describing lobbies and rooms that, in the final analysis, sound much the same. Instead we concentrate on the variables that differentiate one hotel from another: location, size, room quality, services, amenities, and cost.

Restaurants   We provide a lot of detail when it comes to restaurants. Because you will probably eat a dozen or more restaurant meals during your stay, and because not even you can predict what you might be in the mood for on Saturday night, we provide detailed profiles of the best restaurants in and around San Francisco.

Entertainment and Night Life   Visitors frequently try several different clubs or night spots during their stay. Because clubs and night spots, like restaurants, are usually selected spontaneously after arriving in San Francisco, we believe detailed descriptions are warranted. The best night spots and lounges in San Francisco are profiled by category under night life in the same section (see pages 140–162).

Geographic Zones   Once you've decided where you're going, getting there becomes the issue. To help you do that, we have divided the San Francisco Bay area into geographic zones.

Zone 1. Chinatown	Zone 2. Civic Center
Zone 3. Union Square	Zone 4. Financial District
Zone 5. Marina	Zone 6. North Beach
Zone 7. SoMa/Mission	Zone 8. Richmond/Avenues
Zone 9. Waterfront Crescent	Zone 10. Suburban Marin
Zone 11. Yonder Marin	Zone 12. Berkeley
Zone 13. Oakland	Zone 14. South Bay

All profiles of hotels, restaurants, and night spots include zone numbers. If you are staying at the Maxwell Hotel near San Francisco's Union Square, for example, and are interested in a steak dinner, scanning the restaurant profiles for restaurants in Zone 3 (Union Square) will provide you with the best choices.

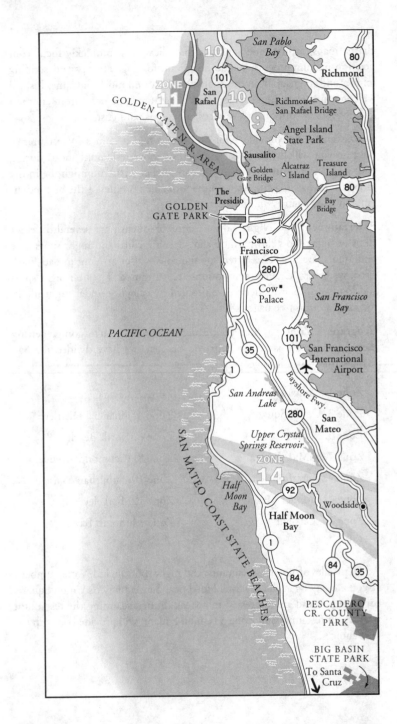

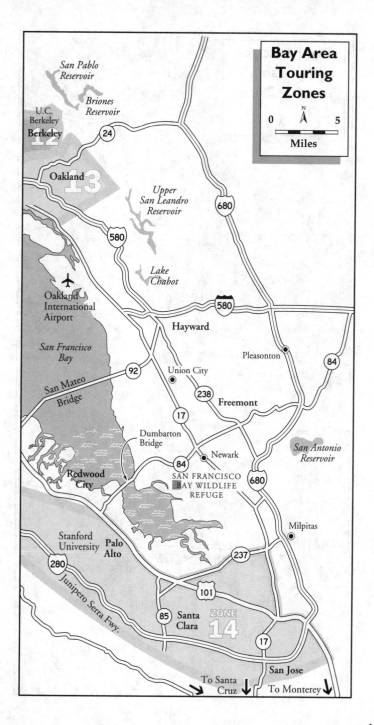

Bay Area Touring Zones

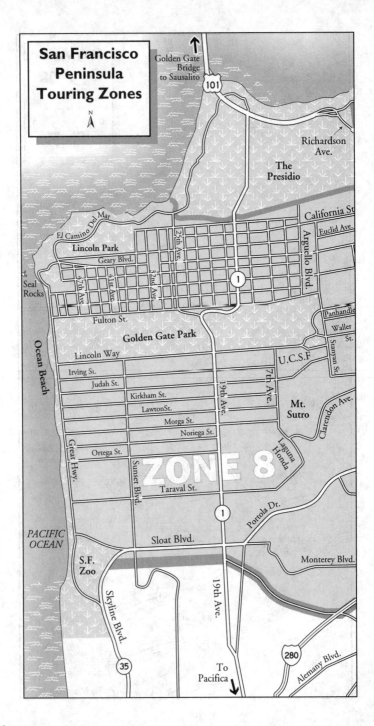

San Francisco Peninsula Touring Zones

N

Golden Gate Bridge to Sausalito

101

Richardson Ave.

The Presidio

California St

El Camino Del Mar

Euclid Ave.

Lincoln Park

Geary Blvd.

25th Ave.

32nd Ave.

Arguello Blvd.

1

Seal Rocks

47th Ave.

41st Ave.

Fulton St.

Golden Gate Park

Panhandle

Waller St.

Ocean Beach

Lincoln Way

U.C.S.F.

Stanyan St.

Irving St.

Judah St.

Kirkham St.

LawtonSt.

Morga St.

Noriega St.

7th Ave.

19th Ave.

Mt. Sutro

Clarendon Ave.

Great Hwy.

Ortega St.

Sunset Blvd.

ZONE 8

Taraval St.

Laguna Honda

PACIFIC OCEAN

Sloat Blvd.

1

Portola Dr.

S.F. Zoo

Monterey Blvd.

Skyline Blvd.

19th Ave.

35

To Pacifica

280

Alemany Blvd.

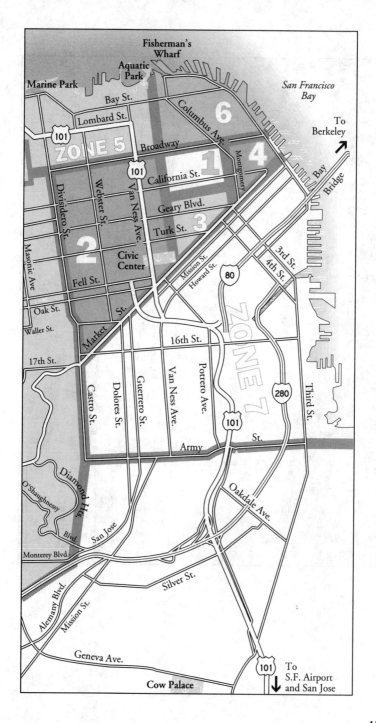

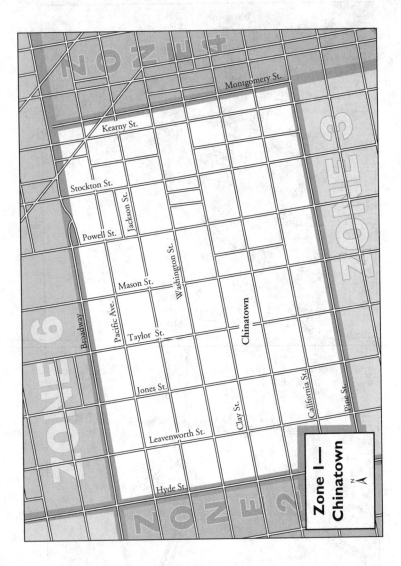

Zone 1—
Chinatown

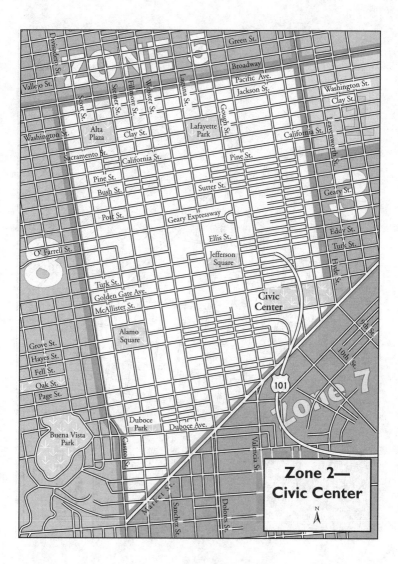

Zone 2—
Civic Center

N

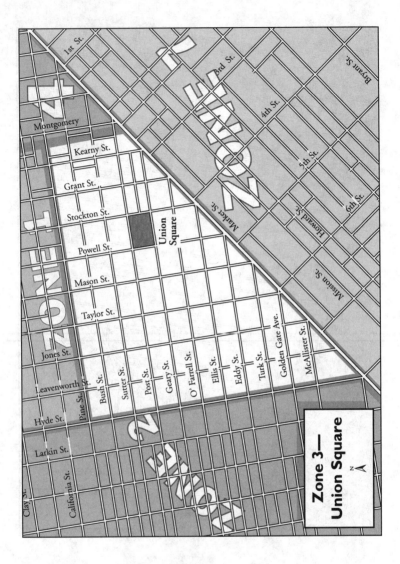

Zone 3—
Union Square

N

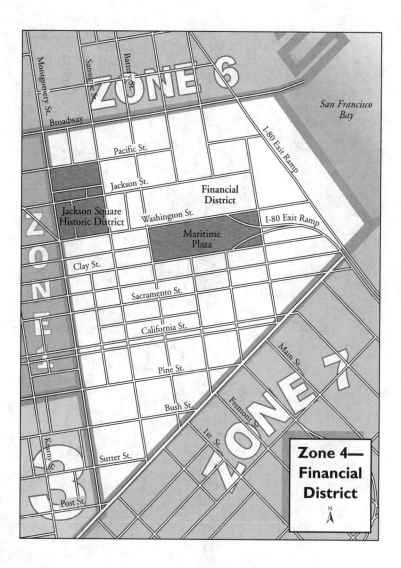

Zone 4—
Financial
District

N

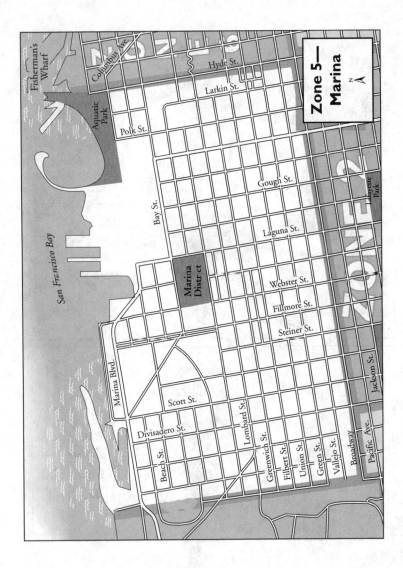

Zone 5—
Marina

N

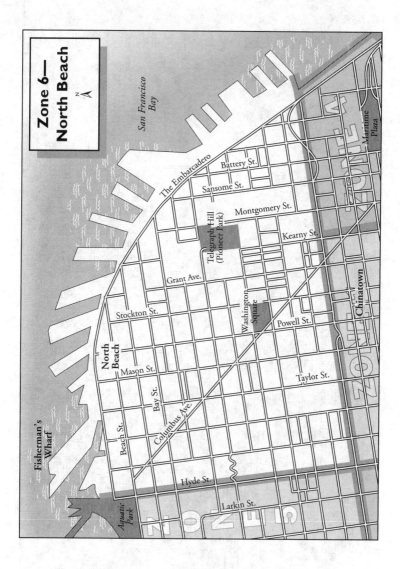

Zone 6—
North Beach

N

San Francisco
Bay

The Embarcadero

Battery St.

Sansome St.

Montgomery St.

Telegraph Hill
(Pioneer Park)

Kearny St.

Grant Ave.

Stockton St.

Washington
Square

Powell St.

North
Beach

Mason St.

Bay St.

Taylor St.

Columbus Ave.

Beach St.

Fisherman's
Wharf

Hyde St.

Larkin St.

Aquatic
Park

Chinatown

Maritime
Plaza

ZONE 4

ZONE 5

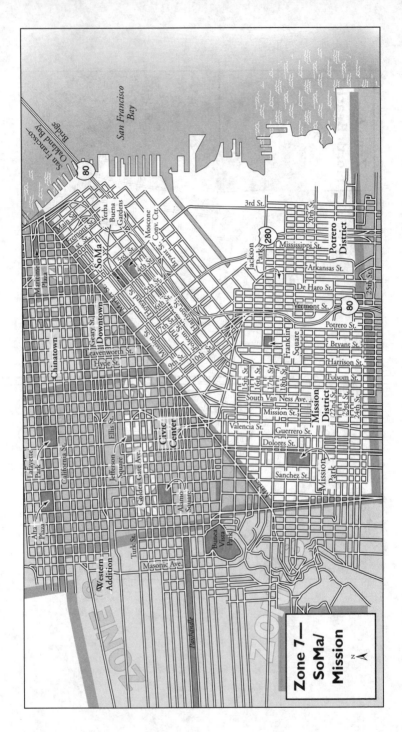

Zone 7—
SoMa/
Mission

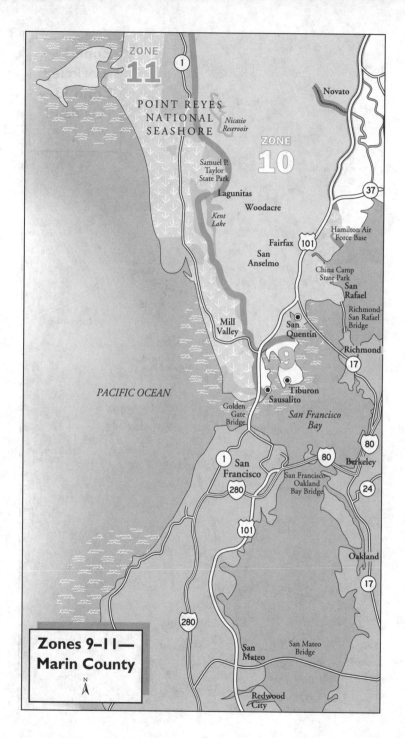

Zones 9–11—
Marin County

N

23

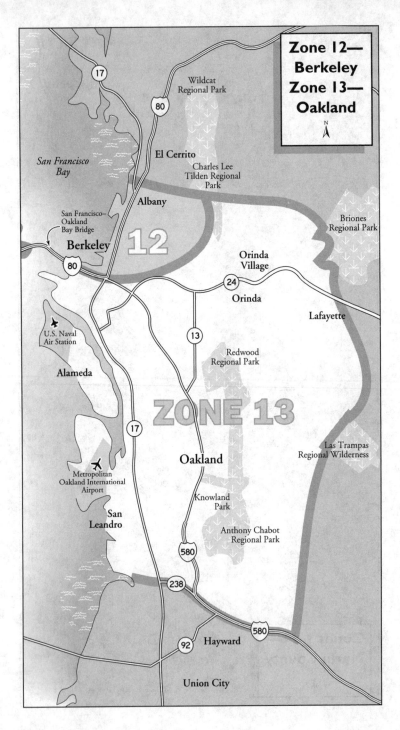

Zone 12—
Berkeley
Zone 13—
Oakland

N

17

80

Wildcat
Regional Park

El Cerrito

San Francisco
Bay

Charles Lee
Tilden Regional
Park

Albany

San Francisco–
Oakland
Bay Bridge

Briones
Regional Park

Berkeley

12

80

Orinda
Village

24

Orinda

U.S. Naval
Air Station

13

Lafayette

Alameda

Redwood
Regional Park

ZONE 13

17

Las Trampas
Regional Wilderness

Oakland

Metropolitan
Oakland International
Airport

Knowland
Park

San
Leandro

Anthony Chabot
Regional Park

580

238

580

92 Hayward

Union City

Planning Your Visit to San Francisco

Understanding the City: A Brief History of San Francisco

After New York City, San Francisco is the most densely populated city in the United States, with more than 700,000 people crowded on a 47-square-mile peninsula. Understanding why so many people choose to live here is easy: The city boasts a mild maritime climate, and its location on a hilly spit of land jutting into San Francisco Bay and overlooking the Pacific Ocean is one of the most beautiful in the world.

While the original residents were largely of German, Italian, and Irish extraction, today San Francisco's mostly middle-class inhabitants are a demographic melting pot of Anglos, Hispanics, African Americans, and Asians. Plus, the city's reputation for tolerance serves as a sort of metaphorical welcome for hippies, gays, and lesbians . . . anyone, really, not in lockstep with traditional American values. San Francisco is still considered by many to be the last bastion of civilization in America.

The Original Natives

Ironically, though, the city is young. The first Spanish settlers arrived just over 200 years ago. But for thousands of years before that, the Bay Area was occupied by Miwok, Ohlone, and Wituk Native American tribes, which lived across much of Northern California. They formed small villages and survived mainly by hunting and fishing. Not much is known about the earliest San

Francisco natives, and the ecologically conscious can only imagine the kinds of lives these Native Americans enjoyed in this beautiful landscape.

One of the first colonists characterized the Indians as "constant in their good friendship, and gentle in their manners." But without any political or social organization beyond the tribal level, it didn't take long after the first Spanish settlement was built for the local tribes to be wiped out, probably through epidemics rather than outright genocide. Today, no Bay Area Native Americans survive on their original homelands.

Early Explorers

As you drink in the view from Fort Point or the visitor center at the southern end of the Golden Gate Bridge, it's hard to imagine that ships cruising up or down the California coast could miss such an impressive sight. But they did. Dozens of European explorers, including heavy hitters such as Juan Cabrillo, Sir Francis Drake, and Sebastian Vizcaino, sailed past for centuries, oblivious of the great harbor beyond. Why? The opening is cloaked in fog for much of the year; even on clear days the East Bay hills rise behind the opening and disguise the entrance to the point of invisibility.

Sir Francis Drake may have came close. In 1579, while on a mission from Queen Elizabeth I to "annoy" the Spanish provinces, he passed by the bay's entrance. Like so many other explorers, he never saw it. Drake anchored the Golden Hind just to the north and sent several landing parties ashore. He was met by a band of Miwoks who greeted him with food and drink; in return, Drake claimed their lands for Queen Elizabeth and named them Nova Albion (New England).

The first Europeans to cast their eyes on the Bay Area and the site of the future San Francisco were in a company of 60 Spanish soldiers, mule skinners, priests, and Indians led by Gaspar de Portola. The small contingent was the advance party of 300 soldiers and clergy on an overland mission from Mexico in 1769 to secure lands north of the colony for Spain and convert the heathens. Somewhere around Half Moon Bay south of San Francisco, Portola sent out two scouting parties, one north up the coast and the other east into the mountains. Both groups returned with extraordinary descriptions of the Golden Gate and the huge bay. On November 4 the entire party gathered on an exposed ridge, overwhelmed by the incredible view. Father Crespi, the priest, wrote that the bay "could hold not only all the armadas of our Catholic Monarch, but also all those of Europe."

First Settlement

It was another six years before the Spanish sent an expedition to explore the bay Portola had discovered. Juan Manuel de Ayala became the first

European to sail into San Francisco Bay in May 1775, when he piloted the San Carlos through the Golden Gate. A year later Captain Juan Bautista de Anza came back with 200 soldiers and settlers to establish the Presidio of San Francisco, overlooking the Golden Gate. He also established a mission three miles to the southeast along a creek he named Nuestra Señora de Dolores—"Our Lady of Sorrows"—from which comes the mission's name, Mission Dolores. (It's the oldest building in San Francisco.)

Four more missions were established in the Bay Area in the following years. Each was similar, with a church and cloistered residence surrounded by irrigated fields, vineyards, and ranch lands. A contingent of soldiers protected the missions, many of which were attacked by Native Americans. To resist fire, the ubiquitous red-tiled roof replaced the thatched roof. By the end of the 18th century, the Bay Area settlements' population remained less than 1,000. Northern California was still a remote outpost and held little appeal for foreign adventurers. While the garrison was strong enough to resist Indian attacks, it would have easily fallen to attacks from the sea, had there been any.

Small towns, called "pueblos," were established to grow food for the missions and to attract settlers. The first, San Jose, was built in a broad, fertile valley south of Mission Santa Clara. Though considered successful, less than 100 inhabitants lived there until well into the 1800s. Another small village, not sanctioned by Spanish authorities, emerged between Mission Dolores and the Presidio around a deep-water landing spot southeast of Telegraph Hill. Called Yerba Buena, or "good grass" (after the sweet-smelling minty herb that grew wild on the nearby hills), it was little more than a collection of shanties and ramshackle jetties. Although not called San Francisco until the late 1840s, this was the beginning of the city.

Mexican Independence and American Settlers

In the 1820s, the Bay Area was still a remote backwater. The mission era ended with the independence of Mexico in 1821; in a few years the missions were secularized, and their lands were handed over to Californios—mostly former soldiers who had settled there after completing their service. The Mexican government hardly exercised any control over distant Yerba Buena and was more willing than the Spanish to let foreigners settle and remain.

In the early part of the decade, a number of American and British started to arrive in the Bay Area. Many were sailors who jumped ship, but some were men of substance. For the most part they fit in with the existing Mexican culture, often marrying into established families and converting to Catholicism. William Richardson, for example, arrived on a whaling ship in 1822 and stayed for the rest of his life. He married the daughter of the

Presidio commander, eventually owned most of southern Marin County, started a profitable shipping company, and ran the only ferry service across the treacherous bay waters.

While the locals were doing well by the 1840s, the Bay Area wasn't seen as having rich natural resources, and as a result it wasn't a major factor in international relations. The U.S. government decided it wanted to buy all of Mexico north of the Rio Grande in the 1830s, but nothing happened until June 1846, when the Mexican-American War broke out in Texas. U.S. naval forces quickly took over the West Coast—the fulfillment of the United States' "manifest destiny" to cover the continent from coast to coast—and captured San Francisco's Presidio on July 9.

At about the same time an interesting—although historically insignificant—event occurred north of San Francisco. An ambitious U.S. army captain, John C. Fremont, had been encouraging unhappy settlers to declare independence from Mexico and set himself up as their leader. He assembled an unofficial force of about 60 sharpshooting ex-soldiers, spread rumors that war with Mexico was imminent, and persuaded settlers to join him. The result was the Bear Flag Revolt. On June 14, 1846, a force descended on the abandoned Presidio in Sonoma, took the retired commander captive, raised a makeshift flag over the plaza, and declared California independent. The flag, featuring a grizzly bear above the words "California Republic," was eventually adopted as the California state flag.

But the republic was short-lived. Three weeks after the disgruntled settlers hoisted the flag, it was replaced by the Stars and Stripes. California was now U.S. territory. Ironically, on January 24, 1848, just nine days before the U.S. government took formal control at the signing of the Treaty of Guadalupe (which ended the war with Mexico and ceded California to the United States), gold was discovered in the Sierra Nevada foothills 100 miles east of San Francisco. It changed the face of the city—and California—forever.

The Gold Rush

James Marshall, contractor of a mill he had just built for John Sutter, discovered gold in the foothills on a 49,000-acre ranch owned by Sutter, a Swiss immigrant whose Sacramento Valley ranch had been granted to him by the Mexican governor of California. Sutter tried to keep the find a secret, but word got out. By the end of May the news was all over California; the editor of the *Californian* announced the suspension of his newspaper because the entire staff had quit. "The whole country from San Francisco to Los Angeles and from the sea shore to the base of the Sierra Nevada," he wrote, "resounds with the sordid cry of gold! GOLD! GOLD!—while the field is left half-planted, the house half-built and everything neglected but the manufacture of shovels and pickaxes." Before the year was over more prospectors arrived from neighboring territories, Mexico, and South America.

At the time gold was discovered, the total population of the Bay Area was around 2,000, about a quarter of whom lived in tiny San Francisco (changed from Yerba Buena the year before). Within a year, 100,000 men—known collectively as Forty-Niners—had arrived in California; it was one of the most madcap migrations in history. While many of the prospectors passed through San Francisco, few stayed long before moving on to the gold fields. About half made a three-month slog across the continent to get there. The rest arrived by ship in San Francisco, which at that time consisted of a few shoddily constructed buildings, abandoned hulks in the harbor, and rats overrunning filthy streets; there was also a shortage of potable drinking water. But by the winter of 1850, the shanty-town settlement began to evolve into a proper city. Former miners set up foundries and sawmills to supply prospectors, while traders arrived to cash in on miners' success, selling them clothing, food, drink, and entertainment.

The city where successful miners came to blow their hard-earned cash now boasted luxury hotels and burlesque theaters (some of which featured the semiclad "spider dance" of Lola Montez). Throughout the 1850s immigrants continued to pour into San Francisco. While many headed on to the mines, enough stuck around to increase the city's population to about 35,000 by the end of 1853. More than half were foreigners, chiefly Mexicans, Germans, Chinese, and Italians.

Early comers to the gold fields made instant fortunes by merely washing nuggets out of streams or scraping gold dust from easily accessible veins in the rock, but it was much more difficult for later arrivals. The real money was being made by merchants, many of whom charged outrageous prices for essentials: $50 for a dozen eggs, $100 for a shovel or pickax. There were reports of exuberant miners trading a shot glass full of gold dust for an equal amount of whiskey—something like $1,000 a shot.

But the real necessities were buckets, shovels, dippers, and pans. Before long, those who supplied everyday items to prospectors were richer than the miners themselves. Levi Strauss, for instance, arrived from Germany to sell tents but ended up converting his supply of canvas into durable pants. Women, too, were in short supply. Hundreds of prostitutes boarded ships in Mexico and South America, knowing their fares would be paid on arrival by captains selling them to the highest bidder.

The Gold Bust

Five years after the discovery of gold, the easy pickings were gone and the freewheeling mining camps evolved into corporate operations. San Francisco swelled from a frontier outpost to a bustling city with growing industry, a branch of the U.S. mint, and a few newspapers. But when revenues from the gold fields leveled out in the late 1850s, the speculative base that had made so many fortunes dried up. Building lots that had been advertised at premium rates couldn't be given away, banks went belly-up, and San Francisco declared bankruptcy following years of political corruption. The freewheeling city descended into near anarchy, and vigilante mobs roamed the streets. By the summer of 1856 the Committee of Vigilance was the city's de facto government and hanged petty criminals in front of enthusiastic mobs. But soon cooler heads prevailed and the city was restored to legitimate governance. The rest of the 1850s was relatively uneventful.

Boom . . .

But whatever chance San Francisco had of becoming placid ended in 1859 when another torrent of riches flowed down the slopes of the Sierras. This time it was silver, not gold. The Comstock Lode, one of the most fantastic deposits ever discovered, was a solid vein of silver mixed with gold that ranged from 10 to more than 100 feet wide and stretched to more than two miles long. It would be an even bigger boom than the gold rush of a decade before.

But most of the silver was buried several hundred feet underground, and mining it would be nothing like the freelance prospecting of the early gold rush. Many of San Francisco's great engineers, including George Hearst, Andrew Hallidie, and Adolf Sutro, put their talents to the formidable task. As the mines went deeper to get at the valuable ore, the mining companies needed larger infusions of capital, which they attracted by issuing shares dealt on the San Francisco Stock Exchange. Speculation was rampant, and the value of shares vacillated wildly depending on daily rumors and forecasts. Fortunes were made and lost in a day's trading; cagier speculators made millions. By 1863 $40 million of silver had been wrenched from the tunnels around the boomtown of Virginia City, 105 miles from San Francisco, and 2,000 mining companies had traded shares on the city's mining exchange, further pumping up the city's economy.

. . . And Bust

While San Francisco enjoyed unsurpassed prosperity in the 1860s, another major development was taking place: the construction of a transcontinental railroad, completed in 1869. While the trains opened up California, they also brought their own problems. The Southern Pacific ensnared San Francisco in its web, creating a monopoly over transportation in the Bay Area. Besides controlling long-distance railroads, the firm also owned the city's streetcar system, the network of ferry boats that crisscrossed the bay, and even the cable-car line that lifted rich San Franciscans up California Street to their Nob Hill palaces.

The coming of the railroad usurped San Francisco's role as the West Coast's primary supply point, and products began to flood in from the East well under prices that local industry could meet. At about the time the Comstock mines began to taper off, a depression set in. A series of droughts wiped out agricultural harvests, followed by the arrival of thousands of now unwanted Chinese workers who had built the railroads. As unemployment rose through the late 1870s, frustrated workers took out their aggression on the city's substantial Chinese population. At mass demonstrations, thousands rallied behind the slogan, "The Chinese Must Go!" For much of the late 19th century, San Francisco wrestled with problems of racism; the need to build a varied, stable economy; and corruption in city politics.

A Golden Age

At the beginning of the early 20th century San Francisco was entering a golden age. The city now boasted a population of some 400,000 inhabitants—about 45% of the population of California (today it's about 4%). Political corruption was still a problem, but the economy was expanding—due in equal parts to the Spanish-American War and the Klondike Gold Rush in Alaska. Both events increased ship traffic in the port, where dockworkers were beginning to organize themselves into unions on an unprecedented scale.

The Great Earthquake

Civic reformers' efforts to reform municipal abuses were well under way when what is probably San Francisco's most mythic event occurred: the Great Earthquake of 1906. On April 18 the city was awakened by violent earth tremors. At 8.1 on the Richter scale, it was the worst earthquake to hit the country before or since (over ten times as strong as the 1989 quake). While the earthquake, which lasted 48 seconds, destroyed hundreds of buildings, the postquake conflagration caused the most damage. Ruptured natural gas mains exploded and chimneys toppled, starting fires across the city that destroyed 28,000 buildings. The fire raged for three days and all but leveled the entire area from the waterfront north and south of Market Street and west to Van Ness Avenue (where mansions were dynamited to form a fire break). Five hundred people were killed in the immense disaster, and a hundred thousand were left homeless. Those who didn't flee the city made camp in what is now Golden Gate Park, where soldiers from the Presidio set up a tent city for about 20,000 displaced San Franciscans.

Recovery

Restoration of the ruined city began almost immediately. Financial assistance flooded in from around the world, $8 million in a few weeks. Even the hated Southern Pacific railroad pitched in, freighting in supplies without charge, offering free passage out of the city, and putting heavy equipment and cranes to work on clearing up rubble.

Much of the reconstruction was completed by 1912, and an era of political reform and economic restructuring was ushered in when James Rolph was elected mayor. The opening of the Panama Canal in 1914, which made the long sea journey around Cape Horn obsolete, and the first transcontinental phone call later that year (from Alexander Graham Bell himself), held great significance for San Francisco. The completion of the Civic Center and the opening of the Panama Pacific International Exhibition (which attracted 19 million visitors) were icing on the cake. The distant war in Europe had few repercussions in San Francisco beyond boosting the economy.

The Roaring Twenties and the Depression

Like most American cities, San Francisco prospered through the 1920s after recovering from a steep drop in employment after World War I. Financiers and industrialists erected the city's first skyscrapers, and the jazz clubs and speakeasies of the Barbary Coast District were in full swing. San Francisco, now completely recovered from the 1906 quake, was the West Coast's premier art and culture center—a role that it passed to Los Angeles in the next decade. It was also a major banking center; the Bank of America, headquartered here, became the largest bank in the world.

After the stock market crash of 1929, San Francisco bore the full brunt of a recession that hit its port activities particularly hard. In 1934 one of the most severe strikes in its history broke out. On July 5—Bloody Thursday—police protecting strike-breakers from angry picketers fired into the crowd, wounding 30 and killing 2 longshoremen. The army was sent in to restore order; in retaliation, unions called a general strike and 125,000 workers put down their tools, halting San Francisco's economy for four days.

It was also an era that saw some of the city's finest monuments take form—for example, Coit Tower. In 1933 Alcatraz Island became the site of America's notorious federal prison. But most importantly, two great structures over San Francisco Bay, the Golden Gate Bridge and the San Francisco–Oakland Bay Bridge, were built. Before the bridges opened, the Bay Area was served by an impressive number of ferry boats; in 1935, their peak year, 100,000 commuters crossed San Francisco Bay by boat each day. Just five years later, the last of the ferries was withdrawn from service, unable to compete with the new bridges.

World War II

Following Japan's attack on Pearl Harbor and the advent of World War II, San Francisco became the main military port on the Pacific; more than 1.5 million servicemen were shipped to the South Pacific from Fort Mason. New shipyards sprang up within months, the number of factories tripled, and the Bay Area was transformed into a massive war machine. The Kaiser Shipyards in Richmond, the largest shipbuilding facility, employed more than 100,000 workers on round-the-clock shifts.

Men and women poured into the region from all over the country for jobs in the plants. Today, Hunters Point, one of the most economically distressed neighborhoods in San Francisco, and Marin City, one of its most affluent suburbs, are remnants of cities built to house the influx of workers who moved to the Bay Area during the war.

The 1950s

Following the war, thousands of GIs returning from the South Pacific passed through San Francisco, and many decided to stay. New neighborhoods such as Sunset, with massive tracts of look-alike housing, were formed, and huge highways were built. The postwar years brought economic prosperity but also created a backlash. As the middle class moved out of the inner city, many of their offspring moved back in. North Beach bars and cafés incubated a wellspring of iconoclastic, anti-establishment youth in what was to become the Greenwich Village of the West Coast. San Francisco columnist Herb Caen labeled them Beatniks, and the name stuck.

The Beat Generation rebelled against the empty materialism of the '50s; many lost themselves in orgies of jazz, drugs, and Buddhism. The new counterculture also fostered a highly personal, expressive blend of prose and poetry. Jack Kerouac wrote the handbook for the Beats, *On the Road,* a novel in a fast, passionate, and largely unpunctuated style. City Lights Bookstore in North Beach became the focal point for the new literary movement, which included poets Lawrence Ferlinghetti (the shop's owner) and the late Allen Ginsberg.

The 1960s

By the early '60s the steam was gone from the Beat movement. Shortly thereafter, though, an offshoot of the anti-establishment trend surfaced—the hippies. Originally the term was a Beat putdown for the inexperienced, enthusiastic young people following in the footsteps of their countercultural elders; the first hippies appeared on college campuses around San Francisco.

There was a difference, though. Hippies were experimenting with a new hallucinogenic drug called LSD (better known by its street name, acid).

Around 1965, hippies began moving into communes in low-rent Victorian houses in the Haight-Ashbury District west of the city's center. It was the beginning of flower power and would culminate in 1967's "Summer of Love," when 100,000 young people converged in the area.

Revolutionary Politics

While hippies tuned into psychedelic music by bands such as Jefferson Airplane, Big Brother and the Holding Company, and the Grateful Dead, across the bay in Berkeley and Oakland it was politics, not acid and acid rock, that topped the agenda. The Free Speech Movement began at the University of California, Berkeley campus in 1964 and laid the ground for more passionate protests against the Vietnam War in the Bay Area and around the country later in the decade.

The most famous protest took place in Berkeley's People's Park, a plot of university-owned land that local activists took over as a community open space. Four days later, an army of police under the command of Edwin Meese (later attorney general under U.S. President Ronald Reagan) teargassed demonstrators and stormed the park, accidentally killing one bystander and seriously injuring more than a hundred others.

In the impoverished flatlands of Oakland, the Black Panthers emerged in a response to the era's overt racism. Formed in 1966 by Bobby Seale, Huey Newton, and Eldridge Cleaver, the Panthers were a heavily armed but outnumbered band of activists who wanted self-determination for blacks. A nationwide organization sprung from the Oakland headquarters; 30 members across the country died in gun battles with police and the FBI.

The 1970s, 1980s, and Contemporary San Francisco

Student unrest, antiwar protests, and flower power spilled over into the early '70s, though at a less fevered pitch. One headline-grabbing event was the 1974 kidnaping of Patty Hearst, who was snatched from her Berkeley apartment by the Symbionese Liberation Army, a small, hardcore group of revolutionaries demanding free food for Oakland's poor in exchange for the rich heiress. Later Hearst helped the group and was photographed wielding a submachine gun in the robbery of a San Francisco bank.

Compared to the '60s, most of the decade was quiet. The Bay Area Rapid Transit (BART) finally opened, and the Golden Gate National Recreation Area was established to protect 75,000 acres of incredibly scenic open areas on both ends of the Golden Gate Bridge. In 1973 the Transamerica Pyramid was completed, receiving mixed reviews from San Francisco critics; today it's a beloved piece of the city's skyline.

New battle lines were being drawn. The city's homosexuals, inspired by the 1969 Stonewall Riots in New York City, began to organize, demanding equal status with heterosexuals. Just as important, gays and lesbians "came out," refusing to hide their sexuality and giving rise to the gay liberation movement. One leader, Harvey Milk, won a seat on the city Board of Supervisors, becoming the first openly gay man to win public office. When he was assassinated in 1978 along with Mayor George Moscone, the entire city was shaken. A riot ensued when Milk's killer, former Supervisor Dan White, was found guilty of manslaughter.

In the '80s, San Francisco's gay community retreated somewhat, hit by a staggering AIDS epidemic that toned down a notoriously promiscuous scene. The gay community, in conjunction with City Hall, continues to fight the disease. And during Mayor (now Senator) Diane Feinstein's term, San Francisco added millions of square feet of office towers to downtown's Financial District (as some bemoaned the Manhattanization of the city).

There were also setbacks. A hundred million people watched on national TV as an earthquake shook San Francisco during a 1989 World Series game between Bay Area rivals the San Francisco Giants and the Oakland As; freeways collapsed and dozens were killed. Two years later a horrific fire in the Oakland hills killed 26 people and destroyed 3,000 homes. In the '90s, most of the problems San Francisco faces are similar to those in other American cities: urban poverty, drug abuse, homelessness, and AIDS. An ongoing economic turndown in California was amplified by post–cold war military cutbacks, which saw the closure of military bases in the Bay Area and the loss of 35,000 civilian jobs.

In spite of such setbacks—and the fact that the center of California's power has shifted south to Los Angeles—San Francisco is seen as being on the leading edge of the nation's future. Nearby Silicon Valley leads the country in high technology, and San Francisco and Marin County set lifestyle trends based on consciousness expansion, Eastern mysticism, and counterculture credos.

New Yorkers may complain that they're too busy living their lives to worry about how to improve them. But are the lifestyles San Franciscans are trying to improve the lifestyles that all Americans will be living next? One thing's for sure: few residents would forsake San Francisco for anyplace else.

San Francisco Neighborhoods

San Francisco's hills, more than anything else, thrill visitors with astounding vistas. Surrounded by the shimmering waters of the bay and the Pacific Ocean, the city's land mass is packed on and around nearly four dozen hills—steep markers that delineate San Francisco's shifting moods and, the higher you get, the price of its real estate. Most commercial square footage is confined to the compact Financial District; much of the rest of the area is residential in nature, providing the charm that makes San Francisco a world-class city that people actually want to live in.

Much remains to be seen at eye-level—a vast potpourri of the natural and the social spread throughout about a dozen distinct neighborhoods hidden away on this narrow peninsula. The best way to enjoy the city is to walk. Armed with a good map, a visitor can hit most of downtown San Francisco's major sights and neighborhoods in a day. A better option is to simply roam. The city's most diverting attractions are best discovered and relished when you're not on a frenzied sight-seeing itinerary. One of the city's charms is its compactness; it's easy to get around on foot or by cable car. There's nearly always a surprise—maybe the view, a cable car rolling by, a gorgeous Victorian house, or a garden full of flowers. A healthy spirit of adventure (and a well broken-in pair of walking shoes) are what it takes to get the most from a visit to San Francisco. Figure on about half a day to get the flavor of a neighborhood before moving on.

The following list of San Francisco's most popular neighborhoods (all safe for exploration on foot, except where noted) starts in the hazily defined downtown area, moves north to the waterfront and Marina District, west to the Presidio, south along the Pacific coast; it turns east at Golden Gate Park and continues easterly toward San Francisco Bay to Haight-Ashbury and Japantown, the Castro and Mission Districts, Twin Peaks, the Avenues, and Hunters Point.

Downtown

The main concentration of urban activity inside San Francisco's 47 square miles is in its oldest and easternmost section, jammed between the waterfront and the steeply rising hills. Constantly shifting its borders due to continuous development, downtown is clustered within a square mile on the northern side of Market Street, San Francisco's main drag that bisects the northeastern corner of the peninsula.

Downtown San Francisco is a real mixed bag and conforms to no overall image. One block may be jammed with international banks and the next with upscale department stores and swank specialty stores; turn the corner and you'll find discount electronics outlets, ethnic markets, and ranting street evangelists. Yet within its confines exist all the hallmarks of an affluent city.

Union Square (Zone 3)

Perhaps the nearest thing to a city center in San Francisco is Union Square, its liveliest urban space. A few acres of concrete and greenery surrounded by huge department stores, swank hotels, and expensive shops, its adjacent streets are jammed with cars and tour buses, upscale shoppers, befuddled tourists, street musicians, beggars and street people bumming quarters, and businesspeople late for appointments. It's all here, from the sleazy to the sublime. Union Square is safe during the day, but it's best to avoid the area after dark.

In addition to giving their credit cards a workout at Neiman-Marcus, Saks Fifth Avenue, or Macy's, visitors can catch a cable car on Powell Street for a ride up Nob Hill or board a motorized trolley for a city tour. Maiden Lane, an elegant, tree-lined alley that extends two blocks east of Union Square from Stockton to Kearny Streets, features exclusive shops and restaurants. Union Square is also the focal point for the city's main hotel district, so for a lot of visitors it's the obvious place to start a walking tour.

For a taste of San Francisco's literary past, stop by **John's Grill** at 63 Ellis Street (between Stockton and Powell Streets). Established in 1908, the restaurant was immortalized by author Dashiell Hammett, who made it a hangout for his best-known fictional character, detective Sam Spade. The place is a repository for Spade/Hammett lore and serves hearty meals such as Sam Spade's favorite pork chops with a baked potato.

Union Square is also San Francisco's primary theater district. The **American Conservatory Theater (ACT)** at the Geary Theater (415 Geary Boulevard) offers both classic and contemporary works (and a penchant for Moliere) in a restored landmark theater that reopened in 1996. The city's premier African American theater company calls the **Lorraine Hansberry Theater** (500 Sutter Street) home, while the **Curran Theatre** (445 Geary Boulevard) and the **Marine's Memorial** (609 Sutter Street) present Broadway musicals from New York.

Chinatown (Zone 1)

North along Grant Avenue and through the flamboyant, green-and-ocher imperial Dragon Gate is bustling Chinatown, a dense warren of restaurants and tacky tourist shops that's the second-largest Chinese community outside of Asia (New York's is number one). Since gold rush days, 24-square-block Chinatown has served as the hub for San Francisco's Chinese population. It's a city within a city, crowded with retail outlets and sidewalk displays jammed with silk, porcelain, teak furniture, handmade jewelry, and the usual tourist gewgaws (the farther you walk up Grant Avenue, the cheaper the postcards get). Walk a little farther to Chinatown's open-air markets, glitzy emporiums, and herbalists' shops filled with exotic herbs and spices. At Grant Avenue and Stockton Street is the main Chinese food-shopping district, crowded with displays of unfamiliar fruits and fish stores with tanks of live eels, fish, frogs, and turtles waiting to be killed on the spot for customers.

If you only have one experience in Chinatown, make it dim sum. The delicious tidbits, generally served for brunch, are a local institution. Most dim sum houses open at 10 a.m. and close by mid- or late afternoon. Typically, waiters circle the restaurant's dining room pushing carts stacked with covered bamboo or stainless-steel containers filled with steamed or fried dumplings, shrimp balls, spring rolls, steamed buns, and Chinese pastries. Just point to what looks appealing; the waiters usually don't speak English and ordering is done by gestures. It's cheap, too—you have to order an awful lot of food to spend more than $10 a person.

For a feel of the real, nontouristy Chinatown, duck into a side alley (such as Waverly Street, which parallels Grant Avenue between Clay and Washington Streets), where you'll see stores that sell lychee wine, Chinese newspapers, dried lotus, and powdered antlers (reputed to restore male virility). Ross Alley, which runs above Grant Avenue between Washington and Jackson Streets, houses small garment shops, laundries, florists, and one-chair barber shops. At the Golden Gate Fortune Cookie Company at 56 Ross Alley, visitors can watch fortune cookies being made in the blink of an eye. Early morning, when shopkeepers are busy setting out their wares, is a good time to get a feel for the real Chinatown.

The Financial District (Zone 4)

Frequently called the "Wall Street of the West," the Financial District lies northeast of Union Square in an area bordered by Embarcadero and Market, Third, Kearny, and Washington Streets. Among the towering skyscrapers are several corporate headquarters and the Pacific Coast Stock Exchange, along with lots of elaborate corporate architecture (including the city's tallest landmark, the Transamerica Pyramid).

Brokers, bankers, and insurance agents pursue wealth during the week on several acres of landfill on and around Montgomery Street; unlike most cities' financial areas, the Financial District remains lively on evenings and weekends, thanks to its many restaurants and nightclubs. What motivates these financial movers and shakers can be studied at several museums that attempt to explain the mysteries of the financial world. The lobby of the **Federal Reserve Bank** (101 Market Street), the **Museum of American Money in the West** (in the basement of the Bank of California, 400 California Street), and the **Wells Fargo History Museum** (420 Montgomery Street) offer insights into the city's rich history. All the museums, by the way, keep bankers' hours.

Visitors can enjoy stunning views of San Francisco from atop **One Embarcadero Center** (one of four high-rise office towers and an interwoven complex of restaurants, movie theaters, and retail stores linked by pedestrian walkways and outdoor courtyards) and the **Bank of America World Headquarters** (555 California Street, from the 52nd-floor cocktail lounge and restaurant that opens to the public after 5 p.m.).

Civic Center and the Tenderloin (Zone 2)

Eight blocks west of Union Square on Geary Boulevard is Van Ness Avenue, a broad north-south boulevard and the main thoroughfare of the Civic Center District, acclaimed by critics as one of the finest collections of beaux arts buildings in the country. **City Hall,** built in 1914, is widely considered one of the most beautiful public buildings in America; on a historical note, it's the building in which Dan White shot Mayor George Moscone and Supervisor Harvey Milk in 1978.

Across the plaza from City Hall is the stately former public library, slated to become the new home of the Asian Art Museum, now in Golden Gate Park. The south end of the plaza contains the **Civic Auditorium** (built in 1913), and on the north side is the **State Office Building** (1926). Also in the neighborhood are a few other distinguished buildings, including the **Veterans Auditorium Building** (1932), the **Opera House,** and the **Louise M. Davies Symphony Hall.** Two blocks away is the contemporary **San Francisco Public Library** (1996), a modern interpretation of the classic beaux arts style.

Surrounding the area is a diverse collection of restaurants, antique shops, and galleries. But Civic Center and its fine collection of buildings (and the adjacent Tenderloin, on the north side of Market Street between the theater district and Civic Center) have become the focal point for San Francisco's most glaring problem, the homeless. Periodically police evict hundreds of street people who converge on the plaza opposite City Hall and its lawns. With suited and gowned San Franciscans heading in and out of the ballet, opera, and symphony, it's not a problem easily disguised. Civic Center and the Tenderloin remain one of the most intensely down-and-out sections of town. Other than attending concerts at Symphony Hall or the Opera House, Civic Center and the Tenderloin should be avoided on foot at night.

South of Market (SoMa) (Zone 7)

Over the last 15 years or so, this dreary area of old factory spaces has been spruced up into galleries, a convention center, fashionable restaurants, museums, gay bars, and nightclubs. SoMa, in fact, is becoming one of San Francisco's most eclectic and artsy frontiers. The biggest change is a new building housing the **San Francisco Museum of Modern Art** (151 Third Street); some critics carp that the $62 million structure is more beautiful than any of the art found inside.

Regardless, SoMa is an up-and-coming area that many are comparing favorably to New York's SoHo, and by night, it's the epicenter of San Francisco's club and dance land. Yet it's a transitional neighborhood that requires extra caution after dark. One added plus for daytime visitors tired of trudging up the city's many hills: SoMa is flat. The district can be divided roughly into four regions: the increasingly developed area around the art museum and the Moscone Convention Center; the nightclub region around 11th and Folsom Streets; the blocks between Third and Fourth Streets, where you'll find the new Yerba Buena Center; and the still undeveloped dock areas of Mission Rock and China Basin. Artists, dancers, and musicians like SoMa for the relatively low rents (by San Francisco standards) for huge spaces they can convert into studios and living quarters.

By day, most of SoMa remains an oddly colorless and semi-industrial neighborhood of warehouses and factory outlets. That's no surprise, considering the area has always been home to industry. Several foundries were located in SoMa in the 1850s, along with rows of prefabricated housing imported from the East, making the neighborhood San Francisco's first industrial population. But in the late 1990s, the city's denizens, including artists, trendsetters, and hipsters of all kinds, descend on a formerly gray landscape lit up by the neon facades of bars and clubs.

If you've already hit the Top of the Mark (see Nob Hill, below), you can further a tradition of drinking cocktails in high places at the Saul Steinbergesque San Francisco Marriott hotel and its 39th-floor bar, the **View Lounge.** Located near Fourth and Market Streets south of Union Square near the edge of SoMa, the bar features concentric parabolic windows that slope backward to form a kind of half-dome, creating the illusion that you're floating over the city in the nose of a helicopter. Drinks are expensive at the View, but you can nurse an under-$4 domestic beer for hours. A historical note: the hotel opened on the day the 1989 earthquake struck. The building sustained no structural damage, but the toll on windows and glassware was high. A sole surviving martini glass is suitably enshrined in the bar.

SoMa is also where you'll find one end of the San Francisco–Oakland Bay Bridge, the longest steel high-level bridge in the world. The eight-mile span took three years to build, and when it opened in 1936 the bridge connected San Francisco and Oakland. It's really two bridges separated by a tunnel on Yerba Buena Island, and one of its foundations extends 242 feet below water, deeper than any other bridge ever built. Today the double-decker Bay Bridge is the busiest thoroughfare in the area.

Nob Hill/Russian Hill (Zones 1, 2, 3, and 6)

In a city renowned for its hills, Nob Hill heads the list. As California novelist and journalist Joan Didion wrote, Nob Hill is "the symbolic nexus of all old California money and power." Its mansions, exclusive hotels, and posh restaurants tower over the rest of the city. While early San Franciscans of wealth preferred lower sections of town, the installation of cable cars in the 1870s turned Nob Hill into a valuable piece of real estate. The generally accepted borders of Nob Hill are Bush Street and Pacific Avenue, and Stockton and Larkin Streets.

For visitors, however, Nob Hill doesn't offer much in the way of sights—unless it's the fantastic views from the top of the hill 376 feet above sea level. Your best bet is to wander, gaze at the exteriors of exclusive clubs (such as the **Pacific Union Club** at 1000 California Street), stop at a hotel bar for a drink, and bask in the aura of privilege and luxury that distinguishes this most famous of San Francisco locales.

Perhaps its most famous landmark is the **Mark Hopkins Inter-Continental San Francisco,** a 392-room hotel at California and Mason Streets; great views are to be had at the **Top O' the Mark** lounge, which dates from 1939 and is a charming place to watch the setting sun. Other posh hotels on Nob Hill include the 600-room **Fairmont Hotel and Tower** (its penthouse suite goes for $6,000 a day, butler, maid, and limo included), the **Stanford Court** (the courtyard is domed in Tiffany-style glass), and the **Ritz-Carlton,** which opened in 1991 and is one of San Francisco's best examples of neoclassical architecture.

More Nob Hill treasures include **Huntington Park,** a flowered square where visitors can see nannies pushing sleek perambulators and walking well-groomed poodles. The great, gray eminence atop Nob Hill on

California Street is **Grace Cathedral,** the largest Gothic structure in the West. Among its many splendors is the cast of the gilded bronze doors created by Lorenzo Ghiberti for the Baptistry in Florence; their ten rectangular reliefs depict scenes from the Old Testament. They stand at the top of the steps to the cathedral's east entrance.

Russian Hill, next door, manages to be both expensive and Bohemian. Home to many rich and famous people, it also has a fair share of artists, struggling writers, and students from the nearby **San Francisco Art Institute.** Again, there's not much here in the way of sights—except for great views, wooded open spaces, picturesque cul-de-sacs, and "the crookedest street in the world" (Lombard Street, with eight turns in one block at its eastern end). Russian Hill, named for a graveyard (long since removed) for Russian seamen, is also where Armistead Maupin's fictional crew in *Tales of the City* made their home. Russian Hill, within walking distance of Union Square, is bordered by Broadway and Chestnut, Taylor, and Larkin Streets.

North Beach (Zone 6)

San Francisco's original waterfront is the aptly named North Beach. Landfill has extended the waterfront farther north, but this old neighborhood has managed to survive gentrification and hang on to vestiges of its original Italian character. One of the city's oldest neighborhoods, North Beach still has the well-worn feel of a pair of old, comfortable shoes. It's a great place for lounging around in cafés and bars, casual shopping and browsing, and exploring side streets on foot.

To get a feel for its melting-pot ethnic mix, stop by **Washington Square,** where you'll see elderly Italians relaxing on a park bench and Chinese going through Tai Chi routines. On the north side of the park are the spires of the Church of St. Peter and Paul, where Joe DiMaggio married Marilyn Monroe. Get up early one morning, stop in a sidewalk cafe for a cappuccino, orange juice, and pastry, and then just wander around. When the caffeine kicks in, consider walking up **Telegraph Hill** to **Coit Tower** and a great vista of San Francisco (see below).

The corner of Grant and Columbus Avenues in North Beach was the crossroads of the Beat world of the '50s. "It was a good time to be in San Francisco," wrote journalist Hunter S. Thompson. "Anybody with half a talent could wander around North Beach and pass himself off as a 'comer' in the new era. I know, because I was doing it. . . . It was a time for breaking loose from the old codes, for digging new sounds and new ideas, and for doing everything possible to unnerve the Establishment."

For a taste of North Beach's literary and Beatnik past, stop in **City Lights Bookstore** (at Columbus Avenue and Broadway), ground zero for the Beat Generation; the small alley that runs down the side of the shop is now called Jack Kerouac Street after the most famous of the '50s beat writers. Also at Columbus and Broadway poetry meets porn on a block of declining strip joints and rock clubs; the most famous is the **Condor Club,** former home of Carol Doda and her silicone-enhanced breasts.

Telegraph Hill (Zone 6)

Bordering North Beach is Telegraph Hill, noted for its great views of the bay, vine-covered lanes, quaint cottages, pastel clapboard homes, and lousy parking. Once the home of struggling writers and artists, Telegraph Hill is now occupied by a wealthier class of people. At the top is **Coit Tower,** named for Lillie Hitchcock Coit, who bequeathed the funds to build this popular tourist landmark.

Getting there, though, can be a chore. Many of the houses dangle precipitously over the steep inclines, and the sidewalks turn to steps as you near the top. An easier option is to take the No. 39 bus to the tower and then walk down the Greenwich Steps, a brick staircase lined with ivy and roses that descends steeply to Montgomery Street. Near the base of the steps is an all glass-brick art-deco apartment house used in the Humphrey Bogart film *Dark Passage*.

Fisherman's Wharf (Zone 5)

Although visitors are hard pressed to find vestiges of its once busy ship-building, fishing, and industrial might, Fisherman's Wharf was once a busy fishing port. Then, about 30 years ago, the area was transformed into a tourist mecca, and that's what it remains today. Here your tourist dollar is pursued with a vengeance at T-shirt shops, fast-food joints, stalls selling sweatshirts and baseball caps, and piers transformed into souvenir complexes, overpriced restaurants, and places to take a cruise on the bay.

In spite of the lamentable statistic that more than 10 million visitors a year come to Fisherman's Wharf, it's tempting to say that, unless you've got restless children in tow, stay away. And while by and large that's good advice, there remain a few good reasons to come (aside from the view, which is great).

Probably the best is **Alcatraz,** 12 minutes away by ferry in San Francisco Bay; it's one of the best places to go in San Francisco and shouldn't be missed. (The ferry leaves from Pier 41; advance reservations are a good idea.) Other worthwhile activities at the wharf include taking a cruise on the bay, renting a bike, or strolling down the **Golden Gate Promenade,** a three-and-a-half-mile paved path by the bay leading to the bridge of the same name. Last but not least, walk out on Pier 41 and wave at the collection of barking sea lions just offshore.

For those restless kids, a cluster of pricey attractions should do the trick. **UnderWater World** is a commercial aquarium where visitors walk through a submerged, transparent tunnel and view Pacific Coast marine creatures. Along Jefferson Street are two rainy-day places: the **Wax Museum** and **Ripley's Believe It or Not** (a favorite with 11-year-old boys regardless of the weather), neither of which offers exhibits that have much to do with San Francisco. Things get better at the **Hyde Street Pier,** where the National Park Service has berthed a collection of real 19th-century ships open to the public. Another block west is the **Maritime Museum,** a gorgeous art-deco building full of nautical treasures.

The wharf also has two refurbished shopping complexes. **The Cannery,** a former fruit-packing factory on Jefferson Street at Leavenworth Street, has three levels of shops, restaurants, and a small (but worthwhile) museum, the **Museum of the City of San Francisco** (third floor). **Ghirardelli Square** at 900 North Point Street (at the western end of Fisherman's Wharf) is a boutique mall that's come a long way since its days as a chocolate factory. Its handsome red-brick facade and red neon sign are San Francisco landmarks.

Fort Mason and Golden Gate Recreation Area (Zones 5 and 8)

A bit west of Fisherman's Wharf is Fort Mason, located on the other side of **Aquatic Park** and the 1,800-foot curving **Municipal Pier** (great spots, by the way, to escape the congestion of the wharf). Millions of GIs shipped out to the South Pacific in World War II from Fort Mason, but today it's a public park. Some locals call it "Fort Culture," for here you'll find in its old, shed-like buildings a variety of nonprofit arts organizations, museums, and galleries.

The best museum by far is the vibrant **Mexican Museum,** which also has an excellent gift shop. Although mainly a daytime destination, Fort Mason attracts crowds at night for performances of its acclaimed **Magic Theatre,** one of the oldest and largest theater companies on the West Coast. At night, the fort's pretty bluff is one the most romantic spots in the city.

Fort Mason also marks the eastern edge of the **Golden Gate National Recreation Area,** almost 70 square miles of gorgeous waterfront property that anchors both ends of the **Golden Gate Bridge.** Because of its national park status, the area is commercial-free (and will stay that way), providing visitors with stunning and uncluttered vistas of sea, bay, and mountains only a few steps from the urban density of downtown San Francisco. Fort Mason is also the start of the **Golden Gate Promenade,** a three-and-a-half-mile paved walkway along San Francisco Bay that ends at **Fort Point National Historical Site,** directly under the Golden Gate Bridge.

The Marina District and Pacific Heights (Zone 5)

Filled with Mediterranean-style houses painted in lollipop colors, the Marina District is home to many of San Francisco's upscale, image-conscious, and moneyed professionals. With the Presidio to the west and Fort Mason to the east, the Marina is one of the city's greenest neighborhoods. Hallmarks include yacht clubs, kite flyers, and joggers, all giving the impression that the Marina would rather be a resort. Ironically, the Marina, built to celebrate the rebirth of the city after the 1906 quake, was the city's worst casualty in the 1989 disaster. Tremors tore through the unstable landfill on which the district is built, and many homes collapsed into smoldering ruins. Rebuilding occurred almost immediately, though, and many of the shimmering new homes are just that—new houses built after the last major earthquake. Nor was the disaster enough to bring rents down; the Marina continues to attract a very well-heeled and smart set.

The Marina's main commercial drag is Chestnut Street, an urban thoroughfare with a swinging-singles reputation; the local Safeway has been dubbed "the Body Shop" for the inordinate amount of cruising that goes on there. A long stretch of turf at Marina Green is popular with the fit, the Lycra-clad, and frisbee-catching dogs.

At the westernmost edge of the Marina is its most notable landmark, the **Palace of Fine Arts** (at Baker and Beach Streets). An interpretation of a classical ruin complete with manicured lawns, ponds, and ducks, it's all that's left of the 1915 Panama Pacific Exhibition. Next door is the **Exploratorium,** a unique science museum with more than 700 hands-on science exhibits for youngsters and adults.

When a cable-car line opened in the Pacific Heights District in 1878, this neighborhood south of Fort Mason and west of Van Ness Avenue quickly evolved into an enclave for San Francisco's nouveaux riche. Attempting to outdo the wooden castles on Nob Hill with mansions featuring Gothic arches, Byzantine domes, and stained-glass windows, the denizens of Pacific Heights created monuments to the bonanza era of the late 19th century. But the opulence and magnificence was short-lived. The earthquake of 1906 reduced the exquisite homes to shambles and the district never fully recovered. Much of the area was rebuilt with luxury apartment houses, and many original Victorian houses remain (including the city's most photographed group of dainty "painted ladies," on the south side of **Alta Plaza Park).**

Today, Pacific Heights, along with the adjacent Cow Hollow and Presidio Heights Districts, are home to more college graduates, professionals, and high-income families than any other city district. A fine collection of

Victorian houses on Union Street has evolved into a premiere shopping area with more than 300 boutiques, restaurants, antique shops, and coffeehouses.

The Presidio, Fort Point, and the Golden Gate Bridge (Zone 8)

After hundreds of years of sporadic military occupation by Spain, Mexico, and the United States, this northwestern tip of the San Francisco peninsula was handed over to the National Park Service in 1994. Now the former army base is in the slow process of evolving into a national park. Blissfully free of developed attractions, the **Presidio** offers miles of eucalyptus-scented roadways, trails, ancient gun fortifications, and incredible views from its sandy buffs. Almost 30 of its 1,500 acres are part of the **San Francisco National Military Cemetery.**

The Presidio's main entrance is at Lombard Street, west of Pacific Heights and the Marina District. Small military buildings remain scattered across the former army post, including the **Presidio Museum,** where visitors can learn more about the military's role in the history of San Francisco. The Presidio's dramatic location (and maybe the most impressive view in the city) is **Fort Point,** the ruins of an old brick fortress overlooking the impossibly scenic Golden Gate, with breathtaking vistas that include the San Francisco skyline on one side and the Marin Headlands across the straight.

Overhead at Fort Point, traffic roars on the **Golden Gate Bridge,** probably the most famous bridge in the world. Formerly thought unbridgeable, the mile-wide Golden Gate between the tip of the San Francisco peninsula and Marin County was finally spanned in 1937, and until 1959 it ranked as the world's longest suspension bridge (4,200 feet). Visitors should consider both driving and walking across the bridge; the drive is thrilling as you pass under the huge towers, and the half-hour walk allows the bridge's enormous size and spectacular views to sink in. A sobering note: About seven people a month commit suicide by jumping off the bridge to the water 260 feet below.

There's a viewing area off the northbound lanes of US 101 with parking and access to trails and the bridge's walkways. (There's no need to cross the bridge by car to return to US 101 southbound.) If you drive across to Marin County, a $3 toll for cars is collected at the southern end of the bridge.

The Beaches, Lands End, the Palace of the Legion of Honor, and Cliff House (Zone 8)

South of the Golden Gate Bridge along the Pacific coastline are some of the city's finest beaches. Former military installations hidden among trees and behind sand dunes provide protection from the wind for picnickers.

The sandy shoreline of **Baker Beach** faces the entrance of Golden Gate, a scenic backdrop for hiking, fishing, and sunbathing; swimming in these treacherous waters, alas, is dangerous. Behind Baker Beach, **Battery Chamberlain** points a 95,000-pound cannon ominously to sea.

A bit farther south, **China Beach** provides an intimate atmosphere on a small beach nestled on a steep shoreline—perfect for family outings and picnics. It's also San Francisco's safest swimming beach (although not as popular as the more accessible Baker Beach).

Hikers are attracted to **Lands End,** a shoreline noted for its absence of cars and abundance of birds, trees, and scenic vistas. Hallmarks are the sound of the ocean, the smell of pine and cypress, and views of coastal scenery. At low tide the wrecks of ships that fell victims to the treacherous water are visible. You can also follow the route of an abandoned turn-of-the-century railroad that once led to Cliff House; stay on the main trail because the cliffs are steep and dangerous. Visitors can also explore defense batteries at **West Fort Miley.**

At the south end of Lands End is the **Palace of the Legion of Honor,** a white-pillared twin of the famous Legion d'Honneur in Paris. Some say its the city's best art museum, but there's no argument about its spectacularly scenic setting overlooking the Pacific Ocean. And with Rodin's "Thinker" in the courtyard, this art museum makes an elegant impression.

Cliff House, a mainstay of San Francisco tourism for more than a century, still attracts plenty of visitors, sometimes by the busload. Just offshore from the restaurant and visitor center are **Seal Rocks,** home base for sea lions and marine birds. Next door are the ruins of the once-elaborate **Sutro Baths,** a turn-of-the-century swimming emporium that could hold 24,000 people in its heyday; it burned to the ground in the 1960s. Come just before sunset for cocktails and a view of Seal Rocks and the setting sun from the restaurant; it's a San Francisco tradition.

Cliff House also marks the northern terminus of **Ocean Beach,** a four-mile stretch of sand and crashing surf that's always windy and wavy. You won't find much in the way of frills or stunning scenery, but the beach is a great place for jogging, walking, and people-watching. Don't go in the water, though. The ocean is always dangerous, even when it looks calm.

Farther down the coast are two more notable San Francisco locales. The **San Francisco Zoo** (at Great Highway and Sloat Boulevard) is Northern California's largest animal emporium and features animals in grassy enclosures behind moats, not pacing in cages. Next is **Fort Funston,** with easy hiking trails, great views of the ocean and coastal scenery, and hang gliders floating overhead. Locals call this place Fort Fun.

Golden Gate Park (Zone 8)

In a city awash in greenery, Golden Gate Park is San Francisco's biggest open space; in fact, it's the largest manmade urban park in the world. The park dazzles visitors with a nearly endless succession of sandy beaches, urban vistas, and rolling coastal hills, and the wide expanse of the Pacific Ocean. Exploration of the 1,040-acre park, which stretches from Haight-Ashbury in the east for 52 blocks to the Pacific coast in the west, could take days. Ideally, the best way to discover Golden Gate Park is to wander aimlessly. That, unfortunately, isn't an option for most visitors. The park slopes gently from east to west and is roughly divided into two parts. The eastern-most part contains all the main attractions—art and science museums, horticultural gardens, bandstands, and the Japanese Tea Garden. The western end is less developed, contains more open space and trails, and has a less-sculpted look. It's also where you'll find a herd of buffalo and a Dutch windmill. Overall the park is safe, but it's a good idea to stay on well-populated paths and avoid the park entirely on foot after dark.

Golden Gate Park's major attractions are the twinned **de Young Memorial Museum** (a gallery of mostly American art) and the **Asian Art Museum** (the largest collection of Asian art in the West); both are major galleries that together could take a day to explore. Across the Music Concourse is the **California Academy of Sciences,** a popular destination for families that includes a planetarium and an aquarium; kids love the place.

The **Japanese Tea Garden** shows how trees, landscape, rocks, and buildings can be arranged into a work of art; you can also get tea and cookies served by kimono-clad waitresses. The **Strybing Arboretum** is 70 gorgeous acres of lawns and trees illustrating the diversity of plant life that thrives in San Francisco's Mediterranean-style climate.

While most people head to the western end of the park to do nothing whatsoever, **Stow Lake** can also feed the urge to loaf. Boats of all types—including the electric, nonrowing kind—are available for rent by the hour, as are bicycles for riding on the nearly flat paths that honeycomb the park. You'll also find rest rooms, drinking water, and a snack bar.

A herd of buffalo roam inside the **BisonPaddock** off JFK Drive at 38th Avenue. You can get close to the shaggy (and once nearly extinct) beasts at their feeding area near the western end. At the edge of the park near the ocean is a tulip garden and a Dutch windmill (a can't-be-missed landmark).

Haight-Ashbury (Zone 8)

At the eastern end of Golden Gate Park and about two miles west of downtown is Haight-Ashbury, a neighborhood that lent its name to an era (and a reputation way beyond its size). Long past its late-'60s heyday, the Haight is still an attraction for a particular brand of tourist. About eight blocks long, the area is surrounded by gorgeous restored Edwardian and Victorian houses. Today, though, there are more homeless than hippies on the blocks around the district's epicenter at Haight and Ashbury Streets. Busloads of tourists snap up tie-dyed T-shirts, upscale boutiques draw shoppers to buy avant-garde lingerie and studded black leather (as well as to browse in the neighborhood's great collection of thrift shops, vintage-clothing stores, and record stores), and the major attraction is a nonstop sideshow of street people.

A neighborhood of more than a thousand Victorian houses in decline in the '50s, the Haight was reborn with the hippie movement of the late '60s. The big houses were subdivided into flats, and the flower children disseminated the values of the counterculture all around Haight Street. But idealism mixed with drugs and unemployment didn't prove to be an effective formula for social improvement. In the '70s and '80s the neighborhood devolved into a place only streetwise natives could navigate safely. With the rise of real estate prices around the city, gentrification has set in—although the drug-dazed, backpack-toting drifters asking for change are still common. Today young execs and upper-middle-class professionals rub shoulders with the homeless remnants of the hippie era. The result is a tense bustle of eclectic eccentrics, perfect for brave people-watchers.

The '60s live on in the Haight in another way: The district is noteworthy for a high level of tolerance, even by San Francisco standards. In addition to its barely hanging on hippie culture, the neighborhood is a haven for new trends in alternative medicine, ecological justice, performance art, and natural foods. Visit anytime during the day, but it's best to avoid the high concentration of street people on foot after dark.

Japantown (Zone 8)

Bounded by Geary Boulevard and California Street, Octavia, and Fillmore Streets, Japantown is called home by only about 4% of San Francisco's Japanese American residents. Most return regularly for shopping and social and religious activities. The construction of **Japan Center** in 1968 was the inspiration for a community-renewal effort, with residents and merchants pitching in to beautify the surrounding blocks. The block-long Buchanan Mall, landscaped with flowering trees and fountains, marks the center's northern entrance.

Full of restaurants and stores, Japan Center is also the home of the **Japanese Consulate** and the **Kabuki Complex,** an eight-screen, ultramodern movie complex. The other highlight at Japan Center is the **Kabuki Hot Springs,** genuine Japanese baths that offer shiatsu massage, steam baths, and other luxuriating facilities.

Compared to Chinatown, Japantown looks bland, well tended, and new. For a taste of ethnicity, visit on weekends, especially in spring and summer, when many Japanese cultural events, from tea ceremonies to martial arts demonstrations and musical performances, take place. Other places of interest include the **Buddhist Church of San Francisco** (Pine Street at Octavia Street), a sumptuous temple filled with what are claimed to be relics of Buddha, and **St. Mary's Cathedral** (where Geary Boulevard meets Gough Street), the city's newest Roman Catholic cathedral (1971); walk inside and gaze at its 190-foot dome.

The Castro District (Zone 7)

While not usually considered a tourist attraction, the Castro District may be San Francisco's most progressive neighborhood. The lesbian and gay community that makes its home in the Castro has contributed significantly to every aspect of the city's life, from economics and the arts to politics. (It's said that no San Francisco politician can win citywide election without the backing of the gay community.)

Some say that the Castro is still the wildest neighborhood in town, and others say that in the late 1990s it's merely a shadow of its former self. It's a good guess that much of the Castro's energy and unabashed hedonism has been channeled into AIDS support groups, care for the sick, and city politics. In the 1970s the gay community transformed the neighborhood into a fashionable, upscale enclave of shops, restaurants, bars, and restored homes.

Probably the best way to explore this attractive neighborhood is a walking tour starting at the Castro Muni station at Market Street. Spend some time strolling along Castro Street between 17th and 19th Streets, the neighborhood's compact business strip, and you'll find plenty of cafés and shops to spend an afternoon browsing and gazing. Be sure to stop by the **Castro Theater,** a beautiful example of Spanish Colonial design built in the 1930s; it's also one of San Francisco's better movie houses, specializing in foreign, repertory, and art films.

The Mission District (Zone 7)

The Mission District, San Francisco's Latino neighborhood, is a vibrant part of town made up of Mexican and, increasingly, Central American immigrants. Named for Mission Dolores, San Francisco's oldest building and the sixth in a chain of Spanish settlements that stretched for 650 miles, the district is hip, low-rent, colorful, and solidly Hispanic working class.

Positioned way south of downtown, the Mission District is also the city's warmest neighborhood and manages to avoid most of the fog that blankets the peninsula in summer. Stretching from the southern end of SoMa to

Army Street in the south, the district is a large neighborhood; luckily it's also served by two BART stations, one at each end.

The Mission is also an international hodgepodge, with large numbers of South Americans, Samoans, Vietnamese, Koreans, and Native Americans moving in; it's considered San Francisco's most transitional neighborhood. For example, an active community of feminists and lesbians has moved into Valencia Street, and cafés and bookstores catering to the crowd have sprung up.

The district's main drag, Mission Street, is a bustling commercial avenue filled with discount shops, used-clothing stores, pawn brokers, cafés, cheap ethnic restaurants, bars, clubs, produce stands, and pool rooms. Salsa and Mexican music blasts from bars, and the air is redolent with the aroma of Hispanic cooking. What a great neighborhood for cheap dining.

Mission Street is also a good place to start a tour of the Mission's 200-odd murals, painted as a result of a City Hall scheme to channel the energy of the district's poor youth; the biggest concentration is along 24th Street between Mission Street and South Van Ness Avenue. More Latino culture is on display at the **Mission Cultural Center** (2868 Mission Street), where visitors can enjoy temporary art exhibits, theatrical productions, and poetry readings. While safe during the day, visitors should use extra caution at night when visiting clubs and restaurants in the district.

Twin Peaks (Zone 8)

Before the skyscrapers were built downtown, Twin Peaks was San Francisco's distinctive landmark. In fact, Market Street was mapped to focus on the hills' voluptuous symmetry. (Spanish explorers first called them "breasts of the Indian girl," but prudish Americans settled on the less-descriptive Twin Peaks.) The peaks' slopes contain curving roads that feature some of the most expensive homes in San Francisco, a testament to the theory that the better the view, the higher the price of real estate.

Luckily, Twin Peaks is one of a few hills in the city spared from development, making a walk, bike ride, or drive to the top very rewarding. (It's also on the itinerary of almost every tour bus in town.) The view may be even more impressive at night, although it can get quite cold and blustery after the sun goes down. Day or night, the view is a spectacular, 360° sight that shouldn't be missed.

The Avenues (Zone 8)

Well beyond downtown and the neighborhoods surrounding it, San Francisco's outlying districts lack the character that helps define the city. In fact, neighborhoods such as the Sunset and Richmond Districts (Zone 8), collectively called the Avenues, resemble the suburbs that encircle most American cities. Full of cookie-cutter housing, the neighborhoods constitute a good part of what makes San Francisco a great place to live, with their openness, greenery, and proximity to the Pacific Ocean and Golden Gate Park. (A major minus: Sunset and Richmond are often shrouded in fog.) But the Avenues isn't a place most visitors should spend their valuable touring time.

Hunters Point

Located in the far southeastern section of San Francisco on its own peninsula, Hunters Point contains the city's largest concentration of public housing; it's also rife with the social and economic problems that plague America's cities. The former site of a major U.S. military shipyard in World War II, Hunters Point housed more than 35,000 workers; much of the housing is still in use. The area is plagued by unemployment, crime, and drug abuse. Visitors have no reason to come here—unless it's passing through to a Giants or 49ers game at 3COM (formerly Candlestick) Park, just south of Hunters Point.

When to Go: A City of Two Seasons

It's important to note that San Francisco does not belong to the California of endless blue skies and year-round summer warmth. Surrounded on three sides by water, the city is regularly swept by winds, yet it boasts one of the most stable climates in the world. Daytime temperatures rarely venture more than 5° from the average 60°. Night temperatures rarely drop lower than 40°, and snow is virtually unheard of.

Almost everywhere else in the Bay Area is warmer than San Francisco, especially in the summer, when Berkeley and Oakland bask in sunshine, and the wine country and other inland valleys sizzle in the heat. Finally, keep in mind that San Francisco's maritime weather is difficult to predict. Warm, sunny mornings often turn overcast and cool by afternoon—just as morning fog often gives way to afternoon sun. Your best bet is to dress in layers and remember that San Francisco weather is predictably unpredictable.

■ The Dry Season ■

San Francisco has two kinds of weather—wet and dry. The dry season starts in April and usually lasts through October (and sometimes a week or two into November). If the virtually rainless months of July and August sound too good to be true, you're right. It *is* too good to be true. There's a catch—the city's fabled fog envelopes the city mornings and evenings during much of the summer, hovering over the Golden Gate and obscuring the bridge. But the fog usually burns off by noon or early afternoon.

Summer is also the most crowded. If you're visiting in the summer, do yourself and your family a favor and pack more than T-shirts, shorts, and sandals; lightweight summer clothing is rarely practical (as the sight of hordes of shivering, shorts-clad tourists at Fisherman's Wharf attests). The city can be decidedly unsummerlike, even in July and August, especially at waterside locales such as the Wharf, Fort Point, the ocean beaches, and the Golden Gate Bridge. A final note: When dense afternoon fogs roll in during the summer months, the temperature can drop as much as 20° in a matter of hours.

■ The Wet Season ■

Winter brings most of San Francisco's rainfall, usually starting sometime in November and continuing through March. Often the rain is quite torrential, especially in December and January. Yet daytime highs rarely plunge much below 60° and the lows hover in the mid-40s, thanks to San Francisco's mild maritime climate. Two days in a row without rain are rare on a winter trip to the city, but crowds are nonexistent and finding a convenient and reasonably priced hotel room is less of a hassle. And San Francisco in the rain is still beautiful.

■ The Shoulder Seasons ■

Visitors who want to enjoy San Francisco when the weather is on its best behavior and want to avoid large crowds have two options: spring and fall. These are the favorite seasons of *Unofficial Guide* researchers. In May and June the hills are at their greenest and are covered with wildflowers. Yet rainfall is nearly nil and daytime highs average in the mid-60s. Crowds at major tourist attractions usually don't pick up until later in the summer when families with children begin to arrive. September and October are San Francisco's warmest months. They're popular months with visitors, but they lack the big crowds that pack the city's attractions during the height of the summer season. Warm, cloudless days are the norm. As an added bonus, it's grape-harvesting season in the wine country, making a one- or two-day excursion to Napa or Sonoma almost imperative. These are the city's least foggy months (although many visitors don't seem to mind the fog).

San Francisco's Average Monthly Temperatures (in Fahrenheit) and Rainfalls (in inches)			
Month	**High**	**Low**	**Rainfall**
January	56.1	46.2	4.48
February	59.4	48.4	2.83
March	60.0	48.6	2.58
April	61.1	49.2	1.48
May	62.5	50.7	0.35
June	64.3	52.5	0.15
July	64.0	53.1	0.04
August	65.0	54.2	0.08
September	68.9	55.8	0.24
October	68.3	54.8	1.09
November	62.9	51.5	2.49
December	56.9	47.2	3.52

■ Avoiding Crowds ■

In general, popular tourist sites are busier on weekends, and Saturdays are busier than Sundays. The summer season by far is the busiest time of year at most attractions. If Alcatraz is on your itinerary (and if you're a first-time visitor to San Francisco, it should be), call in advance for tickets on a weekday, and hit attractions at Fisherman's Wharf on the same day. On summer weekends the wharf is jammed with visitors.

Driving in San Francisco's rush-hour traffic should be avoided. If you're driving to the city on a weekday, avoid hitting town between 7 a.m. and 9 a.m., and 4 p.m. and 6 p.m. If you're driving in on a weekend, you're still not off the hook. Traffic in and around San Francisco on Saturday and Sunday afternoons sometimes exceeds weekday rush-hour intensity. (Our theory: The region around the city, the fifth-largest in the country, registers a population of 6 million. On weekends many residents of San Jose, Berkeley, Oakland, and other towns nearby do what you would if you lived here. They drive to San Francisco.) Try to arrive before noon on weekends and you'll miss the worst of the weekend crush.

■ How to Get More Information on San Francisco ■ before Your Visit

For additional information on entertainment, sight-seeing, maps, shopping, dining, and lodging in San Francisco, call or write

San Francisco Convention and Visitors Bureau
Hallidie Plaza
Powell and Market Streets
P.O. Box 429097
San Francisco, CA 94142
(415) 391-2000
(415) 392-0328 (TDD)

The Convention and Visitors Bureau's Visitor Information Center is in the Benjamin Swig Pavilion on the lower level of Hallidie Plaza at Market and Powell Streets. It's easy to find, and the center's multilingual staff can help answer any questions you may have. Hours are 9 a.m. to 5 p.m. weekdays, and 9 a.m. to 3 p.m. weekends (beginning June 1). The center is closed Easter, Thanksgiving, Christmas, and New Year's Day. For a recorded schedule of events, call (415) 391-2001.

Gays and Lesbians

In San Francisco, "the love that dare not speak its name" is expressed more freely than in any other U.S. city. San Francisco boasts the largest gay and lesbian population of any city in America, with some reports estimating that one-quarter of its total population of 750,000 is gay. Hundreds of restaurants, hotels, shops, and other businesses and services are owned and operated by gays, who enjoy a high level of visibility, acceptance, and political clout in the community at large.

History

The roots of the city's large population of gays and its live-and-let-live ambiance go back to the waning days of World War II, when the U.S. military began purging its ranks of homosexuals and suspected homosexuals, booting them out at the point of embarkation. This was often San Francisco, the major military stepping-off point. Many of the men, officially stigmatized as perverts, stayed in the Bay Area. Another migration occurred in the McCarthy era of the early '50s, when the federal government dismissed thousands of homosexuals from their jobs. Persecution by the U.S. military and cops was common in the postwar years (as it was in other American cities), and in the early 1960s gays began organizing for their civil rights.

By the time the '70s arrived, an estimated one in four San Francisco voters was gay, and homosexuals were an influential minority group. It didn't hurt that proportionately gays tend to vote in larger numbers and contribute to political candidates that support issues important to gays. As gays of the flower-power generation began moving in and restoring Victorian townhouses, Castro Street (formerly an Irish American neighborhood going to seed) became a flourishing enclave and the embodiment of the gay drive for acceptance.

In 1977 the Castro District elected Harvey Milk to the city Board of Supervisors. Milk, a gay activist who organized the district's merchants group, became the first openly gay city official elected in the United States. The drama of gay liberation heightened when former Supervisor Dan White, a former cop and the city's most anti-gay politician, assassinated Milk and pro-gay mayor George Moscone in City Hall in 1978. Six months later, after White was sentenced to only five years for the double murder, a mob marched on City Hall, drawing worldwide attention and headlines. (White, paroled in 1985, eventually committed suicide.)

In the '70s San Francisco became notorious for its bar and bathhouse culture and the anonymous promiscuity that went along with it. But the reputation toned down after the AIDS tragedy struck early in the '80s, causing more than 11,000 deaths in San Francisco. Socially, the city's gay scene has mellowed in the '90s, although gay bars, parades, and street fairs swing better than most.

The '80s also saw a flowering of the city's lesbian culture that parallels the male upswing of the '70s. Today, as in most American cities, the lesbian community is more subtle and less visible than the gay scene (but it's just as powerful politically). Much smaller than the Castro, the main lesbian community is concentrated around 16th and Valencia Streets in the Mission District, while larger lesbian communities are across the bay in Oakland and Berkeley.

In the late '90s, the city's gays and lesbians have escaped the moral backlash provoked by AIDS in other parts of the country, thanks to San Francisco's tolerance and the gay community's support of people with AIDS and their survivors. Gays have, by and large, melded into the mainstream. Gay life is less ghettoized, and gay bars and clubs are scattered all over town. For years the city has had gay and lesbian political leaders, police officers, bureaucrats, and judges. It can be argued that one of the major aims of the gay liberation movement has been met—the acceptance of people regardless of whether they're gay or straight.

Gay Visitors

What's all this mean for gay and lesbian visitors to the city? By and large, you needn't concern yourself with fitting in during a visit to gay-friendly San Francisco. Take, for example, getting a room. While many hotels are gay-owned and cater to a gay clientele, the Bay Area's high level of tolerance just about guarantees that a visitor's sexual orientation—and the gender of his or her roommate—isn't going to be an issue at any hotel in or around San Francisco.

"If you want to be sure, call the hotel manager or concierge and ask if you'll feel comfortable staying in the hotel with your boyfriend or girlfriend," advises Rob Delamater, marketing director for Joie de Vivre, a San Francisco hotel chain. "If you don't get an immediate enthusiastic response, make reservations somewhere else. But because of the city's economic dependence on tourism, anything but a positive response is rare."

Before You Go

Another tip for the computer literate with access to the World Wide Web: Point your browser to **www.gaysf.com,** where you can glean up-to-the-minute information on San Francisco's gay scene. You can also apply for a Gay Passport, a free booklet entitling the holder to free gifts (such as a drink at a bar) and discounts at participating gay-owned city establishments. Order your passport at least two weeks before your trip.

Gay and Lesbian Publications and Community Bulletin Boards

Numerous local newspapers and magazines in San Francisco cater to the gay and lesbian community. The largest and best-known are the *San Francisco Bay Times* (distributed every other Thursday; (415) 227-0800), *San Francisco Frontiers* (distributed every other Thursday; (415) 487-6000) and the weekly *Bay Area Reporter* (distributed on Thursdays; (415) 861-5019); all are free and are distributed to bookstores, bars, and street vending boxes. The newspapers provide complete event calendars and resource listings for gays and lesbians.

Other publications include *Anything That Moves* (a quarterly magazine for bisexuals; (415) 703-7977), *Drummer* (a monthly gay leather and S/M magazine; (415) 252-1195), *Girlfriends* (a monthly magazine for lesbians; (415) 648-9464), *Odyssey* (a gay nightclub and listing guide published every other Friday; (415) 621-6514), and *Q San Francisco* (a "best of" guide for gays and lesbians; (415) 764-0324). An excellent place to find these and other gay and lesbian publications is at the bookstore A Different Light (489 Castro Street; (415) 431-0891).

The San Francisco gay and lesbian community has several information resources by phone. The Pacific Center Lavender Line (phone (510) 841-6224) is a resource for gay activities throughout the Bay Area; it's available from 4 to 10 p.m. weekdays and from 6 to 9 p.m. Saturdays. The *Women's Building of the Bay Area* in the Mission District (phone (415) 431-1180) is a clearinghouse for feminist and lesbian art, entertainment, and resource information; call from 9 a.m. to 5 p.m. weekdays. The *Bisexual Resources Line* (phone (415) 703-7977) provides information and resources for bisexuals in the Bay Area on a recorded message 24 hours a day.

Gay Neighborhoods

The traditional neighborhood for gay men has been the sprawling Castro, now more typified by prepped-up, well-heeled yuppies than the disheveled leftists and ex-hippies that symbolized the early days of the gay liberation movement. SoMa, the city's emerging art and night-life district, features a gay enclave around Folsom Street; the look tends toward black leather and chains. Polk Street and the edges of the Tenderloin District is the tight-blue-jeans-and-pimps zone of young gay transients; it's not the safest part of town at 2 a.m. (or anytime—see below). An enclave of successful gay business executives resides in posh and proper Pacific Heights.

While San Francisco is hands-down the most tolerant city in the country, gay bashing is still alive. Avoid open displays of affection in the Mission District, the largely Hispanic neighborhood where street gangs have attacked gay men. While the Polk Street area has a long gay history, it's now primarily a hustling scene with many bars and porn shops; it's a dangerous area, and more gay bashing is reported here than in any other part of the city.

Calendar of Special Events

San Francisco hosts a variety of annual special events throughout the year, including film, jazz and blues festivals, a cable-car competition, craft fairs, art festivals, street fairs, and ethnic festivals. For exact dates, times, locations, and admission fees (if any), call the phone numbers below before your visit.

January

San Francisco Sports and Boat Show. Cow Palace. Boats, fishing tackle, camping gear, and hunting equipment on display. (415) 469-6065.

Martin Luther King, Jr.'s Birthday Celebration. Various locations. Speeches by civic leaders and entertainment highlight the city's commemoration of Dr. King's life. (415) 771-6300.

Chinese New Year Celebration. The city's largest festival ends with a grand parade from Market and Second Streets to Columbus Avenue. (415) 982-3000.

February

San Francisco Tribal, Folk, and Textile Art Show. Fort Mason. More than 100 folk and ethnic art dealers sell North American pottery, basketry, textiles, and jewelry. (310) 455-2886.

Russian Festival. The Russian Center of San Francisco. Sample Russian foods, desserts, and flavored vodkas; enjoy folk singing, dancing, opera, painting, and crafts. (415) 921-7631.

San Francisco Arts of Pacific Asia Show. Fort Mason. View art of all kinds. (310) 455-2886.

San Francisco Orchid Society's Pacific Orchid Exposition. Fort Mason. An annual expo featuring dozens of floral collections. (415) 546-9608.

TulipMania. Pier 39, Fisherman's Wharf. View more than 40,000 brilliantly colored tulips from around the world. (415) 705-5500.

The Edge Festival.   Dancer's Group Studio Theater. Experimental dance and performances by established artists. (415) 824-5044.

March

Cable Car Appreciation Day.   Union Square. Music, decorations, and memorabilia. (415) 474-1887.

St. Patrick's Day Parade.   Downtown. The Irish have their day on this annual march from Civic Center to Spear Street. (415) 661-2700.

Bouquets to Art.   California Palace of the Legion of Honor. Works by 100 floral designers, lectures by horticultural experts, luncheons, and tea service. (415) 750-3504.

Asian American Film Festival.   Japantown. More than 100 films and videos from more than 20 countries; special programs for children. (415) 252-4800.

Bay Area Music Awards (Bammies).   Bill Graham Civic Auditorium. The Bay Area's best musicians gather for an evening of entertainment and awards. (510) 762-BASS.

April

Whole Life Expo.   The Fashion Center San Francisco. Nutrition, personal growth, alternative healing methods, and environmental issues fill the agenda. (415) 721-2484.

Cherry Blossom Festival.   Japantown. Taiko drumming, martial arts, Japanese food, and music highlight a parade from Civic Center to Japantown. (415) 563-2313.

Easter Parade and Celebration.   Union and Fillmore Streets. Strolling artists, music, outdoor dining, children's activities, and an annual Easter parade. (415) 775-5703.

San Francisco Landscape Garden Show.   Fort Mason. World-famous garden designers and interior designers join forces for this annual show. (415) 750-5108.

Pacific Fine Art Festival.   West Portal Avenue. More than 75 artists show their work. (209) 296-1195.

San Francisco International Film Festival.   April through May; various locations. More than 100 films and videos from around the world. (415) 931-FILM.

Opening Day on the Bay.   San Francisco Bay. Decorated yachts and fire-boats celebrate the Bay Area's maritime heritage. (415) 381-1128.

San Francisco Decorator Showcase.   2520 Pacific Avenue. Top Bay Area designers display the latest design innovations at luxurious San Francisco homes. (415) 749-6864.

May

Cinco de Mayo Celebration.   Mission District. Arts, crafts, and food, as well as a parade to celebrate Mexican independence. (415) 826-1401.

San Francisco Youth Arts Festival.   Golden Gate Park. Area students display their works. (415) 759-2916.

Polish Spring Festival.   San Francisco County Fair Building. Polish food, folk dancing ensembles, polka bands, arts, and crafts. (415) 285-4336.

Traditional Music and Dance Festival.   The Cannery, Fisherman's Wharf. Greek and French music and dancing, music workshops. (415) 771-3112.

***San Francisco Examiner* Bay to Breakers Footrace.**   The Embarcadero to the Great Highway. More than 70,000 costume-clad runners in the world's largest footrace. (415) 777-7770.

Arts and Crafts by the Bay.   Pier 29 between Sansome and Battery Streets. More than 200 artists and craftspeople, food, beer, wine, and continuous entertainment. (415) 956-5316.

Carnaval.   Mission District. San Francisco's Mardi Gras with a parade, street festival, and costume contest. (415) 826-1401.

Union Street Spring Festival of Arts and Crafts.   Union Street. Arts and crafts, wine, food, waiter's races, tea dancing, a fashion show, and street performers. (415) 346-9162.

Min-Sok Festival.   The Presidio. A traditional Korean festival of art and culture. (415) 441-1881.

June

Local 510 Art Show.   Herbst International Exhibit Hall. More than 600 artists showcasing paintings, drawings, metal sculpture, photography; live music, martial arts. (415) 821-7600.

ZooFest for Kids. San Francisco Zoo. A combination of interactive displays, live entertainment, food, drinks, and close-up encounters with animals. (415) 753-7165.

Street Performers Festival. Pier 39, Fisherman's Wharf. Comedians, jugglers, unicyclists, and slack-rope walkers do their thing. (415) 705-5500.

Ethnic Dance Festival. Palace of Fine Arts Theater. Performances by 900 dancers and musicians showcase traditional dance and music. (415) 474-3914.

Animal WingDing. Mission District. A street fair hosted by the San Francisco SPCA; games, live music, food, and a parade. (800) 211-7722.

San Francisco International Lesbian and Gay Film Festival. Castro Theatre and other locations. The second-largest film festival in California showcases more than 350 films and videos from around the world. (415) 703-8650.

North Beach Festival. Grant Avenue and Green Street. San Francisco's oldest street fair offers arts, crafts, and live entertainment. (415) 403-0666.

Stern Grove Midsummer Music Festival. Stern Grove. Mid-June through late August. Some of the world's great performers give free concerts in an outdoor setting. (415) 252-6252.

Juneteenth Festival. Fillmore Street. An annual outdoor event celebrating African American culture. (415) 928-8546.

San Francisco Music Day. Market Street and the Embarcadero. Many bands playing all kinds of music throughout San Francisco. (415) 391-0370.

Midsummer Mozart Festival. Various locations, late June through late July. Hear some of Mozart's most memorable compositions. (415) 392-4400.

KQED International Beer and Food Festival. Concourse Exhibition Center. Sample more than 250 brews, including imports from 20 nations; food and entertainment. (510) 762-BASS.

Lesbian, Gay, Bisexual, Transgender Pride Celebration Festival and Parade. Castro District. San Francisco's celebration of lesbian and gay pride. (415) 864-FREE.

New Orleans by the Bay. Shoreline Amphitheater. More than 40 jazz, blues, zydeco, Dixieland and gospel acts; Cajun, Creole, southern, and international food and crafts. (510) 762-BASS.

Annual Dyke March. Castro and Market Streets. Join more than 40,000 women in a march, followed by a street party in the Castro. (415) 241-8882.

July

San Francisco Chronicle **Fourth of July Waterfront Festival.** Fisherman's Wharf. Live entertainment, food, arts and crafts, fireworks. (415) 777-7120.

Jazz and All That Art on Fillmore. Fillmore Street. Jazz concerts, food, wine, art. (415) 346-9162.

Blues and Art on Polk. Polk Street. Arts, crafts, food, and blues. (415) 346-9162.

San Francisco Marathon. Golden Gate Bridge to Golden Gate Park. A 26.2-mile footrace that finishes at Kezar Stadium. (415) 296-7111.

San Francisco Cable Car Bell Competition. Union Square. Professional bell ringers entertain as they compete for prizes. (415) 6SF-MUNI.

Books by the Bay. Ferry Building area. Forty bookstore booths, author readings and signings, live music, and children's activities. (415) 927-3937.

Folk Art to Funk. Fort Mason. Folk art, antique advertising, toys, country furnishings, vintage clothing, and costume jewelry. (310) 455-2886.

Jazz & Wine Festival. Embarcadero Center. Classic jazz, vintage wine, and arts and crafts. (800) 733-6318.

August

Nihonmachi Street Fair. Japantown and Japan Center. Lion dancers, taiko drummers, Japanese arts and crafts, music, food, and children's events. (415) 771-9861.

Golden Gateway to Gems. San Francisco County Fair Building. Minerals, crystals, and jewelry from all over the world. (415) 564-4230.

ACC Craft Fair. Fort Mason. The largest juried craft fair on the West Coast features necklaces, stoneware, silk scarves, quilts, and more. (415) 896-5060.

Arts & Crafts Art Nouveau Vintage Western Sale. Concourse Exhibition Center. Shop for furniture, accessories, rugs, art, pottery, books, jewelry, vintage clothing, and collectibles. (415) 599-3326.

Comedy Celebration Day. Sharon Meadow, Golden Gate Park. Four hours of comedy from 16 comedians; food, drink, and souvenirs. (415) 777-8498.

Filipino American Arts Exposition. Center for the Arts at Yerba Buena Gardens. An outdoor fair with folk art exhibitions, a film and video festival, and a parade. (415) 436-9711.

Renaissance Pleasure Faire. Blackpoint Forest, Novato. A trip back to Merry Olde England with 1,500 costumed performers, jousting knights, crafts, theater, dance, food, and drinks. (800) 523-2473.

Absolut a la Carte, a la Park. Golden Gate Park. Outdoor dining with 50 restaurants, 40 wineries and microbreweries, celebrity chefs, and music. (415) 383-9378.

Blues & Art on Polk. Polk Street. San Francisco's biggest blues festival, featuring food, drink, blues, and dancing. (415) 346-9162.

Sausalito Art Festival. Sausalito. A top-rated fine arts festival with more than 11,000 original works of art from around the world. (415) 332-3555.

September

A Taste of Chocolate. Ghirardelli Square, Fisherman's Wharf. Watch chocolate dipping, molding, and sculpting demonstrations; enter a chocolate-tasting challenge and collect recipes. (415) 775-5500.

CITIBANK Fall Cup Regatta. Pier 39. America's Cup winners and sailing teams compete in a series of 11-meter fleet races. (415) 705-5500.

Festival of the Sea. Hyde Street Pier. Ship tours, children's activities, maritime music, and storytelling. (415) 929-0202.

Autumn Moon Festival. Grant Avenue between California and Pacific Streets. Multicultural entertainment, traditional lion and dragon dances, Chinese costumes, and children's activities. (415) 982-6306.

Festival de Las Americas. Mission District. A Latin American food festival with dancing, arts and crafts, and entertainment. (415) 826-1401.

El Grito Celebration. Mission District. A commemoration of Mexican Independence Day with music and dancing. (415) 585-2043.

San Francisco Blues Festival. Justin Herman Plaza and Fort Mason. The oldest blues festival in the country. (415) 979-5588.

West Portal Fine Arts Festival. West Portal Avenue. A showcase of art, shops, and restaurants in one of San Francisco's less well-known neighborhoods. (415) 346-9162.

Folsom Street Fair. Folsom Street. A popular fair with arts and crafts, entertainment, and food. (415) 861-3247.

October

Viva! Mexico. Pier 39. Music, dancing, corn-husk doll making, and piñata demonstrations to celebrate Mexican Independence Day. (415) 705-5500.

San Francisco Open Studios. Various locations. More than 500 artists open their doors to the public; the largest visual arts event in the city. (415) 861-9838.

Castro Street Fair. Castro District. An annual fair in the city's predominantly gay district. (415) 467-3354.

Fleet Week. Fisherman's Wharf. A salute to the U.S. Navy with visiting ships and the Blue Angels air show. (415) 705-5500.

Italian Heritage Day Celebration. North Beach, Fisherman's Wharf. A commemoration of Columbus's discovery of America with a Queen Isabella coronation, landing pageant, and Sunday parade. (415) 434-1492.

Great Halloween and Pumpkin Festival. Polk Street. A costume parade, train and pony rides, and pumpkin-carving and pie-eating contests. (415) 346-9162.

San Francisco Jazz Festival. Various locations. One of the world's great jazz festivals. (415) 398-5655, (800) 627-5277.

Grand National Rodeo, Horse, and Stock Show. Cow Palace. Bull, saddle bronc, and bareback bronc riding. (415) 469-6065.

Sukkot, the Festival of the Booths. Sacramento and Lake Streets. A harvest festival celebrating the Jewish holiday of Sukkot; 100 artists and craftspeople, Klezmer music, dancing, and Judaica. (415) 346-9162.

Whole Life Expo. The Fashion Center San Francisco. Nutrition, personal growth, and alternative healing methods. (415) 721-2484.

Halloween San Francisco. Civic Center. A lesbian, bisexual, transgender, and gay community event. (415) 777-5500.

November

Harvest Festival and Christmas Crafts Market. Concourse Exhibition Center. An arts and crafts fair for the holiday season. (707) 778-6300.

San Francisco Bay Area Book Festival. Concourse Exhibition Center. 250 authors, 330 publisher and bookstore booths, panel discussions, and a new writers showcase. (415) 908-2833.

San Francisco International Auto Show. Moscone Center. The latest and greatest in automobiles. (415) 673-2016.

ACGA Holiday Clay and Glass Festival. San Francisco County Fair Building. More than 90 ceramic and glass artists sell their wares. (510) 865-0541.

December

Celebration of Craftswomen. Fort Mason. Craftswomen display their latest inventions and innovations. (415) 252-8981.

Art Deco 50s Holiday Sale. Concourse Exhibition Center. More than 200 dealers sell furniture, accessories, rugs, art, pottery, and collectibles from the 1920s to 1950s. (415) 599-3326

Christmas at Sea. Hyde Street Pier. Caroling, storytelling, hot cider, cookies, children's crafts, and Santa. (415) 929-0202.

PART TWO

Hotels

Deciding Where to Stay

San Francisco hotels generally offer good values, interesting Pacific urban architecture and decor, and remarkably diverse amenities. As a generalization, service at San Francisco hotels, if not quirky, is somewhat differently defined. At the bar your drinks may not come any faster than they would at home, and your room-service breakfast may arrive cold. But ask the bartender or food server, "What should I do next?" and you're in for a spirited and opinionated discourse on the city.

The idea that information is the most valuable service a hotel can offer is novel in most cities. In San Francisco, however, hotels that don't even have room service or a bar may publish their own guidebooks and pamphlets on attractions, or they may have 24-hour concierge service. With 32% of San Francisco guest rooms scoring four stars or higher, the quality of guest rooms is exceptionally high. Plus, guest rooms in the Bay Area are reasonably priced. On average, rooms here are less expensive than rooms in New York City, Washington, DC, Chicago, and other comparable destinations. This combination of high-quality rooms and reasonable rates makes San Francisco attractive for both leisure and business travelers.

Hotels dot the San Francisco peninsula and Bay Area suburbs, so you need not be more than ten minutes from tourist attractions or businesses. As in most cities, guest-room rates are higher in more desirable areas. The steepest rates are generally found within walking distance of Union Square, and some of the best hotel bargains are located in less fashionable neighborhoods. Of these, many have excellent on-premises security and may be of particular interest to those who plan to tour by car.

A distinctive characteristic of San Francisco's hotel scene is an artful marriage of historic architecture with modern interior design. Some of the city's hotels are modern, but the vast majority are housed in older buildings. Historic hotel buildings include some of the world's oldest skyscrapers and quaint Victorian and Edwardian mansions.

Step inside the nicer San Francisco hotels and you'll find some of the more inventive interior design you'll encounter in this country. Though palatial room size is not characteristic of San Francisco hotels, utilizing square footage wisely is. In both common areas and guest rooms, the *Unofficial Guide* hotel inspectors were impressed by how creatively form and function are blended. Several of San Francisco's nicest hotels have such ergonomically exact guest rooms that we were reminded of Tokyo. The comfortable integration of modern technology such as in-room fax machines, microwaves, and coffeemakers is noteworthy in guest rooms that are sometimes smaller than 200 square feet.

In San Francisco, you are more likely to find a guest room suited to your individual needs than in destinations where hotel homogeneity rules. The **Nob Hill Lambourne,** for example, offers a state-of-the-art, in-room treadmill and an honor bar with healthy foods for quite reasonable rates. Similarly, the **Hotel Triton** boasts 24 environmentally sensitive guest rooms and suites designed by Jerry Garcia and nature artist Wyland.

The decor runs the gamut of historical and modern styles. Classic opulence, signaled by airplane hangar–sized lobbies, chandeliers the size of canoes, and richly textured upholstery can be found at hotels such as the **Fairmont** and the **Westin Saint Francis.** There is also an emphasis on modern interior decorating. Using elements of art deco, art nouveau, and modern art, the finished interior in the modern design style contains whimsically curved lines, bold patterns, and metallic and bright colors. You can see one of the best examples of this style at the **Hotel Diva,** where black and primary colors accent the theme of brushed chrome. Another is the newly renovated **Hotel Monaco,** which uses lush textures such as velvet and deep colors, including eggplant and ruby, to create a look of futuristic affluence.

San Francisco hotels market and cater to diverse groups, and hotel amenities and their ambience reflect this trend. While some properties target business or leisure travelers, others have more specific target markets. These include rock 'n' rollers—both professionals and fans—at the **Phoenix Inn,** opera fans at the **Inn at the Opera,** wine lovers at many Bay Area hotels, and spa junkies at others. Magic fans should try the **Mansions Bed and Breakfast,** where a magic show dinner theater is included with the price of a room. And aspiring actors and film buffs will want to check out the **Hotel Bijoux,** which offers a small movie theater and a 24-hour hotline to current San Francisco film shoots and casting-call opportunities.

■ A Few Noteworthy Properties ■

San Francisco is home to a few noteworthy properties that we have not ranked and rated because their clientele is so narrowly defined.

Those wishing to relive the Summer of Love may want to stay at the **Red Victorian Bed, Breakfast, and Art Center.** Owned and run by veteran flower child Sami Sunchild, the bed-and-breakfast is in the heart of the historic Haight-Ashbury neighborhood. Each of its 18 rooms is decorated with a different theme, ranging from the Summer of Love room and the Rainbow room to the Japanese Tea Garden room and the Teddy Bear room, replete with 50 or so stuffed bears.

Guests of the "Red Vic" are encouraged to socialize at the breakfast table, and reclusive types may find this aspect of the bed-and-breakfast overwhelming if not downright annoying. Outgoing folks will probably have a lot of fun, as Ms. Sunchild conducts breakfast like a love-in; each guest is encouraged to tell the others where they are from and what they do for a living. Tip: if you make your living working for a right-wing political organization, conducting experiments that include vivisection, or designing weapons, you'll want to lie. When one guest told the group he was a social worker from New Zealand, Ms. Sunchild almost squealed with delight as she exclaimed, "See, we take care of the people who take care of the world!" Room rates at the Red Victorian Bed, Breakfast, and Art Center range from $60 to $130. For more information, call (415) 864-1978.

If you are looking for a narrowly focused bed-and-breakfast for gay men, try the **Black Stallion,** located in the Castro District. Billing itself as "San Francisco's only Leather/Levi/Western Bed and Breakfast," the Black Stallion's common areas are clothing-optional. Occupying the top two floors of a black Victorian building, eight rooms share bathrooms, a lounging area, a kitchen, and a sun deck. The bottom floor is occupied by a private social club to which bed-and-breakfast guests are also admitted. Room rates at the Black Stallion range from $50 to $100. Call (415) 863-0131 for information and reservations.

House O' Chicks is a women's bed-and-breakfast in the Castro District. Two guest rooms share a bathroom; one guest room has a TV and VCR, the other has a stereo, and both have a homey atmosphere. Innkeeper Dorie Lane tells prospective guests that "it's like coming to a friend's house and she has a room all made up for you." Common areas include the living room, dining room, library, and kitchen, and all rooms contain original women's artwork. Room rates are $75 for single occupancy, and $85 for double occupancy. Call (415) 861-9849 for information and reservations.

Most of the other hotels and bed-and-breakfasts in the Castro District are places where everyone will feel comfortable, though they are particularly convenient for gay travelers wishing to explore shops and clubs in the Castro area.

Bock's Bed and Breakfast offers three guest rooms with private entrances in a 1906 Edwardian mansion and has a strict nonsmoking policy. Call (415) 664-6842.

The **Delores Park Inn** has received various awards, offers four antique-furnished guest rooms and one suite, and is a favorite stay-over for visiting celebrities. It also has a strict nonsmoking policy. Call (415) 621-0482.

The **Castillo Inn** has four guest rooms that share one bathroom, and a two-bedroom suite at another location. This bed-and-breakfast on Henry Street in the heart of the Castro District is also strictly nonsmoking. Call (800) 865-5112.

By now you may be wondering, "Can't I just get a normal room in San Francisco?" The answer, of course, is yes. For those whose tastes tend to be more conservative, traditional hotel rooms are not hard to come by. But you will need to ask for what you want. In San Francisco, the difference between name-brand corporate hotels and freestanding, proprietary, or "boutique" hotels is not clearly delineated. This is because many of the corporate hotels in San Francisco occupy older buildings that once housed freestanding and family-owned hotels. Don't expect cookie-cutter guest rooms just because you're staying at your favorite name-brand hotel. If you prefer to stay in a rectangular room with the bathroom adjacent to the front door, two double beds, and a picture window opposite the front door, be sure to shop around.

Getting a Good Deal on a Room

■ **Money-Saving Tips** ■

To say that you receive good value for your lodging dollar in San Francisco doesn't mean that San Francisco is cheap. If you are looking for ways to save money beyond getting a discount on the price of a room, consider the following.

1. Stay in a less-than-fashionable neighborhood. San Francisco is made up of many distinct neighborhoods, and this emphasis on address reflects itself in pricing. Unless you need to be there for convenience, it may not be worth it to you to stay on Nob Hill when the same level of room in North Beach may be half the cost. The most expensive area is Union Square then Nob Hill.

2. Seek a suite that includes a kitchen. Several hotels offer this option; suites can accommodate four or more people and help save on restaurant bills.

3. Stay at the worst room at a good hotel instead of the best one at a lesser hotel. Ask for the smallest room, lowest floor, worst view. The cost differential can be considerable, although the rest of the hotel services, amenities, and public rooms remain the same. You're getting the biggest bang for your buck.

4. Avoid room service and minibars. Bring food up from groceries, delis, or convenience stores. Or make like a resident and have a restaurant deliver (allowed at some hotels, frowned on at others — check first). Neighborhood restaurants, especially the "ethnics," are good and reasonable. If you eat like a local rather than a tourist, you will save money this way.

5. Skip the in-house movies. Bring a book. Better yet, walk down the street to see dramatic stories and sights beyond fiction.

6. Try a bed-and-breakfast. They are plentiful in the Bay Area and range from accommodations in houseboats and Victorian mansions to Junior's room when he's away at college. For information and options call Bed & Breakfast California at (800) 872-4500.

■ **Getting a Discounted Rate** ■

Because San Francisco is popular year-round, room rates tend not to fluctuate much. Even so, the market is highly competitive and there are deals to be had for the smart shopper. Check out deals through ads, agents, special events, and openings. These include weekend and convention deals, frequent-mileage clubs, automobile or other travel clubs, senior rates (some with age requirements as low as 50 years), military or government discounts, corporate or shareholder rates, packages, long-stay rates (usually at least five nights), and travel industry rates. Some hotels might even give lower rates if you are visiting because of bereavement or medical problems. You can also try some of the following.

Surf the Net

Check out the Internet. Last-minute bargains are now available online. You can judge comparative value by seeing a listing of hotels—what they offer, where they are located, and what they charge.

Special Weekend Rates

Most hotels that cater to business, government, and convention travelers offer special weekend discount rates that range from 15% to 40% below normal weekday rates. Find out about weekend specials by calling individual hotels or consulting your travel agent.

Getting Corporate Rates

Many hotels offer discounted corporate rates (5–20% off rack rate). Usually you do not need to work for a large company or have a special relationship with the hotel to obtain these rates. Simply call the hotel of your choice and ask for their corporate rates. Many hotels will guarantee you the discounted rate on the phone when you make your reservation. Others may make the rate conditional on your providing some sort of verification, for instance a fax on your company's letterhead requesting the rate, or a company credit card or business card upon check-in. Generally the screening is not rigorous.

Preferred Rates

If you cannot book the hotel of your choice through a half-price program (see below), you and your travel agent may have to search for a smaller discount, often called a preferred rate. A preferred rate might be a discount available to travel agents to stimulate their booking activity or a discount initiated to attract a certain class of traveler. Most preferred rates are promoted through travel industry publications and are accessible only through an agent.

We recommend sounding out your travel agent about possible deals. Be aware, however, that the rates shown on agents' computerized reservations systems are not always the lowest rates obtainable. Zero in on a couple of hotels that fill your needs in terms of location and quality of accommodations, and then have your agent call the hotel for the latest rates and specials. Hotel reps are almost always more responsive to travel agents because agents represent a source of additional business. Again, there are certain specials that hotel reps will disclose only to agents. Travel agents also come in handy when the hotel you want is supposedly booked. A personal appeal from your agent to the hotel's director of sales and marketing will get you a room more than half the time.

Half-Price Programs

Larger discounts on rooms (35–60%) in San Francisco or anywhere else are available through half-price hotel programs, often called travel clubs. Program operators contract with an individual hotel to provide rooms at deep discounts, usually 50% off, on a "space available" basis. Space available in practice means that you can reserve a room at the discounted rate whenever the hotel expects to be at less than 80% occupancy. A little calendar sleuthing to help you avoid special events and citywide conventions will increase your chances of choosing a time when these discounts are available.

Most half-price programs charge an annual membership fee or directory subscription rate of $25–125. Once you're enrolled, you'll receive a membership card and a directory listing participating hotels. You will notice immediately that there are many restrictions and exceptions. Some hotels, for instance, "black out" certain dates or times of year. Others may only offer the discount on certain days of the week or require you to stay a certain number of nights. Still others may offer a much smaller discount than 50% off the rack rate.

Programs specialize in domestic travel, international travel, or both. More established operators offer members between 1,000 and 4,000 hotels to choose from in the United States. All of the programs have a heavy concentration of hotels in California and Florida, and most have a very limited selection of participating properties in New York or Boston. Offerings in other cities and regions of the United States vary considerably. The programs with the largest selections of San Francisco hotels are Encore, ITC-50, Great American Traveler, Quest, Privilege Card, and Entertainment Publications. Each of these programs lists between 20 (Quest) and 53 (Entertainment Publications) hotels in the greater San Francisco area.

Encore	(800) 444-9800
Entertainment Publications	(800) 445-4137
ITC-50	(800) 987-6216
Great American Traveler	(800) 548-2812
Privilege Card	(800) 236-9732
Quest	(800) 742-3543

One problem with half-price programs is that not all hotels offer a full 50% discount. Another slippery problem is the base rate against which the discount is applied. Some hotels figure the discount on an exaggerated rack rate that nobody would ever have to pay. A few participating hotels may deduct the discount from a supposed "superior" or "upgraded" room rate, even though the room you get is the hotel's standard accommodation. Though hard to pin down, the majority of participating properties base discounts on the published rate in the *Hotel & Travel Index* (a quarterly reference work used by travel agents) and work within the spirit of their agreement with the program operator. As a rule, if you travel several times a year, your room rate savings will easily compensate you for program membership fees.

A noteworthy addendum: deeply discounted rooms through half-price programs are not commissionable to travel agents. In practical terms this means that you must ordinarily make your own inquiry calls and reservations. If you travel frequently, however, and run a lot of business through your agent, he or she will probably do your legwork, lack of commission notwithstanding.

Wholesalers, Consolidators, and Reservation Services

If you do not want to join a program or buy a discount directory, you can take advantage of the services of a wholesaler or consolidator. Wholesalers and consolidators buy rooms or options on rooms (room blocks) from hotels at a low, negotiated rate. Then they resell the rooms at a profit through travel agents or tour operators, or directly to the public. Most wholesalers and consolidators have a provision for returning unsold rooms to participating hotels, but they are not inclined to do so. The wholesaler's or consolidator's relationship with any hotel is predicated on volume. If they return rooms unsold, the hotel may not make as many rooms available to them the next time around. Thus wholesalers and consolidators often offer rooms at bargain rates, anywhere from 15–50% off rack, occasionally sacrificing their profit margins in the process, to avoid returning the rooms to the hotel unsold.

When wholesalers and consolidators deal directly with the public, they frequently represent themselves as "reservation services." When you call, you can ask for a rate quote for a particular hotel or ask for their best available deal in the area you prefer. If there is a maximum amount you are willing to pay, say so. Chances are the service will find something that will work for you, even if they have to shave a dollar or two off their own profit. A list of services that sell rooms in San Francisco follows.

Accommodations Express	(800) 444-7666
California Reservations	(800) 576-0003
Central Reservations Service	(800) 548-3311
Hotel Reservations Network	(800) 964-6835
Players Express Vacations	(800) 458-6161
Quikbook	(800) 789-9887
RMC Travel	(800) 245-5738
San Francisco Reservations	(800) 677-1550

The discount available (if any) from a reservation service depends on whether the service functions as a consolidator or a wholesaler. Consolidators are strictly sales agents who do not own or control the room inventory they are trying to sell. Their discounts are determined by the hotels with rooms to fill and vary enormously depending on how desperate the hotel is to unload the rooms. When you deal with a room reservation service that operates as a consolidator, you pay for your room as usual when you check out of the hotel.

Wholesalers have longstanding contracts with hotels that allow the wholesaler to purchase rooms at an established deep discount. Some wholesalers hold purchase options on blocks of rooms, while others actually pay for rooms and own the inventory. Because a wholesaler controls the room inventory, it can offer whatever discount it pleases consistent with current demand. In practice, most wholesaler reservice discounts fall in the 10–40% range. When you reserve a room with a reservation service that operates as a wholesaler, you must usually pay for your entire stay in advance with your credit card. The service then sends you a written confirmation and usually a voucher (indicating prepayment) for you to present at the hotel.

Our experience has been that the reservation services are more useful for finding rooms when availability is scarce than for obtaining deep discounts. When we called the hotels ourselves, we were often able to beat the reservation services' rates when rooms were generally available. When the city was booked, however, and we could not find a room by calling the hotels ourselves, the reservation services could almost always get us a room at a fair price.

▪ How to Evaluate a Travel Package ▪

Hundreds of San Francisco package vacations are offered to the public each year. Packages should be a win-win proposition for both the buyer and the seller. The buyer only has to make one phone call and deal with a single salesperson to set up the whole vacation—transportation, rental car, lodging, meals, attraction admissions, and even golf and tennis. The seller, likewise, only has to deal with the buyer once, eliminating the need for separate sales, confirmations, and billing. In addition to streamlining sales, processing, and administration, some packagers also buy airfares in bulk on contract like a broker playing the commodities market. Buying a large number of airfares in advance allows the packager to buy them at a significant savings from posted fares. The same practice is also applied to hotel rooms. Because selling vacation packages is an efficient way of doing business, and because the packager can often buy individual package components (airfare, lodging, etc.) in bulk at a discount, savings in operating expenses realized by the seller are sometimes passed on to the buyer. This means that, in addition to convenience, the package is an exceptional value. In any event, that's the way it is supposed to work.

In practice, all too often the seller cashes in on discounts and passes none on to the buyer. In some instances, packages are loaded with extras that cost the packager next to nothing but inflate the retail price sky-high. As you would expect, the savings to be passed along to customers do not materialize.

When considering a package, you should choose one that includes features you are sure to use; whether you use all the features or not, you will most certainly pay for them. Second, if cost is of greater concern than convenience, make a few phone calls and see what the package would cost if you booked its individual components (airfare, rental car, lodging, etc.) on your own. If the package price is less than the à la carte cost, the package is a good deal. If the costs are about the same, the package is probably worth buying just for the convenience.

If your package includes a choice of rental car or airport transfers (transportation to and from the airport), take the car if your hotel offers free (or at least affordable) parking. Take the transfers if you plan to spend your time in the area from Nob Hill and Union Square down to the San Francisco Bay. If you want to run around town or go on excursions outside the city, take the car. And if you take the car, be sure to ask if the package includes free parking at your hotel.

Tour operators, of course, prefer to sell you a whole vacation package. When business is slow, however, they will often agree to sell you just the lodging component of the package, usually at a nicely discounted rate.

Hotel-Sponsored Packages

In addition to tour operators, packages are frequently offered by hotels. Usually "land only" (i.e., no airfare included), the hotel packages are sometimes exceptional deals. Promotion of hotel specials tends to be limited to the hotel's primary markets, which for most properties is California, Washington, Oregon, Arizona, Hawaii, Nevada, Texas, Illinois, and New York. If you live in other parts of the country, you can take advantage of the packages but probably will not see them advertised in your local newspaper. An important point regarding hotel specials is that the hotel reservationists do not usually inform you of existing specials or offer them to you. In other words, you have to ask.

■ Helping Your Travel Agent Help You ■

When you call your travel agent, ask if he or she has been to San Francisco. If the answer is no, be prepared to give your travel agent some direction. Do not accept any recommendations at face value. Check out the location and rates of each suggested hotel and make sure the hotel is suited to your itinerary.

Because some travel agents are unfamiliar with San Francisco, your agent may try to plug you into a tour operator's preset package. This essentially allows the travel agent to set up your whole trip with a single phone call and still collect an 8–10% commission. The problem with this scenario is that most agents will place 90% of their San Francisco business with only one or two wholesalers or tour operators. In other words, it's the line of least resistance for them and leaves you with very little choice.

Travel agents will often use wholesalers who run packages in conjunction with airlines, such as Delta Vacations or American Airlines' Fly-Away Vacations. Because of the wholesaler's exclusive relationship with the carrier, these trips are easy for travel agents to book. However, they will probably be more expensive than a package offered by a high-volume wholesaler who works with a number of airlines in a primary San Francisco market.

To help your travel agent get you the best possible deal, do the following:

1. Determine where you want to stay in San Francisco, and if possible choose a specific hotel. This can be accomplished by reviewing the hotel information in this guide and by writing or calling hotels that interest you.

2. Check out the hotel deals and package vacations advertised in the Sunday travel sections of the *Los Angeles Times, San Francisco Examiner,* or *Dallas Morning News* newspapers. Often you will

be able to find deals that beat the socks off anything offered in your local paper. See if you can find specials that fit your plans and include a hotel you like.

3. Call the hotels or tour operators whose ads you have collected. Ask any questions you have about their packages, but do not book your trip with them directly.

4. Tell your travel agent about the deals you find and ask if he or she can get you something better. The deals in the paper will serve as a benchmark against which to compare alternatives your agent proposes.

5. Choose from the options that you and your travel agent uncover. No matter which option you select, have your agent book it. Even if you go with one of the packages in the newspaper, it will probably be commissionable (at no additional cost to you) and will provide the agent some return on the time invested on your behalf. Also, as a travel professional, your agent should be able to verify the quality and integrity of the deal.

■ If You Make Your Own Reservation ■

As you poke around trying to find a good deal, there are several things you should know. First, always call the specific hotel rather than the hotel chain's national, toll-free number. Quite often, the reservationists at the national number are unaware of local specials. Always ask about specials before you inquire about corporate rates. Do not be reluctant to bargain. If you are buying a hotel's weekend package, for example, and want to extend your stay into the following week, you can often obtain at least the corporate rate for the extra days. Do your bargaining, however, before you check in, preferably when you make your reservations.

Hotel and Motel Toll-Free 800 Numbers	
Best Western	(800) 528-1234 U.S. and Canada
	(800) 528-2222 TDD
Comfort Inn	(800) 228-5150 U.S.
Courtyard by Marriott	(800) 321-2211 U.S.
Days Inn	(800) 325-2525 U.S.
Doubletree Hotels	(800) 222-8733 U.S. and Canada
Econo Lodge	(800) 424-4777 U.S.
Embassy Suites	(800) 362-2779 U.S. and Canada
Fairfield Inn by Marriott	(800) 228-2800 U.S.
Hampton Inn	(800) 426-7866 U.S. and Canada
Hilton	(800) 445-8667 U.S.
	(800) 368-1133 TDD
Holiday Inn	(800) 465-4329 U.S. and Canada
Howard Johnson	(800) 654-2000 U.S. and Canada
	(800) 654-8442 TDD
Hyatt	(800) 233-1234 U.S. and Canada
Loew's	(800) 223-0888 U.S. and Canada
Marriott	(800) 228-9290 U.S. and Canada
	(800) 228-7014 TDD
Quality Inn	(800) 228-5151 U.S. and Canada
Radisson	(800) 333-3333 U.S. and Canada
Ramada Inn	(800) 228-3838 U.S.
	(800) 228-3232 TDD
Renaissance Hotels and Resorts	(800) 468-3571 U.S. and Canada
Residence Inn by Marriott	(800) 331-3131 U.S.
Ritz-Carlton	(800) 241-3333 U.S.
Sheraton	(800) 325-3535 U.S. and Canada
Wyndham	(800) 822-4200 U.S.

Hotels and Motels: Rated and Ranked

■ What's in a Room? ■

Except for cleanliness, state of repair, and decor, most travelers do not pay much attention to hotel rooms. There is, of course, a discernible standard of quality and luxury that differentiates Motel 6 from Holiday Inn, Holiday Inn from Marriott, and so on. In general, however, hotel guests fail to appreciate the fact that some rooms are better engineered than others.

Contrary to what you might suppose, designing a hotel room is (or should be) more complex than picking a bedspread to match the carpet and drapes. Making the room usable to its occupants is an art, a planning discipline that combines form and function.

Decor and taste are important, certainly. No one wants to spend several days in a room with a decor that is dated, garish, or even ugly. But beyond the decor, several variables determine how livable a hotel room is. In San Francisco, for example, we have seen some beautifully appointed rooms that are simply not well designed for human habitation. The next time you stay in a hotel, pay attention to the details and design elements of your room. Even more than decor, these will make you feel comfortable and at home.

It takes the *Unofficial Guide* researchers quite a while to inspect a hotel room. Here are a few of the things we check and suggest you check, too.

Room Size   While some smaller rooms are cozy and well designed, a large and uncluttered room is generally preferable, especially for a stay of more than three days.

Temperature Control, Ventilation, and Odor   The guest should be able to control the temperature of the room. The best system, because it's so quiet, is central heating and air-conditioning controlled by the room's own thermostat. The next best system is a room module heater and air-conditioner, preferably controlled by an automatic thermostat but usually by manually operated button controls. The worst system is central heating and air without any sort of room thermostat or guest control.

The vast majority of hotel rooms have windows or balcony doors that have been permanently sealed. Though there are some legitimate safety and liability issues involved, we prefer windows and balcony doors that can be opened to admit fresh air. Hotel rooms should be odor free and smoke free, and they should not feel stuffy or damp.

Room Security Better rooms have locks that require a plastic card instead of the traditional lock and key. Card and slot systems allow the hotel to change the combination or entry code of the lock with each new guest. A burglar who has somehow acquired a conventional room key can afford to wait until the situation is right before using the key to gain access. Not so with a card-and-slot system. Though larger hotels and hotel chains with lock-and-key systems usually rotate their locks once each year, they remain vulnerable to hotel thieves much of the time. Many smaller or independent properties rarely rotate their locks.

In addition to the entry lock system, the door should have a deadbolt and preferably a chain that can be locked from the inside as well. A chain by itself is not sufficient. Doors should also have a peephole. Windows and balcony doors should have secure locks.

Safety Every room should have a fire or smoke alarm, clear fire instructions, and preferably a sprinkler system. Bathtubs should have a nonskid surface, and shower stalls should have doors that open outward or slide side to side. Bathroom electrical outlets should be high on the wall and not too close to the sink. Balconies should have sturdy, high rails.

Noise Most travelers have been kept awake by the television, partying, or amorous activities of people in the next room, or by traffic on the street outside. Better hotels are designed with noise control in mind. Wall and ceiling constructions are substantial, effectively screening routine noise. Carpets and drapes, in addition to being decorative, also absorb and muffle sounds. Mattresses mounted on stable platforms or sturdy bed frames do not squeak even when challenged by the most acrobatic lovers. Televisions are enclosed in cabinets and have volume governors so that they rarely disturb guests in adjacent rooms.

In better hotels, the air-conditioning and heating system is well maintained and operates without noise or vibration. Likewise, plumbing is quiet and positioned away from the sleeping area. Doors to the hall and adjoining rooms are thick and well fitted to better block out noise.

If you are easily disturbed by noise, ask for a room on a higher floor, off main thoroughfares, and away from elevators and vending machines.

Darkness Control Ever been in a hotel room where the curtains would not quite meet in the middle? Thick, lined curtains that close completely in the center and extend beyond the edges of the window or door frame are required. In a well-planned room, the curtains, shades, or blinds should almost totally block light at any time of day.

Lighting Poor lighting is a common problem in American hotel rooms. The lighting is usually adequate for dressing, relaxing, or watching television, but not for reading or working. Lighting needs to be bright over tables and desks, and beside couches and easy chairs. Since so many people read in bed, there should be a separate light for each person. A room with two queen beds should have individual lights for four people. Better bedside reading lights illuminate a small area, so if one person wants to sleep and another wants to read, the sleeper will not be bothered by the light. The worst situation by far is a single lamp on a table between beds. In each bed, only the person next to the lamp has sufficient light to read. This deficiency is often compounded by weak light bulbs.

In addition, closet areas should be well lit, and there should be a switch near the door that turns on room lights when you enter. A desirable but seldom seen feature is a bedside console that allows a guest to control all or most lights in the room from bed.

Furnishings At a bare minimum, the bed(s) should be firm. Pillows should be made with nonallergenic fillers, and a blanket should be provided in addition to the sheets and a spread. Bedclothes should be laundered with fabric softener and changed daily. Better hotels usually provide extra blankets and pillows in the room or on request, and they sometimes place a second top sheet between the blanket and spread.

There should be a dresser large enough to hold clothes for two people during a five-day stay. A small table with two chairs, or a desk with a chair, should be provided. The room should be equipped with a luggage rack and a three-quarter- to full-length mirror.

The television should be color and cable-connected; ideally, it should have a volume governor and a remote control. It should be mounted on a swivel base and preferably enclosed in a cabinet. Local channels should be posted on the set, and a local TV program guide should be supplied. The telephone should be touch-tone and conveniently situated for bedside use, and it should have on or near it clear dialing instructions and a rate card. Local white and Yellow Pages should be provided. Better hotels install phones in the bathroom and equip room phones with long cords.

Well-designed hotel rooms usually have a plush armchair or a sleeper sofa for lounging and reading. Better headboards are padded for comfortable reading in bed, and there should be a nightstand or table on each side of the bed(s). Nice extras in any hotel room include a small refrigerator, a digital alarm clock, and a coffeemaker.

Bathroom Two sinks are better than one, and you cannot have too much counter space. A sink outside the bath is a great convenience when one person bathes as another dresses. Sinks should have drains with stoppers.

Better bathrooms have a tub and shower with a nonslip bottom. Tub and shower controls should be easy to operate. Adjustable shower heads are preferred. The bath needs to be well lit and should have an exhaust fan and a guest-controlled bathroom heater. Towels and washcloths should be large, soft, fluffy, and generously supplied. There should be an electrical outlet for each sink, conveniently and safely placed.

Complimentary shampoo, conditioner, and lotion are a plus, as are robes and bathmats. Better hotels supply tissues and extra toilet paper in the bathrooms. Luxurious baths feature a phone, a hair dryer, and sometimes a small television or even a Jacuzzi.

Vending   Complimentary ice and a drink machine should be located on each floor. Welcome additions include a snack machine and a sundries (combs, toothpaste) machine. The latter are seldom found in large hotels that have restaurants and shops.

■ Room Ratings ■

To distinguish properties according to relative quality, tastefulness, state of repair, cleanliness, and size of standard rooms, we have grouped the hotels and motels into classifications denoted by stars. Star ratings in this guide apply to San Francisco–area properties only and do not necessarily correspond to ratings awarded by Mobil, AAA, or other travel critics. Because stars carry little weight when awarded in the absence of commonly recognized standards of comparison, we have linked our ratings to expected levels of quality established by specific American hotel corporations.

Room Star Ratings		
★★★★★	Superior Rooms	Tasteful and luxurious by any standard
★★★★	Extremely Nice Rooms	What you would expect at a Hyatt Regency or Marriott
★★★	Nice Rooms	Holiday Inn or comparable quality
★★	Adequate Rooms	Clean, comfortable, and functional without frills (like a Motel 6)
★	Super Budget	

Star ratings apply to room quality only and describe the property's standard accommodations. For most hotels and motels, a "standard accommodation" is a hotel room with either one king bed or two queen beds. In an all-suite property, the standard accommodation is either a one- or two-room suite. In addition to standard accommodations, many hotels offer luxury rooms and special suites that are not rated in this guide. Star ratings for rooms are assigned without regard to whether a property has restaurant(s), recreational facilities, entertainment, or other extras.

In addition to stars (which delineate broad categories), we also employ a numerical rating system. Our rating scale is 0–100, with 100 as the best possible rating, and zero (0) as the worst. Numerical ratings are presented to show the difference we perceive between one property and another. For instance, rooms at the **Sherman House,** the **Archbishop's Mansion,** and the **Westin Saint Francis** are all rated as four and a half stars (★★★★½). In the supplemental numerical ratings, the Sherman House is rated a 95, the Archbishop's Mansion is rated a 93, and the Westin Saint Francis is a 90. This means that within the four-and-a-half-star category, the Sherman House and Archbishop's Mansion are comparable, and both have slightly nicer rooms than the Westin Saint Francis.

The location column identifies the greater San Francisco area where you will find a particular property.

■ How the Hotels Compare ■

Cost estimates are based on the hotel's published rack rates for standard rooms. Each "$" represents $40. Thus a cost symbol of "$$$" means a room (or suite) at that hotel will cost about $120 a night.

Below is a hit parade of the nicest rooms in town. We've focused strictly on room quality and have excluded any consideration of location, services, recreation, or amenities. In some instances, a one- or two-room suite can be had for the same price or less than that of a hotel room.

If you use subsequent editions of this guide, you will notice that many of the ratings and rankings change. In addition to the inclusion of new properties, these changes also consider guest-room renovations or improved maintenance and housekeeping. A failure to properly maintain guest rooms or a lapse in housekeeping standards can negatively affect the ratings.

Finally, before you begin to shop for a hotel, take a hard look at this letter we received from a couple in Hot Springs, Arkansas:

We cancelled our room reservations to follow the advice in your book [and reserved a hotel room highly ranked by the Unofficial

Guide]. *We wanted inexpensive, but clean and cheerful. We got inexpensive, but [also] dirty, grim, and depressing. I really felt disappointed in your advice and the room. It was the pits. That was the one real piece of information I needed from your book! The room spoiled the holiday for me aside from our touring.*

Needless to say, this letter was as unsettling to us as the bad room was to our reader. Our integrity as travel journalists, after all, is based on the quality of the information we give our readers. Even with the best of intentions and the most conscientious research, however, we cannot inspect every room in every hotel. What we do, in statistical terms, is take a sample. We check out several rooms selected at random in each hotel and base our ratings and rankings on those rooms. The inspections are conducted anonymously and without the knowledge of the management. Although unusual, it is certainly possible that the rooms we randomly inspect are not representative of the majority of rooms at a particular hotel. Another possibility is that the rooms we inspect in a given hotel are representative, but that by bad luck a reader is assigned a room that is inferior. When we rechecked the hotel our reader disliked, we discovered our rating was correctly representative, but that he and his wife had unfortunately been assigned to one of a small number of threadbare rooms scheduled for renovation.

The key to avoiding disappointment is to snoop around in advance. We recommend that you ask for a photo of a hotel's standard guest room before you book, or at least get a copy of the hotel's promotional brochure. Be forewarned, however, that some hotel chains use the same guest-room photo in their promotional literature for all hotels in the chain; a specific guest room may not resemble the brochure photo. When you or your travel agent call, ask how old the property is and when your guest room was last renovated. If you arrive and are assigned a room inferior to that which you had been led to expect, demand to be moved to another room.

How the Hotels Compare in San Francisco				
Hotel	Zone	Star Rating	Quality Rating	Cost ($ = $40)
The Pan Pacific Hotel	3	★★★★★	97	$$$$$–
Mandarin Oriental	4	★★★★★	96	$$$$$$$–
The Ritz-Carlton	1	★★★★★	96	$$$$$$–
Hotel Nikko	3	★★★★½	95	$$$$$+
The Sherman House	5	★★★★½	95	$$$$$$–
The Archbishop's Mansion	2	★★★★½	93	$$$$+

How the Hotels Compare in San Francisco (continued)

Hotel	Zone	Star Rating	Quality Rating	Cost ($ = $40)
Inn Above the Tide	9	★★★★½	93	$$$$–
Nob Hill Lambourne	3	★★★★½	93	$$$$–
ANA Hotel San Francisco	7	★★★★½	92	$$$$$–
Campton Place Hotel	3	★★★★½	92	$$$$$$–
The Prescott Hotel	3	★★★★½	92	$$$$+
Sheraton Palace Hotel	7	★★★★½	92	$$$$$$+
Casa Madrona	9	★★★★½	91	$$$–
Claremont Resort	12	★★★★½	91	$$$$–
Fairmont Hotel	1	★★★★½	91	$$$$$–
Hotel Monaco	3	★★★★½	91	$$$$$–
Hotel Majestic	2	★★★★½	90	$$$–
Renaissance Stanford Court Hotel	1	★★★★½	90	$$$$$$–
The Westin St. Francis	3	★★★★½	90	$$$$$$–
White Swan Inn	3	★★★★½	90	$$$+
The Clift Hotel	3	★★★★	88	$$$$$+
Grand Hyatt San Francisco	3	★★★★	88	$$$$$$–
Westin Hotel San Francisco Airport	SFIA	★★★★	88	$$$$+
The Donatello	3	★★★★	86	$$$$–
Embassy Suites Hotel	10	★★★★	86	$$$$–
Hotel Triton	3	★★★★	86	$$$$+
Hyatt Regency San Francisco	4	★★★★	86	$$$$$$
Hyatt Regency San Francisco Airport	SFIA	★★★★	86	$$$$+
Warwick Regis Hotel	3	★★★★	86	$$$–
Hyatt Fisherman's Wharf	6	★★★★	85	$$$$+
Parc Fifty Five	3	★★★★	85	$$$$$–
San Francisco Hilton and Towers	3	★★★★	85	$$$$+
San Francisco Marriott	7	★★★★	85	$$$$$–
Wyndham Garden Hotel	10	★★★★	85	$$+
Embassy Suites SFO	SFIA	★★★★	84	$$$$+
Galleria Park Hotel	3	★★★★	84	$$$$$
Mark Hopkins Inter-Continental	3	★★★★	84	$$$$$+
San Francisco Airport Marriott	SFIA	★★★★	84	$$$$–

How the Hotels Compare in San Francisco (continued)

Hotel	Zone	Star Rating	Quality Rating	Cost ($ = $40)
Berkeley Marina Marriott	12	★★★★	83	$$$–
Inn at the Opera	2	★★★★	83	$$$
Sheraton at Fisherman's Wharf	6	★★★★	83	$$$$–
Crowne Plaza	SFIA	★★★½	82	$$$+
Hotel Diva	3	★★★½	82	$$$–
Hotel Juliana	3	★★★½	82	$$$$–
Hotel Milano	7	★★★½	82	$$$+
Waterfront Plaza Hotel	13	★★★½	82	$$$+
Harbor Court Hotel	7	★★★½	81	$$$$$–
Holiday Inn Financial District	1	★★★½	81	$$$–
Crowne Plaza Union Square	3	★★★½	81	$$$$+
Hotel Rex	3	★★★½	81	$$$$$–
The Huntington Hotel	1	★★★½	81	$$$$$+
Oakland Airport Hilton	OIA	★★★½	81	$$$$–
San Francisco Marriott Fisherman's Wharf	6	★★★½	81	$$$$–
Alamo Square Inn	2	★★★½	80	$$$–
Doubletree Hotel San Francisco Airport	SFIA	★★★½	80	$$$+
Kensington Park Hotel	3	★★★½	80	$$$–
Union Street Inn	5	★★★½	80	$$$$–
Holiday Inn Fisherman's Wharf	6	★★★½	79	$$$$
Howard Johnson Hotel Fish. Wharf	6	★★★½	78	$$$–
Shannon Court Hotel	3	★★★½	78	$$+
Hotel Griffon	7	★★★½	77	$$$$–
Monticello Inn	3	★★★½	77	$$$+
Hotel Bijou	3	★★★½	76	$$–
The Mansions	2	★★★½	76	$$$+
Radisson Miyako Hotel	2	★★★½	76	$$$$–
Beresford Arms	3	★★★½	75	$$$–
Oakland Marriott City Center	13	★★★½	75	$$$–
Edward II Inn	5	★★★	74	$$–
Golden Gate Hotel	3	★★★	73	$$–
The Inn at Union Square	3	★★★	73	$$$

How the Hotels Compare in San Francisco (continued)

Hotel	Zone	Star Rating	Quality Rating	Cost ($ = $40)
The Carlton	2	★★★	73	$$$+
The Handley Union Square Hotel	3	★★★	72	$$$−
The Maxwell	3	★★★	72	$$$−
Savoy Hotel	3	★★★	72	$$$−
Marina Inn	5	★★★	71	$$+
Sir Francis Drake Hotel	3	★★★	71	$$$$−
Stanyan Park Hotel	8	★★★	71	$$+
Villa Florence	3	★★★	71	$$$$+
The Abigail Hotel	2	★★★	70	$$−
Hotel Vintage Court	3	★★★	70	$$$+
Amsterdam Hotel	3	★★★	69	$$−
Andrews Hotel	3	★★★	69	$$−
Park Plaza	SFIA	★★★	68	$$$−
Petite Auberge	3	★★★	68	$$$−
Cartwright Hotel	3	★★★	67	$$$−
Cow Hollow Motor Inn and Suites	5	★★★	67	$$−
Hotel Durant	12	★★★	67	$$$−
Queen Anne Hotel	2	★★★	67	$$$−
Best Western Grosvenor Hotel	SFIA	★★★	66	$$+
Hotel Californian	3	★★★	66	$$−
King George Hotel	3	★★★	66	$$$
Ramada Plaza Fisherman's Wharf	6	★★★	66	$$$$$−
Park Plaza Hotel	OIA	★★★	65	$$$−
The Phoenix Inn	2	★★★	65	$$+
Clarion Bedford Hotel	3	★★½	64	$$$−
Hampton Inn Oakland Airport	OIA	★★½	64	$$+
Laurel Motor Inn	8	★★½	64	$$+
Ramada Limited Golden Gate	5	★★½	64	$$−
Best Western Miyako Inn	2	★★½	63	$$−
Comfort Inn by the Bay	5	★★½	63	$$$$−
Travelodge San Francisco Airport North	SFIA	★★½	63	$$−
Grant Plaza	3	★★½	62	$$−

How the Hotels Compare in San Francisco (continued)

Hotel	Zone	Star Rating	Quality Rating	Cost ($=$40)
Holiday Inn Oakland Airport (interior rooms)	OIA	★★½	62	$$$–
Travelodge Bel Aire	5	★★½	62	$$–
Travelodge by the Bay	5	★★½	62	$$+
Buena Vista Motor Inn	5	★★½	61	$$+
Hotel Sheehan	3	★★½	60	$$+
Pacific Motor Inn	5	★★½	60	$$$–
Red Roof Inn	SFIA	★★½	60	$$
Vagabond Inn Airport	SFIA	★★½	60	$$–
Days Inn at the Beach	8	★★½	59	$$–
Days Inn Oakland Airport	OIA	★★½	59	$$–
Holiday Lodge	2	★★½	59	$$+
Ramada San Francisco Airport	SFIA	★★½	59	$$$–
Commodore International Hotel	3	★★½	58	$$–
Holiday Inn Oakland Airport (exterior rooms)	OIA	★★½	58	$$$–
Hotel Beresford	3	★★½	58	$$+
Marina Motel	5	★★½	58	$$–
Seal Rock Inn	8	★★½	58	$$+
Super 8 Motel	5	★★½	58	$$
Best Western Canterbury Hotel	3	★★½	57	$$$–
Days Inn Fisherman's Wharf	5	★★½	57	$$+
Villa Inn	10	★★½	57	$$–
Chelsea Motor Inn	5	★★	55	$$–
Town House Motel	5	★★	54	$$–
The Fitzgerald	3	★★	53	$$+
Redwood Inn	5	★★	53	$$–
Star Motel	5	★★	53	$$–
Pacific Heights Inn	5	★★	52	$$+
Travelodge Golden Gate	5	★★	52	$$–
Travelodge on Columbus	6	★★	51	$$+
Capri Motel	5	★★	48	$$–

	Star	Quality	Cost
How the Hotels Compare in the Wine Country			
Hotel	Rating	Rating	($=$40)
Auberge du Soleil	★★★★★	96	$$$$$$$
Cottage Grove Inn	★★★★½	93	$$$$–
Napa Valley Lodge	★★★★½	93	$$$+
Cedar Gables Inn	★★★★½	91	$$$–
The Inn at Southbridge	★★★★½	91	$$$$$$$–
Vintage Inn	★★★★½	90	$$$$$–
Vintner's Inn	★★★★	89	$$$+
Sonoma County Hilton Santa Rosa	★★★★	87	$$$–
Marriott Hotel Napa Valley	★★★★	85	$$$–
Silverado Country Club and Resort	★★★★	84	$$$
El Dorado Hotel	★★★★	83	$$$$
Rancho Caymus	★★★★	83	$$$$–
Harvest Inn	★★★½	82	$$$$+
Mount View Hotel	★★★½	82	$$$–
Sonoma Mission Inn and Spa	★★★½	82	$$$$$
Fountaingrove Inn	★★★½	81	$$$+
Napa Valley Railway Inn	★★★½	76	$$$–
Sonoma Hotel	★★★½	75	$$+
Best Western Sonoma Valley Inn	★★★	73	$$$–
Brannon Cottage Inn	★★★	73	$$$+
Falcon's Nest	★★★	73	$$$–
Hotel St. Helena	★★★	71	$$$$–
El Peublo Inn	★★★	68	$$
El Bonita Motel	★★★	66	$$$–
John Muir Inn	★★★	65	$$+
Chateau Hotel	★★½	64	$$+
Calistoga Inn	★★½	61	$+
Dr. Wilkinson's Hot Springs	★★½	60	$$–

■ The Best Deals ■

Now that we've listed the nicest rooms in town, let's reorder the list to rank the best combinations of quality and value in a room. As before, the rankings are made without consideration of location or the availability of restaurant(s), recreational facilities, entertainment, and/or amenities. Once again, each lodging property is awarded a value rating on a 0–100 scale. The higher the rating, the better the value.

A reader recently complained to us that he had booked one of our top-ranked rooms in terms of value and had been very disappointed in the room. We noticed that the room the reader occupied had a quality rating of ★★½. We would remind you that the value ratings are intended to give you some sense of value received for dollars spent. A ★★½ room at $30 may have the same value rating as a ★★★★ room at $95, but that does not mean the rooms will be of comparable quality. Regardless of whether it's a good deal or not, a ★★½ room is still a ★★½ room.

Listed below are the best room buys for the money, regardless of location or star classification, based on averaged rack rates. Note that sometimes a suite can cost less than a hotel room.

The Top 30 Best Deals in San Francisco

Hotel	Quality Rating	Star Rating	Cost ($ = $40)
1. Casa Madrona	91	★★★★½	$$$−
2. Wyndham Garden Hotel	85	★★★★	$$+
3. Hotel Majestic	90	★★★★½	$$$−
4. Hotel Bijou	76	★★★½	$$−
5. White Swan Inn	90	★★★★½	$$$+
6. Nob Hill Lambourne	93	★★★★½	$$$$−
7. Berkeley Marina Marriott	83	★★★★	$$$−
8. Warwick Regis Hotel	86	★★★★	$$$−
9. Edward II Inn	74	★★★	$$−
10. Amsterdam Hotel	69	★★★	$$−
11. Shannon Court Hotel	78	★★★½	$$+
12. The Abigail Hotel	70	★★★	$$−
13. Alamo Square Inn	80	★★★½	$$$−
14. Inn at the Opera	83	★★★★	$$$
15. Golden Gate Hotel	73	★★★	$$−
16. Cow Hollow Motor Inn and Suites	67	★★★	$$−

The Top 30 Best Deals in San Francisco (continued)

Hotel	Quality Rating	Star Rating	Cost ($=$40)
17. Inn Above the Tide	93	★★★★½	$$$$–
18. Claremont Resort	91	★★★★½	$$$$–
19. Beresford Arms	75	★★★½	$$$–
20. Andrews Hotel	69	★★★	$$–
21. The Prescott Hotel	92	★★★★½	$$$$+
22. Holiday Inn Financial District	81	★★★½	$$$–
23. Marina Inn	71	★★★	$$+
24. Kensington Park Hotel	80	★★★½	$$$+
25. Hotel Californian	66	★★★	$$–
26. Grant Plaza	62	★★½	$$–
27. Westin Hotel San Francisco Airport	88	★★★★	$$$$+
28. Howard Johnson Hotel Fish. Wharf	78	★★★½	$$$–
29. Oakland Marriott City Center	75	★★★½	$$$–
30. Stanyan Park Hotel	71	★★★	$$+

The Top 10 Best Deals in the Wine Country

Hotel	Quality Rating	Star Rating	Cost ($=$40)
1. Cedar Gables Inn	91	★★★★½	$$$–
2. Napa Valley Lodge	93	★★★★½	$$$+
3. Sonoma County Hilton Santa Rosa	87	★★★★	$$$–
4. Marriott Hotel Napa Valley	85	★★★★	$$$–
5. Calistoga Inn	61	★★½	$+
6. Sonoma Hotel	75	★★★½	$$+
7. Silverado Country Club and Resort	84	★★★★	$$$
8. Cottage Grove Inn	93	★★★★½	$$$$–
9. Vintner's Inn	89	★★★★	$$$+
10. Napa Valley Railway Inn	76	★★★½	$$$–

PART THREE

Visiting San Francisco on Business

Not All Visitors Are Headed for Fisherman's Wharf

While most of the 3.5 million overnight visitors who come to San Francisco each year are tourists, not every visitor has an itinerary centered around strolling through Chinatown, taking a ferry to Alcatraz, or hanging around Fisherman's Wharf. In fact, nearly 1.5 million people who came to San Francisco in 1996 were meeting, convention, and trade-show delegates. And many other visitors each year are men and women on business trips.

Located about 50 miles north of Silicon Valley, San Francisco is a center for high-technology business and manufacturing. Corporations with a major presence in San Francisco include Chevron, Hewlett-Packard, Bank America, Intel, Apple Computer, Sun Microsystems, Wells Fargo, Seagate Technology, and The Gap.

The city is also a major center for higher education. It's the home of San Francisco State University, the University of San Francisco, Hastings College of Law (University of California), the University of California Medical Center, the San Francisco Art Institute, and other public and private colleges. Across the bay is the University of California, Berkeley, one of the world's great research institutions. As a result, San Francisco attracts many visiting academics, college administrators, and students and their families.

In many ways, the problems facing business visitors on their first trip to San Francisco don't differ much from the problems of folks in town intent on seeing its best-known tourist attractions and breathtaking scenery. Business visitors need to be in a hotel that's convenient; they want to avoid the worst of the city's traffic, they face the same problems getting around an unfamiliar city, and they want to know the locations of San Francisco's best restaurants. This book can help. For the most part, though, business visitors aren't nearly as flexible about the timing of their visit as folks who pick San Francisco as a vacation destination. While we advise that the best times to visit are the shoulder seasons between winter and summer, the necessities of business may dictate that August, when the city is often shrouded in fog, or January, the rainiest month, is when you pull into town.

Much of the advice and information presented in the *Unofficial Guide* is as valuable for business visitors and convention-goers as it is for tourists. As for our recommendations on seeing the Bay Area's many attractions, who knows? Maybe you'll find the time to squeeze a morning or afternoon out of your busy schedule, grab this book, and spend a few hours exploring some of the places that draw millions of visitors to San Francisco each year.

■ The Moscone Center ■

San Francisco is home to one major convention center, the 1.3-million-square-foot Moscone Center, actually two convention venues (Moscone North and Moscone South) on adjacent, 11-acre blocks bounded by Mission, Folsom, Third, and Fourth Streets near the heart of downtown. Named for San Francisco Mayor George R. Moscone (murdered in 1978 along with Supervisor Harvey Milk), this modern, $330 million convention center (747 Howard Street, San Francisco, CA 94103; (415) 974-4000) is located in the booming area South of Market District (called SoMa), four blocks south of Union Square.

Because Moscone Center was built close to the action in one of America's most exciting cities, convention-goers never feel trapped here. Within walking distance are 20,000 hotel rooms, the city's major shopping district, the Powell Street cable cars to **Chinatown, Nob Hill,** and **Fisherman's Wharf,** and many of San Francisco's best restaurants. Wait, there's more. Next door is the new **San Francisco Museum of Modern Art (SFMOMA),** and across the street is the **Yerba Buena Center,** with a park, art gallery, theaters, and cafés. Without a doubt, San Francisco and the Moscone Center add up to one of the best convention destinations in the world.

In the future, it's going to get even better. Already evolving into San Francisco's premier neighborhood for art, cuisine, and night life, SoMa will be adding new attractions over the next few years. The long-awaited **Children's Center at Yerba Buena Gardens** is scheduled to open in 1998 and will include an NHL regulation-size ice-skating rink, the Studio for Technology and the Arts, a bowling center, gardens, a 1903 Charles Looff carousel, and a daycare center. The **Sony Urban Entertainment Center,** a cinema, retail, and entertainment complex, will occupy an adjacent corner.

Already home to the **San Francisco Museum of Modern Art,** the **Ansel Adams Center,** the **California Historical Society,** the **Cartoon Art Museum,** and several art galleries, SoMa will also become home to two other established San Francisco museums—the **Mexican Museum** and the **Jewish Museum**; both should be in new digs near the Moscone Center in the next two or three years.

The Layout

Moscone South, which opened in 1981, offers 260,560 square feet of primary exhibit area in a column-free space that can be divided into three halls. (The distinctive arches that make the hall column-free also reduce usable floor space by about 40%.) Forty-one flexible meeting rooms provide more than 60,000 square feet of meeting space. The lobby-level, 42,675-square-foot Esplanade Ballroom (a newer facility added in 1991) accommodates more than 5,000 delegates and is surrounded by terraced patios.

Across the street and connected to Moscone South by an underground concourse and a pedestrian sky bridge is the smaller Moscone North, which opened in 1992 and contains 181,440 square feet of exhibit space in two halls and up to 53,410 square feet of flexible meeting space in 17 rooms. The lobby provides a striking entrance to the exhibit level; delegates descend on escalators and stairs illuminated by skylights.

Both buildings are modern, bright, and airy, featuring extensive use of skylights and large expanses of glass that admit ample light to the mostly underground site. Outside, the two buildings are enhanced by landscaped walkways, gardens, patios, sculptures, and a walk-through fountain. In a nice touch, the meeting rooms on the mezzanine level in Moscone South have windows that overlook the main hall.

All major exhibit areas and most meeting rooms are on one underground level linked by the underground concourse; additional meeting rooms are located on Moscone South's mezzanine level. Twenty completely enclosed loading docks are located on the same level as the main halls, providing direct drive-in access to both exhibit halls.

A note to exhibitors: All installation and dismantling of exhibits, and all handling of materials require union labor, including signs and carpet laying. But union labor isn't required for the unpacking and placement of exhibitors' merchandise in the booth, nor is it required if the display can be installed by one person in less than 30 minutes without the use of tools.

Services

Two business centers, one each in the lower lobbies of Moscone North and Moscone South, provide access to photocopying services, transparencies, fax, overnight mail, UPS, office supplies, and cellular phone rental. The centers are open during event hours, and major credit cards are accepted for purchases and services.

Nursing services are on site during events at first-aid stations in Moscone North, Moscone South, and the esplanade level. A gift shop in the Moscone South lower lobby sells souvenirs. Hungry? Each convention group works with the Moscone Center to set up food service, so food availablility differs with each convention. However, the neighborhood is full of places to eat, ranging from fast food and cafés to gourmet fare. The closest places to grab a quick bite to eat are the two cafés located in Yerba Buena Center and the Museum of Modern Art café, which offers reasonably priced sandwiches, salads, desserts, beer, and wine (closed Wednesdays).

Parking and Public Transportation

The Moscone Center has no on-site parking. But 5,000 parking spaces can be found within walking distance in garages and parking lots and on the street. Still, dealing with a car in this dense city scene is a hassle. With so many hotels, restaurants, museums, art galleries, and public transportation within walking distance of the convention center, why bother with a car?

Consider using San Francisco's excellent public transportation systems instead. Powell Street Station, only two blocks from the convention center, provides access to BART (Bay Area Rapid Transit) and Muni Metro (streetcars); adjacent are the Powell Street cable-car lines to Nob Hill and Fisherman's Wharf (although the wait in line to get aboard a cable car can be lengthy during peak tourist seasons).

Muni Metro will get you to the Financial District and the city's outlying neighborhoods, while BART can whisk you beyond the city to Oakland and Berkeley. Muni buses and cable cars will get you just about everywhere else. Plus, there are cabs. Our advice: Do yourself a favor and don't drive.

Lodging within Walking Distance of the Moscone Center

While participants in citywide conventions lodge all over town, a couple of hotels are within particularly easy walking distance of the Moscone Center: the **San Francisco Marriott** (55 Fourth Street) offers 1,500 rooms; the **Sheraton Palace** (2 New Montgomery Street) has 550 rooms; the **ANA Hotel** (50 Third Street) has 667 rooms; and the **Galleria Park Hotel** (191 Sutter Street) offers 177 rooms.

Convention Rates: How They Work and How to Do Better

If you're attending a major convention or trade show, the meeting's sponsoring organization has probably negotiated "convention rates" with a number of hotels. Under this arrangement, hotels agree to "block" a certain number of rooms at an agreed upon price for conventioneers. In the case of a small meeting, only one hotel may be involved; but "city-wide" conventions may involve almost all downtown and airport hotels.

Because the convention sponsor brings big business to San Francisco and reserves many rooms, often annually, it usually can negotiate volume discounts substantially below rack rate. But some conventions and trade shows have more bargaining clout and negotiating skill than others, and your convention sponsor may not be one of them.

Once a convention or trade show sponsor completes negotiations with participating hotels, it sends its attendees a housing list that includes all the hotels serving the convention, along with the special convention rate for each. You then can compare these convention rates with the rates using the strategies covered in the previous section.

If the negotiated convention rate doesn't sound like a good deal, try to reserve a room using a half-price club, a consolidator, or a tour operator. Remember, however, that many of the deep discounts are available only when the hotel expects to be at less than 80% occupancy, a rarity when a big convention is in town.

Strategies for Beating Convention Rates:

1. Reserve early. Most big conventions and trade shows announce meeting sites one to three years in advance. Get your reservation booked as far in advance as possible using a half-price club. If you book well ahead of the time the convention sponsor sends out the housing list, chances are good that the hotel will accept your reservation.

2. Compare your convention's housing list with the list of hotels presented in this guide. You may be able to find a suitable hotel not on the housing list.

3. Use a local reservations agency or consolidator. This is also a good strategy if you need to make reservations at the last minute. Local reservations agencies and consolidators almost always control some rooms, even in the midst of a huge convention or trade show.

■ Convention and Trade-Show Calendar ■

The Moscone Center can have a considerable impact on San Francisco when, say, 65,000 exhibitors and trade-show attendees come into town and snatch up almost every hotel room in the city. Luckily, though, the large conventions and trade shows register no discernible effect on the availability of restaurant tables or traffic congestion; it's just hotel rooms that get scarce. Use the following list of major 1998 and 1999 Moscone Center conventions and trade shows when you plan your trip to San Francisco.

Convention and Trade-Show Calendar		
Dates	**Convention Event**	**Attendees**
1998		
April 4–9	San Francisco Gourmet Show	20,000
April 18–23	Society of Experimental Biology	25,000
April 26–May 1	DB Expo '98	12,000
May 12–18	American Institute of Architects	15,000
June 15–20	Design Automation	15,000
July 13–16	Semicon	65,000
July 22–26	USA West NA Square Dance Association	10,000
Aug. 1–6	San Francisco International Gift Fair	30,000
Aug. 9	International Conference of Applied Psychology	15,000
Aug. 13–19	American Psychological Association	15,000
Aug. 22–25	Western Restaurant	20,000
Aug. 31–Sept. 4	Seybold Seminars	40,000
Sept. 8–12	Wintis/Support Services	20,000
Sept. 15–22	American Academy of Family Physicians	18,000
Oct. 10–15	Direct Marketing Association	15,000
Oct. 24–28	American Dental Association	40,000
Nov. 9–14	Oracle Corporation	32,000
1999		
Jan. 17–20	International Fancy Food and Confection	17,000
April 10–14	NA School Boards Association	22,000

Convention and Trade-Show Calendar		
Dates	**Convention Event**	**Attendees**
Feb. 6–10	NA Auto Dealers	25,000
Feb. 19–25	San Francisco International Gift Fair	30,000
April 18–21	DB Expo '99	12,000
July 11–15	Semicon	65,000
Aug. 7–12	San Francisco International Gift Fair	30,000
Aug. 16–21	Embedded Systems Conference	11,500
Aug. 31–Sept. 3	Seybold San Francisco	15,000
Sept. 27–30	American Society for Microbiology	15,000
Oct. 11–15	American College of Surgeons	20,000

PART FOUR

Arriving and Getting Oriented

Coming into the City

■ By Car ■

San Francisco is located on the tip of a peninsula linked to the mainland by two bridges. As a result, visitors arriving in San Francisco by car enter the city by one of three routes: from the south on US 101, from the east on Interstate 80 (via the San Francisco–Oakland Bay Bridge), or from the north on US 101 (on the Golden Gate Bridge).

US 101 and a parallel interstate highway, Interstate 280, link the city to the rest of the peninsula to the south, including Palo Alto, Santa Clara, and San Jose, located at the southern end of San Francisco Bay. US 101 is also the coastal highway that continues farther south to Gilroy, Salinas, San Luis Obispo, Santa Barbara, and Los Angeles, 400 miles away. A more scenic— and significantly slower—option that hugs the coast is California Route 1, which leads directly to Santa Cruz, Carmel, Big Sur, and Morro Bay.

Travelers coming from the east on I-80 (which goes through Sacramento, Reno, Salt Lake City, Omaha, Chicago, and other points east before reaching New York City) pass through Oakland before crossing San Francisco Bay on the Bay Bridge and entering downtown San Francisco. It's also the route for people coming to the Bay Area on Interstate 5, the north-south interstate through California's Central Valley (and the fastest driving route from Los Angeles).

Drivers coming through Oakland are confronted with a maze of inter-state highways that link together to form a kind of beltway around San

Francisco. In addition to the San Francisco–Oakland Bay Bridge, San Francisco Bay is crossed by two more bridges to the south (these connect with the San Francisco peninsula well south of the city). Interstate 580 crosses San Pablo Bay north of San Francisco, where it connects the East Bay city of Richmond with San Rafael. But visitors bound for San Francisco can ignore the confusing jumble of highways that bind together the populous Bay Area surrounding the city.

US 101 to the north, via the Golden Gate Bridge, links San Francisco to Marin County and the rest of Northern California, including San Rafael, Petaluma, Healdsburg, and Eureka. Again, California Route 1 is the slow and scenic option; the two-lane road follows the coast north.

■ By Plane ■

Most domestic and foreign visitors who fly to San Francisco land at the San Francisco International Airport, 14 miles south of downtown directly on US 101. It's the fifth-busiest airport in the United States, and it's undergoing a major expansion. Luckily, many domestic flyers have a choice: Oakland International Airport, a smaller, more convenient facility is worth considering, especially if you can get a direct flight from your hometown. Oakland International is located five miles south of downtown Oakland, across San Francisco Bay (about 24 miles from downtown San Francisco.)

San Francisco International Airport (SFO)

Seventy-four percent of visitors arrive by air, most of them through the San Francisco International Airport (SFO); it handled 38 million passengers in 1996. A $2.4 billion construction project is under way to ready the airport for a projected volume of 51 million passengers in 2006. Plans include a new international terminal, an airport rail-transit system, a BART (Bay Area Rapid Transit) station, and elevated roadways. The centerpiece of the program is a 2-million-square-foot international terminal scheduled for completion in spring 2000. Because of the huge project, navigating the roadways surrounding the airport will be a real headache for the next couple of years, especially for first-time visitors.

The Layout   SFO handles an average of 108,000 passengers a day on 54 passenger airlines. It's a horseshoe-shaped facility with three major terminals: the South Terminal, the International Terminal, and the North Terminal. The terminals surround a parking garage and are linked by indoor corridors featuring changing art exhibits (nice to know if you've got time to kill). Each terminal features shops, restaurants, and newsstands, and the International Terminal has a small boutique shopping mall. Five airport information booths, open from 8 a.m. to midnight, are located in the baggage claim areas; multilingual agents can provide information on ground transportation, Bay Area lodging, and cultural events.

Arriving From your gate, follow the signs down to the baggage area on the lower level. Then for most folks it's back to the main level to reach rental car shuttles, door-to-door vans, public transportation, and hotel shuttles . . . a major inconvenience only slightly mitigated by nearby elevators. Cabs and limos, however, are outside the lower-level doors. Short-term parking is across the street from the terminals in the parking garage; from the North Terminal take the escalator up to reach the garage. From the International and South Terminals, take a shuttle van (available at the curb outside on the arrival level) to the garage.

Getting Downtown

Driving If you're renting a car, you'll find rental agency counters on the lower baggage level. Next, haul your luggage up to the arrival level, walk outside to the outer curb, and board the appropriate rental car agency bus, which will whisk you through the confusion of new construction to the car rental lots. After picking up your car keys, get explicit directions to US 101, which goes to downtown San Francisco. (It's a good idea to call ahead to your hotel for turn-by-turn driving directions.)

To reach Market Street near Union Square (the main downtown hotel district), take US 101 to I-280 north; then take the Sixth Street exit. Market Street is about six blocks from the end of the exit; across Market Street, Sixth Street becomes Taylor Street, a one-way street heading north toward Fisherman's Wharf. It's about a 25-minute drive to downtown from the airport (longer during rush hour).

Cabs and Shuttles Cabs are available outside the baggage area near the yellow column at all terminals. Typical fares to downtown San Francisco are about $30; up to five riders can split the cost. Door-to-door shared van service to downtown San Francisco, available outside the doors of the arrival level on the center island, is reasonably priced, starting at around $10 per person (free for children ages 12 and under). The vans leave every 15 to 20 minutes between 6 a.m. and 11 p.m. Reservations aren't required unless you're arriving after 11 p.m.

Major shuttle van services include **SuperShuttle** (phone (415) 558-8500) and **Yellow Airport Shuttle** (phone (415) 282-7433). **SFO Airporter** (phone (415) 495-8404) only goes to these major downtown hotels: Westin Saint Francis, San Francisco Hilton and Towers, and San Francisco Marriott (every 15 minutes); and ANA Hotel, Grand Hyatt, Park 55, Hyatt Regency,

Sheraton Palace, and Holiday Inn Union Square (every 30 minutes). You can also make reservations for your return trip on any of the shuttle services. For more information, call one of the van services or the SFO transportation hotline: (800) SFO-2008.

Public Transportation   Travelers on a budget with only one bag (but no luggage) and plenty of time, can take a **SamTrans** bus to the Transbay Terminal at First and Mission Streets in downtown San Francisco; the 7F Express leaves from the upper level about every 30 minutes. The one-way fare is $2.50. The slower, cheaper 7B Local is another option, and you can bring luggage; the fare is $1. Call (800) 660-4287 for more information.

A free **CalTrain-SFO Shuttle** (upper level) provides a ten-minute bus ride to a commuter train station at nearby Millbrae, where you can catch the next train to downtown San Francisco; a one-way fare is about $4, and you purchase tickets from the conductor after you board. On weekdays, trains run about every 10 minutes during rush hour and about every 30 minutes the rest of the day and on weekdays and holidays. The commuter trains arrive at Third and Townsend Streets in the SoMa District, where you can grab a cab or bus to downtown. And it's okay to carry luggage. For more information, call (800) 532-8405.

Oakland International Airport (OAK)

Smaller is better at Oakland International Airport (OAK), across the bay from San Francisco and five miles south of downtown Oakland. With only two terminals and everything on one level, Oakland is a lot less confusing to weary travelers. It's also new, bright, and attractive. While Oakland is the obvious airport choice if your destination is in the East Bay area, it's also the hassle-free alternative to SFO for San Francisco–bound travelers—at least, the ones who can book a direct flight from their hometowns.

The Layout   Terminal 1 handles all domestic and international airlines, with the exception of Southwest Airlines, which claims all of Terminal 2. From your gate, follow signs to the baggage area near the entrance and to the right. Ground transportation is outside the door, including shuttle vans to downtown San Francisco (to the left of Terminal 1 under the covered walkway). Most rental car agencies are across the street; no need to take a shuttle bus to a remote lot. Shuttles to the BART station in Oakland and bus service are located outside the terminals.

Getting Downtown

Driving   To reach downtown San Francisco from Oakland International, exit the airport and take Hegenberger Road to Interstate 880 north.

Follow signs for I-80, which takes you across the double-decker San Francisco–Oakland Bay Bridge. The first two exits after the bridge take you downtown. It's about a 30-minute drive (longer during rush hour).

Cabs and Shuttles Cabs are usually available outside the baggage areas between Terminal 1 and Terminal 2; a typical fare to downtown San Francisco is $40 and can be split between riders. Door-to-door, shared-ride shuttle services to downtown San Francisco include **RBJ Airporter** ($17 per person, no reservation required), **E-Z Way Out** ($20 per person, 24-hour advanced reservation required; phone (510) 430-9090) and **Bayporter Express** ($20 per person, reservation required; phone (415) 467-1800).

Public Transportation Shuttle service to the BART Oakland Coliseum station is $2 one way (50 cents for children, disabled, and seniors). From there, take a BART train to one of four downtown San Francisco stations on Market Street ($2.75 one way). **AC Transit's Line 58** bus connects the airport with the Alameda/Oakland Ferry and downtown Oakland's Jack London Square. One-way fare is $1.10; exact fare is required. The ferry provides a scenic trip across San Francisco Bay to the city's Ferry Terminal and Pier 39 in Fisherman's Wharf. One-way fares are $3.75 for adults, $1.50 for children ages 5–12, and $2.50 for seniors, disabled, and active military personnel. For ferry schedules, call (510) 522-3300.

▪ By Train ▪

Amtrak's staffed ticket office, waiting room, and baggage check is located in the Ferry Building at the foot of Market Street. Motor coaches transport departing and arriving passengers to the Amtrak train station in Emeryville, near Oakland, and to three other downtown San Francisco points: Pier 39 in Fisherman's Wharf, the Hyatt Regency in the Financial District, and Macy's near Union Square.

The motor coach trip from Emeryville takes about ten minutes; your luggage is checked through to your final stop downtown (or, for departing passengers, to your train). Cities with daily round-trip service to San Francisco are Los Angeles and San Diego (eight trips a day), Sacramento (four trips a day), Seattle and Portland (one trip a day), and Chicago (one trip a day). For exact schedule and fare information, call Amtrak at (800) USA-RAIL

■ Where to Find Tourist Information in San Francisco ■

If you're short on maps or need more information on sight-seeing, restaurants, hotels, shopping, or things to do in San Francisco and the Bay Area, there are several places to stop and pick up maps and brochures.

- In downtown San Francisco: **San Francisco Convention and Visitors Bureau,** Hallidie Plaza at Powell and Market Streets (lower level). Phone (415) 391-2000. Open weekdays 9 a.m. to 5 p.m. and weekends 9 a.m. to 3 p.m.; closed Easter, Thanksgiving, Christmas, and New Year's Day.

- In Marin County: **Marin County Convention and Visitors Bureau,** Avenue of the Flags, San Rafael. Phone (415) 472–7470. Open weekdays 9 a.m. to 5 p.m.

- In Napa Valley wine country: **Napa Valley Conference and Visitors Bureau,** 1310 Napa Town Center, Napa. Phone (707) 226-7459. Open daily 9 a.m. to 5 p.m.

- In Sonoma wine country: **Sonoma County Convention and Visitors Bureau,** 5000 Roberts Lake Road, Suite A, Rohnert Park. Phone (707) 586-8100 or (800) 326-7666. Open daily 9 a.m. to 5 p.m.

A Geographic Overview of San Francisco and the Bay Area

San Francisco, with more than 700,000 residents, is the second most densely populated city in the country (after New York). The city, on the West Coast of the United States about halfway between the northern and southern ends of California, is situated on the tip of a hilly peninsula jutting into San Francisco Bay and, to the west, overlooking the Pacific Ocean. San Francisco is the epicenter of a larger metropolitan area with a total population of about 6 million, making it the fifth-largest urban area in the United States.

California, the most populous state in the union (and its third largest), is bordered to the east by Arizona and Nevada. To the north is Oregon and the Pacific Northwest; to the south is the international border with Mexico. Along California's nearly 800-mile coastline, which forms the western edge of the state, is the Pacific Ocean. The largest city in California is Los Angeles, 400 miles to the south; the state capital is Sacramento, about 90 miles northeast of San Francisco.

■ Earthquakes ■

Geologically, the city sits on the boundary between the Pacific Plate and the North American Plate, which are tectonic plates that slide horizontally past each other in opposite directions. The San Andreas fault, the active frontier between the two plates, runs vertically through California and is the source of tremors that can be extremely violent. Resulting earthquakes have left indelible marks on San Francisco, especially the quake of April 1906, estimated to have reached 8.25 on the Richter scale, and the more recent quake in October 1989, which hit 7.1.

All along the fault the risk of earthquakes is constant, and seismologists are unable to predict when they'll occur or how severe they'll be. It's not the shifting of the plates that causes the most damage and deaths, but the resulting explosions, fires, collapsing buildings and freeways, and landslides. Since the 1989 quake, many buildings in San Francisco have been strengthened to withstand tremors, and shelters (such as the one at the Moscone Convention Center) are stocked as emergency relief sites. In addition, most hotels have their own evacuation procedures. For more detailed information on what to do in the unlikely event of a tremor while you're in San Francisco, check the local phone directory, which has pages full of detailed advice.

■ Scenic Beauty ■

In spite of the ever-present risk of the "Big One"—the mythic quake that's a constant source of angst and black humor to denizens of the city—San Francisco remains everyone's favorite. One reason is its breathtakingly beautiful location. It's not just that the city is surrounded by water on three sides. Across the Golden Gate lie the Marin Headlands with windswept mountain ridges covered in chaparral (dense, scrubby brushland), the peaks of Mount Tamalpais, protected valleys with giant redwood trees, and rocky ocean beaches. Both ends of the Golden Gate Bridge, probably the most famous bridge in the world, are anchored in the Golden Gate National Recreation Area, more than 75,000 acres of parkland managed by the National Park Service; it's a recreational mecca to San Franciscans.

North of the Marin Headlands is Point Reyes National Seashore, a windswept peninsula on the Pacific coast covered with woodlands, prairies, and marshes. A geologic "island" cut off from the mainland by the San Andreas fault, Point Reyes was discovered by Sir Francis Drake in 1579. Today it is a carefully preserved sanctuary for more than 350 species of birds and a paradise for botanists and nature lovers in general, who with a little luck can spot elk, lynx, coyotes, and falcons. In the winter, visitors can watch migrating whales at an overlook near the 1870 Point Reyes Lighthouse.

Closer to the city in San Francisco Bay (one of the greatest natural harbors in the world) are more outdoor attractions. Angel Island, only reachable by ferry from Tiburon, Oakland, and San Francisco, is a state park with picnic tables, hiking and biking trails, woods, and the spooky ruins of a military garrison that served as a quarantine station for Asian immigrants until November 1940 (it was known as the "Ellis Island of the West"). Alcatraz, notorious as a federal penitentiary that once harbored America's most dangerous criminals, is now making a comeback as a nature and wildlife habitat.

South of San Francisco is just as scenic. California Route 1 follows the dramatic Pacific coast past towns and villages such as Half Moon Bay and a nearly endless succession of beaches and state parks. The Santa Cruz Mountains, running down the spine of the San Francisco peninsula, provide a dramatic backdrop to crashing ocean waves and offer fantastic views of the ocean and bay along Skyline Boulevard, which follows the mountain ridges.

▪ The Bay Area and Nearby Cities ▪

To the east across San Francisco Bay are the cities of Oakland and Berkeley, reached by the double-decker San Francisco–Oakland Bay Bridge. To the north, the Golden Gate Bridge links the peninsula to Marin County and the upscale suburban towns of Sausalito, Tiburon, Marin City, and Mill Valley. (Both bridges, by the way, are major rush-hour bottlenecks as commuters make their way in and out of San Francisco.) These cities and towns, along with suburbs to the south of San Francisco, make up the Bay Area.

North of San Francisco on US 101 above Marin County are the small cities of Petaluma and Santa Rosa (57 miles away), and, slightly to the east, the wine country valleys, Napa and Sonoma (about 60 miles away). About 125 miles north along the rugged coastline is Mendocino, a small picturesque town that was once a logging village and became a haven for artists in the 1950s. The Oregon state line is almost 400 miles to the north.

The Sierra Nevada mountains and the Nevada state line are about 200 miles east of the city. Yosemite National Park, southeast of San Francisco in the Sierra Nevada range, is 184 miles away. Fifty miles south along the peninsula (below the southern end of San Francisco Bay) are San Jose and Silicon Valley. South along the coast are the cities of Santa Cruz (80 miles), Monterey (115 miles), Santa Barbara (320 miles), Los Angeles (400 miles), and San Diego (550 miles).

▪ The Major Highways ▪

San Francisco's major highway, US 101, links Seattle and San Diego along the California coast. The freeway threads its way through the city on Van Ness Avenue after crossing the Golden Gate Bridge at the northwestern tip of the city and continues south along the peninsula to San Jose and beyond.

Interstate 80 crosses the San Francisco–Oakland Bay Bridge and continues northeasterly to Sacramento. Interstate 80 also intersects with I-580 and I-880 in Oakland. Interstate 580 (the Eastshore Freeway) heads north toward Richmond and then swings west across San Pablo Bay to San Rafael and US 101, north of San Francisco. To the south, I-880 follows the eastern shore of San Francisco Bay south toward San Jose, while I-580 swings east toward Stockton and an intersection with I-5, the inland interstate link that runs from Vancouver to San Diego.

Below San Francisco, I-280 begins south of the city and parallels US 101 toward Redwood City, Stanford, and Sunnyvale; its northern end is one of the most beautiful stretches of interstate highway in the country. US 101 (here called the Bayshore Freeway) follows the western shore of San Francisco Bay on a more direct route to the cities of Palo Alto, Santa Clara, and San Jose.

■ The Layout ■

San Francisco occupies a land area of about 46 square miles on a 32-mile-long peninsula. Twin Peaks, the geographic center of the city (and, before skyscrapers, its most distinctive landmark), is 900 feet high. While confusing at first, the city's layout is quite simple. Downtown streets are laid out on a grid pattern, with the exceptions of Market Street and Columbus Avenue, which cut across the grid at right angles to each other. Many of the city's 42 hills can seem to distort this pattern at first, but later they become useful landmarks and reference points.

Because most of the city's streets are laid out on a grid, finding an address is easy if you know the nearest cross street. When you ask for directions, always find out the nearest cross street and which neighborhood your address is located in. Most of San Francisco's streets are very long, with numbers typically ranging from 1 to 4000. Street numbers get higher going from east to west and from south to north. Distances are measured in blocks, with numbers rising by 100 from block to block.

Most San Franciscans refer to streets by their names without specifying "street" or "avenue," except when the street or avenue has a number, not a name: for example, Third Avenue, 23rd Street. (There is no 13th Street or 13th Avenue.) Twenty-five parallel streets with numbers are located in South of Market, while 46 numbered parallel avenues (Second to 48th) cross Richmond—a neighborhood sometimes called, appropriately enough, the Avenues. It's important not to get them confused.

It would be nice if street addresses along Market, Mission, and other streets in the SoMa District had street numbers that corresponded with the intersecting numerical streets, but they don't. For example, the Cartoon Art Museum at 814 Mission Street is located between Fourth and Fifth Streets, not Eighth and Ninth.

Throughout the northwest sector of the city (downtown to Fisherman's Wharf) and in the cookie-cutter neighborhood of Sunset, streets are one way, with the exceptions of Columbus Avenue, Market Street, and Van Ness Avenue. When traffic on a street only goes one way, the traffic in the two streets on either side of it move in the opposite direction.

■ Major Arteries and Streets ■

Market Street is San Francisco's main drag. Many of the city's buses and streetcars follow this route from the outlying suburbs past the Castro and

Mission Districts, Civic Center, SoMa, and Union Square to the downtown Financial District. Underground, subways operated by BART and light-rail trains operated by Muni Metro load and disgorge passengers at seven underground stations located along Market Street.

The tall office buildings clustered downtown are at the northeast end of Market Street; one block beyond lie the Embarcadero and the bay. The building with the tall tower at the end of the street is the Ferry Building, one of a few major structures to survive the 1906 earthquake and fire. The Embarcadero curves along San Francisco Bay from south of the Bay Bridge to the northeast perimeter of the city and ends at Fisherman's Wharf, San Francisco's famous cluster of piers and tourist attractions. (The elevated freeway used to continue along the bay west of the wharf but was almost completely removed after the 1989 earthquake, much to the relief of many San Franciscans, who can now enjoy unimpeded views of the bay.) Beyond Fisherman's Wharf are Aquatic Park, Fort Mason, the Presidio, and Golden Gate National Recreation Area, all linked by the Golden Gate Promenade, a three-and-a-half-mile pedestrian walkway.

From the eastern perimeter of Fort Mason, Van Ness Avenue runs due south back to Market Street; it's also US 101 south of the Golden Gate Bridge. The rough triangle formed by these three major thoroughfares— Market Street to the southeast, the Embarcadero and the waterfront to the north, and Van Ness Avenue to the west—contains most of the city's major tourist attractions and neighborhoods of interest to visitors.

■ Other Major Streets ■

A few other major thoroughfares that visitors are bound to encounter include Mission Street, which parallels Market Street to the south in SoMa; it's also the main street in the Mission District south of downtown. Montgomery Street in the Financial District links to Columbus Avenue in North Beach, while Bay, Jefferson, and Beach Streets are major east-west arteries in and around Fisherman's Wharf.

Grant Avenue is Chinatown's touristy main street, while Powell Street runs north-south from Market Street to the bay past Union Square; it's also a major cable-car route, as the street climbs Nob Hill. Lincoln Boulevard is the major road through the Presidio, a former army base at the northwest corner of the city that's now part of Golden Gate National Recreation Area.

Geary Boulevard, California Street, and Broadway are major east-west streets downtown; Geary goes the distance to the Pacific Ocean, where it merges with Point Lobos Avenue just before reaching Cliff House, a major tourist landmark. Visitors following signs for US 101 on Van Ness Avenue to reach the Golden Gate Bridge will make a left onto Lombard Street, then zoom past the Palace of Fine Arts as they approach the famous span.

At the southern end of Market Street (just past Twin Peaks) the name changes to Portola Drive; turn right on Sloat Boulevard to reach the San Francisco Zoo and Ocean Beach. There you'll find Great Highway, which parallels the ocean. Turn right on Great Highway and head north to reach the western end of Golden Gate Park (look for the Dutch windmill). The park's main drag is John F. Kennedy Drive, which is closed to traffic on Sundays. At the eastern end of Golden Gate Park are Fell and Oak Streets, which head east to Van Ness Avenue and Market Street.

Things the Natives Already Know

■ **Customs and Protocol** ■

With a population of only about 750,000, San Francisco scarcely ranks as a major U.S. city. Yet it's considered the capital of Northern California, just as Los Angeles is considered the capital of Southern California. The city is also constantly invigorated by an influx of immigrants from Asia and Central America.

An established city, San Francisco is proud of its traditions and its reputation as the intellectual center of the West Coast. Built on a peninsula, the city could have turned into another haughty Manhattan. But its population, concerned about the environment, has resisted the spread of skyscrapers, preserving San Francisco's largely residential character. Throw in San Francisco's temperate climate and remarkably liberal character, and casualness is a byword in the City by the Bay.

Eating in Restaurants   By and large, it's hard not to think of a situation where casual clothing isn't appropriate for dining in the Bay Area, with the exception of a small number of exclusive restaurants and clubs that require jackets and ties for men and equally formal attire for women. Although people tend to get more dressed up for dinner downtown, you'll still find plenty of casual restaurants, especially ethnic eateries such as Thai, Indonesian, Mexican, and Vietnamese. If in doubt, call ahead or dress casual-chic: nice looking, but no T-shirts or running shoes.

Tipping   Is the tip you normally leave at home appropriate in San Francisco? The answer is yes. Just bear in mind that a tip is a reward for good service. Here are some guidelines.

Porters and Skycaps $1–1.50 a bag.

Cab Drivers   A lot depends on service and courtesy. If the fare is less than $8, give the driver the change and $1. Example: If the fare is $4.50, give the cabbie fifty cents and a buck for tip. If the fare is more than $8, give the driver the change and $2. If you ask the cabbie to take you only a block or two, the fare will be small, but your tip should be large ($3–5) to make up for his or her wait in line and to partially compensate him or her for missing a better-paying fare. Add an extra dollar to your tip if the driver handles a lot of luggage.

Parking Valets $2 is correct if the valet is courteous and demonstrates some hustle. $1 will do if the service is just okay. Pay only when you check your car out, not when you leave it.

Bellmen and Doormen   When a bellman greets you at your car with a rolling luggage cart and handles all of your bags, $5 is about right. The more luggage you carry yourself, of course, the less you should tip. Add another $1 or $2 if the bellman opens your room. For calling a taxi, tip the doorman $1.

Waiters   Whether in a coffee shop or an upscale eatery, or ordering room service from the hotel kitchen, the standard gratuity range is 15–20% of the tab, before sales tax. At a buffet or brunch where you serve yourself, leave a dollar or two for the person who brings your drinks. Some restaurants, however, are adopting the European custom of automatically adding a 15% gratuity to the bill, so check before leaving a cash tip.

Cocktail Waiters and Bartenders   Here you tip by the round. For two people, $1 a round; for more than two people, $2 a round. For a large group, use your judgment: is everyone drinking beer, or is the order long and complicated? Tip accordingly.

Hotel Maids   When you check out, leave a $1–2 per day for each day of your stay, provided service was good.

How to Look and Sound Like a Native   Cosmopolitan city that it is, San Francisco can be a tough place to blend in. Mecca to artists, performers, intellectuals, and folks of every describable (and sometimes indescribable) sexual bent, the city is where most of America's new personal and social trends materialize. Yet if it's important to you not to look like A Visitor on Holiday, we offer the following advice.

1. Don't go to Fisherman's Wharf.
2. If you do go to Fisherman's Wharf, don't wear shorts and a T-shirt; freezing, underdressed tourists huddling for warmth at the wharf is an enduring San Francisco cliché.
3. Guys: Shave your head, grow a goatee, and dress in black.
4. Gals: Shave your head, pierce an eyebrow, and dress in black.
5. Don't call cable cars "trolleys."
6. Don't pronounce Ghirardelli with a soft "g"; the square's name is pronounced "GEAR-ar-delly."
7. Don't call it "Frisco."

■ Publications for Visitors ■

San Francisco has two daily newspapers, the *San Francisco Chronicle*, published in the morning, and the *San Francisco Examiner*, which comes out in the afternoon; the publications combine on Sundays for one big edition. Both newspapers cover local, national, and international news, and Friday editions feature up-to-the-minute information on weekend entertainment.

Free weekly tabloid papers include the *San Francisco Bay Guardian* and the *SF Weekly.* Both offer coverage on everything from art to politics and generally provide more detailed information on local night life and entertainment than the dailies. *Where San Francisco* is a free monthly magazine for tourists offering information on shopping, dining, and entertainment, as well as maps and listings of things to do while you're in town; look for a copy in your hotel room. *Bay City Guide,* found in many museums and shops, is a free monthly magazine; it provides maps and listings of things to do for visitors.

San Francisco Magazine is the city's leading glossy magazine, and it focuses on dining, the arts, entertainment, and ten-best lists. *San Francisco Arts Monthly* is a tabloid listing the city's visual and performing arts calendars. *Street Sheet,* sold by homeless and formerly homeless people on the city's streets for a buck, provides a street-level view of homelessness and helps the homeless earn money. *The Bay Area Reporter*, distributed free on Thursdays, covers the gay community, including in-depth news, information, and a weekly calendar of goings-on for gays and lesbians.

■ San Francisco on the Air ■

Aside from the usual babble of format rock, easy listening, and country music stations, San Francisco is home to a few radio stations that really stand out for high-quality broadcasting. Tune in to what hip San Franciscans listen to:

San Francisco's High-Quality Radio Stations		
Format	**Frequency**	**Station**
Jazz	91.1 FM	KCSM
NPR	91.7 FM	KQED
Talk, classical, community affairs	94.1 FM	KPFA
Classical	102.1 FM	KDFC
Rock	104.5 FM	KFOG
Rock	105.3 FM	KTIS

■ **Access for the Disabled** ■

Steep hills aside, travelers with mobility problems are likely to find San Francisco more in tune with their needs than most other U.S. cities; it's considered one of the most barrier-free towns around. Nearly all buildings and public transportation are equipped for easy access. In compliance with the American Disabilities Act, direction signs, toilets, and entrances are adapted for blind and disabled visitors. In addition, many theaters (both movie and stage) offer special audio equipment for hearing-impaired people.

Parking spaces reserved for handicapped people with disabled permits are marked by a blue-and-white sign and a blue curb; frequently a wheelchair outline is painted on the pavement. Disabled persons may pay a $6 fee and present a state-of-origin permit or plaque with photo I.D. to get a temporary permit at the Department of Motor Vehicles (1377 Fell Street); there's a service window reserved for the disabled.

Most street corners downtown have dropped curbs and most city buses have wheelchair lifts. Major museums throughout the Bay Area are fitted with wheelchair ramps, and many hotels offer special accommodations and services for wheelchair-bound visitors.

All Muni Metro and BART stations are wheelchair accessible. In addition, wheelchair-boarding platforms are located at many stops, including some islands on Market Street. In addition, Muni operates more than 30 accessible bus lines. For a complete listing of transit lines, including a chart indicating which lines offer disabled access, pick up a copy of the Official San Francisco Street and Transit Map, available at most newsstands for $2. Call (415) 923-6336 (touch-tone only) to get recorded schedule information. For more information on disabled access to public transportation or a Muni Access Guide, write to the Accessible Services Program, 949 Presidio, San Francisco, CA 94115, or call (415) 923-6142 or (415) 923-6366 (TDD).

A Paratransit Taxi Service provides discount taxi service to qualified disabled persons unable to use fixed Muni lines; to get a certificate, call the San Francisco Paratransit Broker at (415) 543-9650. Golden Gate Transit, which operates buses between the city and Marin County, publishes a handbook on accessible equipment and procedures; to get a copy of *Welcome Aboard,* call (415) 923-2000 (voice) or (415) 257-4554 (TDD).

■ **Time Zone** ■

San Francisco is in the Pacific time zone, which puts it three hours behind New York, two hours behind Chicago, one hour behind the Rocky Mountains, and eight hours behind Greenwich Mean Time.

■ Phones ■

The San Francisco area is served by three area codes: (415) inside the city and Marin County, (510) in Alameda and Contra Costa Counties in the East Bay (including Oakland and Berkeley), and (650) to the south in San Mateo County and around San Francisco International Airport. Calls from pay phones range from 25 to 35 cents (depending on which carrier owns the pay phone); if you talk for more than three minutes, additional payments may be requested. To call outside the (415) area code, dial 1 plus the appropriate area code and the seven-digit number.

■ Liquor, Taxes, and Smoking ■

Liquor and grocery stores and some drug stores sell packaged alcohol from 6 to 2 a.m. daily. Most restaurants, bars, and nightclubs are licensed to serve a full line of alcoholic beverages during these hours, although some have permits to sell beer and wine only. The legal drinking age is 21.

An 8.5% sales tax is added to purchases in San Francisco. If your purchases are shipped to a destination outside of California, they're exempt from the sales tax. An 8.5% tax is added to restaurant bills, and hotels tack on a 12% room tax to the bill.

San Francisco has stiff antismoking laws, making it illegal to light up in offices, public buildings, banks, lobbies, stores, sports arenas, stadiums, and theaters, as well as in all restaurants without bars and on public transportation.

How to Avoid Crime and Keep Safe in Public Places

■ Crime in San Francisco ■

San Francisco, like any large city, has its share of violent crime, drug abuse, and poverty. But the good news for visitors is that by and large the city is safe. Unlike some towns, such as Chicago (synonymous with gangsters and "smash-and-grab"—breaking a car window and stealing a purse) and Miami (where tourists have been shot while driving from the airport), San Francisco ranks low among U.S. cities for serious crime, and it has the statistics to prove it. According to the FBI, San Francisco recorded 24 murders in the first half of 1997, compared to 120 in New Orleans and 135 in Washington, DC, two cities of comparable size (with considerably more urban squalor). Not only is the city's violent crime rate relatively low, it's getting lower—part of a national trend that saw the violent crimes of murder, forcible rape, robbery, and aggravated assault drop by 5% in the first half of 1997. In the first half of 1996, San Francisco had 45 murders, almost double the number in 1997.

Downtown San Francisco, where tourists and business visitors spend most of their time, is unusually safe for a large city. "One good thing is that we've got a very lively downtown with lots of different things going on at all hours of the day. It's never completely dead," notes Dewayne Tully, a police service aid with the San Francisco Police Department. "Even the Financial District, an area usually dead at night in most cities, has lots of clubs and restaurants." Because of crowds and 24-hour foot, horse, motorcycle, and car patrols by San Francisco's finest, few visitors to San Francisco are victims of street crime.

■ Places to Avoid ■

This doesn't mean visitors should let their guard down. "The major tourist areas are relatively safe," Tully says. "But often visitors are victims of personal crimes—car boosting, pickpockets, purse snatchings. They've got to be wary, especially in crowded areas and on crowded buses."

Beyond downtown, some neighborhoods require extra caution, especially at night. In Golden Gate Park, stick to well-populated paths during the day and don't go at night. The Tenderloin, on the downtown side of the

Civic Center, attracts undesirable types; this depressing area should be avoided at all hours. South of downtown, Market Street gets seedy and is a haven for vagrants from about Fifth Street west to Gough Street. In fact, it's best to avoid all of Market Street and Union Square after dark.

The Mission District, currently San Francisco's hottest neighborhood, requires extra caution at night; take a cab to restaurants and clubs, and don't wander the side streets. The same goes for SoMa, another booming neighborhood in a state of transition. Haight-Ashbury, with its overflow of panhandlers and vagrants, is also best avoided after dark.

More advice: San Francisco's legions of homeless aren't usually a threat to visitors; just keep contact with panhandlers to a minimum. Also, avoid using public transportation late at night and in the wee hours of the morning. In other words, use common sense. "Awareness is the key," says Pam Matsuda of SAFE, a San Francisco crime-prevention education group. "People put down a suitcase in the lobby of their hotel and the next thing they know, it's gone."

If you are the victim of a crime or witness one, you can get immediate police, fire, or medical assistance by dialing 911 from any pay phone without inserting money. For nonemergency help (for instance, to report a car break-in), dial 553-0123. For more information on personal safety in San Francisco, call SAFE at (415) 673-SAFE.

While we recommend that visitors stay away from unsafe public housing projects (such as the ones in Hunters Point, a part of the city far from downtown and not on any tourist agenda) and other economically deprived areas, keep in mind that crime can happen anywhere. It is common for tourists in San Francisco to ask a police officer which areas to avoid as they explore the city on foot. Police know, and tell these tourists, that they can be robbed or mugged just about anywhere. We are not discussing "areas." Rather, we are talking about neighborhoods—places where people live and work, where they go to school and church. Singling out neighborhoods as unsafe is not only disparaging, but it also stimulates a false sense of security about the safety of so-called "good" neighborhoods. San Francisco is a big city, and the big-city rules of common sense apply wherever you are.

1. Be alert and understand that crime can occur anywhere.

2. Walk in populated, well-lit areas, preferably in the company of others.

3. Be suspicious of anyone who approaches you.

Most of San Francisco is pretty safe during the day, but after dark you should stick to the more populated streets. Don't leave a lot of money or travelers checks in your hotel room, even though the employees are probably dependable. And if you buy any valuables that might be easily pawned, such as silver, gems, or electronics, ask the hotel to lock them in the safe.

■ Having a Plan ■

Random violence and street crime are facts of life in any large city. You've got to be cautious and alert, and you've got to plan ahead. When you're out and about, remember that you must use caution because you're on your own; if you run into trouble, it's unlikely that police or anyone else will be able to come to your rescue. You must give some advance thought to the ugly scenarios that could occur and consider preventive measures and an escape plan, just in case.

Not being a victim of street crime is sort of a survival-of-the-fittest thing. Just as a lion stalks the weakest member of the antelope herd, muggers and thieves target the easy victims. Simply put, no matter where you are or what you are doing, you want potential felons to think of you as a bad risk.

On the Street   For starters, you're always a less appealing target if you're with other people. Second, if you must be out alone, act alert, be alert, and always have at least one arm and hand free. Muggers and thieves gravitate toward preoccupied folks, the kind found plodding along staring at the sidewalk, both arms encumbered by briefcases or packages. Visible jewelry (on men or women) attracts the wrong kind of attention. Men, keep your billfolds in your front trouser or coat pocket. Women, keep your purses tucked tightly under your arm; if you're wearing a coat, put it on over your shoulder-bag strap. If you're wearing rings, turn the setting palm-in.

Here's another tip: men can carry two wallets. Carry an inexpensive wallet in your hip pocket with about $20 in cash and some expired credit cards. This is the one you hand over if you're accosted. Your real credit cards and the bulk of whatever cash you have should be in a money clip or a second wallet hidden elsewhere on your person. Women can carry a fake wallet in their purse and keep the real one in a pocket or money belt.

If You're Approached   Police will tell you that a felon has the least amount of control over his intended victim during the few moments of his initial approach. A good strategy, therefore, is to short-circuit the crime scenario as quickly as possible. If a felon starts by demanding your money, for instance, quickly take out your billfold (preferably your fake one) and hurl it in one direction while you run shouting for help in the opposite direction. The odds are greatly in your favor that the felon will prefer to collect your silent billfold rather than pursue you. If you hand over your wallet and just stand there, the felon will likely ask for your watch and jewelry next. If you're a woman, the longer you hang around, the greater your vulnerability to personal injury or sexual assault.

Secondary Crime Scenes   Under no circumstances, police warn, should you allow yourself to be taken to another location—a "secondary crime scene" in police jargon. This move, they explain, gives the criminal more privacy and consequently more control. A thief can rob you on the street quickly and efficiently. If he tries to move you to another location, whether by car or on foot, it is a certain indication that he has more than robbery in mind. Even if he has a gun or knife, your chances are infinitely better if you run away. If the criminal grabs your purse, let him have it. If he grabs your coat, slip out of the coat. Hanging onto your money or coat is not worth getting mugged, sexually assaulted, or murdered.

Another maxim: never believe anything a criminal tells you, even if he's telling you something you desperately want to believe—for example, "I won't hurt you if you come with me." No matter how logical or benign he sounds, assume the worst. Always, always break off contact as quickly as possible, even if that means running.

In Public Transport   When you ride a bus, always take a seat as close to the driver as you can; never ride in the back. Likewise, on BART (the subway), sit near the driver's or conductor's compartment. These people have a phone and can summon help in the event of trouble.

In Cabs   At night, it's best to go to one of the hotel stands or call for a cab on the phone. Once you have secured a cab, check the driver's certificate, which by law must be posted on the dashboard. Address the cabbie by his last name (Mr. Jones or whatever) or mention the number of his cab. This alerts the driver to the fact that you are going to remember him and/or his cab. Not only will this contribute to your safety, it will keep your cabbie from trying to run up the fare.

If you need to catch a cab at the train stations, bus terminals, or airports, always use the taxi queue. Taxis in the official queue are properly licensed and regulated. Never accept an offer for a cab or limo made by a stranger in the terminal or baggage claim. At best, you will be significantly overcharged for the ride. At worst, you may be abducted.

■ Personal Attitude ■

While some areas of every city are more dangerous than others, never assume that any area is completely safe. Never let down your guard. You can be the victim of a crime, and it can happen to you anywhere. Women leaving a restaurant or club alone should never be reluctant to ask to be escorted to their car or assisted in hailing a taxi.

Never let your pride or sense of righteousness and indignation imperil your survival. This is especially difficult for men, particularly in the presence of women. It makes no difference whether you are approached by an aggressive drunk, an unbalanced street person, or an actual criminal; the rule is the same. Forget your pride and break off contact as quickly as possible. Who cares whether the drunk insulted you if everyone ends up back at the hotel safe and sound? When you wake up in the hospital with a concussion and your jaw sewn shut, it's too late to decide that the drunk's filthy remark wasn't really all that important.

Felons, druggies, some street people, and even some drunks play for keeps. They can attack with a bloodthirsty hostility and hellish abandon that is beyond the imagination of most people. Believe me, you are not in their league (nor do you want to be).

■ Self-Defense ■

In a situation where it is impossible to run, you'll need to be prepared to defend yourself. Most police insist that a gun or knife is not much use to the average person. More often than not, they say, the weapon will be turned against the victim. The best self-defense device for the average person is Mace. Not only is it legal in most states, it's nonlethal and easy to use.

When you shop for Mace, look for two things. The dispenser should be able to fire about eight feet, and it should have a protector cap so it won't go off by mistake in your purse or pocket. Carefully read the directions that come with your device, paying particular attention to how it should be carried and stored and how long the active ingredients will remain potent. Wear a rubber glove and test-fire your Mace, making sure you fire downwind.

When you are out about town, make sure your Mace is easily accessible, say, attached to your keychain. If you are a woman and you keep your Mace on a keychain, avoid the habit of dropping your keys (and the Mace) into the depths of your purse when you leave your hotel room or car. The Mace will not do you any good if you have to dig through your purse for it. Keep your keys and your Mace in your hand until you safely reach your destination.

■ Carjackings and Highway Robbery ■

With the recent surge in carjackings, drivers also need to take special precautions. "Keep alert when you're driving in traffic," one police official warns. "Keep your doors locked, with the windows rolled up and the air-conditioning or heat on. In traffic, leave enough space in front of you so that you can make a U-turn and aren't blocked in. That way, if someone approaches your car and starts beating on your windshield, you can drive off." Store your purse or briefcase under your knees when you are driving, not on the seat beside you.

Also be aware of other drivers bumping you from the rear or driving alongside you and gesturing that something is wrong with your car. In either case, do not stop or get out of your car. Continue until you reach a very public and well-lit place where you can check things out and, if necessary, get help.

▪ Ripoffs and Scams ▪

A lively street scene is an incubator for ripoffs and scams. Although pickpockets, scam artists, and tricksters work throughout San Francisco, they are particularly thick in Union Square, along the Embarcadero and Fisherman's Wharf, and at BART stations. While some scams are relatively harmless, others can be costly and dangerous.

Pickpockets work in teams, sometimes using children. One person creates a diversion, such as dropping coins, spilling ice cream on you, or trying to sell you something, and a second person deftly picks your pocket. In most cases your stolen wallet is almost instantaneously passed to a third team member walking by. Even if you realize immediately that your wallet has been lifted, the pickpocket will have unburdened the evidence.

Because pickpockets come in all sizes and shapes, be especially wary of any encounter with a stranger. Anyone from a man in a nice suit asking directions to a six-year-old wobbling toward you on in-line skates could be creating a diversion for a pickpocket. Think twice before giving assistance, and be very aware of other people in your immediate area. Don't let children touch you or allow street peddlers to get too close. Be particularly wary of people whose hands are concealed by newspapers or other items. Oh yeah, one more thing: if somebody does spill ice cream on you, be wary of the good Samaritan who suddenly appears to help you clean up.

The primary tip-off to a con or scam is someone approaching you. If you ask help of somebody in a store or restaurant, you are doing the approaching and the chances of being the victim of a scam are quite small. When a stranger approaches you, however, regardless of the reason, beware.

Most travelers carry a lot more cash, credit cards, and other stuff in their wallet than they need. If you plan to walk in San Francisco or anywhere else, transfer exactly what you think you will need to a very small, low-profile wallet or pouch. When the *Unofficial Guide* authors are on the street, they carry one American Express card, one VISA card, and a minimum amount of cash. Think about it. You do not need your gas credit cards if you're walking, and you don't need all those hometown department store credit cards if you're away from home.

Do not, repeat, *do not* carry your wallet and valuables in a fanny pack. Thieves and pickpockets can easily snip the belt and disappear into the crowd with the pack before you realize what's happened. As far as pockets are concerned, front pockets are safer than back pockets or suitcoat pockets, though pickpockets (with a little extra effort) can get at front pockets, too. The safest place to carry valuables is under your arm in a holster-style shoulder pouch. Lightweight, comfortable, and especially accessible when worn under a coat or vest, shoulder pouches are available from catalogs and most good travel stores. Incidentally, avoid pouches that are worn on your chest and suspended by a cord around your neck. Like the fanny pack, they can be easily cut off or removed by pickpockets.

■ More Things to Avoid ■

When you do go out, walk with a minimum of two people whenever possible. If you have to walk alone, stay in well-lit areas with plenty of people around. Be careful about whom you ask for directions. (When in doubt, shopkeepers are a good bet.) Don't count your money in public, and again, carry as little cash as possible. At public phones, if you must say your calling card number to make a long-distance call, don't say it loud enough for strangers around you to hear.

While this litany of warnings and precautions may sound grim, it's really commonsense advice that applies to visitors in any large American city. Finally, remember that millions of visitors a year still flock to San Francisco, making it one of the most visited destinations in the United States. The overwhelming majority encounter no problems with crime.

■ The Homeless ■

If you're not from a big city or haven't visited one in a while, you're in for a shock when you come to San Francisco, where there is a large homeless population. The homeless are more evident in some areas than others, but you're likely to bump into them just about anywhere.

Who Are These People? "Most are lifelong San Francisco residents who are poor," says Joan Alker, assistant director of the National Coalition for the Homeless, an advocacy group headquartered in Washington. "The people you see on the streets are primarily single men and women. A disproportionate number are minorities and people with disabilities—they're either mentally ill, or substance abusers, or have physical disabilities."

Are They a Threat to Visitors? "No," Ms. Alker says. "Studies show that homeless men have lower rates of conviction for violent crimes than the population at large. We know that murders aren't being committed by the homeless. I can't make a blanket statement, but most homeless people you see are no more likely to commit a violent crime than other people."

Should You Give the Homeless Money?   "That's a personal decision," Ms. Alker says. "But if you can't, at least try to acknowledge their existence by looking them in the eye and saying, 'No, I can't.'" While there's no way to tell if the guy with the Styrofoam cup asking for a handout is really destitute or just a con artist, no one can dispute that most of these people are what they claim to be: homeless.

Ways to Help   It's really a matter for your own conscience. We confess to being both moved and annoyed by these unfortunate people—moved by their need and annoyed that we cannot enjoy the city without running a gauntlet of begging men and women. In the final analysis, we find it easier on the conscience and spirit to carry an overcoat or jacket pocket full of change at all times. The cost of giving those homeless who approach you a quarter does not add up to all that much, and it is better for the psyche to respond to their plight than to deny or ignore their presence.

There is a notion, perhaps valid in some instances, that money given to a homeless person generally goes toward the purchase of alcohol or drugs. If this bothers you excessively, carry granola bars for distribution or buy some inexpensive gift coupons that can be redeemed at a McDonald's or other fast-food restaurant for coffee or a sandwich.

We have found that a little kindness goes a long way, and that a few kind words delivered along with your quarter or granola bar brighten the day for both you and your friend in need. We are not suggesting a lengthy conversation or prolonged involvement, just something simple like, "Sure, I can help a little bit. Take care of yourself, fella."

Those moved to get more involved in the nationwide problem of homelessness can send inquiries—or a check—to the National Coalition for the Homeless, 1612 K Street, NW, Suite 1004, Washington, DC 20006.

Keep It Brief and Don't Play Psychologist   All of the people you encounter on the street are strangers. They may be harmless, or they may be dangerous. Either way, maintain distance and keep any contacts or encounters brief. Be prepared to handle street people in accordance with your principles, but mostly just be prepared. If you have a druggie in your face wanting a handout, the last thing you want to do is pull out your wallet and thumb through the twenties looking for a one-dollar bill. As the sergeant on *Hill Street Blues* used to say, be careful out there.

PART FIVE

Getting around San Francisco

Driving Your Car

Because of its compact size and excellent (if often crowded) public transportation system, San Francisco isn't a town that requires visitors to have a car. Most of the major sights and attractions are in close proximity to one another, and getting to the ones that aren't is fairly easy on Muni, the city's public transportation system.

That said, we still think having a car—or at least access to one for a day or two—is a nice option for visitors. Much of Northern California's scenic splendor lies just beyond the city, and breaking up a vacation or business trip with a one-day excursion to Point Reyes, the wine country, or, say, Half Moon Bay can be a major highlight to an otherwise hectic week in the city.

If you're driving to San Francisco, your best bet is to use your car sparingly after parking it at your hotel. Driving in downtown and the Financial District requires patience, as traffic is usually intense. The same goes for North Beach, Chinatown, and Telegraph Hill, areas infamous for traffic congestion and scarce parking. Our advice is to keep your car in your hotel's garage and use it sparingly for excursions away from downtown and beyond the city, or in the evenings.

■ Time of Day ■

San Francisco's weekday rush hour starts before 7 a.m. and lasts until around 9 a.m.; it picks up again around 4 p.m. and goes to about 6 p.m. In between, traffic is congested but usually flows—at least beyond downtown and Fisherman's Wharf.

Weekends, on the other hand, can be just as bad as weekday rush hours—and often worse. While traffic on Saturday and Sunday mornings is usually light, it picks up around noon and doesn't let up until well into the evening. Remember, about 6 million people live in the Bay Area, and on weekends many of them jump in their cars and head to San Francisco.

■ Parking ■

Finding a place on the street to park your car downtown is tough. When you do find a spot, the meter is often timed to only allow a half-hour of parking (not a lot of time to go sight-seeing or attend a business meeting). Traffic cops and meter maids patrol diligently, and the meters, unless posted otherwise, are in effect Monday through Saturday, usually from 8 a.m. to 6 p.m. Center-city parking garages cost anywhere from $10 to $25 a day; check with your hotel to see if you can get a reduced rate at a nearby garage that allows unlimited access to your car.

Colored curbs in San Francisco indicate reserved parking zones. Red means no stopping or parking; yellow indicates a half-hour loading limit for vehicles with commercial plates, yellow and black means a half-hour loading limit for trucks with commercial plates; green, yellow, and black indicates a taxi zone; and blue is reserved for vehicles marked with a California-issued disabled placard or plate. Green is a ten-minute parking zone for all vehicles, and white is a five-minute limit for all vehicles.

San Francisco cops don't take parking regulations lightly, and any improperly used spot can become a tow-away zone. Watch for street-cleaning signs and stay out of parking lanes opened up for rush-hour traffic. Many residential neighborhoods have permit parking, and a parking ticket can cost you more than $20, plus $100 for towing and additional charges for storage. Parking in a bus zone or wheelchair-access space can set you back $250, while parking in a space marked handicapped or blocking access to a wheelchair ramp costs $275. If you get towed, go to the nearest district police department for a release and then pick up your car at the towing company.

When you're parking on San Francisco's steep hills, there is only one way to rest easy: curb your wheels. Turn the front tires away from the curb when your car is facing uphill (so that if the brake fails the car rolls back into the curb), and toward the curb when your car is facing downhill (so that the car can roll forward into the curb, effectively using it as a block). Because even the best brakes can fail, curbing your wheels is the law in San Francisco (and you'll see plenty of street signs to remind you).

Public Transportation

San Francisco Municipal Railway, commonly called Muni, is a citywide transportation system that consists of all cable cars, streetcars (called Muni Metro), conventional buses, and electric buses. All fares are $1 for adults and 35 cents for seniors, disabled passengers (with a valid Regional Transit Connection Discount Card), and children ages 5–17; children ages 4 and under ride free. Cable-car fare is $2 per person (kids ages 4 and under ride free). One-dollar bills are accepted on most buses, but the drivers don't give change. If you need a transfer, ask for one when you board; it's free and valid for two hours and a maxi-mum of two rides in any direction.

Many San Franciscans feel a fierce devotion to the system; some affection-ately call it "Joe Muni." No wonder; it's a European-style transportation system that gets people around the city cheaply and efficiently. You're never more than a couple of blocks from a bus stop or train station. Not that it's without some drawbacks—buses can get incredibly crowded, especially at rush hour and on weekends, and occasionally you may have to wait for a bus while fully loaded buses pass by without stopping. Yet despite its problems, riding Muni is a great way for visitors to learn the city and meet its people.

■ A Money-Saving Tip ■

Muni passports allow unlimited use of all buses, cable cars, and Muni Metro streetcars in San Francisco. It's a great money-saving deal that makes it even easier and more convenient to use San Francisco's public transportation. In addition, Muni passports provide discounts at dozens of city attractions, including museums, theaters, and bay tours.

Muni passports come in three versions: one-day ($6), three-day ($10), and seven-day ($15). Pocket-sized and easy to use, the passports are available at locations throughout the city, including the **San Francisco Convention and Visitors Bureau Visitor Information Center** (in Hallidie Plaza at Powell and Mason Streets), **TIX Bay Area** (Stockton Street on Union Square), and **Muni** (949 Presidio, Room 239). Be sure to pick up a copy of the Official San Francisco Street and Transit Map for $2. To use a pass-port, scratch off the dates of the day (or days) you're using the pass and simply show it to the driver, who will wave you aboard.

▪ Cable Cars ▪

After the Golden Gate Bridge, cable cars are probably San Francisco's most famous symbol. There's no question about it—every visitor has to ride one at least once. The cars, pulled by cables buried underneath the streets, operate on three lines from 6:30 to 12:30 a.m. daily at about 15-minute intervals.

The first San Francisco cable car made its maiden voyage in 1873. By 1906, just before the earthquake, the system hit its peak, with 600 cars on a 110-mile route. But the system was heavily damaged by the quake and fire, and many lines weren't rebuilt. Electric trolleys took over some routes, and the number of cable cars dwindled over the years. In 1955 the city voted to save the famous hill climbers, and in 1984 it spent more than $60 million on a two-year renovation of the system, including new track and cable vaults, renovation of the Cable Car Barn, and restoration of the cars, which were given a new coat of shiny maroon, blue, and gold paint, as well as new brakes, seats, and wheels. Today there are 44 cable cars in all, with 27 in use at peak times. An average of 13 million people travel on the 17 miles of tracks each year—more than 35,000 people a day.

How They Work

What makes the cable cars move? Each six-ton car attaches itself to a cable that's continuously running beneath the street. (Go to the Cable Car Barn and see the huge electric motors that move the cables on 14-foot diameter wheels.) The cars move at a steady nine and a half miles an hour when the cable-car operator mechanically grips the cable; he releases it to stop the car. Tension can be adjusted to keep the cable from slipping.

Three Lines

There are three cable-car lines in San Francisco. The most popular route for tourists is the Powell-Hyde line, which starts at the Powell and Market Street turntable south of Union Square. The line skirts Union Square, climbs Nob Hill (with good views of Chinatown), goes past the Cable Car Barn, crosses Lombard Street, and descends to Hyde Street to the turntable near Aquatic Park and Fisherman's Wharf. The Powell-Mason line starts at the same place, but after the Cable Car Barn it passes by North Beach and ends at Bay Street. For the best views on either line, try to face east.

The California line runs from California and Market Streets to Van Ness Avenue, passing through the Financial District and Chinatown; it's used more by commuters than tourists (a tourist attraction in itself). At Nob Hill the Powell lines cross over the California line, so passengers can transfer between lines (but they have to pay again). At the end of all lines, all passengers must get off.

For each of the three lines, the return journey follows the outward route, so riders can catch different views from the other side of the car. If you'd rather sit than stand, you're more likely to be successful if you board at the end of the line. During peak tourist seasons and on weekends, lines are long to board the cars at the turntables where the cars get turned around, and boarding at cable-car stops along the routes can be impossible as the cars rumble by, full of smiling, camera-toting tourists.

Safety Tips

As much fun as the cable cars are to ride, it's important to keep safety in mind when you're on one. If it's not crowded—not likely in the summer or fall after 9 a.m. or so—you can choose to sit or stand inside, sit outside on a bench, or stand at the end of the car. Adventurous types and some cable-car purists prefer hanging on to a pole while standing on a side running board. But wherever you decide to ride, hang on tight.

Try not to get in the way of the gripman, who operates the grip lever that holds and releases the cable pulling the car; he needs a lot of room. A yellow stripe on the floor marks an off-limits area, and passengers should stay out of it. Be extra cautious while the car is moving. Passing other cable cars is exciting because they pass so close, but be careful not to lean out too far. And be careful getting on and off. Often cable cars stop in the middle of busy intersections; you don't want to step in front of a moving car or truck.

▪ Buses ▪

Bus service in San Francisco reaches into all parts of the city and beyond. Some are powered by standard diesel engines, and others are powered by overhead electric cables. All buses are numbered and display their destinations on the front. Along the streets, bus stops are indicated by signs displaying the Muni logo; the route numbers of the buses serving the stop are listed below the sign. Some bus stops have three-sided glass shelters, with route numbers painted on the exterior and route maps posted inside. Along Market Street, some buses stop at the curb while others stop at islands in the street.

The buses only stop at designated stations every two or three blocks along the route. When you board, give the driver $1 or flash your Muni passport; if you need a transfer, get it now. If you're not sure about where to get off, ask the driver to let you know when you're near your destination. Drivers are usually considerate and glad to help.

Most bus lines operate from 6 a.m. to midnight, after which there is an infrequent Night Owl service; for safety's sake, take a cab at those late hours. Popular tourist bus routes include numbers 5, 7, and 71, which go to

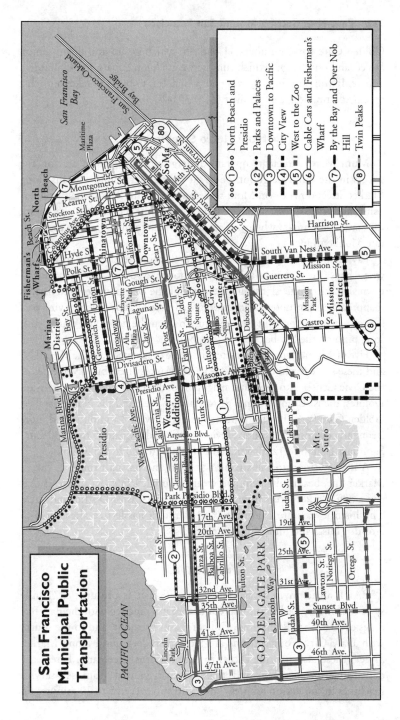

San Francisco
Municipal Public
Transportation

LEGEND:
1 North Beach and Presidio
2 Parks and Palaces
3 Downtown to Pacific
4 City View
5 West to the Zoo
6 Cable Cars and Fisherman's Wharf
7 By the Bay and Over Nob Hill
8 Twin Peaks

PACIFIC OCEAN

GOLDEN GATE PARK

San Francisco Bay

San Francisco-Oakland Bay Bridge

Maritime Plaza

Fisherman's Wharf

North Beach

Marina District

Presidio

Lincoln Park

Mt. Sutro

Mission District

Western Addition

Chinatown

Downtown

SoMa

Civic Center

Golden Gate Park; numbers 41 and 45, which go up and down Union Street; and number 30, which runs between Union Square and Ghirardelli Square. If you need help figuring out which bus or buses to take to reach a specific destination, call Muni at (415) 391-2000.

■ Muni Metro Streetcars ■

Muni Metro streetcars operate underground downtown and on the streets in the outer neighborhoods. At four underground stations along Market Street downtown, Muni shares quarters with BART, the Bay Area's commuter train system. Orange, yellow, and white illuminated signs mark the station entrances; when you get inside the terminal, look for the separate Muni entrance.

Pay or show your Muni passport and go down to the platform. To go west, choose the outbound side of the platform; to go east, choose the downtown side. Electronic signs with the name of the next train begin to flash as it approaches. The doors open automatically; stand aside to let arriving passengers depart before you step aboard. To open the doors and exit at your stop, push on the low bar next to the door.

Five of Muni Metro's six streetcar lines are designated J, K, L, M, and N, and these share tracks downtown beneath Market Street but diverge below the Civic Center into the outer neighborhoods. The J line goes to Mission Dolores; the K, L, and M lines go to Castro Street; and the N line parallels Golden Gate Park. The sleek trains run about every 15 minutes and more frequently during rush hours. Service is offered daily from 5 to 12:30 a.m., Saturdays from 6 to 12:30 a.m., and Sundays from 8 to 12:20 a.m.

A new addition to the streetcar system (and its sixth route) is the F-Market line, beautiful green- and cream-colored, 1930s-era streetcars that run along Market Street from downtown to the Castro District and back. The historic cars are charming, and they're a hassle-free alternative to crowded buses and underground terminals.

■ BART ■

BART, an acronym for Bay Area Rapid Transit, is a futuristic, 71-mile system of high-speed trains that connects San Francisco with the East Bay cities of Oakland, Richmond, Concord, and Fremont, and to the south, with Daly City. Four stations are located underground along Market Street (these also provide access to Muni Metro streetcars). Fares vary depending on distance, and tickets are dispensed from self-service machines in the station lobbies. The trains run every 15 to 20 minutes on weekdays from 4 a.m. to midnight, on Saturdays from 6 a.m. to midnight, and on Sundays from 8 a.m. to midnight.

The good news for most visitors is that they can forget about BART, a commuter system that makes it possible for downtown workers to reach affordable housing across San Francisco Bay and to the south of the city. Tourists without a car, however, can use BART to reach excellent attractions in Berkeley and Oakland. In a few years the system will extend to San Francisco International Airport.

■ Ferries ■

In the days before the Golden Gate and Bay Bridges were built, Bay Area commuters relied on hundreds of ferries to transport them to and from the northern counties and the East Bay. Although no longer a necessity, ferries continue to operate in smaller numbers, transporting suburban commuters who prefer a tension-free boat ride across the bay to the headache of rush-hour traffic. The ferries are also favorite ways for local residents and visitors to enjoy San Francisco's incredible scenery. On weekends, many suburban families leave their cars at home and take the ferries for fun and relaxation.

One person's commute can be another's excursion. Although the ferries don't offer the narrated audio tours of the commercial sight-seeing cruises offered at Fisherman's Wharf, they're less expensive. Food and bar service are offered on board, but the modern ferries only transport foot traffic and bicycles, not cars.

The Ferry Building at the foot of Market Street is the terminus for ferries to Sausalito and Larkspur. For prices and schedules, call (415) 923-2000. Private ferry service to Sausalito, Tiburon, and Angel Island (weekends and holidays in winter, daily the rest of the year) operates from Piers 39 and 41 at Fisherman's Wharf. For more information, call the **Blue & Gold Fleet** at (415) 773-1188.

■ Taxis ■

Unlike New York and Chicago, cabs in San Francisco tend to be expensive and scarce. You may be able to hail a moving taxi downtown, but in general it's better to call and make arrangements for pickup. Another option is to head toward a cab stand at a major hotel, but the wait can be long during rush hour and in bad weather.

San Francisco taxis have rooftop signs that are illuminated when the cab is empty. Rates are $1.70 for the first mile and $1.80 for each additional mile. Major cab companies include **Veteran's Cab,** (415) 552-1100 or

552-1300; **Yellow Cab,** (415) 626-2345; **City Cab,** (415) 468-7200; **DeSoto Cab,** (415) 673-1414; and **Luxor Cab,** (415) 282-4141.

▪ Walking ▪

Exploring San Francisco on foot reveals the city's richness and detail like nothing else; it's really the best way to get around this remarkably compact town. Major tourist areas are within a half-hour or less of one another. Hills, especially Nob Hill and Telegraph Hill, can leave you gasping for breath at the top, but the views are worth the effort.

Most street intersections are marked with green and white signs bearing the name of the cross street; this can get confusing along Market Street, where street names are different on each side of the thoroughfare. Street names are also frequently imprinted in the pavement at corners. Often, electronic "walk" signs indicate when it's safe (and legal) to cross the street.

Always watch for right-turning vehicles, which can turn right on red lights when traffic is clear. Jaywalking is common but illegal, and it technically could result in a $50 fine. Visitors not from the West Coast will be pleasantly surprised at the consideration most San Francisco drivers show to pedestrians; just make a move toward stepping off the curb and most cars will come to a stop to let you cross the street.

Where to Walk

The Bay City is a walker's paradise, making virtually all parts of the city excellent places to explore on foot. A hit list of great walking destinations must start with **Chinatown** and **North Beach,** two adjacent neighborhoods that can only be appreciated on foot. Neither neighborhood offers much in the way of specific attractions such as museums, but they're attractions in their own right, full of shops, restaurants, cafés, and activity. In Chinatown, make sure you get beyond Grant Street, a very touristy thoroughfare; walk along Stockton Street instead.

Other excellent walking destinations include the **Golden Gate Promenade,** a spectacularly scenic, three-and-a-half-mile path along the waterfront linking Fort Mason and the Golden Gate Bridge (also a breathtaking place to walk, if windy), **Golden Gate Park, Ocean Beach,** the **Mission District** (during the day, when it's usually sunny and always festive), and the **Presidio,** which has miles of trails leading to scenic overlooks.

PART SIX

Entertainment and Night Life

Performing Arts

While San Francisco has to fight off a reputation for provincialism when it comes to the arts, it's the only city on the West Coast to boast its own professional symphony, ballet, and opera companies. They benefit from thriving support of the city's upper crust, who wine and dine their way through glittering fundraisers. Other hallmarks of the San Francisco cultural milieu include free summer music concerts and a thriving theater scene.

■ Classical Music ■

Louise M. Davies Symphony Hall (201 Van Ness Avenue at Hayes Street; (415) 864-6000) is the permanent home of the **San Francisco Symphony.** Conductor Michael Tilson Thomas and many of the world's best-known soloists and guest conductors offer a year-round season of classical music, as well as occasional performances by off-beat musical and touring groups. Ticket prices vary by concert, but the least expensive seats are generally around $20. Call about the availability of standby tickets on the day of a concert; they sometimes cost less than $20.

A night at the opera in San Francisco is no small affair. The newly renovated **War Memorial Opera House** in the Civic Center District is an opulent venue for the **San Francisco Opera Association,** which has been getting rave reviews since the building opened in 1932. Rated the best of the city's top cultural trio (symphony, opera, ballet), the San Francisco Opera consistently wins critical acclaim for operatic warhorses as well as obscure Russian opuses that other companies prefer not to tackle.

With its considerable international weight, the San Francisco Opera pulls in heavy hitters such as Placido Domingo, Marilyn Horne, Joan Sutherland, and others. The three-month main season starts at the end of September, and opening night is one of the main social events on the West Coast. Tickets start at more than $40, but standing room costs considerably less. For ticket and schedule information, call (415) 864-3330.

■ Ballet ■

The **San Francisco Ballet** also calls the War Memorial Opera House home. The oldest and third-largest ballet company in the United States has a four-month season lasting from February to May. The San Francisco Ballet was the first company in the country to perform "The Nutcracker" as a Christmas event (and still does each December) and offers consistently excellent productions of full-length neoclassical and contemporary ballets. Tickets run from $7 to $100. For ticket and schedule information, call (415) 865-2000.

■ Summer Classical Music Festivals ■

The **Stern Grove Midsummer Music Festival** is the nation's oldest (since 1938) free summer music festival. The festival presents 11 outdoor concerts on Sunday afternoons from June through August at the sylvan **Sigmund Stern Grove** in San Francisco. Performances include the San Francisco Ballet, Symphony, and Opera, as well as a diverse mix of blues, jazz, popular, and world music. Come early with a blanket to this magnificent, eucalyptus-lined grove. For schedule information, call (415) 252-6252.

Midsummer Mozart presents a summer season of the works of Mozart in many venues around the Bay Area. The **Festival Orchestra** is conducted by George Cleve and features well-known soloists. Chamber concerts are presented on the first Saturday of the month during the year at the **Legion of Honor.** Tickets range from $18 to $36. For schedule and ticket information, call (415) 954-0850.

■ Theater ■

The majority of San Francisco's theaters congregate downtown around the Theater District, just west of Union Square. The **American Conservatory Theater** (ACT) is the Bay Area's leading theater group, offering celebrated classics and new works on the stage of the recently restored **Geary Theater** (450 Geary Boulevard at Taylor Street). Celebrated thespians to appear in ACT productions include Olympia Dukakis, John Turturro, and Jean Stapleton. The season runs from September through July, and tickets range from $11 to $51. For more information, call the box office at (415) 749-2ACT.

Three downtown theaters concentrate on Broadway productions; call (415) 551-2000 for schedule and ticket information. The **Curran Theatre** (445 Geary Boulevard at Taylor Street) tackles the bigger shows, such as Andrew Lloyd Webber's *The Phantom of the Opera* under the direction of its original London production team; the open-ended run began in 1993. The recently restored **Golden Gate Theatre** (1 Taylor Street at Market Street) is the city's most elegant theater. The **Orpheum Theatre** (1192 Market at Eighth Street) focuses on cabaret and song and dance performances.

After the ACT, **The Magic Theater** in Fort Mason is the city's busiest and largest company—and consistently rated the most exciting. The company specializes in the works of contemporary playwrights and emerging talent; Sam Shepard traditionally premieres his new plays here. For schedule and ticket information, call (415) 441-8822.

In the heart of San Francisco, the **Center for the Arts at Yerba Buena Gardens** presents art and art education in an attractive venue. Attractions include award-winning theater groups, film and video presentations, and free outdoor events. The center is located at 701 Mission Street across from the Moscone Convention Center in SoMa. For ticket information, call (415) 978-ARTS.

■ Ticket Agencies ■

BASS Tickets offers tickets for theater, sports, concerts, and other Bay Area events by phone or through outlets at **Tower Records** (Bay and Columbus Streets) and **Wherehouse Records** (30 Powell Street and 165 Kearny Street). A service charge is added to the ticket price. To charge by phone or to get a recorded events schedule, call (800) 225-2277 outside of California or (510) 762-2277.

TIX Bay Area sells half-price, day-of-performance tickets for selected theater, dance, and music events (cash only), as well as full-price, advance-sale tickets for local performing events (by credit card). A service charge is added to ticket prices. TIX is located on the Stockton Street side of Union Square. Call (415) 433-7827 for information.

Mr. Ticket (2065 Van Ness Avenue) is the Bay Area's largest ticket agency offering premium seating for sports, concerts, and theater at market prices. Major credit cards are accepted, and delivery is available. For more information, call (800) 424-7328 outside the (415) and (510) area codes, and (415) 775-3031 from San Francisco.

San Francisco Night Life

You've just landed in one of the best night-life cities in the Western world. Do you want to dance? Free form, rhumba, tango, or swing? Dressed in formal, leather, or naked (well, almost)? Do you want to drink microbrews with local Bohemians, shoot darts with the Irish, sing off-key with tourists, or prowl a singles meat market where hormones are as thick as San Francisco fog? Do you want fancy, not so fancy, or downright dirty? Straight, gay, bi, all of the above, or just confused? San Francisco opens its Golden Gate to you.

Any style, taste, gender, or orientation can be found here, but one of the most important trends in San Francisco night life and culture is the "retro" scene. Choose your decade: 1940s big-band elegance, '50s swing, even '60s groove ('70s disco rarely rears its blow-dried head). Take a trip to a vintage clothing store or just come as you are. Step into a retro club and through the portals of time. The bouncer is dressed in a zoot suit or bears a faint resemblance to Elvis. The bartender is shaking martinis, there's a cigarette girl making her rounds, the dance floor is full of jitterbugs, and the only way you can tell that the girl in the '40s hairdo and the poodle skirt isn't Rosie the Riveter is by the ring in her nose. Retro does not preclude piercings and tattoos.

A related aspect of this scene, permeating all night-life culture, is the return of "cocktail nation." Skillful mixologists are now almost as highly regarded as the DJs who mix the music. Gone, mercifully, are the days when a club-hopper ordered just a glass of white wine or some crazy brain-food drink, or a slam-dunk to a cheap drunk. The martini in classic form and many variations, along with its cousin the Cosmopolitan, are among the most popular drinks.

Along with this return to Happy Days is a sense of elegance and a restoration of polite behavior. In a retro club, and even in a not-so-retro club, it is not considered chic, progressive, or relevant to talk with a loud or foul mouth, energetically condemn the establishment, or dress like a slob to show one's lemming-like individualism. San Francisco, always a more civilized place than most, is these days even more civilized.

The city is also one of the most important musical centers of the nation. All kinds of jazz, rock, punk, acid, and even orchestral music have been incubated here. The only thing you won't find here is country/western music. You'll have to head south to San Jose for line dancing and cowboy hats. The lack of country music notwithstanding, virtually every neighborhood in the city has a variety of music venues. They're so common and plentiful that they're taken for granted.

Some practical considerations: Most of the clubs listed are located in a contiguous swath running from North Beach (quaint, excellent views, less fog) through the Union Square area (uptown, elegant) to the SoMa and Mission Districts (leading edge, alternative). And since San Francisco is a small city, clubs are not far apart. Most are situated near other clubs, so if you don't find one to be your cup of tea, just check out its neighbors. In North Beach all you have to do is walk along Broadway, peering down the side streets as you go. At Union Square just stand on a corner and point yourself in any direction. In the SoMa and Mission Districts the greatest concentration of clubs is on Folsom Street, between 7th and 11th Streets. It's a good idea to go by foot or taxi. Driving under the influence is a serious affair here, and the cops will frequently set up drunk-driver checks on the main streets.

A good way to see the city by night without having to drive is travel with **3 Babes & a Bus.** Every Saturday and sometimes on Friday, for $30 Paula, Donna, and Susan will load you and yours onto a party bus with a highly mixed and totally unpredictable crowd of revelers and take you on a nocturnal tour of the city, stopping at three or four of the more popular clubs. You won't have to pay cover charges, you get priority admittance and one free drink, and you leave the driving and often impossible parking to them. This is also a good way to meet other revelers. Gentlemen should be advised that bachelorette parties are frequent patrons of the 3 Babes (phone (415) 552-2582).

Very recently a new law took effect in California that effectively bans smoking in enclosed public places such as bars and restaurants. The law enjoys wide popular support, as most Californians are nonsmokers. But bar and nightclub operators have complained loudly that the law is seriously hurting their business. The lower house of the state legislature has repealed the law in response to those complaints. At press time, the state senate has yet to vote on the matter, so the law is still in effect. Which way will the senate go? The smart money isn't betting. You will want to be aware of this since a number of entries in this section mention the "smoke friendliness" of the establishment. We've left those remarks in the text, since, if the senate follows the lower house and repeals the law, you'll need the information. If the senate does not repeal, those remarks are easily ignored.

Up-to-the minute club information is listed in the *San Francisco Guardian* and *San Francisco Weekly,* free weekly newspapers available at any newsstand. The Sunday edition of the *San Francisco Examiner* provides the "pink section" that lists nearly every entertainment happening in town.

Ever since the gold rush of 1849, San Francisco has been a city of revels. Many locals live for it. Some make it an art form. People from Los Angeles and Seattle fly in for it. And now you're in the middle of it. Tip a dollar per drink, pace yourself, and don't forget your trench coat.

BIMBO'S 365 CLUB

Classic big-band nightclub

Who Goes There: Very mixed crowd

1025 Columbus Avenue
   (415) 474-0365   Zone 6 North Beach

Cover: Varies
Minimum: Two drinks
Mixed drinks: $4.50
Wine: $4–6

Beer: $3–4
Dress: Varies
Food available: None

Hours: Vary

What goes on: A wide range of musical entertainment from lounge to jazz to rock and soul. The big draws these days are retro nights, when guys and dolls wear zoot suits, circle skirts, tuxedos, and full-length gowns. The Preservation Hall Jazz Orchestra or Mr. Rick's martini band might play after Work That Skirt gives free dance lessons. Tap and bubble dancers often round out the program.

Setting & atmosphere: Beautifully restored, 1940s-style nightclub with a large stage and dance floor, roving photographer and cigarette girl, and the famous Dolphina, the nude lady in a giant fish bowl. Put on your black and white and step into another, better time.

If you go: Call for information and reservations.

BISCUITS & BLUES

Blues supper club

Who Goes There: Eclectic crowd of blues lovers

550 Geary Boulevard
   (415) 292-2583   Zone 3 Union Square

Cover: $10
Minimum: None
Mixed drinks: $3.50
Wine: Bottles, $14–28; $4–7 by the
   glass

Beer: $3
Dress: Casual
Food available: Full menu

Hours: Daily, 5 p.m.–2 a.m.

(Biscuits & Blues)

What goes on: Dedication to the preservation of the blues. All manner of people with a liking for blues music come to eat Southern country cooking and listen raptly to some great, not-so-great, and someday-great practitioners of this uniquely American musical form.

Setting & atmosphere: The type of basement venue that was first a necessity, then a statement, and now the norm for jazz, blues, and other non-mainstream music clubs. It's close, cramped, and intimate, with candles on the tables and splashes of modern art. Tables are arranged in a horseshoe around the stage and small dance floor. Movie actor Danny Glover is a part owner, and his culinary background is reflected in a menu, which features fried chicken and biscuits (quite good), hush puppies (not so good), deep-fried dill pickles (you be the judge), and black-eyed peas. Some good beers, a short wine list, and a fine collection of single-malt scotch.

If you go: The kitchen can be glacially slow. Smoking is permitted only in the bar area until food service stops at about 10 p.m., when smoking is extended to the whole place. People start dancing at about the same time.

BLUE LAMP

Smoky old blues bar

Who Goes There: Neighborhood regulars,
European budget travelers, all ages, ethnic

561 Geary Boulevard
   (415) 885-1464   Zone 3 Union Square

Cover: Saturday, $5	Dress: Casual; anything goes in the
Minimum: None	Tenderloin
Mixed drinks: $3–6	Specials: Blue Lamp Ale on draft, $3
Wine: $3.50	Food available: None
Beer: $2.75–3.50	

Hours: Daily, 11–2 a.m.

What goes on: Local blues, rock, and acoustic bands starting at 10 p.m. Amateur musicians take turns jamming the blues on Sundays after 9 p.m. Just belly up to the bar and let Michael serve you a cold one. One pool table is open, and a working jukebox plays while you're waiting for the band to set up.

Setting & atmosphere: You don't have to squint too hard to see Scarlett O'Hara's Tara grown old. Dimly lit chandeliers hide the age on the antique burgundy curtain-cum-wallpaper decor. The fireplace is empty, and sports plays on televisions at both ends of the bar.

If you go: Know that there ain't a whole lot of women. Men, you won't find your future bride here. Women, Mr. Right Now is here for the taking if you can get him to leave the pool table.

BRUNO'S

Jazz bar

Who Goes There: Glamorous Bohemians

2389 Mission Street
   (415) 550-7455   Zone 7 SoMa/Mission

Cover: $3–5
Minimum: None
Mixed drinks: $3.50–5
Wine: $6
Beer: $3.50

Dress: Evening casual
Food available: Bar menu, which is a
   brief selection of the full menu
   available in the adjoining restaurant

Hours: Monday–Saturday, 6 p.m.–2 a.m.; Sunday, closed

What goes on: Live music every night from gospel to Latin to smoky blues and cool jazz. People hiding out or snuggling in the big booths in the dark depths of the long, narrow main room. Perfectly coiffed and made-up women displaying themselves with studied nonchalance. The proclaiming of "cocktail nation" with every perfect martini or Cosmopolitan shaken.

Setting & atmosphere: Nightclub chic done with restraint. Artistically and subtly lit with black, red, and green. Paneled in wood and appointed with red leather, it's just glamorous and stylish enough. It makes you want to stay. You'll feel hip but not tragically so.

If you go: Go on a slow night. On weekends this place is too popular for its own good.

THE CAFE

Gay and lesbian

Who Goes There: Women seeking women, men seeking men

2367 Market Street at Castro Street
(415) 861-3846   Zone 7 SoMa/Mission

Cover: None
Minimum: None
Mixed drinks: $3.50
Wine: $2.50–4.75

Beer: $1.25–3
Dress: Everything from jeans to drag
Food available: None

Hours: Daily, noon–2 a.m.

What goes on: The question is, what doesn't go on? Originally set up by women to be one of the premier lesbian social centers, the Cafe has become extremely popular among gay male fun-seekers. Mostly a dance house for high-energy techno music, but there's a pool table for variety.

Setting & atmosphere: A dark, neon-lit, coed dance club that overlooks the Castro. It's hot and hopping in here, but there's an outdoor balcony where you can take a breather. Don't bother coming if you don't want to be checked out; this is definitely a spot where you'll be hit on, unless you're obviously straight. The drinks are cheap and the staff is friendly.

If you go: You better not care about secondhand smoke, or PDA (public displays of affection) for that matter. On weekends it's nearly impossible to get in, so start early. And don't worry about taking the time to go to the bank; there's an ATM in the back by the bar.

CAFE DU NORD

Swing club

Who Goes There: 20- to 30-something hipsters, swing enthusiasts

2170 Market Street
(415) 979-6545   Zone 8 Richmond/Avenues

Cover: $3 and sometimes more for
  bigger venues; no cover before 8 p.m.
Minimum: None

Mixed drinks: $3.25–4.75; specialty
  liquors, $4.25–7.50
Wine: $3.25–6.50

(Cafe Du Nord)

Beer: $3.25–3.50

Dress: 1920s to 1960s retro; dress to impress

Specials: Happy hour daily, 4–7 p.m.: $2 martinis and manhattans; well, beer on draft, wine by the glass, $2.50

Food available: American continental with European flair; Wednesday–Saturday, 6:30–11 p.m.

Hours: Sunday–Tuesday, 6 p.m.–2 a.m.; Wednesday, 4 p.m.–2 a.m.; Thursday–Saturday, closed

What goes on: If you're not swing dancing to the music of the ten-piece big band in the back room or admiring the women's '20s-era dress and hairdos, then chances are you're sipping a martini in a dark corner with your date. Swing on Saturdays and Sundays; salsa and free lessons on Tuesdays.

Setting & atmosphere: If you get past the weekend line, you'll walk downstairs to this basement cabaret that was a speakeasy in the 1920s. There are oil paintings alongside black and white photos dimly lit by converted gas lamps. Experienced swing and salsa dancers inspire you to take lessons. If the scene is too fast, escape back past the bar and cuddle up with a love interest on an antique couch. The polished wood floors and trim compliment the specialty liquors and well-dressed hipsters. If you're not here on a date, it's quite possible you'll leave with one.

If you go: Don't worry if you're not dressed retro; they'll still let you in, and you won't be snubbed. Forget about getting in after 10:30 p.m., when Lavay Smith and her Red Hot Skillet Lickers are playing. A long line usually forms on weekends after 9 p.m., but you can always get in on weekdays.

CAFE ISTANBUL

Turkish coffee house

Who Goes There: The quiet, the tired, the bleary-eyed club-hopper

525 Valencia Street
   (415) 863-8854   Zone 7 SoMa/Mission

Cover: None

Minimum: None

Mixed drinks: None

Wine: None

Beer: None

Dress: Casual

Specials: Belly dancing

Food available: Sandwiches, salads, soups, Turkish and Greek snacks and desserts

(Cafe Istanbul)

Hours: Closed for remodeling at press time; please call for hours

What goes on: A recovery room in the night scene of the Mission District. No alcohol and no dancing (except for the belly dancers on Wednesdays and Saturdays), but a chance to decompress with a delicious cup of rich, black, steamy Turkish coffee and a bite to eat. People come here to wind down after an evening's revels or just to catch their breath in the midst of an all-nighter.

Setting & atmosphere: *Arabian Nights* setting; a golden glow in the foggy San Francisco evening. Low tables, stools, throw pillows, brass artifacts, and the smell of coffee and rosewater.

If you go: On belly-dancing nights you'll need reservations after 8:30 p.m.

CLUB DELUXE

Retro hot spot

Who Goes There: Gen-X retro hipsters, Haight Street locals

1509 Haight Street
   (415) 552-6949   Zone 8 Richmond/Avenues

Cover: Varies	Beer: $3–5
Minimum: None	Dress: Vintage
Mixed drinks: $3.50–8	Food available: None
Wine: $3–5	

Hours: Daily, 3 p.m.–2 a.m.

What goes on: Sipping cocktails, lounging like a lizard, and looking cool. This is the place to show off your latest find from Buffalo Exchange just down the street.

Setting & atmosphere: A step back from the 1960s tie-dye world of Haight-Ashbury to the hip, art deco 1940s. Smooth leather booths and slick Formica tables accessorize the suspenders, skirts, suits, and 'dos of the impressively retro and ultimate retro crowd. Quality local jazz and swing bands play Wednesday through Sunday after 9 p.m.

If you go: Known among locals to have the best Bloody Mary in town. Parking, like everything else, can sometimes be crazy on Haight Street. Try a few blocks up from the strip or take the 6, 7, 33, or 43 Muni bus.

THE ELBO ROOM

Neighborhood pub cum dance club

Who Goes There: Local Bohemians

647 Valencia Street
  (415) 552-7788   Zone 7 SoMa/Mission

Cover: $3–5	Beer: $2.75–3.50
Minimum: None	Dress: Casual
Mixed drinks: $3.50	Specials: None
Wine: $3–4	Food available: None

Hours: Daily, 5 p.m.–2 a.m.

What goes on: In the large bar downstairs, neighborhood regulars drink beer, shoot darts, and schmooze. One expects to see Archie Bunker in his younger days. Upstairs, acid jazz and Latin musicians play for a very discriminating crowd of music aficionados and polished dancers (beginners are welcome, too). On nights with no live music, talented DJs work the sounds.

Setting & atmosphere: Look at it with one eye and you'd call it "working class." Look at it with the other eye and you might call it "Bohemian." Either way it's unpretentious, and unventilated as well. People here don't mind sweating.

If you go: Don't go tired or hungry.

ESSEX CLUB

Retro supper club and jazz joint

Who Goes There: People who dress for the evening

847 Montgomery Street
  (415) 397-5969   Zone 5 North Beach

Cover: None	Beer: $3–5
Minimum: None	Dress: Dressy
Mixed drinks: $4	Food available: Full menu in the
Wine: $3–5	adjoining restaurant

Hours: Sunday–Thursday, 5:30 p.m.–1 a.m.; Friday and Saturday, 5:30 p.m.–2 a.m.

(Essex Club)

What goes on: Entertainment on three levels. The main bar is a rather sedate, old San Francisco establishment where a tuxedo is not out of place. A cool jazz trio provides the music. Upstairs, serious jazz is played on weekends in the more casual Scarlet Room, a saloon-like venue. The cigar room and the wine cellar reside in the basement. Decorated with murals, casks, and bottles, this is the place where you can puff on a stogie, sip brandy, and shoot pool in a swanky joint.

Setting & atmosphere: In the former Ernie's restaurant, a beloved and sorely missed San Francisco institution that was the site of Hitchcock movies and celebrity dinners for decades. The color scheme has changed, but that special, elegant San Francisco excess is still there.

If you go: Call ahead for information on martini nights and dress code.

FILLMORE

Rock and roll ballroom

Who Goes There: Those looking to see a great band
or needing a nostalgia fix

1805 Geary Boulevard (at Fillmore Street)
  (415) 346-6000   Zone 2 Civic Center

Cover: $12.50 and up
Minimum: None
Mixed drinks: $3–6
Wine: $3.50–4
Beer: $2.75–3.50

Dress: Varies
Food available: American cuisine
  upstairs amid a selection of
  infamous vintage psychedelic
  concert posters

Hours: Doors usually open at 7 or 8 p.m.; show starts an hour later

What goes on: "Return to the sixties" parties, big-name and on-the-rise rock concerts, formal sitdown dinners. This rock-and-roll landmark continues to put out the San Francisco sound that made it famous in the 1960s.

Setting & atmosphere: Distinct San Francisco soul still lives and breathes direct from the Fillmore. The place that birthed the Grateful Dead, Janis Joplin, and Santana still gives the leg up to climbing young quality bands. This hall features the largest collection of historic concert posters on view in the world. It has a spacious feel to it, and there's plenty of ground floor for getting a good view. A few tables and chairs are in the balconies off to the sides.

(Fillmore)

If you go: You can always find a listing of upcoming events in the Sunday "pink pages." Tickets are on sale at BASS (phone (510) 762-2277), subject to a service charge. Advance tickets are on sale at the Fillmore box office Sunday, 10 a.m.–4 p.m. only, with a limit of six tickets per person. The hall is available to rent for parties or events and holds 1,000.

GOLD CLUB

High-class strip club, bar, and restaurant

Who Goes There: Mixed male crowd

650 Howard Street
(415) 536-0300   Zone 7 SoMa/Mission

Cover: $10 after 7 p.m.	Dress: Casual to dressy
Minimum: None	Specials: Happy hour daily, 3–7 p.m.
Mixed drinks: $5	Food available: Full menu of steak,
Wine: $3.50–4	chicken, fish; adequate but
Beer: $2.75–3.50	nothing fancy

Hours: Monday–Friday, 11:30–2 a.m.; Saturday and Sunday, 6 p.m.–2 a.m.

What goes on: The males of the species from all stations in life and all ages over 21 come here to eat red meat, drink whiskey, smoke cigars, and howl at the moon (and whatever else is being displayed at the time). Tuxedo-clad bachelor parties are often seen here.

Setting & atmosphere: Formerly a modern dance venue with DJ, light show, and full bar. Two floors surround a central stage backed by a mirror and fronted by a fireman's pole; some of the best-looking nearly naked ladies in town perform (topless only). Cost: $10.

If you go: You'll never feel sleazy or tawdry in a place like the Gold Club. For a fee they can even come pick up you and your party in a limousine. The upper floor is known as the VIP Lounge and has an extra cover of $10. The women are mostly intelligent and articulate. Check the prices carefully on the wine list; they are high.

GOLD DUST LOUNGE

Barbary Coast saloon

Who Goes There: Mixed crowd of tourists and local regulars

247 Powell Street
  (415) 397-1695   Zone 3 Union Square

Cover: None
Minimum: None
Mixed drinks: $3.50
Wine: $3–5

Beer: $3–3.50
Dress: Anything goes
Food available: None

Hours: Daily, 6 a.m.–2 a.m.

What goes on: Live Dixieland jazz in a bawdy and gaudy San Francisco classic saloon established in 1933. Its central location and the sound of rollicking good times spilling onto the street may explain why tourists from all over the world find themselves here. There's no room to dance, but people do anyway.

Setting & atmosphere: Like a lot of older joints in the city, it's deep, narrow, and often tightly packed; it's hard not to get friendly with the people next to you. A lot of rich wood, brass, gilt, and paintings of turn-of-the-century nymphs and satyrs cavorting in what were once considered risqué postures. This is the San Francisco of old movies fame.

If you go: Brush up on your foreign language skills; you may have a chance to use them. And be prepared to sing along with the band.

GREAT AMERICAN MUSIC HALL

Rock concert hall

Who Goes There: Music enthusiasts of all types

859 O'Farrell Street (at Polk and Larkin)
  (415) 885-0750   Zone 3 Union Square

Cover: Varies according to venue
Minimum: None
Mixed drinks: $3–4
Wine: $3–5

Beer: $2.75–3.50
Dress: Casual to impressive
Food available: Assorted appetizers,
  finger food

(Great American Music Hall)

Hours: Vary

What goes on: A variety of nationally or internationally recognized music shows ranging from local bands on their way up to Latin ensembles, folk, country, and even jazz. Occasionally San Francisco radio stations sponsor select bands or events where you can get free stuff.

Setting & atmosphere: The fact that this turn-of-the-century bordello theater has been preserved is one of the things that makes San Francisco so special. Although it can get a bit smoky, the gold rococo balcony, wood floors, high fresco ceiling, and marble columns make this a timeless classic. For your favorite bands, come early and scream away Beatlemania-style up front by the stage.

If you go: The hall is available to rent for events and parties of up to 600. Be on the lookout for a touch of the dangerous and the lewd; next door is the famous Mitchell Brothers' O'Farrell Theater, described by Hunter S. Thompson as "the Carnegie Hall of public sex in America."

HARRY DENTON'S STARLIGHT ROOM

Rooftop dance club

Who Goes There: A well-dressed mixed crowd

450 Powell Street
   (415) 392-7755   Zone 3 Union Square

Cover: $5	Dress: Dressy
Minimum: None	Specials: Happy hour,
Mixed drinks: $4	Monday–Friday, 5–8 p.m.
Wine: $5.75–10	Food available: Hors d'oeuvres
Beer: $4–5	

Hours: Daily, 4:30 p.m.–2 a.m.

What goes on: Party, party, party! Dance to a wide variety of music, heavy on rock and retro. Cocktail culture asserts itself in style. Socialites, yuppies, tourists, other club owners, the odd Bohemian stuffed into a jacket and tie, and Harry Denton himself (no dancing on the bar unless accompanied by Harry) are drawn to the Starlight Room like moths to a flame; they all party and dance to the Starlight Orchestra's repertoire, which runs the gamut from the 1940s to the 1990s.

(Harry Denton's Starlight Room)

Setting & atmosphere: Exuberantly elegant decor and staff on the top floor of the Sir Francis Drake hotel. At the bar, where stylish women smoke Monte Cristo cigars, the sound of the cocktail shaker never stops. Through the big picture windows the stars twinkle, and overhead, yes, that's you looking into the mirrored ceiling. The atmosphere is thick and heady, the crowd is at capacity, and there is so much energy that it will be a long time before you sleep again.

If you go: Go early or late, unless you're a party animal. Make sure you have a supply of one- and five-dollar bills for tipping the waiters and bartenders and the coat-check girl. Call for information on entertainment and private parties.

HARVEY'S

Gay bar

Who Goes There: Locals, gay pilgrims, and straight looky-loos

500 Castro Street
(415) 431-4278   Zone 7 SoMa/Mission

Cover: None	Beer: $2.50–3.50
Minimum: None	Dress: Casual
Mixed drinks: $3.50	Food available: None
Wine: $3.25–6.25	

Hours: Daily, 11–2 a.m.

What goes on: A hard core of locals using it as their neighborhood pub and tourists of any persuasion who come to pay homage or gawk. Named after Harvey Milk, the assassinated gay city supervisor, this was once a place where members of the local gay community came to relax and take pride. Now many locals are embarrassed by its notoriety.

Setting & atmosphere: Like a Hard Rock Cafe with a gay theme. Lots of media and sports memorabilia tacked to the walls. Despite the fact that most of the patrons are gay men and the bartenders are lesbians, the place is almost distressingly "normal" looking and there are no wild goings on. It's just a neighborhood good-time bar. A gay "Cheers."

If you go: Be cool.

HIGHBALL

Swing dance club

Who Goes There: 20- to 30-somethings

473 Broadway
   (415) 397-9464   Zone 6 North Beach

Cover: $5	Beer: $3–3.50
Minimum: None	Dress: Casual, some retro
Mixed drinks: $3.25	Specials: Free swing dance lessons
Wine: $3–5	Food available: None

Hours: Vary

What goes on: Dancing to the music of big bands. A mostly young crowd that can jitterbug as well as their great-grandparents. The small bar in the corner serves up small drinks and some good beers on tap, but people come here mainly to dance to the music, both live and recorded.

Setting & atmosphere: Deep, narrow, and dark; you could call it intimate and close or tightly packed. The dance floor is so small that dancing often spills out between the small tables. But it's cool. Girls dancing together and guys in bowties, surrounded by leopard-skin drapes, red globe lights, ferns, and photos of jazz greats. It's like an alien's image of what a 1940s nightclub would look like. Nothing but fun.

If you go: Be prepared to rub elbows. You'll smell like cigarette smoke when you leave. But there's no pretension here, nobody tragically hip.

JULIE'S SUPPER CLUB

Eclectic supper club

Who Goes There: Well-dressed 20- to 30-somethings

1123 Folsom Street
   (415) 861-0707   Zone 7 SoMa/Mission

Cover: $5	Beer: $3.75
Minimum: None	Dress: Evening casual
Mixed drinks: $4.25–4.75	Food available: Full menu
Wine: $6–7	

(Julie's Supper Club)

Hours: Monday–Saturday, 5:30 p.m.–2 a.m.; Sunday, closed

What goes on: The dancing-est nondance club in town. Live jazz, blues, and R&B keep the atmosphere charged with dance fever even though there's no dance floor. Diners usually remain seated, but people at the bar will carve out any space they can to boogie. It can get crowded and loud; that's how they like it.

Setting & atmosphere: *Happy Days* meets the *Jetsons*. A 1950s vision of space-age decor. Mint green, mouthwash blue, and splashes of neon punctuated with a curvy bar and black and white photos of '50s celebrities. Yeah, it's weird. But it's good weird.

If you go: Call ahead for dinner reservations and the musical menu. No cover charge if you're having dinner. This is a fun and friendly place, although it can get intense. If it gets to be too much, there are many respites nearby. Julie's is at the foot of a **T** intersection formed by Folsom and 11th Streets; you'll find the greatest concentration of clubs in the SoMa area right here. Just start walking westward.

LI PO

Bar

Who Goes There: Locals in the know and accidental tourists

916 Grant Avenue
(415) 982-0072   Zone I Chinatown

Cover: None	Beer: $2.50
Minimum: None	Dress: Casual
Mixed drinks: $3.25	Specials: Li Po Special Snifter
Wine: $2.50–4	Food available: None

Hours: Daily, 2 p.m.–2 a.m.

What goes on: Drinking in the dark. Pinball on a "Creature of the Black Lagoon" machine. Low conversations in the nooks and crannies of an ancient labrynthine structure. A few Chinese-speaking Chinese and a lot of hip white folks from North Beach speaking English. A good place for spies to meet.

Setting & atmosphere: Dark and cavernous. Like a subterranean Chinese shrine to money and Miller Genuine Draft. The main room is dominated by a Chinese deity and currency from around the world tacked to the wall. Chinese lanterns and brewing-company neon leap out at you. If you've ever been a sailor in old Hong Kong, you'll feel nostalgic. If you've seen the movie *Suzy Wong*, you'll feel like you just stepped onto the set. It's a cliché with drinks.

If you go: It's so garish and in such bad taste that it will charm you from the moment you enter.

MAD MAGDA'S RUSSIAN TEA ROOM

Tea room

Who Goes There: Artsy, new age, journal writers, mixed crowd

579 Hayes Street (at Laguna and Octavia)
  (415) 864-7654   Zone 2 Civic Center

Cover: None
Minimum: None
Mixed drinks: None
Wine: $4
Beer: $2.25–3.25
Dress: Anything goes
Specials: Homemade blintzes ($5.50) and shiksa ($4.50) Saturday and Sunday until 7 p.m.
Food available: Russian sandwiches, pizzettes, crepes, salads, and soups. Magda's famous borscht is served daily. Magda also supplies a nice assortment of countertop cakes, brownies, muffins, and lemon bars.

Hours: Sunday, 9 a.m.–7 p.m.; Monday and Tuesday, 7 a.m.–9 p.m.; Wednesday–Friday, 7 a.m.–midnight; Saturday, 9 a.m.–midnight

What goes on: Most come to hang out, write in their journals, escape the night-life frenzy, or have a bite to eat. Then there are those who come just for the psychic readings.

Setting & atmosphere: Magda's is right at the end of Hayes Street, a melting pot of art galleries, antique shops, presymphony restaurants, cafés, and boutiques. Here, the straight and narrow prepare to come out with their new-age selves, sit at a table near the mystic booth, and eavesdrop on a psychic reading. The Whisper Garden in the back patio is a wonderful place to spend a sunny afternoon when the coastal neighborhoods are covered in fog. The long, narrow room in front is decorated with the latest local art on one side and colorful Russian mosque sculptures on the other.

If you go: Get a tarot reading ($15) from Violet or one of the other psychics. They relate enough to your life and are really fun if you're there with a group. Also, don't forget to put your extra pennies in the wishing well by the cash register; your dreams just might come true!

MAKE-OUT ROOM

Neo-Bohemian hipster bar

Who Goes There: Gen Xers looking for alternatives

3225 22nd Street (near Mission Street)
  (415) 647-2888   Zone 7 SoMa/Mission

Cover: Occasional, $3	Beer: $3
Minimum: None	Dress: Casual
Mixed drinks: $3	Food available: None
Wine: $3.50 – 4	

Hours: Daily, 6 p.m.–2 a.m.

What goes on: Occasional live music, usually folk or rock. The main attraction is getting away from the usual smoke-filled, shoulder-to-shoulder, ear-shattering trauma that is the delight of so many club-hoppers. You can hear the music, but you can hear the conversation, too. You can shoot pool and you won't get a cue in the gut when you turn around. You can enjoy a microbrew or a cocktail at the bar or a booth or table and feel that you're in a happening place, but it won't overwhelm.

Setting & atmosphere: This place is cavernous. It looks almost like a high school gym decorated for a dance. The big space, high ceiling, and darkness sprinkled with colored lights feel outdoorsy, especially when the doors are open and the fog rolls in.

If you go: Be cool. Relax. Enjoy. Pssst: people don't really make out here.

MARTUNIS

Cocktail lounge as art

Who Goes There: Mixed crowd of gay and straight

4 Valencia Street
  (415) 241-0205   Zone 7 SoMa/Mission

Cover: None	Beer: $2.75 – 3.50
Minimum: None	Dress: Evening casual
Mixed drinks: $5	Food available: None
Wine: $3.50	

Hours: Daily, 2 p.m.–2 a.m.

(Martunis)

What goes on: A variety of cool jazz and other lounge music accompanied by the cheerful clinking of cocktail glasses. Music might be a trio or just a singer at the copper-topped piano bar. Classic cocktails and new inventions are served up large, with a smile. If you sit at the piano, you might be asked to sing.

Setting & atmosphere: It might have been called the Black Room, a Yin to the Red Room's Yang. It's dark in here. And the heavy drapes, thick carpet, and indirect lighting make it more so. Even when you come in at night, you have to let your eyes adjust. But it gives you the sense of being far away in some cozy, friendly getaway where all the strangers are just friends you haven't met.

If you go: Don't go on an empty stomach. The drinks are huge, and you'll be bombed before you know it.

NOC NOC

Cave bar

Who Goes There: Gen Xers, 30-something locals

557 Haight Street (at Fillmore and Steiner Streets)
(415) 861-5811   Zone 2 Civic Center

Cover: None	Beer: $3.25
Minimum: None	Dress: Casual, alternative
Mixed drinks: None	Specials: Sake: $3, small; $5, large
Wine: $3.25	Food available: Bar snacks

Hours: Daily, 5 p.m.–2 a.m.

What goes on: Either starting off the night or closing it down. Gen Xers come here to be mellow and avoid those who care to see and be seen. Perfect postdate spot for the tragically hip and alternative.

Setting & atmosphere: The Stone Age meets *Road Warrior*. A small cave den littered with hieroglyphics, metal levers, bombs, and airplane wings. Scattered large throw pillows and pit booths are great for intimate chatting. A cozy escape from the harried lower Haight scene.

If you go: Great locations for a crawl. The Toronado, known by beer connoisseurs for its wide selection on draft and bottled, is just a few doors down. Also a stone's throw away are the British hangout Mad Dog in the Fog, Midtown, and Nickie's BBQ. Note that these bars specialize in beer; you'll have to go elsewhere if you want a decent cocktail.

OCCIDENTAL GRILL

Saloon and restaurant

Who Goes There: Financial District suits, locals, 30-somethings

453 Pine Street
  (415) 834-0484   Zone 4 Financial District

Cover: None
Minimum: None
Mixed drinks: $5
Wine: $4.50–15, by the glass
Beer: $4

Dress: Business, sports jackets
Specials: Martinis
Food available: Full menu of meat-
  and-potatoes fare, elegantly done

Hours: Monday–Friday, 11:15 a.m.–until ?

What goes on: The original building came down in the 1906 earthquake, but this is the site of the birthplace of the martini. First concocted by "Professor" Jerry Adams and served to his "patients" at the Occidental, it is still being poured, at a rate of 200 a day, in a form little changed since 1863.

Setting & atmosphere: Brick walls, rich wood, and long brass rail in the bar. Starched white tablecloths and booths with padded seats in the restaurant. 1920s and '30s crooners on the sound system, including Satchmo, der Bingle, Rudy Valley, and Lena Horne. As is common in the city, it's high class without being snooty. In the spirit of frontier egalitarianism, it's what's in your pocket, not your pedigree.

If you go: A sign above the door reads, "Smoking prohibited except in designated areas such as the bar, where we invite you to enjoy a cigar without fear of imprisonment or public stoning." Be prepared for well-dressed men and women smoking fat cigars in the designated area and talking shop. On the plus side, when bothersome sellers of flowers, drugs, illegal weapons, or souvenirs wander in, they are quickly ushered out with the stern admonition, "It's against our regulations!"

PIER 23

Jazz bar/restaurant

Who Goes There: Locals, sailors, and jazz aficionados

Pier 23
   (415) 362-5125   Zone 6 North Beach

Cover: $5 on Saturday	Beer: $3–3.50
Minimum: None	Dress: Casual
Mixed drinks: $3.25	Food available: Meat and potatoes,
Wine: $3.50–5	seafood, pizza

Hours: Monday–Saturday, 11–2 a.m.; Sunday, 11a.m.–9 p.m.

What goes on: In the afternoons you can sit at the beaten copper bar, drink, and watch the parade of watercraft on the bay. In the evenings, dine and listen to popular local jazz bands of all kinds. One of the more popular performers is Melanie Schaefer, who played two saxophones at once and called herself "bisaxual."

Setting & atmosphere: An airy waterfront version of a smoky, late-night jazz basement. It's an old-time dockside cafe with a concrete floor; the pier in the back serves as a patio and a place for the fireboats to tie up. A cheery place with lots of regulars.

If you go: The bands play inside, where there's limited seating for dinner, so many dine outside on the pier and listen to the music being piped out. If you do this, remember the highly changeable San Francisco weather and bring a coat.

PLOUGH AND THE STARS

Irish pub

Who Goes There: Irish gents and lasses, Richmond-area locals

116 Clement Street, between Second and Third
   (415) 751-1122   Zone 8 Richmond/Avenues

Cover: $3 on weekends	Dress: Casual
Minimum: None	Specials: Happy hour, weekdays,
Mixed drinks: $3.50–3.75	4–6 p.m.
Wine: $3.50–3.75	Food available: Cheese and crackers
Beer: $3.50–3.75	during Friday happy hour

(Plough and the Stars)

Hours: Daily, 2 p.m.–2 a.m.

What goes on: "Home of traditional Irish music in the Bay Area"; quality local bands play nightly after 9:30 p.m. Pool, darts, and chewing the fat with the regulars.

Setting & atmosphere: Accents are thick, and so is the Guinness. No one comes here just once, so make yourself comfortable at the long wooden tables or pull up a stool and chat with the regulars at the bar. It's easy to forget you're in San Francisco, not Ireland, amid the acoustic ballads beneath the Irish Republic flag. It's sometimes hard to have an intimate conversation when everyone is clapping their hands to the music.

If you go: Feel free to do the Irish crawl. Though Plough and Stars is known among locals to have the best Guinness in town, there's a plethora of Irish hangouts just a jig away, including the Bitter End, Ireland 32s, Pat O'Shea's, and the Front Room.

THE RED ROOM

Retro cocktail lounge

Who Goes There: Hipsters in their 20s and 30s

827 Sutter Street
   (415) 346-7666   Zone 3 Union Square

Cover: None	Beer: $3.50–4
Minimum: None	Dress: Dressy
Mixed drinks: $4–7	Food available: None
Wine: $6–7	

Hours: Daily, 5 p.m.–2 a.m.

What goes on: A 1950s lounge lizard meets *Details* magazine. Young yuppies who are too cool to cop to the term come to this oh-so-hip location to advance the cause of cocktail culture. Aside from the decor, nothing distracts the patrons from themselves and their long-stemmed glasses.

Setting & atmosphere: Red. Crimson. Vermillion. Sanguine. Longer wavelengths of the visible light spectrum. It's red, by God, red! The ceiling, the floor, the wallpaper, the drapes. Even the lights are red, though you should read nothing into that. The place is small and smoky, with a horseshoe bar commanded by an Amazon and her assistant; they slosh out a variety of martinis into cocktail glasses the size of bull horns.

(The Red Room)

If you go: Go early. The terminally hip tend to crowd this place so much in the evening that a doorman has to ask guests to form a line; they're allowed in only after a reverential wait. But don't let this deter you. Before the hordes of hip descend it's a great place for a predinner cocktail. All that red is somehow soothing when accompanied by a well-made martini.

SAVOY TIVOLI

Meat-market nightclub

Who Goes There: The young and the restless

1434 Grant Avenue (Green and Union Streets)
   (415) 362-7023   Zone 6 North Beach

Cover: None
Minimum: None
Mixed drinks: $3.50–6
Wine: $4.75
Beer: $2.50–3.50
Dress: Casual seductive

Specials: Schnapps, $1.50
Food available: Wonderful North Beach Italian cuisine all over the neighborhood. Management allows you to bring in any food, but no drinks.

Hours: Monday–Friday, 5–2 a.m.; Saturday, 3–2 a.m.; Sunday, closed

What goes on: A neighborhood party for those on the make. For those who can concentrate, there are three pool tables.

Setting & atmosphere: Every bit of this large North Beach bar is packed on weekends. The overflow hangs out of the wall-sized open windows in the heated patio facing the street. Partygoers are mostly in their 20s, and they're ready for some serious action. The jukebox is enough to keep this popular bar rocking.

If you go: Get ready to be checked out. This is a desperate singles haven and a fun place despite its meat-market reputation. It's surrounded by great eateries and other bars. Conveniently located; a perfect stop after a nice dinner when entertaining out-of-towners.

TOP O' THE MARK

Rooftop lounge and dance floor

Who Goes There: Well-dressed 30s and up, tourists and regulars

999 California Street
   (415) 392-3434   Zone 3 Union Square

Cover: Weeknights, $6; weekends, $10
Minimum: None
Mixed drinks: $5.50–8
Wine: $5.50–14
Beer: $4–5.50

Dress: Evening casual to dressy
Specials: The view at sunset
Food available: Finger foods, elegant
  hors d'oeuvres

Hours: 3 p.m.–until ?

What goes on: Dancing, romancing, schmoozing, and boozing. Musical offerings include in-house pianists, cool jazz combos, and retro groups. People come here for swing and ballroom dancing, sunset cocktails, business talks, romantic assignations, and conspiracies.

Setting & atmosphere: Understated elegance on the most romantic rooftop in town, on top of the Mark Hopkins hotel, on top of Nob Hill. The elevated dance floor is in the center of the room and surrounded by plush seating along the huge windows that give a near 360° view of the city. Despite the price and the sophistication, it's never intimidating, always welcoming, almost homey.

If you go: Valet parking is $21. Take a taxi or the California line cable car and get off right at the Mark.

TOSCA'S

Opera bar

Who Goes There: Mostly locals, 30-something and up

242 Columbus Avenue
   415 (391-1244)   Zone 6 North Beach

Cover: None
Minimum: None
Mixed drinks: $3.50–3.75
Wine: $3.50–4.75

Beer: $3.50–3.75
Dress: Come as you are
Specials: Irish coffee
Food available: None

Hours: Daily, 5 p.m.–2 a.m.

(Tosca's)

What goes on: Conversation and playing the jukebox. It's the only one in town with selections only from the world of opera. A lot of locals, including a few celebs, camp out here. In the back is an invitation-only pool room said to be a fave of Sam Shepard and Francis Ford Coppola.

Setting & atmosphere: A big place for a bar. All wood with red upholstered booths and a long bar on which sit dozens of Irish coffee glasses already charged with whiskey, sugar, and cream, waiting to be filled with hot coffee.

If you go: Afternoon to early evening is best, especially when the fog rolls in. At night the thunderous base notes of the disco in the basement can be felt through the floor.

TROCADERO

Leading edge, gothic, kinky dance club

Who Goes There: Mostly 20-somethings
with a smattering of all the human race

520 Fourth Street
    (415) 495-6620   Zone 7 SoMa/Mission

Cover: $10	Beer: $4
Minimum: None	Dress: Use your imagination
Mixed drinks: $4	Food available: Bar snacks
Wine: $5	

Hours: Monday–Friday, 11 p.m.–6 a.m.

What goes on: The question is, what doesn't go on? Especially on Wednesday nights when it's "bondage go-go." While the band thunders on the main lower floor and the Goths, Primitives, and Neotribals dance to their separate demons, the "leather crowd" comes out to play upstairs. Have you been naughty? Need a spanking? Wildly costumed sadists will oblige you by tying you up and whipping the daylights out of you. And they never lack for willing subjects. They'll also demonstrate their techniques and sell you copies of their "toys."

Setting & atmosphere: Two floors of black-lit, hard-rock techno-dungeon. The stage acts often resemble a Star Trek version of the *Clash of the Titans,* but the patrons are even more entertaining. You will be amazed at how many tattoos and piercings one body can accommodate. It all looks scary, but don't worry; they won't bite.

If you go: Wear leather and check your inhibitions at the door. Don't gawk.

PART SEVEN

Exercise and Recreation

A City of Two Seasons

Most of the folks on our *Unofficial Guide* research team work out routinely. Some bike, run, or lift weights, and others play tennis or do aerobics. When it comes to outdoor recreation, we discovered yet another reason San Francisco is so great: the weather. Its Mediterranean climate is invariably spring-like year-round. Daytime temperatures average in the 60s in the summer, and winter highs range from the high 40s to the high 50s. You could say San Francisco is "air-conditioned"—the result of a unique combination of waters, winds, and topography. During much of the summer a fog bank hugs the cold currents off the Northern California coast (while in the Central Valley to the east temperatures soar to 100° or more). Because air always travels from cooler to warmer surfaces, the mist moves toward the mountainous shore. Denied access along a nearly 600-mile front, the fog pushes through the continental wall at the mouth of San Francisco Bay. As the land cools, the vapor dissipates.

At dawn on a typical morning in July or August, San Francisco lies blanketed in fog. But the fog soon begins to break up over the East Bay and fades to translucence around Fisherman's Wharf, Telegraph Hill, and the Financial District. By noon the city is usually basking in bright sunlight. Late in the afternoon, the fog is usually back.

■ Getting a Handle on San Francisco's Weather ■

San Francisco, because of its unusual geographical position, is usually cooler than the surrounding Bay Area—an important point to keep in mind when you're planning a day trip. There's an apt, if oversimplified, adage: for every ten miles you travel away from the city, the temperature goes up 10°. When it's a comfortable 65° in the city, it's often in the 80s across the Golden Gate in Marin County to the north, on the peninsula to the south, and in Oakland to the east. In Sacramento, nearly 100 miles to the east, things can be simmering at 100°.

One more thing about summer in San Francisco—it almost never rains, and an overcast sky rarely results in precipitation. Which brings us to the city's other major season: winter. November through March is the rainy season, when the Bay Area gets virtually all of its rainfall. January, the rainiest month, averages nearly four and a half inches of rain. And snow? The city rarely sees the white stuff.

Fall is the warmest and sunniest season; daytime averages approach 70° and the fog is at its minimum. Spring, with only trace amounts of rain and daytime highs in the low to mid-60s, is the other season that's popular with the *Unofficial Guide* research crew and outdoor enthusiasts.

Indoor Sports

■ Free Weights and Nautilus ■

Many of the major hotels in San Francisco have a spa or fitness room with weight-lifting equipment, or they have reciprocity with a nearby health club that extends privileges to hotel guests. For an aerobic workout, most of the fitness rooms offer a Lifecycle, Stairmaster, or rowing machine.

■ Fitness Centers and Aerobics ■

Many San Francisco fitness centers are coed and accept daily or short-term memberships. **Club One** has five locations with free weights, Nautilus, aerobic equipment, Jacuzzis, steam rooms, aerobics classes, and certified fitness professionals. Locations are Citicorp Center (1 Sansome Street; (415) 399-1010), Yerba Buena (350 Third Street; (415) 512-1010), Embarcadero Center (2 Embarcadero Center; (415) 788-1010), Nob Hill (950 California Street; (415) 834-1010), and Jackson Square (30 Hotaling Place; (415) 837-1010). The daily rate is $15.

Pacific Heights Health Club at 2356 Pine Street (at Fillmore Street; (415) 563-6694) provides separate gyms for men and women; equipment includes a full line of Nautilus, free weights, Stairmaster and Lifecycle cardiovascular workout machines, a full spa, and towel and locker service. The daily guest fee is $10. **24 Hour Fitness** has seven locations in the city, including 100 California Street (phone (415) 434-5080) and 1200 Van Ness Avenue (phone (415) 776-2200). Equipment includes Nautilus, free weights, and aerobic machines; the daily rate is $15.

At two of the four locations of **Pinnacle Fitness,** guests can swim at indoor pools after working out on Cybex weight-training gear or free weights; all locations have steam rooms. The clubs with pools are at 1 Post Street (phone (415)781-6400) and 3200 California Street (phone (415) 440-2242); the other locations are 435 Spear Street in the Hills Plaza on the Embarcadero (phone (415) 495-1939) and 61 Montgomery Street (across from the Sheraton Palace hotel; (415) 543-1110). The daily fee is $15.

■ Exercising in Your Hotel ■

You work out regularly, but here you are stuck on a rainy San Francisco day in a hotel without an exercise room. Worse, you're out of sorts from overeating and sitting in airplanes, and not being able to let off steam. Don't despair. Unless your hotel is designed like a sprawling dude ranch, you have stairs to play on. Put on your workout clothes and find a nice interior stairwell, which all hotels are required to have in case of fire. Devise a step workout consistent with your fitness level.

Bob's Plan (for a ten-story hotel): from your floor, descend to the very bottom of the stairwell. Walk up ten flights and down again to get warmed up. Then, taking the stairs two at a time, bound up two floors and return to the bottom quickly but normally (i.e., one step at a time). Next bound up three floors and return. Add a floor after each circuit until you get to the top floor. Then reverse the process, ascending one less floor on each round trip: nine, eight, seven floors, etc. You get the idea. Tell somebody where you'll be in case you fall down the stairs or something. Listen to your body and don't overdo it. If your hotel has 30 stories, don't feel compelled to make it to the top.

Joe's Plan (for a ten-story hotel): sit in the stairwell on the fourth-floor landing with a six-pack of Bud and laugh at Bob every time he chugs past. Thank God that you are not a Type-A obsessive-compulsive. If steps aren't your gig, you might consider buying a Reebok Slide exerciser. Self-contained and complete—and weighing less than 12 pounds—the slide can be spread out on your hotel room floor for a great workout. Take it with you wherever you travel.

Outdoor Sports

■ Walking ■

San Francisco, which reminds some people of a European city, is a great town for walking. Whether you're exploring fascinating neighborhoods such as Chinatown or North Beach or checking out the magnificent scenery on a stroll along San Francisco Bay, you'll find that this compact city is best appreciated—and most approachable—on foot. Folks who are fit and enjoy using their own two feet should bring comfortable walking shoes and regularly give themselves a rest by taking a bus, cable car, or Muni Metro streetcar.

Along the Bay

San Francisco's premier walking destination is the **Golden Gate Promenade,** a three-and-a-half-mile paved footpath that starts in Fort Mason (just west of Fisherman's Wharf) and ends at the famous bridge of the same name. As the trail follows the shoreline along San Francisco Bay, it passes through Marina Green, the Yacht Harbor, Crissy Field, and the Presidio; it ends at Fort Point (a Civil War–era brick fortress). Along the way are picnic areas, rest rooms, restaurants, beaches, drinking water, fishing piers, quiet stretches of shoreline, and breathtaking views. To lengthen the walk, hike the **Coastal Trail** along the Pacific coast to Cliff House. Temperatures can change rapidly along the shoreline, and wind is often strong; bring a jacket or sweater.

Visitors can begin a stroll in **South Beach Harbor** on the east side of the city facing Oakland. Start at Pier 40 and walk north along the promenade past the new marina, new apartment complexes, and South Beach Park, where artists sometimes set up their easels on the lawn beneath the colossal red-and-silver Mark di Suvero sculpture "Sea Change." It's a place where picnickers and dog-walkers gather to watch the boats. As you walk north, the Bay Bridge soon arches above; curving along the sidewalk for nearly half a mile is a ribbon of glass blocks lit with fiber-optic cable and set in concrete; some of it is raised for use as benches or tables. This public art is a nice place to relax and watch the bay and the parade of joggers, skaters, and strollers.

City Walks

There are other great places to walk in San Francisco. In the northwest corner of the city, the 1,480-acre **Presidio** has 11 miles of trails in a variety of landscapes, including coastal bluffs, forested hills, and historic architectural settings (such as the old army buildings on the main post). You can pick up a trail map at the visitor center, open from 9 a.m. to 5 p.m. daily. **Golden Gate Park** features miles of walking, multipurpose bicycle, and bridle paths. Probably the best place for walkers is **Strybing Arboretum** near the Japanese Tea Garden. The beauty and tranquility of the many gardens inside the 70-acre arboretum and its manicured lawns are unsurpassed.

If your hotel doesn't have a Stairmaster, simply go outside. City stair climbs not only provide a great workout, the views are great, too. The **Filbert Street Steps** scale the sheer eastern face of Telegraph Hill; the 377 steps wind through verdant flower gardens and charming 19th-century cottages. The steps are located between Sansome Street and Telegraph Hill. The **Lyon Street Steps,** between Green Street and Broadway, contain four sets of steep stairs totaling 288 steps. Start at Green Street and go all the way to the top, past manicured hedges and flower gardens, to an iron gate that leads to the Presidio. A block east, on Baker Street, is another set of 369 steps that descend to Green Street.

Along the Pacific beaches, walkers and hikers can explore trails at **Lands End,** where they'll find San Francisco's natural coastline; just be sure to stick to the main trails because the cliffs are steep and dangerous. **Ocean Beach** provides an exhilarating view of the ocean and the tang of salt air on four miles of sand and ocean surf. Resist the urge to wade in, though; the water is always dangerous, even when it looks calm. **Fort Funston** has miles of easy trails (including a wheelchair-accessible loop trail), a gentle short walk revealing stunning coastal scenery, and hang gliders floating overhead as they take advantage of the area's high cliffs and strong winds. Be sure to stay clear of the hang gliders' landing and takeoff area.

Islands in the Bay

In San Francisco Bay there are two destinations great for walking, but they require a ferry ride; both are worth it. **Angel Island State Park,** located about a mile southeast of Tiburon, has amazing views of the San Francisco skyline and the spooky ruins of a long-closed immigration center. A number of foot trails go to the island's highest peak (780 feet); there are also paved and unpaved roads (but no traffic). Ferries leave from four ports: Tiburon, Fisherman's Wharf, Vallejo, and Oakland/Alameda. Tiburon, a few miles north of the Golden Gate Bridge, is the closest and has hourly trips to the island (in winter, weekends only); the cost is $7 a person.

Alcatraz Island, infamous for its federal penitentiary ruins, is also an evolving ecological preserve—and a great walking destination. The absence of four-footed predators has made the island a haven for birds, as well as thriving populations of crabs, starfish, and other marine animals living in tide pools. Visitors can see all this on the **Agave Trail,** which follows the island's shoreline. Ferries to Alcatraz leave from Pier 41 at Fisherman's Wharf; it's almost always necessary to make reservations in advance.

■ Running ■

You'll see plenty of runners on the sidewalks downtown. But for visitors who would rather avoid traffic, large crowds, and stoplights, there are plenty of other options. Flat but usually windy, the **Golden Gate Promenade** offers runners a paved and scenic route for a workout; the round trip from Fort Mason to the Golden Gate Bridge is seven miles. Not that you have to stop at the landmark span; you can run across the bridge on its pedestrian walkway to Marin County or continue along the Pacific coast on the **Coastal Trail.**

Usually less windy, **Golden Gate Park** has plenty of paved roads and miles of pedestrian, bike, and bridle paths on rolling terrain; the main drag, Kennedy Drive, is closed to traffic on Sundays. On the east side of the city in **South Beach,** a promenade heads north along the shoreline toward the Bay Bridge; it's a favorite destination for joggers and runners.

Although most folks drive or take a tour bus, a more exhilarating way to get to the summit of **Twin Peaks** and its stupendous view is to run or walk. Routes include the back roads from the University of California Medical Center or either of the two main roads that lead to the top. The best time is early morning when the city is quiet and the air is crisp; just make sure you pick a morning that's not fogbound. Watch for traffic and be sure to jog beyond the parking lot to the highest vantage point.

■ Tennis ■

More than 140 tennis courts are operated throughout the city by the San Francisco Recreation and Parks Department. All are available free on a first-come, first-served basis, with the exception of 21 courts in **Golden Gate Park,** where a fee is charged and reservations must be made in advance for weekend play. The courts are located off Kennedy Drive opposite the Conservatory; individual and group lessons are available.

To make weekend reservations at a court in Golden Gate Park, call (415) 753-7101 on the preceding Wednesday evening between 7 and 9 p.m., the preceding Thursday between 9:15 a.m. and 5 p.m., or the preceding Friday between 9:15 and 11:30 a.m. (Call Wednesday evening to avoid disappointment.) The nonresident court fee is $8 for a 90-minute play period. For more information and the locations of other courts around San Francisco, call the parks department at (415) 753-7100.

▪ Road Bicycling and In-Line Skating ▪

In downtown San Francisco, most visitors will want to leave bicycling and in-line skating to bike messengers and street-savvy natives. Yet skinny-tire cyclists and skaters don't need to go far to find some excellent places to spin the cranks or skate the black ice. The **Golden Gate Promenade** starts in Fort Mason (just west of Fisherman's Wharf) and follows the bay shore for three and a half miles to the bridge of the same name (which has a pedestrian-bike lane). The scenery from the bridge is spectacular, and it's usually very windy. Across the bridge in Marin County at the end of the Vista Point parking lot is a bike lane that parallels US 101 and then turns off to Alexander Avenue through Sausalito.

The **Presidio** has 14 miles of paved roads, open to cyclists and in-line skaters, that weave through groves of trees and wind past military housing. Because most of the old military post's roads were laid out in horse-and-buggy days, all grades are easy to moderate. **Golden Gate Park** has seven and a half miles of designated paved trails for bikes that extend from the tip of the Panhandle through Golden Gate Park to Lake Merced. In addition, some roads (such as Kennedy Drive, the main drag) are closed to car traffic on Sundays; it's mecca for San Francisco in-line skaters.

With its three bicycle lanes, the flat, three-mile sidewalk along **Ocean Beach** (Great Highway) provides a great workout and can be incorporated into a longer tour of the Sunset District. Ride south on the Great Highway for two miles past the San Francisco Zoo to Sloat Boulevard and turn right onto Lake Merced Boulevard; then ride for five miles around the lake and nearby golf course.

For another variation along the Pacific shoreline, ride north along the Great Highway from Lake Merced toward Cliff House. Just before you get there, gear down for a 200-foot ascent. Then veer right onto Point Lobos Avenue and turn right onto 43rd Avenue. Then it's all downhill to Golden Gate Park; enter at Chain of Lakes Drive East, which takes you back to Kennedy Drive. Turn right and continue west to the Great Highway, which takes you back to Lake Merced.

A San Francisco classic for the thin-tire set is a 19-mile loop ride across the Golden Gate Bridge to Sausalito and Tiburon that returns you to San

Francisco on a ferry. The ride can start at the parking lot at the south end of the bridge or at Fisherman's Wharf; after the one-and-a-half-mile bridge crossing, descend into Sausalito on Alexander Avenue, ride into Tiburon, and catch the ferry to Fisherman's Wharf. Check with a local bike shop for turn-by-turn directions and a map; it's also a good idea to check the ferry schedule by calling (800) 229-2784.

Renting Bikes and In-Line Skates

Bike and skate rentals are widely available throughout San Francisco; some shops also provide guided tours. **Bay Bicycle Tours & Rentals** at the Cannery in Fisherman's Wharf (phone (415) 436-0633) rents 21-speed hybrid (city) bikes starting at $5 an hour and $25 a day; helmet, rear rack and bag, lock, maps, tour info, and water bottles are included. They also offer a guided tour across the Golden Gate Bridge to Sausalito and a return to San Francisco by ferry for $35.

American Rentals doesn't just rent bicycles (starting at $5 an hour), they also rent motor scooters (starting at $45 a day) and motorcycles (starting at $150 for 24 hours). The shop is located at 2715 Hyde Street (at the last cable-car stop between North Point and Beach); call (415) 931-0234. **Blazing Saddles** rents computer-equipped bikes for self-guided tours of San Francisco, the Marin Headlands, Muir Woods, and Mount Tamalpais. Mountain bike rentals start at $5 an hour; also available for rent are road bikes, city bikes, tandems, kids' bikes, and car racks. The shop is located at 1095 Columbus Avenue (at Francisco); call (415) 202-8888.

Downtown at 599 Post Street, **Bay Area Rentals** offers bikes for rent starting at $3 an hour; locks and bike racks are $5 a day each. Call (514) 202-8841 for more information. In Golden Gate Park, **Surrey Bikes & Blades** rents in-line skates starting at $6 an hour and bikes at $5 an hour; the shop, located at Stow Lake (closed Wednesdays and rainy days) also rents tandem bikes, electric bikes, and pedal-powered surreys. For more information, call (415) 668-6699.

Skates on Haight, half a block from Golden Gate Park in Haight-Ashbury, rents in-line skates for $8 an hour; the price includes head, knee, and wrist protection. The shop is open daily; call (415) 752-8375 for more information. Across the street, **Park Cyclery** rents bikes starting at $5 an hour. The shop is closed Thursdays; call (415) 751-7368 for more information.

At Angel Island State Park in San Francisco Bay, **Angel Island Company** rents 21-speed mountain bikes for exploring traffic-free roads and paths on the island. Basic rentals start at $9 an hour or $25 a day and include a helmet. Open daily April through October, and weekends only in November and mid-February through March; closed mid-November through mid-February. Call (415) 897-0715 for more information on rentals and (800) 229-2784 for ferry schedules from Pier 43 in Fisherman's Wharf.

▪ Mountain Biking ▪

While fat-tire mountain bikes are fine for riding on San Francisco's streets and paved trails, off-road afficionados who prefer the feel of dirt between their knobbies should look farther afield, but not too far. Across the Golden Gate Bridge lies Marin County, where popular myth says mountain biking was invented 20 years ago.

The holy of holies is Mount Tamalpais, affectionately known as Mount Tam. It's so popular a destination among fat-tire fanatics that the sport has been banned from single-track trails, and cops armed with radar guns give out tickets to cyclists who exceed 15 miles an hour on the fire roads. The most popular route is the technically easy, but aerobically demanding, Old Railroad Grade to the historic West Point Inn and the East Peak. There are lots of scenic spots along the way, and the reward is a breathtaking (not that you'll have much breath left), 360° view of San Francisco Bay. And, as they say, it's all downhill from here.

To reach the **Old Railroad Grade** (an unpaved fire road), load your bike onto your car and take US 101 north across the Bay Bridge to the Tiburon Boulevard/East Blithedale Avenue exit. Then turn left, heading under US 101 and west onto East Blithedale Avenue. Take East Blithedale as it turns into West Blithedale Avenue and go past an intersection with Eldridge Road. About a mile later, Old Railroad Grade branches off to the right over a wooden bridge. Park as close to this bridge as you can. Unload your bike and ride across the bridge. Note: Don't ride alone, and stop by a bike shop for a map and more detailed directions before you plunge into the wilderness.

A little closer to San Francisco is **Angel Island State Park,** located in San Francisco Bay about a mile from Tiburon. Take the ferry from Fisherman's Wharf or Tiburon to get there; bikes are permitted on the ferry. You can also rent one on the island (see above), but rentals are cheaper on the mainland. There are about eight miles of easy, unpaved fire roads to explore, and the scenery is terrific, especially from the upper fire road. Alas, mountain bikes are not permitted on trails on the island and ferry service is limited to weekends in the winter.

▪ Beaches ▪

With San Francisco's mild climate, it's just too chilly to hang out at the beach on most days. But sometimes, after the fog clears and the sun comes out, one of the best ways to spend an afternoon is oceanside, enjoying the view, people-watching, building sand castles, or just loafing.

But not swimming. Pacific waters are fiercely cold and often treacherous to boot. The only beaches considered safe for swimming are **Aquatic Park** next to the Hyde Street Pier and **China Beach,** a small cove on the western edge of the South Bay. But you swim at your own risk; neither beach provides lifeguards.

Ocean Beach, located at the end of Golden Gate Park below Cliff House, is the city's largest beach; it's four miles long. While not especially scenic, this is a great place for strolling, sunbathing, and people-watching, but again, not for swimming. The water is treacherous even when it looks calm.

Nude Beaches

Many beaches around San Francisco allow nudity, with the interesting caveats that you don't touch anybody and nobody complains. (If you equate nudity with sex, keep in mind that in the Golden Gate National Recreation Area, where many of the nude beaches are located, public sex is a federal offense.) Other negatives to lounging in the buff at San Francisco beaches include cool temperatures, fog, wind, rocky beaches with little or no sand, and gawkers. In addition, many of the beaches are difficult to reach, requiring long walks on narrow, steep paths lined with poison oak.

One of the top-rated nude beaches is at **Lands End** on the western edge of the city. It's a rocky beach with a few sandy spots and a couple of wind-protected nooks. Most visitors are gay men, and the beach has a reputation as a gay cruising spot. But on nice days there's a killer view. To get there, drive to the dirt parking lot just above Cliff House on the Great Highway and follow the trail at the far end of the lot.

North Baker Beach may be America's most popular nude beach because of its proximity to a major city. Other lures include a safe parking lot and clean sand. Recently, car-sized boulders tumbled onto the north (nude) end of the beach, creating nice spots for sunbathing sheltered from the wind. Nudity isn't permitted on the south end of the beach. To get there, walk north from the west end of Gibson Road, just off Bowley Street (which is west of Fort Point, off Lincoln Boulevard). Follow a well-marked trail that begins near Lincoln Boulevard; when you reach the sand, head north toward the nude area. The beach can get extremely crowded on warm days; other problems include fog, wind, noise, gawkers, and occasional sexual activity.

Red Rock Beach and **Muir Beach,** both located in Marin County, are two popular "clothing optional" (nude) beaches close to the city. To reach them, take US 101 north over the Golden Gate Bridge to the Stinson Beach/Highway 1 exit, which leads to Shoreline Highway. Follow the signs to

Stinson Beach, turning left onto Highway 1 at the first stoplight (Tam Junction). Follow Highway 1 about six miles to Muir Beach at milepost 5.7; park in the public lot, which can fill up early on summer weekends. From the main (not nude) beach, walk north over the rocks to the nude area, several hundred yards or so of wide, sandy beach protected from the winds by a nearby cliff.

On to Red Rock Beach: about six miles past Muir Beach, park in the large unpaved area on the ocean side just past the Steep Ravine Environmental Campground (a gated road). Hike down a gravelly path to the beach and be sure to watch out for poison oak. You'll find places to eat and shop in the town of Stinson Beach.

■ Sea Kayaking ■

San Francisco's spectacular marine setting is perfect for exploration by water. And a sea kayak—a stable, covered boat similar to a canoe but propelled by a double-bladed paddle—is just the ticket for exploring hidden coves and bays. **Sea Trek Ocean Kayaking Center** offers tours for novices around Angel Island, Sausalito, and Point Reyes. Rentals for single and double kayaks start at $15 an hour. Wetsuits, paddle jackets, sprayskirts, paddles, pumps, and paddle floats are included with rentals. Call (415) 488-1000 for more information.

Blue Waters Kayaking in Marin County offers instruction, rentals, and tours in Point Reyes and Tomales Bay; no experience is necessary for some tour packages. Half- and full-day tours led by a naturalist start at $45 a person; an all-day introductory kayaking course is $79. Sea kayak rentals start at $25 an hour. For reservations and more information, call (415) 669-2600.

■ Rock Climbing ■

When the urge hits to go climbing or bouldering, you don't have to jump in the car and drive to Yosemite. **Mission Cliffs** is the world's largest indoor climbing gym (2295 Harrison Street at 19th Street). Beginners are welcome; a first-time basic safety class is $5 (plus the day-pass fee and $6 for shoes and harness). The nonmember rate is $8 before 3 p.m. on weekdays and $16 after 3 p.m. on weekdays and all day on weekends. For more information, call (415) 550-0515.

■ Hang Gliding ■

With its persistent coastal winds, San Francisco is an excellent place to go hang gliding. The **San Francisco Hang Gliding Center** specializes in tandem hang-gliding flights. You can see some of Northern California's most beautiful terrain while flying with Bodhi Kroll, a pro with an unblemished 12-year safety record. The center is at 977 Regal Road in Berkeley (phone (510) 528-2300). The basic tandem flight is $149.95, and transportation to the site is available. If you'd rather just watch, head for Fort Funston south of Ocean Beach, where hang gliders launch off 200-foot cliffs and soar on coastal breezes.

▪ Sailing ▪

San Francisco Bay, one of the largest and most beautiful harbors in the world, is also a major yachting center—although sailing on the bay is challenging even for the most experienced sailor. Certified skippers can charter anything from day sailors to luxury yachts and sail past all the landmarks that make the bay so famous. Don't know a spinnaker from a jib? You can also learn how to sail while you're on vacation in San Francisco.

Cass' Marina charters day sailors that accommodate up to six people, starting at $105 a day on weekdays; each boat is equipped with toilet facilities and life vests. Cruising boats for large daytime outings or overnight charters start at $200 a day; weekend, five-day, and weekly rates are also available. Cass' offers a full compliment of instructional courses for beginners to advanced sailors. A basic keelboat certification course with 29 hours of instruction is $700; completion qualifies you to bareboat (no crew) charter a cruising sailboat. Private instruction is available for $200 for three hours (for one or two people). Cass' Marina is located at 1702 Bridgeway at Napa Street in Sausalito (across the bay from San Francisco); phone (415) 332-6789 for more information.

Also in Sausalito is **Atlantis Yacht Charters,** where you can charter 30-foot and longer yachts. Bareboat charters start at $210 a day for an Ericson 30 that sleeps four; a Nordic 44 goes for $450 a day midweek and sleeps seven adults. Skippered charters start at $295 for four hours midweek; the price includes captain, yacht, and fuel. For more information, call (800) 65-YACHT.

▪ Horseback Riding ▪

San Francisco's only equestrian center is **Golden Gate Park Stables,** located in Golden Gate Park at Kennedy Drive and 36th Avenue. Guided, one-hour rides in the park are $25 a person; the minimum age is 8. Also offered are guided, one-and-a-half-hour rides along the Pacific at Ocean Beach for $35 a person. Riding instruction and pony rides for children are also available. Reservations are required; call (415) 668-7360.

■ Windsurfing ■

Good coastal winds make San Francisco one of the top spots in the country for windsurfing. The premier location in the city is **Crissy Field,** where experienced board sailors frolic on wind and waves. Newcomers can learn the basic skills of this difficult sport in the more gentle environment of Lake Merced and its consistent, gentle breezes. The **San Francisco School of Windsurfing** offers a two-day beginner course at the freshwater lake for $130 a person ($115 a person for groups of three or more). After land instruction, students work in the water until they become proficient at the skills of sailing in light winds; once certified, they can rent equipment at Lake Merced. For more information, call the school at (415) 763-3235.

■ Golf ■

San Francisco has two municipal golf courses that are open to the public. Golden Gate Park Course (47th Avenue and Fulton Street; (415) 751-8987) is a small nine-hole course covering 1,357 yards. It is open every day, 6 a.m. until dusk. Green fees are $10 during the week and $13 on weekends. Lincoln Park Golf Course (34th Avenue and Clement Street; (415) 221-9911) offers 18 holes and covers 5,081 yards. The oldest course in the city, it offers beautiful views and fairways. It is open every day, 6:30 a.m. until dusk. Green fees are $23 during the week and $27 on weekends.

■ Fishing ■

Deep-sea fishing charter boats leave Fisherman's Wharf daily, depending on weather and season. Catches in the Pacific waters beyond the Golden Gate include salmon, sea bass, halibut, striped bass, bonito, shark, tuna, and albacore. Licenses (required), rods, and tackle are available on board; plan for wind and some rough seas, and bring motion-sickness preventatives and warm clothing. **Miss Farallones,** a 50-foot charter boat, sets out on sport-fishing expeditions from Fisherman's Wharf most days and can carry up to 38 passengers. For rates and more information, call (510) 352-5708.

Freshwater fishing is available at **Lake Merced,** south of downtown where Skyline Boulevard meets the Great Highway at the Pacific coast. Large trout and some catfish and bass are stocked in the 360-acre lake, which is open year-round. Anglers must purchase a $9.70 one-day fishing license and pay a $4 access fee. Rowboats and canoes are available for rent for $9 an hour, $20 a half-day, and $25 all day. Electric boat rentals start at $13 an hour. You can also fish from the bank of the lake, which stocks trophy trout of two pounds and more. For more information, call (415) 753-1101.

■ Whale-Watching ■

Each year gray whales embark on one of the longest migrations of any mammal, and the coast near San Francisco is one of the best places to observe these giant mammals during their 6,000-mile journey between their Arctic feeding grounds and Baja California. The nonprofit **Oceanic Society** offers naturalist-led expeditions year-round to observe the whales and nature cruises to the Farallon Islands, stark granite cliffs 27 miles from the Golden Gate that teem with marine life.

Gray whale cruises depart from San Francisco at 9:30 a.m. on selected dates from December to May and last six hours, returning to the dock at 4 p.m. Rates for adults start at $48; bring your own lunch and beverages. The expedition transports guests under the Golden Gate Bridge and north along the Marin coast to search for gray whales off the Bolinas and Point Reyes areas.

Farallon Islands nature cruises depart at 8:30 a.m. on selected dates from June through November and last eight hours. Rates for adults start at $60; bring your own lunch and beverages. The cruise sails under the Golden Gate Bridge and goes west to the Farallon Islands, where a quarter-million seabirds nest and visible marine mammals include California sea lions, Steller's sea lions, northern elephant seals, harbor seals, and possibly humpback and blue whales.

All cruises are aboard the **New Superfish,** a 63-foot Coast Guard–certified, fully insured motor vessel with an open observation deck and indoor salon, and a passenger capacity of 49. Off-street parking is available at the harbor at Fort Mason. Youths ages 14 and under must be accompanied by an adult, and children ages 9 and under aren't permitted on the boat. Reservations are required; call (800) 326-7491 or (415) 474-3385 for a schedule, and make reservations at least two weeks in advance (although it's possible to get aboard at the last minute if there are cancellations).

Bring rain gear and warm clothing; the cruises depart rain or shine. Don't forget binoculars, a camera with a telephoto lens, sunscreen, and motion-sickness medicine. More advice: get a good night's sleep; eat a high-carbohydrate, high-protein, nongreasy breakfast; and bring crackers to nibble and ginger ale to sip to help avoid queasiness on the cruise.

Spectator Sports

By and large, San Franciscans are sports enthusiasts—not just in partici-patory activities such as running, biking, and tennis. In fact, Bay Area fans' dedication to their professional sports teams can verge on the obsessive. How much so? To the tune of more than half a billion dollars. Voters recently approved a new $525 million stadium complex at Candlestick Park for the San Francisco 49ers that's scheduled to open in 2000. The profes-sional sports scene in the Bay Area includes football, baseball, basketball, and horse racing.

■ Pro Teams ■

Baseball

The National League **San Francisco Giants** play home games at 3Com (formerly Candlestick) Park, infamous for its winds, cold, and fog. The park, soon to be replaced by a 75,000-seat stadium complex, is located at Giants Drive and Gilman Avenue (about eight miles south of downtown). The sea-son starts in April and goes through October. Tickets are usually available up until game time, but the seats can be regrettably far from the on-field action. Tickets are available through BASS/Ticketmaster (phone (510) 762-2277). Special express bus service is offered by Muni on game days and leaves from Market Street; call (415) 673-6864 for more information. And don't forget to bring a coat; it can get chilly in this windy stadium.

The American League **Oakland Athletics,** the 1989 world champs, play at the sunnier Oakland Coliseum across the bay (take the Hegenberger Road exit off I-880). The stadium seats 50,000 fans and is served by BART's Coli-seum station. Tickets to home games are available from the coliseum box office or by phone from BASS/Ticketmaster (phone (510) 762-2277).

Football

The **San Francisco 49ers,** five-time Super Bowl champs, play home games at 3Com Park Sundays from August through December. They're best known for their intelligence, speed, and grace. Good luck getting tickets, though. The games sell out early in the season, but sometimes select tickets are available; call the box office at (415) 468-2249. If you're willing to pay an inflated price, tickets may be available from ticket agents before game days and from scalpers at the gate; expect to pay up to $100 for a seat. Talk to your hotel concierge or stop by City Box Office (141 Kearny Street; (415) 392-4400). Muni operates special express buses to the park, located about eight miles south of downtown, from Market Street on game days; call (415) 673-6864 for more information.

The Bay Area has two pro football teams again. Across the bay are the 49ers' arch enemy, the **Oakland Raiders,** who returned to Oakland from Los Angeles in 1995 after abandoning the city for sunny Southern California 13 years before. Known as blue-collar heroes, the team charges country-club prices; expect to pay at least $60 for a ticket. Home games are played at the Oakland Alameda County Coliseum off I-880. For ticket information, call (800) 949-2626.

Basketball

The Bay Area's NBA team is the **Golden State Warriors,** who play in the newly renovated Oakland Coliseum Arena across the bay. The season runs from November through April; most games start at 7:30 p.m. Tickets are available at the arena, located at the Hegenberger Road exit off I-880, south of downtown Oakland (phone (510) 986-2222), or from BASS/Ticketmaster at (510) 762-2277.

■ Horse Racing ■

The Bay Area is home to two horse-racing tracks. Scenic **Golden Gate Fields,** located in the East Bay on Gilman Street (off I-80 in Albany, ten miles northeast of San Francisco), features thoroughbred racing from January to March and from April to the end of June. For post times and more information, call (510) 559-7300.

The autumn racing closest to San Francisco is at **Bay Meadows,** south of San Francisco in San Mateo (on US 101 at the Hillsdale exit). The thoroughbred and quarter-horse track hosts races Wednesday through Sunday from August through January. It's one of the oldest, busiest, and most beautiful ovals in California. For more information and post times, call (415) 574-7223.

■ Amateur Sports ■

Local college gridiron action is provided by the University of California **Golden Bears,** who play at Memorial Stadium across the bay in Berkeley. For game times and ticket information, call (510) 642-5150 or (800) GO-BEARS; tickets are usually available on game day. From November to March the Bears men's basketball squad plays at the Oakland Coliseum Arena—until the new $40 million Haas Pavilion opens on campus in January 1999.

The University of San Francisco **Dons** men's basketball team provides on-the-court excitement from November to March at the War Memorial Gymnasium on campus (5300 Golden Gate Avenue). Games start at 7 p.m.; for tickets and schedules, call (415) 422-6USF or BASS/Ticketmaster at (510) 762-2277.

PART EIGHT

Shopping in San Francisco

In the gold rush days of miners, soldiers, sailors, and scoundrels, folks used to come into the already wicked city of San Francisco to shop. The city has long since been eclipsed by Los Angeles as a West Coast center of consumer excess, but it still has unmatched treasures. It's still a frontier town, although today the frontiers are different; multimedia and technology, global commerce, and artistic innovation are some of the new territories.

San Francisco's merchants still know how to separate fools from their gold. Shopping is about more than getting the goods; it's about the neighborhood. And shopping in these distinct neighborhoods (they even have their own "microclimates") is a good way to glimpse the city's kaleidoscope of cultures.

Real San Franciscans wouldn't be caught dead in a mall or a superstore for something they can find at a neighborhood place for less. In a city that loves its neighborhoods, supporting small businesses and local artists and craftspeople who sell their wares is a matter of civic pride, a way of voting with your wallet, a mix of economic necessity, political conscientiousness, and style. It's a way of saying, "I like where I live, and I want it to stay as individualistic and eccentric as I am." The locals don't say "I'm going shopping." (How suburban!) They say, "I'm going to the Haight (or the Castro or Cow Hollow or the Mission)." They have a thing for shops with personality. Neighborhoods are notorious for banning chains from their enclaves and supporting mom-and-pop operations (even if the mom and pop in question are a pair of 20-something, mom-and-mom entrepreneurs).

If you time your visit right, you can catch some of the best shopping values (and best people-watching) at the annual spring and summer street fairs thrown by the city's major neighborhoods. The biggies are the Union Street fair (late May) and the Haight, Castro, and Folsom Street fairs (September and October).

Here's a look at San Francisco shopping, with an eye on the specialties (and peculiarities) of the Bay Area—its fixations on food, wine, recycled and earth-friendly merchandise, and of course, sex, drugs, and rock and roll. This is the birthplace of such stylish hometown enterprises as Levi Strauss, The Gap, Banana Republic, Esprit, Williams-Sonoma, and Bebe. It's also the hothouse of trends; the current craze for tattooing and piercing was born here.

Those hunting for bargains might pick up Sally Socolich's definitive *Bargain Hunting in the Bay Area* (published by Chronicle Books), which maps out discount shopping in the city and surrounding areas. If you want some shopping guidance, consider a shopping tour such as **A Simple Elegance Shopping Tour** (phone (415) 661-0110) and **Shopper Stopper Shopping Tours** (phone (707) 829-1597). You might also check online at the San Francisco Web sites, including **Microsoft's Sidewalk** (www.sidewalk.com) and **CitySearch San Francisco** (www.citysearch7.com); both are updated with up-to-the-minute information.

Like many other aspects of the city, shopping is a mellow, laid-back, sensual affair. Combined with a stop at one of the area's almost ridiculously plentiful cafés, window-shopping is as satisfying as shelling out the cash. When you go home (if you do), you can take back something more than a loaf of airport gift-shop sourdough, a Hard Rock Cafe T-shirt, and a case of Rice-A-Roni.

■ **The Neighborhoods** ■

Union Square

While not exactly a neighborhood, Union Square, San Francisco's renowned shopping district, is the closest the city comes to a downtown, at least in terms of shopping. There's an enormous underground public parking lot beneath the 2.6-acre green park at the center of the square; the park above is peopled with chess players, street artists and musicians, street characters, and bustling shoppers from around the world.

Framing this colorful square are the main shopping streets (Stockton Street, Powell Street, Geary Boulevard, and Post Street) and the city's densest concentration of major department stores, tony boutiques, restaurants and cafés, big hotels, and corner flower stands.

Moving clockwise from the Saint Francis Hotel on Powell Street, you'll find the following: **Disney Store** (400 Post Street at Powell Street; (415) 391-6866); **Borders Books and Music** (400 Post Street; (415) 399-1633); **Saks Fifth Avenue** (384 Post Street; (415) 986-4300), **Tiffany** (350 Post Street at Union Square; (415) 781-7000); and **Neiman Marcus** (150 Stockton Street at Geary Boulevard; (415) 362-3900), which each year sends the city's most spectacular Christmas tree soaring to the top of its stained-glass dome. A megalithic **Macy's** (170 O'Farrell Street at Stockton Street; (415) 397-3333), which took over the building vacated by the sadly folded San Francisco institution I. Magnin & Co., sprawls over three city blocks and includes a **Boudin's Bakery** where you can get clam chowder in a sourdough bread bowl; the massive, three-story **F.A.O. Schwarz** (48 Stockton Street at O'Farrell Street; (415) 394-8700) has a Barbie boutique the size of most other department stores' women's clothing sections.

Like elsewhere in the country, chain stores are moving into San Francisco, robbing the Union Square shopping zone of some of its legendary exclusivity. The square has been recently colonized by the theme park–like megastores **Niketown** (278 Post Street; (415) 392-6453), **Disney Store,** and **Virgin Records** (2 Stockton Street at Market Street; (415) 397-4525), the shopping equivalents of Planet Hollywood and Hard Rock Cafe.

The dozens of tony boutiques on the side streets offer shopping with an international feel and "if you have to ask . . ." prices: **Celine of Paris, Gucci** (200 Stockton Street; (415) 392-2808), **Hermes** (212 Stockton Street; (415) 391-7200), **Louis Vuitton, Alfred Dunhill of London** (250 Post Street at Stockton Street; (415) 781-3368), and **Cartier** (231 Post Street between Grant and Stockton Streets; (415) 421-3714).

Tangential to the square is Maiden Lane, a narrow, car-free alley that once housed ladies of the evening. Now the quaint street features pricey shops and restaurants, including a three-floor **Chanel** (155 Maiden Lane between Grant and Stockton Streets; (415) 981-1550), the Paris-based **Christofle** silversmiths (140 Maiden Lane at Post Street; (415) 399-1931), and an outpost of Seattle's **Sur La Table** (77 Maiden Lane at Post Street; (415) 732-7900), a gourmet kitchenware boutique. Also worth searching out is **Robison's** (135 Maiden Lane; (415) 421-0310), the oldest pet shop in America. If you can afford to browse on Maiden Lane, nearby you'll find the equally elegant and snooty **Emporio Armani Boutique** (1 Grant Street between Market and O'Farrell Streets; (415) 677-9400), in the 1911 Security Pacific Bank building.

Also in Union Square area are a handful of San Francisco–based stores, including 150-year-old **Shreve & Co.** jewelers (200 Post Street at Grant Street; (415) 421-2600) and the equally venerable **Gumps** (135 Post Street between Kearny and Grant Streets; (415) 982-1616), one of the world's most beautiful and unusual department stores. Gumps features china, crystal, Asian art treasures, antiques, and one-of-a-kind objects and furniture.

These old-timers are balanced out by fresh-faced young merchandisers near Union Square like fun and funky **Urban Outfitters** (80 Powell Street; (415) 989-1515), the **Williams-Sonoma** flagship store (150 Post Street between Kearny and Grant Streets; (415) 421-2033), **Crate & Barrel** (125

Grant Street at Maiden Lane; (415) 986-4000), and **Banana Republic** (256 Grant Street at Sutter Street; (415) 788-3087).

San Francisco–based **The Gap** recently opened a sleek, stark, three-story flagship store at Union Square (890 Market Street at Powell Street; (415) 788-5909) right next to the tourist-choked cable-car turnaround on Market Street. And it's wired; you can mix and match clothing components ("you want a belt with that?") on a computer screen while lounging on a sofa. Across Market Street from the cable-car turnaround is the **San Francisco Shopping Center** (865 Market Street at Fifth; (415) 495-5656), a multilevel enclosed urban mall anchored by **Nordstrom** (phone (415) 243-8500), with its five-floor spiral escalator, and a "mall-esque" array of shops including **Abercrombie & Fitch,** the **Body Shop,** and the **Warner Bros.** store.

Pacific Heights/Cow Hollow/Marina

The city's second-largest upscale shopping zone covers three linked neighborhoods: the five blocks of Fillmore Street between Geary Boulevard and Jackson Street, the six-block stretch of Union Street from Gough to Steiner Streets (also known as Cow Hollow because it evolved from grazing pasture to browsing nirvana), and the seven blocks of Chestnut Street known as the Marina District.

The beautifully preserved Victorian and Edwardian homes of Union Street, many of which survived the 1906 earthquake, now house hip, upscale, yuppie boutiques and cafés and offer some of the city's best window-shopping (just be careful not to get run over by a baby stroller pushed by one of the area's fast-moving power moms). Fillmore has evolved from a run-down area into a gauntlet of chic boutiques and restaurants. And the Marina is another warren of cute shops catering to the moneyed.

Chinatown

More car chases are filmed in Chinatown than in any other neighborhood of this cinematic city. A visit to this famous, fascinating district— home to more than 200,000 Chinese Americans (the Chinese community is second in size only to New York's Chinatown)—begins at the large, ornate gateway at the intersection of Grant and Bush Streets, just above Union Square. Don't even think of driving in Chinatown. You'd miss all the sights, sounds, tastes, and smells of the bustling streets, where you'll encounter otherworldly vegetables, live animals, exotic spices, herbs, ivory, jade, pearls, and other prizes amid the Oriental kitsch. Shops like **Dragon House** (315 Grant Street between Sutter and Bush Streets; (415) 421-3693) and the **China Trade Center** (838 Grant Street between Clay and Washington Streets), which is a three-floor mini-mall, encapsulate the best of

Chinatown and minimize the jostling. But half the adventure is getting lost in this intriguing world and discovering a few treasures among the trinkets.

Bordering Chinatown is the formerly Italian neighborhood known as North Beach, the main stomping grounds of the Beat poets and artists who made **City Lights Bookstore** and **Caffe Trieste** their home. You'll find hours of browsing potential on the streets bordering Washington Square Park, and the plentiful Italian cafés and pastry shops alone are a shopping experience.

Japantown

Sunday is the busiest shopping day in Japantown, and the five-acre enclosed mall **Japan Center** is its heart. The shops and boutiques contain everything from antique kimonos and scrolls to ultramodern furniture and electronics. Favorite shops for Westerners are **Kinokinuya Stationery and Gifts** (1531 Webster Street at Post Street; (415) 567-8901), with its fascinating array of intricate notecards and writing implements, and **Kinokinuya Book Store** (1531 Webster Street at Post Street; (415) 567-7625), which has a vast assortment of books and magazines in Japanese and English. The complex also includes the **Kabuki Theater** multiplex cinema and the Kabuki Japanese hot springs, where you can steam, soak, and sigh away a hard day's shop.

The Haight

To many visitors and residents, the time warp known as Haight Street is still synonymous with hippies. Even though the famous corner of Haight and Ashbury Streets is now bounded by a Ben & Jerry's and a Gap, and even though music and fashion have passed through punk and techno, the Haight has managed to hang onto its 1960s reputation. A mishmash of head shops, secondhand stores, record and book shops, and the city's most alternative shopping experiences line Haight Street from Masonic to Stanyan Streets.

Some of the street's colorful landmarks include **Pipe Dreams** (1376 Haight Street between Central and Masonic Streets; (415) 431-3553), a venerable head shop with the usual drug accoutrements and jewelry, T-shirts, and maybe even a blacklight poster or two; and **Bound Together,** a truly anarchist bookstore (369 Haight Street between Central and Masonic Streets; (415) 431-8355).

South of Market

Otherwise known as SoMa (mostly in guidebooks; you won't hear many San Franciscans actually calling it that), the sprawling, industrial warehouse–filled South of Market area, with clusters of outlet and discount stores, is a focal point for bargain hunters. An enormous **Costco** dominates an entire city block; other discount stores include **Tower Records Outlet, Bed Bath & Beyond, Trader Joe's, Yerba Buena Square,** and **Burlington Coat Factory.**

Because the nightclub scene also thrives in SoMa, there's a host of leather and fetish stores and other purveyors of "underground" attire and accessories, including **Stormy Leather** and the **Leather Outlet.**

The Castro

In the sunny, predominantly gay and lesbian neighborhood known as the Castro, you never know what you'll see. A controversy recently erupted over a bookstore's window display, which featured an anatomically correct porn star. A self-sufficient village, the Castro has become the equivalent of an island resort overrun with pricey boutiques offering gifts, trendy clothing, coffee, burritos, more coffee, more burritos, and fruit juice. Don't-miss shops include the neoclassic **Cliff's Hardware Store,** sort of Mayberry R.F.D. circa 2021, and **Hello, Gorgeous!,** a combination museum, memorabilia boutique, and shrine to the divine diva Barbra Streisand.

■ The Malls ■

Despite what you may have seen in movies like *Clueless* and *Valley Girl,* malls no longer define the California shopping experience (and anyway, that was Southern California). The Bay Area is almost actively anti-mall, and neighborhood shopping is de rigueur. But if you must mall it, there are several not unattractive options.

Too fancy to be called a mall, the seriously stylin' **Crocker Galleria** (Post and Sutter Streets at Kearny Street; (415) 393-1505), in the heart of the downtown Financial District, was fashioned after the Galleria Vittorio Emanuele in Milan. The galleria offers 50 shops, restaurants, and services, including **Versace** and **Nicole Miller** boutiques and a charming rooftop park. Parking is free on Saturday with a $10 purchase (which, in a place that sells $50 undershirts, should take about ten seconds).

By the waterfront is the monumental **Embarcadero Center,** a complex of four office towers housing two levels of restaurants, movie theaters, and shops including **The Limited, Ann Taylor, Banana Republic, The Gap, Crabtree and Evelyn, Pottery Barn,** and **Sam Goody,** plus a few interesting local boutiques like **Essentiel Elements,** an aromatherapy bath and skincare shop, and **Earthsake,** which offers exquisite eco-friendly objects for the home. The whole thing is topped by the SkyDeck, an observation deck with one of the best panoramas of the Bay Area; it's open to the public.

The **Stanford Shopping Center** (180 El Camino Real, Palo Alto, phone (800) 772-9332), which is owned by Stanford University, offers the most concentrated upscale retail experience in the area, with **Bloomingdales, Neiman Marcus, Macy's, Nordstrom, Tiffany, Smith & Hawken,** and the new **Crate & Barrel Furniture Store.**

San Francisco's only genuine enclosed mall in the city limits is **Stonestown Galleria** (19th Avenue at Winston Street; (415) 564-8845) in the outer Sunset District. The mall includes a substantial 120 shops anchored by **Nordstrom, Eddie Bauer,** and **Williams-Sonoma.**

■ Specialty Shops ■

Alternative Shopping

San Francisco specializes in eccentrics and subcultures (this is, after all, a city with a church—St. John Coltrane African Orthodox Church— devoted to jazz music), so shoppers can always expect the unexpected. Along with tattooing, body-piercing has become hot stuff (some say the craze began here), and body modification is one souvenir that keeps on giving. If you decide to get a new perforation while you're here, you might as well get something cool to put in it. For body jewelry and other accessories, visit the **Gauntlet** (2377 Market Street near Castro Street; (415) 431-3133) and **Body Manipulations** (3243 16th Street between Guerrero and Dolores Streets; (415) 621-0408).

The Beats go on, and so do the hippies, at least in the memories and imaginations of most visitors. For Beat memorabilia, **City Lights Bookstore** (261 Columbus Avenue at Broadway; (415) 362-8193) in North Beach is un-Beat-able; a window-shopping stroll through the Haight District will turn up all sorts of hippie flashbacks, from head shops to vintage rock concert poster peddlers.

Shopping in the city is certainly a left-field (and right-brain) experience— nowhere more so than at **Left Hand World** (Pier 39; (415) 433-3547), which sells everything imaginable in a left-hand version. Hip shoppers and grown-up kids find themselves kitschy-cooing over **Uncle Mame's** (2241 Market Street near Noe Street; (415) 626-1953), whose larger-than-life proprietor provides a loving home for misfit toys and all-but-forgotten fads—everything you weren't allowed to have as a kid. And kid-aged kids love the **Sanrio** flagship store (39 Stockton Street near Market Street; (415) 981-5568) in Union Square, with two floors of Hello Kitty and her cloyingly cute chums. The Castro's **Hello, Gorgeous!** (548 Castro Street above 18th Street; (415) 864-2678) is a combination museum, shop, and shrine devoted to the (still) living memory of drag queen inspiration Barbra Streisand. **Wig Factory** (3143 Mission Street between Army and Precita Streets; (415) 282-4939) displays the city's most outlandish collection of wigs (and in San Francisco, that's really saying something).

More silliness: **House of Magic** (2025 Chestnut Street at Fillmore Street; (415) 346-2218) is an old-fashioned, all-purpose magic supply store with the usual unusual array of gag gifts and gadgets. **Game Gallery** (in the Embarcadero Center) and **Gamescape** (333 Divisadero Street at Oak Street; (415) 621-4263) specialize in games for all ages, ranging from casual board games and puzzles, to fantasy and strategy games, to computer games. Gamescape also sells used games.

For shopping of an *X-Files* bent, check out **Botanica Yoruba** (998 Valencia Street) and **Curios and Candles** (289 Divisadero Street; (415) 863-5669), which offer candles, potions, herbs, and incantations for every need or desire—sort of a "Pagans R Us." **Three Eighty One** (381 Guerrero Street at 16th Street; (415) 621-3830) is an exceedingly eccentric gift shop crammed with the city's weirdest candles and borderline sacrilegious stuff. Check out the sequined Mexican wrestling masks (and mousepads!). One of the most unusual and off-the-beaten-path shops in town, **Paxton Gate** (1204 Stevenson Street between Market and Mission Streets; (415) 255-5955) may be the world's most bizarre gardening store, as evidenced by its displays of eerie air plants, mounted bugs and butterflies, and stuffed and costumed mice.

Amid the usual bazaars and holiday sales, there's an annual crafts fair for people who hate Christmas; **Naughty Santa's Bizaare Bazaar** is presented by Space Cowgirls/Sounds Good! in early December and features gifts by more than 50 fringe artisans at the **SOMAR Gallery** (934 Brannan Street).

Antiques

San Franciscans are in love with history, and the antique stores are stocked with everything from ultrapricey traditional pieces and 1950s kitschware to last month's fads.

In the area once known as the Barbary Coast, **Jackson Square,** San Francisco's first designated historic district (it was the only group of downtown buildings to survive the 1906 earthquake and fire) has fittingly become the city's official antique district. Bounded by Jackson, Washington, Montgomery, and Sansome Streets, the square, which showcases its pieces like small museums, houses **John Doughty Antiques** (619 Sansome Street; (415) 398-6849), with 18th- and 19th-century English antiques; **Drum & Company** (472 Jackson Street; (415) 788-5118), with 18th- and 19th-century continental furniture; **Highgate Antiques** (425 Jackson

Street; (415) 397-0800), with period, English, and continental furniture; and **Chaliss House** (463 Jackson Street; (415) 397-6999), with period furniture and works of art.

Market Street near the Civic Center has evolved into an unofficial antiques district. **Grand Central Station Antiques** (1632 Market Street between Franklin and Gough Streets; (415) 252-8155) is like a classic jumble sale, with two floors of fun finds. Next door at **Beaver Bros. Antiques** (1637 Market Street between Franklin and Gough Streets; (415) 863-4344), you can rent the merchandise; the two-floor shop is the city's biggest prop-rental outfit, supplying furniture and colorful clutter for movie and TV sets.

Perhaps the most pleasurable antique shopping is on **Russian Hill** at spots like **Russian Hill Antiques** (2200 Polk Street at Vallejo Street; (415) 441-5561) and **J. Goldsmith Antiques** (1924 Polk Street between Jackson and Pacific Streets; (415) 771-4055), specializing in early American furniture, collectibles, and toys; and **Naomi's Antiques to Go** (1817 Polk Street between Washington and Jackson Streets; (415) 775-1207), specializing in every sort of American dishware from the 1920s to the 1950s (sorry, those aren't the prices).

Bargains/Thrift

Although shopping in San Francisco may not be the way of life or contact sport it is in Los Angeles or New York, the locals are nevertheless competitive about what they get. And how they get it. If you compliment a San Franciscan about his new computer bag or her little black dress, be prepared to hear the tale of how cheap it was at a thrift store (or at a sidewalk sale or on the Net). The more obscure the source and the lower the price, the better. Never underestimate the talent it takes to emerge from **Community Thrift** with something cheap that you'll actually use or wear! In San Francisco, people try on and toss off new personas the way other folks change underwear. Previously owned and recycled everything, from clothes to records to kitchenware, is big business. Nostalgia cycles seem to speed up in this town and Bohemian, artist-friendly neighborhoods like the Haight and the upper Mission have particularly high concentrations of vintage and thrift stores, but you can go on a bargain bender even in snooty Pacific Heights.

American Rag (1305 Van Ness Avenue at Sutter Street; (415) 474-5214) has the largest and trendiest selection of retro rags in town, but the prices don't really qualify as thrift. Gargoyles guard the carnival-like exterior of the Haight's **Wasteland** (1600 Haight Street at Belvedere Street; (415) 863-3150), and if you can bear the famously loud and obnoxious music, you'll be rewarded with great finds. **Community Thrift** is a veritable secondhand department store

(625 Valencia Street; (415) 861-4910) where you can specify which of more than 30 charities you want your purchase to benefit. Other old faithfuls include **Crossroads Trading Co.** (1901 Fillmore Street, (415) 775-8885; or 2231 Market Street, (415) 626-8989) and **Buffalo Exchange** (1555 Haight Street between Clayton and Ashbury Streets, (415) 431-7733; 1800 Polk Street at Washington Street, (415) 346-5726). The enormous new **Goodwill** store (1580 Mission Street at South Van Ness Avenue; (415) 826-5759) is as brightly lit as any grocery store, and it's always chock-full of new and old trash and treasure.

For a highbrow rummage-sale experience, try the Pacific Heights version. Rich folks unload their castoffs at the **Next-to-New Shop** (2226 Fillmore Street between Sacramento and Clay Streets; (415) 567-1628), which gets its goods from the Junior League of San Francisco, and at **Repeat Performance Thrift Shop** (2223 Fillmore Street between Sacramento and Clay Streets; (415) 563-3123), which benefits the San Francisco Symphony.

Secondhand shopping isn't confined to clothing. The trend for recycled merchandise extends to books, CDs, records, and even cookware. **Cookin'** (339 Divisadero Street near Haight Street; (415) 861-1853) is like your grandmother's attic, filled with classic kitchen gadgets, dishware, cook-books, and anything else the gourmet in you might desire.

The SoMa District is full of big game for bargain hunters, and you can find particularly good sport at the **Esprit Outlet Store** (499 Illinois Street; (415) 957-2540), with discounts of up to 70% off Esprit clothes for women, teens, and kids; **New York Cosmetics & Fragrances** (318 Brannan Street at Second; (415) 543-3880), with discounts on fragrances and beauty products; and **Yerba Buena Square,** an urban outlet mall (899 Howard Street at Fifth; (415) 543-1275), anchored by a **Burlington Coat Factory Warehouse** and **The Shoe Pavilion.** Not so far away is the **Six Sixty Factory Outlet Center** (660 Third Street at Townsend Street; (415) 227-0464), with bargains on many name brands.

Near the holidays, in early November and May before Mother's Day, the merchants of the **Gift Center** (888 Brannan Street at Eighth; (415) 861-7733) offer their samples and overstock on four levels of the building. It's like the world's biggest garage sale; there's something for everyone, and you can have a nice lunch or a drink at the **Pavilion Cafe and Deli** (phone (415) 552-8555). And the nearby **Fashion Center** (699 Eighth Street between Townsend and Brannan Streets; (415) 789-5373) opens its doors to the public four or five times a year (usually in March, July, September, and November) for sample sales representing more than 6,000 lines of clothing and accessories.

Books and Magazines

Since many come to San Francisco to be writers, artists, and musicians (or just to be near them), the city has an unusually well-read population and plenty of well-stocked and personable bookstores. The big guys are here, of course—including **Borders Books & Music** (400 Post Street at Powell Street; (415) 399-1633), a superstore with four stories of books, music, and videos, and **Barnes and Noble** (2552 Taylor Street; (415) 292-6762).

But as is the case with other shoppers in San Francisco, book enthusiasts are loyal to their neighborhood booksellers. Many bookstores stay open late and function as people-browsing salons at night. One of the city's favorite bookstores, **A Clean Well-Lighted Place for Books** (Opera Plaza, 601 Van Ness Avenue at Golden Gate; (415) 441-6670), offers frequent readings, book signings, and bountiful sale and remainder tables. You'll find (or stumble over) more than a million used books, records, and magazines in the overstuffed **McDonald's Bookstore** (48 Turk Street near Market Street; (415) 673-2235), affectionately known as "A Dirty, Poorly Lit Place for Books." **A Different Light** is a remarkably well-stocked gay and lesbian bookstore that functions as a de facto community center (489 Castro Street at Eighteenth; (415) 431-0891) . Beat HQ and the publishing home and hangout of Jack Kerouac and Allen Ginsberg, **City Lights Booksellers & Publishers** (261 Columbus Avenue between Pacific Street and Broadway; (415) 362-8193) is probably San Francisco's best-known bookstore. You still may find founder-poet Lawrence Ferlinghetti hanging around; he'll pose for pictures if it's a good day.

Magazine lovers should check in at **Harold's International Newsstand** (524 Geary Boulevard between Taylor and Jones Streets; (415) 441-2665). **Naked Eye News and Video** (533 Haight Street; (415) 864-2985) specializes in culture rags and 'zines—the more obscure, the better. **The Magazine** (920 Larkin Street; (415) 441-7731) is one of many strangely wonderful shops in town; it's where all those old magazines you threw away wind up, and its obsessively catalogued gay and straight porn section is a miracle of modern library science. Or something.

For the best used bookstore, it's a tie between Russian Hill's **Acorn Books** (1436 Polk Street at California Street; (415) 563-1736) and Richmond's bewildering, maze-like **Green Apple Books** (506 Clement Street at Sixth; (415) 387-2272), which stays open until midnight.

Bookstores cater to almost every specialized taste. One of the best children's bookstores in the city is **Charlotte's Webb** (2278 Union Street; (415) 441-4700). Find books from an African American perspective at **Marcus Books** (1712 Fillmore Street; (415) 346-4222). **William Stout Architectural**

Books (804 Montgomery Street at Jackson Street; (415) 391-6757) is one of the best of its kind in the country. **Fields Book Store** (1419 Polk Street between Pine and California Streets; (415) 673-2027) seriously specializes in spiritual and new age books. Not so seriously, **Comics and Comix** (650 Irving Street; (415) 665-5888) offers classics and alternative specimens. And travelers can map out their lives at **Rand McNally Map & Travel Store** (595 Market Street; (415) 777-3131) and the charming little **Get Lost Travel Books Maps & Gear** (1825 Market Street at Pearl Street; (415) 437-0529).

Clothing

Sure, San Francisco may be less image conscious and clothes crazy than, say, Los Angeles; but as low key and dressed down as San Franciscans are, they like to look good. Fortunately, there are plenty of places to dress up (or down).

For women, Union Square is shopping nirvana, offering all the famous fashion names in boutiques and department stores. Union Street has more than 40 clothing boutiques from trendy to traditional in its ten-block shopping area, including San Francisco–based **bebe** (2095 Union Street; (415) 563-2323), which has classic suiting for the chic and slim contemporary woman, and **girlfriends** (1824 Union Street; (415) 673-9544), whose distinctive logo items have become coveted souvenirs. For the unpredictable San Francisco weather, layering is essential. Stop at **House of Cashmere** (2764 Octavia Street near Union Street; (415) 441-6925) and **Three Bags Full** (2181 Union Street; (415) 567-5753) for handknit sweaters and sportswear. At **Carol Doda's Champagne and Lace** (1850 Union Street; (415) 776-6900) in a picturesque Union Street alley, San Francisco's famous former stripper sells lingerie and bodywear for women of every size. **Canyon Beachwear** (1728 Union Street; (415) 885-5070) is San Francisco's only women's specialty swimwear shop. And **Darbury Stenderu** (541 Hayes Street; (415) 861-3020) displays breathtakingly beautiful clothing and furniture of handpainted silk velvet in a gallery shop in the emerging Hayes Valley boutique neighborhood.

Look sharp, men. San Francisco's snazzy Mayor Willie Brown is friendly with the equally dandyish proprietor of **Wilkes Bashford** (375 Sutter Street between Grant and Stockton Streets; (415) 986-4380), who keeps Brown in fedoras and tailored suits in an opulent atmosphere; Don Johnson shops here, too. For more traditional men's clothing, **Cable Car Clothiers** (246 Sutter Street between Kearny and Grant Streets; (415) 397-4740) at Union Square and **The Hound** (140 Sutter Street; (415) 989-0429) are good bets for the jacket-and-tie set. On the other side of the couture coin, the new **Saks Fifth Avenue Men's Store** (384 Post Street; (415) 986-4300) stocks gear by

Versace, Gaultier, and Dolce and Gabbana, and San Francisco–based **Billy-blue Menswear** (73 Geary Boulevard; (415) 781-2111) creates stylish modern classics. For nightlifers, **Dal Jeets** (541 Valencia Street between 16th and 17th Streets; (415) 626-9000) has off-the-wall clothes for street and clubwear, and the clothing and underwear shop **Rolo** (450 Castro Street between 18th and Market Streets, (415) 626-7171; or 2351 Market Street at Noe Street, (415) 431-4545) is so up to date it's futuristic.

Creativity and the Decorative Arts

San Francisco is known for its creativity and free spirit. Start beautifying your life with a stop at **FLAX** (1699 Market Street at Valencia Street; (415) 552-2355), a distinctive arts supply superstore with paints and paper, furniture, lighting, framing, wrapping paper, and unusual jewelry and toys. Be sure to check out the always unpredictable bargain basement, **Primary Values,** open Tuesday through Saturday, 11 a.m. to 4 p.m. **Arch** (407 Jackson Street between Sansome and Montgomery Streets; (415) 433-2724) sells architectural and art supplies and surprising gifts in a Jackson Square shop. **Art & Craft Supplies Outlet** (41 14th Street; (415) 431-7122) is a right-brain sort of store— cluttered but creative. It has art, craft, and party supplies at 50 percent or more off original retail prices, plus some things you never knew you wanted.

You can actually rent a painting (with an option to buy) from the **San Francisco Museum of Modern Art Rental Gallery** (Building A, Fort Mason Center at Buchanan Street and Marina Boulevard; (415) 441-4777). The gallery's goal is to give exposure to new artists, and if you decide the work looks good over your couch, half of the rental fee goes toward the purchase price.

Flowers and Plants

The Bay Area is one of the nation's premier flower-growing areas, and the city is abloom with talented florists like **Fioridella** for the social set (1920 Polk Street; (415) 775-4065) and the Castro's more avant-garde **Ixia** (2331 Market Street between Noe and Castro Streets; (415) 431-3134). You can make your own arrangements after a visit to the **San Francisco Wholesale Flower Market** (at Fifth and Sixth Streets between Brannan and Bryant Streets), which fills an entire city block with blooms and branches. Some parts of the market are accessible only to professionals with badges, but several outlets offer fresh and unusual flowers, plants, and paraphernalia at budget prices.

If you want an arrangement to last longer, walk across the street to **Silks** (635 Brannan Street between Fifth and Sixth Streets; (415) 777-1354), which specializes in eternal silk flowers. **Coast Wholesale Dry Flowers & Baskets** (149 Morris Street in the Flower Market; (415) 781-3034) is a warehouse with dried versions of nearly every plant on earth. For more exotic specimens, try **Red Desert** (1632 Market Street between Franklin and Gough Streets; (415) 552-2800), an aptly sand-floored shop with a collection of cacti and succulents. **The Palm Broker** (1074 Guerrero Street; (415) 626-7256) specializes in palm trees and variants for that Southern California look.

Food

Perhaps because San Francisco is the home of California cuisine, restaurant dining has become one of the city's most popular participatory sports, and locals watch the trades and power plays of big-name chefs the way they watch their quarterbacks. Many of the city's foodies, known for their sophisticated tastes and obsession with fresh local ingredients, will tell you they live here because it's so near the source of wonderful produce. And with the Napa Valley and Sonoma wine country so close, almost everyone knows something about wine.

A few food specialty stores, including an outpost of Seattle's **Sur La Table** (77 Maiden Lane; (415) 732-7900), can be found in Union Square. In North Beach, you can't go wrong at many of the Italian bakeries and delis; start at the century-old deli **Molinari's** for first courses (373 Columbus Avenue at Vallejo Street; (415) 421-2337) and finish with dessert from **Dianda's** (565 Green Street between Grant and Stockton Streets; (415) 989-7745). In Chinatown, **The Wok Shop** (718 Grant Street between Sacramento and Commercial Streets; (415) 989-3797) specializes in everything you need for cooking Chinese cuisine, including cookbooks, spices, and sauces. And for the perfect end to the meal, **Golden Gate Fortune Cookies** (56 Ross Alley off Jackson Street; (415) 781-3956) makes traditional fortunes, and, um, more modern ones. **Joseph Schmidt Confections** (3489 16th Street; (415) 861-8682) is the city's premier (and quite imaginative) chocolatier, especially famed for its chocolate sculptures. Bring back your souvenirs in chocolate.

Even something as mundane as grocery shopping can provide a California experience at places like **Real Food Company** (2140 Polk Street between Vallejo Street and Broadway; (415) 673-7420); **Whole Foods** (1765 California Street; (415) 674-0500), a gourmet megastore; and **Rainbow Grocery & General Store** (1745 Folsom at Division Street; (415) 863-0965), a crunchier, co-op version of Whole Foods, with pierced, tattooed staffers ringing up your bulk food items. **Trader Joe's** (555 Ninth Street at Brannan Street; (415) 863-1292) has become a favorite for its discount gourmet snacks, health foods, and fresh juices, and a great selection of wines and beers.

Coffee is still the craze in hypercaffeinated San Francisco, and you can find a café selling java and whole beans on almost every corner. But **Eureka Coffee** (2747 10th Street between Bryant and York Streets) in SoMa sells coffee beans. Only. Roasted fresh on the premises, at up to half the prices you'll pay at Starbucks, et al.

Another distinctive San Francisco shopping experience is an early morning visit to one of the weekly farmers markets. On Wednesday and Sunday at United Nations Plaza (Market Street between Grove and Fulton Streets, near the Civic Center), the **Heart of the City Farmers' Market** replaces the panhandlers with dozens of booths featuring fresh-from-the-farm fruits, vegetables, and flowers. And Saturday morning the outdoor **Ferry Plaza Farmers' Market** opens (in the Embarcadero at the Ferry Building), with cooking demonstrations and craftspeople adding to the flavor. Chinatown's open produce markets, which have the feel of exotic farmers' markets, are open every day.

Plump Jack Wines (3201 Fillmore Street at Greenwich Avenue; (415) 346-9870) in the Marina is a companion store to the Getty-owned **Plump Jack Cafe,** and it's one of the best places in San Francisco to find impressive and obscure labels. Free delivery is available anywhere in the city. The name says it all—the **Napa Valley Winery Exchange** (415 Taylor Street between Geary Boulevard and O'Farrell Street; (415) 771-2887) is a wine boutique specializing in hard-to-find vintages and labels from nearby Napa. They ship. So does the **Cannery Wine Cellar and Gourmet Market** (in the Cannery, 2801 Leavenworth Street at Jefferson Street; (415) 673-0400), which showcases a hearty array of California labels, plus beers and single-malt scotches. Other good spots for California wines are **D&M Liquors** in Pacific Heights (2200 Fillmore Street at Sacramento Street; (415) 346-1325) and **Wine Club** (953 Harrison Street; (415) 512-9086), which sells wine from jug to connoisseur at just above wholesale prices. For spirits of another sort, head to the Financial District for a visit to **John Walker & Co. Liquors** (175 Sutter Street between Montgomery and Kearny Streets), the city's largest specialty and import liquor merchant.

Insider Shops

Cliff's Hardware (479 Castro Street between 18th and Market Streets; (415) 431-5365), with its friendly, small-town feeling, everything-but-the-kitchen-sink stock, and outlandish window displays, has become a Castro institution. **Whole Earth Access** (401 Bayshore Boulevard at Flower Street; (415) 285-5244) discounts cutting-edge technology (plus furniture, sports clothing, and natural-fiber home items) in an appealingly eco-friendly, high-tech setting. **Fillamento** (2185 Fillmore Street at Sacramento Street;

(415) 931-2224) is an eye-filling boutique department store full of surprising furniture and housewares, including one-of-a-kind works by local artists and artisans. If you need a gift but are stumped about what to give, turn the problem over to the staff at **dandelion** (55 Potrero Street at Alameda Street; (415) 436-9500), which has 40 minidepartments on two floors and celebrates "the home and sharing great things with friends." **Quantity Postcards** stocks hundreds of postcards from the comfortingly antique to the shockingly modern. Try the North Beach location (1441 Grant Street between Green and Union Streets; (415) 986-8866), which features an earthquake simulator, and the Haight location (1427 Haight Street at Masonic Street; (415) 255-1199). **See's Candy** is an old-fashioned candy shop, and the kind people behind the counter give you a free sample if you buy something and sometimes even if you don't. Stores are located throughout the city (phone (800) 347-7337). **Bepple's** (1934 Union Street, (415) 931-6225; or 2142 Chestnut Street, (415) 931-6226) is a Pacific Heights café specializing in huge, home-baked pies brimming with fruit. Anne Rice fans and other Gothic fanciers flock to **Vampire Technology** (351 Ninth Street between Folsom and Harrison Streets), a somewhat scary SoMa shop specializing in handmade rubber clothing, furniture, and art for the modern urban vampire. Seriously.

Real insiders skip Crate & Barrel and Home Depot and go right to the source—the supply stores. If you need a few dozen martini glasses or those cool white china coffee cups, who ya gonna call? **Economy Restaurant Fixtures** (1200 Seventh Street; (415) 625-5611). And if you had a hammer, you wouldn't need **Discount Builders Supply** (695 Mission Street; (415) 621-8158), would you? Paper mavens find their staples at **Patrick & Co.** (560 Market Street; (415) 546-4952).

And if you need something at any hour, there's a good chance you'll find it (or something that will do until the shops open) at one of the city's all-purpose, 24-hour stores, including **Safeway** (2020 Market Street at Church Street; (415) 861-7660) and **Walgreen's** (498 Castro Street at 18th; (415) 861-6276).

Kids

Kids will get a kick out of a visit to the **Basic Brown Bear Factory** (444 De Haro Street at 17th; (415) 626-0781), where they can watch a bear-making demonstration and pick out their own cuddly pal. Pacific Heights and the Marina are the spots for the stroller set; **Dottie Doolittle** (3680 Sacramento Street between Locust and Spruce Streets; (415) 563-3244), **Jonathan-Kaye by Country Living** (3548 Sacramento Street between Laurel and Locust Streets; (415) 563-0773), and **Mudpie** (1694 Gough

Street; (415) 771-9262) are just a few of the upscale kidswear boutiques for label-savvy Pacific Heights tots.

Museum Shops

San Francisco is rich with museums, and the museum shops are full of take-home treasures. Consider these shops your own ace team of personal shoppers. The **Ansel Adams Center for Photography** gift shop and bookstore (250 Fourth Street between Howard and Folsom Streets; (415) 485-7000) feature the best of Ansel Adams and other California photographers. The **California Historical Society** (678 Mission Street at Fourth; (415) 357-1860) has beautiful graphics of California's parks, including Muir Woods and Alcatraz. The **Cartoon Art Museum** (814 Mission Street between Fourth and Fifth Streets; (415) 227-8666) offers more than 11,000 works, including comic book pages, animation cells, and editorial cartoons. There are three museums in Golden Gate Park, each with its own unique shop. The **Academy Store** in the California Academy of Sciences (Golden Gate Park; (415) 750-7330) focuses on science and natural history, with dinosaur models, earth-friendly gifts, and a boutique devoted to the work of Far Side cartoonist Gary Larson, who has his own gallery at the museum. Across the courtyard is the **de Young Memorial Museum** (Golden Gate Park; (415) 750-3642), which sells books and objects related to recent shows, including its show on the Beats and California artisans; the **Asian Art Museum of San Francisco** (Golden Gate Park near Eighth and Fulton Streets; (415) 379-8801), linked to the de Young, is the largest museum in the Western hemisphere devoted to the arts of Asia. It represents 6,000 years of history and 40 Asian cultures. Among the treasures you can take home are a carved-while-you-wait soapstone "chop" with your name in Chinese or a luxurious kimono. The internationally famous **Exploratorium** (360 Lyon Street next to the Palace of Fine Arts; (415) 563-7337) is an interactive, hands-on science museum, and its gift shop is full of intriguing science kits, games, and puzzles for children of all ages. The two-year-old **San Francisco Museum of Modern Art** (150 Third Street; (415) 357-4035) is already a San Francisco landmark, and its innovative museum store has racked up high sales.

Music

The birthplace of acid rock, a hotbed of jazz, and a historically culture-craving town full of classical music buffs and operaholics, San Francisco is rich in record stores. There are two **Tower Records** locations (Castro: Market and Noe Streets, (415) 621-0588; Fisherman's Wharf: Columbus Avenue and Bay Street; (415) 885-0500) and a **Tower Records Outlet** (660 Third Street near Brannan Street; (415) 957-9660); these are really fun to shop.

The **Virgin Megastore** (2 Stockton Street at Market Street; (415) 397-4525) has three sprawling, noisy floors of CDs, cassettes, videos, CD-ROMs, books, magazines, a café, and its own DJ. It's a good place to listen before you buy, and the import section is tops. **Rough Trade Records** (1529 Haight Street; (415) 621-4395) is the Tower Records of indie, alternative, and punk music.

The used records scene is a way of life. The new kid on the old-music block is **Amoeba** (1855 Haight Street; (415) 831-1200), which recently opened a superstore in a Haight Street bowling alley. Other places to search for that Holy Grail–like CD or record: **Streetlight** (3979 24th Street between Sanchez and Noe Streets; (415) 282-3550), **Record Finder** and **Haight's Reckless Records** (1401 Haight Street at Masonic Street; (415) 431-3434), and **Recycled Records** (1377 Haight Street at Masonic Street; (415) 626-4075). Vinyl lives on at **Grooves** (1797 Market Street at Elgin Park; (415) 436-9933) and **Medium Rare Records** (2310 Market Street near Castro Street; (415) 255-RARE), which specializes in all sorts of campy old platters.

Then there's the new and the next. San Francisco has a thriving dance culture and techno scene, and the hippest kids shop where the local DJs get their discs: **CD Record Rack** (3897 18th Street at Sanchez Street; (415) 552-4990) and **soundworks** (228 Valencia Street at Clinton Park; (415) 487-3980).

Sex Sells

With its (well-deserved) anything-goes reputation, San Francisco is synonymous with sex. Here's where to get your sensual supplies. **Good Vibrations** (1210 Valencia Street between 23rd and 24th; (415) 974-8980) is a friendly, nonfurtive store that's been women-owned and -operated for 20 years; it sells sex supplies, books, and videos. Check out the vibrator museum. **Jaguar** (4057 19th Street between Castro and Hartford Streets; (415) 863-4777) carries an eye-popping array of men-on-men erotica and supplies. **Dark Garden Unique Corsetry** (321 Linden Alley at Gough Street; (415) 431-7684) and **Romantasy** (2191 Market Street at Sanchez Street; (415) 487-9909) cater more to straight people, offering erotic fantasy wear, magazines, and videos. Often voted "best place to buy drag" in local alternative weeklies, **Foxy Piedmont** (1452 Haight Street) is a glitzy showgirl shop, but most of the showgirls are guys. Piedmont has been dressing strippers and drag queens for 25 years. **Lady Boutique** (2644 Mission Street between 22nd and 23rd; (415) 285-4980) has wigs, gowns, lingerie, accessories, and shoes and boots up to size 15.

Stormy Leather (1158 Howard Street between Seventh and Eighth; (415) 626-1672) specializes in leather and vinyl fetish wear for women. **A Taste of Leather** (317-A Tenth Street between Folsom and Harrison Streets) carries a full range of leatherwear for out on the street and (one hopes) the bedroom. **Leather Etc.** (1201 Folsom Street at Eighth; (415) 864-7558) for men and women, has lots of sexy clothes. **Leather Zone** (2352 Market Street between Castro and Noe Streets; (415) 255-8585) sells new and used jackets and custom items.

Touristarama

If you absolutely must go home with an Alcatraz shot glass, miniature cable car, or "fog dome," all this tourist merchandise and more (mind-bogglingly more) is conveniently concentrated in the boardwalk-like waterfront area known as Fisherman's Wharf. Shopping for nonessentials and unnecessary items is plentiful at the wharf's street vendors and souvenir booths, as well as at **Pier 39,** the famous amusement area with lounging sea lions; the **Anchorage** (2800 Leavenworth Street between Beach and Jefferson Streets; (415) 775-6000); **Ghirardelli Square** (900 North Point; (415) 775-5500), with its clusters of 70 specialty shops surrounding the delightfully old-fashioned **Ghirardelli Chocolate Manufactory and Soda Fountain** (phone (415) 474-3939); and the **Cannery,** where you can take a breather from shopping with the live entertainment in the courtyard.

PART NINE

Sight-Seeing Tips and Tours

Touring San Francisco

One of the world's most spectacular cities, San Francisco is filled with stately mansions, ornate Victorians, and world-class museums perched atop hills that slope down to a blue bay. There is much to see, yet it's manageable when taken in neighborhood by neighborhood. The hills are steep, but San Francisco is remarkably compact. And like the consummate Californian, San Francisco is continually reinventing itself, working on self-improvement, getting in shape. The Marina District, devastated by the 1989 earthquake, is thriving with new and rebuilt Mediterranean-style houses in lollipop colors. The waterfront is reawakening, the Presidio is being transformed into a national park, and major projects such as the Yerba Buena Gardens are changing the face of the city.

Half the fun of discovering this town is simply wandering around and stumbling on great views, interesting shops, a location used in a favorite movie, and things that even the locals may not be aware of. While metropolitan, San Francisco is small; if you get disoriented, just remember that downtown is east, and the Golden Gate Bridge is north. And if you do get lost, you can't go too far because the city is surrounded by water on three sides. Here are some hints for first-time visitors.

▪ Taking an Orientation Tour ▪

Visitors to San Francisco can't help but notice the regular procession of open-air tour buses—"motorized cable cars" is probably a more accurate term—that prowl Union Square, Fisherman's Wharf, North Beach, and major tourist spots such as Fort Point. Not to be confused with real cable cars (the rubber tires are a dead giveaway), the trolleys operated by Gray Lines and Cable Car Charters offer regularly scheduled shuttle buses along regular routes that include the city's top attractions. Between stops, a tour guide discusses the city's cataclysmic fire of 1906, Barbary Coast days during the gold rush, and the flower-power era of the '60s.

The guides also suggest good places to eat and drop tidbits of interesting and often funny San Francisco trivia. Our advice: If this is your first visit, take one of the tours early in your trip, even on the first day. The narrated tours are a no-brainer for jet-lagged or otherwise exhausted visitors who want spoon-fed details of San Francisco's major sights while learning the lay of the land. Think of the tours as an educational system that not only gets you to the most well-known attractions, but provides a timely education on the city's history and scope. On Gray Line motorized "cable cars," your ticket allows unlimited reboarding privileges for that day, so you can get off at any scheduled stop to tour, eat, shop, or explore, and you can reboard on a later bus. On either service you can determine which sights warrant another day of exploration. Tour buses run about every 30 minutes (every hour in the winter), and boarding locations include some of the city's most popular attractions.

Gray Line

Both of the guided tours that operate a regular route in and around downtown San Francisco are good values. **Gray Line** features San Francisco–style motorized cable cars and a tour guide on trips lasting one and a quarter hours and two hours (longer during evening rush hour). On the shorter tour, passengers can get off and reboard at Union Square, Pier 39 in Fisherman's Wharf, and the Embarcadero Center in the Financial District. On the longer tour, visitors can get off and reboard at Pier 39, the Palace of Fine Arts, Fort Point, the Golden Gate Bridge, the Presidio, and Union Square. If it rains, tours may be canceled or an enclosed vehicle may be substituted.

Reservations aren't required for either tour. The cost for the one-and-a-quarter-hour tour is $16 for adults and $8 for children ages 5–11. For the longer tour, the price is $22 for adults and $11 for children ages 5–11. Departures begin at 10 a.m. daily and continue about every half-hour until 4 p.m.; during the winter, the tours depart hourly. Passengers can pay an additional $10 and go on a bay cruise departing from Fisherman's Wharf. Tickets for both tours can be purchased at booths in Union Square or at Pier 39 in Fisherman's Wharf. For more information call (800) 826-0202 or (415) 558-9400.

Cable Car Charters

Cable Car Charters offers one-hour narrated tours on open-air motorized "cable cars" that depart on the hour and the half-hour from A. Sabella's Restaurant at Jefferson and Taylor Streets, across from Pier 41 in Fisherman's Wharf. Sights on the tour include Ghirardelli Square, Coit Tower, Union Square, and the Financial District. The cost is $12 for adults and $5 for children ages 12 and under; passengers stay with the bus for the entire trip (no reboarding on a later bus). A two-hour San Francisco tour departs daily at 2 p.m., taking passengers across the Golden Gate Bridge; it visits Pacific Heights, provides views of Alcatraz, and stops at the Palace of Fine Arts. Tickets are $18 for adults and $5 for children. For more information, call (800) 562-7383 or (415) 922-2425.

▪ Specialized Tours ▪

Gray Line offers several general-interest tours around the city and special tours to destinations beyond San Francisco. A three-hour deluxe city tour via motor coach takes visitors to the city's major attractions, including the Civic Center, Mission Dolores, Twin Peaks, Golden Gate Park, and Cliff House. Reservations are required for the tour, which departs daily at 9 a.m., 10 a.m., 11 a.m., 1:30 p.m., and 2:30 p.m. (with an additional 3:30 p.m. departure May through September). The price is $28 for adults and $14 for children ages 5–11.

Tours to Muir Woods and Sausalito are offered by Gray Line daily and leave at 9 a.m., 10 a.m., 11 a.m., 1:30 p.m., and (May through October) 2:30 p.m.; they last three hours. The cost is $28 for adults and $14 for children ages 5–11. In addition, Gray Line offers day tours to Yosemite, the wine country, and Monterey, as well as airplane and helicopter tours. Coach tours from San Francisco include pick-up and drop-off at your hotel. For more information or to make reservations, call (800) 826-0202 or (415) 558-9400.

Tower Tours leads a deluxe city tour to Chinatown, North Beach, Telegraph Hill and Coit Tower, the Marina District, the Presidio, Cliff House and Seal Rocks, and Golden Gate Park. Scheduled stops on the tour (which uses minibuses with large windows, not motor coaches) are Vista Point at the Golden Gate Bridge, Cliff House above Seal Rocks, the Japanese Tea Garden in Golden Gate Park (small admission fee not included), and Twin Peaks (weather permitting).

Trips depart daily at 9:15 a.m., 11 a.m., and 2 p.m. The cost of the three-hour tour is $28 for adults and $13 for children ages 5–11. Tower Tours also offers day trips to Muir Woods and Sausalito, the wine country,

Yosemite, and Monterey and Carmel. All tours include pick-up and return to your hotel; meals aren't included. For more information, call (415) 434-8687.

Off-the-beaten-track tours of San Francisco architecture and the city's best sights are offered by **Quality Tours.** A customized, seven-passenger Chevy Suburban provides more comfort and greater visibility than a bus, and it can handle Lombard Street, "the crookedest street in the world." Rates are $55 an hour for one to four passengers and $60 an hour for five to seven passengers. Pick-up and drop-off at your hotel is included. In addition, custom tours are available. For more information and reservations (required), call (650) 994-5054.

▪ Bay Cruises ▪

Visitors can enjoy spectacular views of the city skyline, the Golden Gate and Bay Bridges, and Alcatraz Island on narrated cruises around San Francisco Bay. **Red & White Fleet** offers a Golden Gate Bridge cruise that passes Fort Mason, the Presidio, and Fort Point before going under the famous bridge. The cruises, which last an hour, depart from Pier 43 in Fisherman's Wharf every 45 minutes, from 10 a.m. to 6 p.m. in the summer and from 10 a.m. to 4:45 p.m. in the winter. The price is $16 for adults, $12 for seniors and children ages 12–18, and $8 for children ages 5–11.

Red & White also offers its "Round the Rock" boat tour, which pulls in close and cruises around Alcatraz without docking; a narrator describes the island prison's infamous past. It's a good alternative for folks who would rather not tackle the steep climbing required on the prison tour. The 45-minute tour departs on the half-hour from 10:30 a.m. to 4:30 p.m. in the summer and less frequently the rest of the year. The cost is $11 for adults, $9 for seniors and teens, and $7 for children ages 5–11.

Blue & Gold Fleet offers one-hour cruises in San Francisco Bay departing from Pier 39 in Fisherman's Wharf every day except Christmas. The boats leave every half-hour from 10 a.m. to 7 p.m. spring through fall, and every 45 minutes from 10 a.m. to 4 p.m. in the winter. The price is $16 for adults, $12 for seniors and children ages 12–18, and $8 for children ages 5–11. Blue & Gold also offers ferry service to Sausalito and Tiburon from Pier 41, a Muir Woods tour, and a Napa-Sonoma wine country tour. For more information, call (415) 773-1188; to make advance reservations, call (415) 705-5555.

For an elegant introduction to the San Francisco Bay, enjoy a champagne brunch aboard the **San Francisco Spirit,** a three-deck, 150-foot charter vessel that can accommodate up to 700 passengers. The two-hour cruise departs every Sunday at 11:30 a.m. from Pier 39 in Fisherman's Wharf. The cost is $50 a person; the children's rate is $25, and kids ages 4 and under are free. For reservations, call (415) 788-9100.

■ Air Tours ■

For 50 years **San Francisco Seaplane Tours** has whisked visitors aloft from the waters of the San Francisco Bay on flights over the city and its famous landmarks. Thirty-minute sight-seeing rides from Pier 39 in Fisherman's Wharf leave daily from 9 a.m. to sunset; the price is $89 for adults and $59 for children (minimum of two passengers). Flights are also offered from Sausalito, including a 30-minute city and bay tour ($74 for adults, $49 for children) and a 45-minute ride over Mount Tamalpais, north along the Pacific coast, and over the city ($89 for adults, $59 for children). Champagne sunset tours leave 30 minutes before sundown and take passengers over San Francisco at dusk; the ride lasts 35–40 minutes and costs $104 a person. Reservations are recommended for all tours and required for the sunset tour; call toll-free (888) 732-7526 for more information.

San Francisco Helicopter Tours and Charters offers jet helicopter flights daily from San Francisco International Airport, about a half-hour south of downtown. Fifteen-minute flights ($79 for adults, $69 for children ages 11 and under) provide spectacular views of downtown and Fisherman's Wharf. Twenty-minute flights ($99 for adults, $79 for children) add the Golden Gate Bridge to the itinerary, while 30-minute tours ($129 for adults, $99 for children) include all of the above plus the California coast around Cliff House and Seal Rocks. Hotel pick-up and return is included in the price; the maximum number of passengers is four. For more information and reservations (required), call (800) 400-2404.

■ Walking Tours ■

San Francisco is best seen up close, and the best way to do that is on a walking tour. **City Guides Walking Tours,** presented by the San Francisco Friends of the Library, provides more than 200 trained volunteers who conduct about 20 different history walks each month. The one- to two-hour tours are led daily year-round, rain or shine. And here's the good part: the guided walks are free. An expanded schedule, offered in May and October, provides more than 40 different walks, with more than 125 free tours available. Walking tours are offered of San Francisco's most famous (and, in some cases, infamous) districts, as well as hidden neighborhoods most tourists miss.

No reservations are required; just meet at the place and time designated in the current tour schedule. Wear comfortable shoes (although tours are not strenuous unless so listed) and look for the City Guide, who should be wearing a badge. For a recorded schedule of walks, call (415) 557-4266. You can pick up a printed walk schedule at the San Francisco Convention and Visitors Bureau, Hallidie Plaza at Powell and Market Streets.

Victorian Home Walk takes visitors on tours of the city's famed Victorian houses, with an emphasis on exploring neighborhoods off the beaten tourist path. Tours depart daily at 11 a.m. from Union Square; rates for two or more are $20 a person. The walk lasts about two hours, and transportation is included. For more information or to make reservations (required), call (415) 252-9485.

Feel like a native on **Helen's Walk Tour,** a three-hour exploration of Union Square, Chinatown, and North Beach offered Monday through Thursday. The walk begins at 9 a.m. "under the clock" in the lobby of the Saint Francis Hotel on Union Square. The cost for two people is $100; family and group rates are available. For more information and to make reservations, call (510) 524-4544.

Bay Ventures offers a variety of walking tours in and around San Francisco, including walks emphasizing sculpture and fountains, movie locations, the waterfront, graveyards, and the city's art-deco treasures. Prices start at $18 a person and the walks vary from three to four hours. For more information and reservations, call (510) 234-4834.

Learn about San Francisco's history on the **San Francisco Then . . . and Now** walking tour, which takes visitors through Union Square, Chinatown, North Beach, and the former Barbary Coast. The tours depart from the Flood Building, 870 Market Street, at 11 a.m. on weekends and holidays. The cost is $20 a person (children ages 17 and under free), and no steep hills are encountered on the three-hour walk. For more information or to make reservations, call (415) 931-4021.

Roger's Custom Tours offers a variety of ways to explore the city on foot, including a three-hour San Francisco High Points tour ($39.95 for adults, $25 for children ages 11 and under), a 90-minute Golden Gate Bridge tour ($25 for adults, $10 for children), and a two-hour Chinatown tour ($25 for adults, $10 for children). Foreign language and custom tours are also available; the $40-an-hour custom tour includes transportation in a luxury car (maximum four people). For more information, call (650) 742-9611.

Relive the '60s on the two-hour **Haight-Ashbury Flower Power** walking tour. Learn about the Summer of Love and the Diggers, and see shrines to the late Jerry Garcia (of the Grateful Dead). The tours depart at 9:30 a.m. on Tuesdays and Saturdays at the corner of Stanyan and

Waller Streets in the Haight; the cost is $15 per person. Reservations are required; call (415) 863-1621.

For free, in-depth walking tours of Golden Gate Park, call **Friends of Recreation & Parks** at (415) 263-0991. A variety of guided walks are offered throughout the week, including tours of the Japanese Tea Garden and Stern Grove. **Cruisin' the Castro** is an award-winning tour with an emphasis on the neighborhood's history; sights include Harvey Milk's camera shop and the AIDS quilt museum. The walk, offered daily, starts at 10 a.m. and lasts four hours; brunch is included. The cost is $35 a person; students and seniors pay $30. For reservations, call (415) 550-8110.

For a look at the history, folklore, and food of Chinatown, take a **Chinatown Adventure Tour** with the "Wok Wiz," cookbook author Shirley Fong-Torres. The walks are offered daily at 10 a.m. and last about two hours; you can finish the tour with a dim sum lunch. The cost is $37 a person ($25 a person without lunch). Reservations are required; call (800) 281-9255.

All About Chinatown takes visitors on a behind-the-scenes walk of this colorful neighborhood, covering its history, culture, and traditions. Tours leave daily at 10 a.m. from 812 Clay Street. The two-hour walk finishes with a dim sum lunch. The cost is $35 a person (lunch included; $25 without lunch); children ages 7 and under go free. For more information and reservations, call (415) 982-8839.

▪ Touring on Your Own: Our Favorite Itineraries ▪

If your time is limited and you want to experience the best of San Francisco in a day or two, here are some suggested itineraries. The schedules assume you're staying at a downtown hotel, have already eaten breakfast, and are ready to go around 9 a.m. If you've got two days, make reservations for a morning ferry ride to Alcatraz Island and for Beach Blanket Babylon (Wednesday through Sunday evenings) before you hit town.

Day One

1. Walk to Union Square or Fisherman's Wharf and tour San Francisco's major sights on one of the open-air, motorized "cable car" services; Gray Line offers unlimited reboarding privileges for the day. You can also pay an additional $10 for a one-hour narrated cruise of San Francisco Bay.

2. At Fisherman's Wharf, skip touristy Pier 39 and walk west to the Hyde Street Pier, where you can explore real 19th-century ships; or walk another block or two to the National Maritime Museum,

which is free and chock-full of nautical goodies. Or, if it's a nice day, take a bay cruise.

3. For lunch, try the clam chowder served in a bowl of sourdough bread at Boudin's Bakery in Fisherman's Wharf; it's fast and cheap ($5).

4. On the "cable car" tour, stop at the Golden Gate Bridge. Don't just gaze at the scenery from the overlook near the visitor center; walk onto the bridge for even better views. Take a jacket (it gets very windy).

5. Back at Union Square after your circuit on the "cable car," walk up Grant Avenue to Chinatown; to get the real flavor of this exotic neighborhood, walk a block west to Stockton Street, which is less touristy.

6. Continue walking north through Chinatown to Columbus Avenue; now you're in North Beach. Settle in at a nice sidewalk café for a latte and primo people-watching; then browse at City Lights Bookstore, a North Beach landmark.

7. For a spectacular view of San Francisco, hike up Telegraph Hill to Coit Tower; if your legs and feet aren't up for the steep walk, take the No. 39 bus (board near Washington Square). After savoring the view (at its best around sunset), walk down the Greenwich Steps, a brick staircase lined with ivy and roses that descends steeply to Montgomery Street. Near the base of the steps is a glass-brick, art-deco apartment house used in the Humphrey Bogart film *Dark Passage*.

8. Have dinner at The Stinking Rose (825 Columbus Avenue in North Beach), which features "garlic seasoned with food." This fun restaurant is popular with locals as well as tourists.

Day Two

1. Get to Fisherman's Wharf for a morning ferry ride to Alcatraz. Allow at least two hours to explore the prison ruins and island.

2. Have lunch at Greens (in Building A at Fort Mason), with a full view of the Golden Gate Bridge and the Marin Headlands. It's an outstanding vegetarian restaurant (not sprouts and tofu) in a former enclosed pier with polished wood floors and a serene atmosphere. Call ahead for reservations: (415) 771-6222.

3. Stop at the Mexican Museum in Fort Mason, and then explore the Marina District and its beautiful waterside houses. If you've got time, stroll the park-like grounds of the Palace of Fine Arts.

4. Take the cable car from the Beach and Hyde Streets turnaround (Powell-Mason line) or the turnaround near Taylor and Bay Streets (Powell-Hyde line); both head toward Union Square as they pass through Nob Hill. If it's a nice day, hop off and explore Nob Hill and Russian Hill. At sunset, order cocktails at the Top O' the Mark lounge in the Mark Hopkins Inter-Continental San Francisco, a 392-room hotel at California and Mason Streets.

5. Have dinner at John's Grill (63 Ellis Street near Union Square), where you can pay homage to Dashiell Hammett and Sam Spade while enjoying 1930s dining at its best.

6. Enjoy an evening of zany entertainment at Beach Blanket Babylon (at Club Fugazi in North Beach), San Francisco's long-running musical revue famous for its excellent singers, enormous hats, and stunning costumes. Advance reservations are required.

If You've Got More Time

If you're spending more than two days in town or if this is not your first visit, consider some of these options.

1. Drive or take a bus up Van Ness Avenue to Union Street and Pacific Heights, where you'll find some of the best examples of San Francisco's famed Victorian houses. The Union Street shops are an upscale retail experience, with more than 300 boutiques, restaurants, antique shops, and coffeehouses.

2. Visit the California Palace of the Legion of Honor, a world-class European art museum in Lincoln Park with a spectacular view of the Pacific and the Marin Headlands. It's also a location used in Hitchcock's classic thriller *Vertigo*. Drive or take the No. 38 bus from Union Square.

3. Spend at least half a day in Golden Gate Park. The Japanese Tea Garden is a work of art, while the de Young and Asian Art Museums will thrill culture vultures. Families should head to the California Academy of Sciences. Other options include renting a bike or rowboat.

4. Go to Sausalito or Tiburon for lunch and an afternoon. You can drive, but taking the ferry from Fisherman's Wharf is a better way to reach these two upscale, bay-side communities across from San Francisco.

5. Serious shoppers will want to exercise their credit cards around Union Square, where they'll find the city's major department stores and many high-end specialty shops. Discount shoppers should head to SoMa, which is loaded with warehouse retail spaces. On-the-edge fashion victims and vintage-clothes browsers should head to Haight-Ashbury.

6. If you've got a car, make the trip across the Golden Gate Bridge to Muir Woods (giant redwoods) and Mount Tamalpais (a knock-your-socks-off view of San Francisco Bay and the Pacific). You can do both in half a day.

7. Drive up Twin Peaks for its stunning view of the city (from its highest location). Hint: go at night (and take a jacket or sweater).

8. The San Francisco Museum of Modern Art is the city's newest art emporium, and even if you're not a big fan of modern art, the building alone is worth the price of admission. It's a knockout.

9. Don't miss Fort Point. While the Civil War–era brick fortress isn't much to get excited about, the view, framed by the Golden Gate Bridge, is. It's got our vote as the most scenic spot in the city (and not just because it's the place where Jimmy Stewart pulls Kim Novak out of the water in Hitchcock's *Vertigo*).

10. Take a drive along the city's western edge south of the Golden Gate Bridge, and you'll see yet another reason why San Franciscans love living here. The views of the Pacific and the coast are spectacular. Good places to explore include Seal Rocks, Cliff House, Ocean Beach, and Fort Funston.

San Francisco for Children

Question: After taking the kids on the requisite trips to Fisherman's Wharf and the Golden Gate Bridge, what else can a parent do to entertain kids on a San Francisco vacation? Answer: A lot. San Francisco offers plenty of fun-filled places and things to do that will satisfy the most curious—and fidgety—kids. Their folks will have fun, too.

The *Unofficial Guide* rating system for attractions includes an "appeal to different age groups" category with a range of appeal from one star (★), don't bother, to five stars (★★★★★), not to be missed. To get you started, we've provided a list of attractions in and around San Francisco most likely to appeal to children.

Top 10 Attractions for Kids
Alcatraz
California Academy of Sciences
Cliff House
Exploratorium (school-age children)
Fort Point
Hyde Street Pier (San Francisco Maritime Historical Park)
Lawrence Hall of Science (Berkeley)
Ripley's Believe It or Not! Museum
San Francisco Zoo
UnderWater World

More Things to Do with Children

San Francisco has more for kids to enjoy than museums, a zoo, and vistas of the bay. A cable-car ride never fails to delight, especially if children can sit in the open-air section of the car on a steep hill. The icing on the cake is a stop at the Cable Car Museum near Chinatown (it's free). Golden Gate Park has the Children's Playground, with a carousel that's fun for toddlers. You can also rent a boat on Stow Lake; bicycles, in-line skates, and roller skates are also available for rent. Another kid-pleasing attraction in the giant park is the Bison Paddock.

Great Views and Walks While a visit to a highbrow art museum may not be every child's idea of a good time, most kids will like the view of the Pacific Ocean and the Golden Gate Bridge from atop 200-foot cliffs near the California Palace of the Legion of Honor in Lincoln Park. Children also enjoy taking a bay cruise and seeing San Francisco from the water. And don't forget another place popular with both children and adults: Lombard Street, "the crookedest street in the world," so steep that the road has to zigzag to make the descent (between Hyde and Leavenworth Streets).

Great places to walk include the Golden Gate Promenade (a three-and-a-half-mile, paved walkway that starts near Fisherman's Wharf and follows the bay shore west to the bridge of the same name) and Ocean Beach, a four-mile stretch of sand beginning just south of Cliff House. Forget your bathing suits, though—the water is always treacherous. At Fort Funston, south of Ocean Beach, the scenery is great and kids can watch hang-gliders floating overhead.

Indoor Fun Kids climbing the hotel walls? Let them work it off at **Mission Cliffs,** the world's largest indoor climbing gym (2295 Harrison Street at 19th Street; (415) 550- 0515). Another option is **Jungle Fun and Adventure** (555 Ninth Street in the Toys R Us shopping center; (415) 552-4386), a massive indoor playland where kids of all ages can work off energy on cargo nets, slides, and tubes; there are also crafts and games.

Rainy Days Need an idea for a rainy day? Go shopping. All children enjoy the wonderland of toys, **F.A.O. Schwarz,** a three-floor megastore packed with toys, dolls, games, books, and stuffed animals; the 25-foot-high singing clock is as impressive as it is annoying. The toy emporium is near Union Square at 48 Stockton Street (near O'Farrell Street); phone (415) 394-8700. And don't forget the other classic rainy-day option—a movie. The **AMC Kabuki 8** in Japantown is an eight-screen theater complex that's sure to be playing something the kids will enjoy.

Let's Eat! And what about something to eat? Kids love **Planet Hollywood,** where the theme decor is better than the food; it's noisy, too. The restaurant is located at 2 Stockton Street; phone (415) 421-7827. Other dining spots children enjoy include the **Hard Rock Cafe,** featuring great burgers, rock memorabilia, and a deafening sound level (1699 Van Ness Avenue; (415) 885-1699); and **Mel's Drive-In,** straight out of *American Graffiti* and as American as it gets, with greasy fries, frothy milkshakes, and Patsy Cline crooning on the table-top jukeboxes (2165 Lombard Street, (415) 921-3039; or 3355 Geary Boulevard, (415) 387-2244).

Pro Sports, a Scenic Lake, and Some Really Big Amusement Parks
Depending on the season and ticket availability, take the gang to a 49ers, Giants, Golden State Warriors, Oakland As, or Oakland Raiders game. Speaking of Oakland, the kids will enjoy sailing on Lake Merritt or taking a ride on the **Merritt Queen,** a miniature Mississippi sternwheeler that plies the lake on weekends. Youngsters enjoy **Children's Fairyland** on the north shore of Lake Merritt; it's one of the most imaginative children's parks in the country; call (510) 452-2259 for information.

Farther afield are some kid-pleasing attractions that are still near San Francisco. **Marine World Africa USA** is a 160-acre theme park with wildlife of all kinds, including elephants, seals, butterflies, and giraffes. Admission also includes a variety of shows. The park is a 45-minute drive northeast of the city in Vallejo. You can also take a ferry from Fisherman's Wharf. For more information, call (707) 643-6722.

Paramount's **Great America** is a giant amusement park filled with rides such as the Top Gun Jetcoaster and the Days of Thunder Racetrack, both based on Paramount movies; it's just the place for the roller-coaster crowd. The park is a one-hour drive south of San Francisco in Santa Clara; just drive south on US 101 until you see the signs. The park is open March through September. For more information, call (408) 988-1776.

Helpful Hints for Tourists

■ How to Get into Museums for Half-Price ■

Save up to $30 when you visit San Francisco's most popular museums and attractions with a **CityPass,** a book of tickets that cuts the price of admission in half. Participating attractions are the California Academy of Sciences, California Palace of the Legion of Honor, Exploratorium, M. H. de Young Memorial Museum, San Francisco Bay Cruise, San Francisco Museum of Modern Art, and San Francisco Zoo.

The passes cost $29.95 for adults, $19.95 for seniors ages 65 and older, and $17.95 for children ages 12–17. Children ages 11 and under pay the regular, reduced fare at each attraction. Ticket books are sold at the participating attractions and are good for seven days, beginning with the first day you use them. Don't remove the individual tickets from the booklet; just present the CityPass at each attraction, the clerk at the site removes the ticket, and you walk in.

■ When Admission Is Free ■

Many San Francisco museums that usually charge admission open their doors for one free day a month. If you'd like to save a few bucks during your visit, use the following list when planning your touring itinerary. And don't forget that summer is the season of free events and outdoor concerts.

- Asian Art Museum (first Wednesday of the month)
- California Academy of Sciences (first Wednesday of the month)
- California Historical Society (first Tuesday of the month)
- California Palace of the Legion of Honor (second Wednesday of the month)
- Center for the Arts at Yerba Buena Gardens (first Thursday of the month)
- M. H. de Young Memorial Museum (first Wednesday of the month and the first Saturday of the month between 10 a.m. and noon)
- Exploratorium (first Wednesday of the month)
- Mexican Museum (first Wednesday of the month)

- Hyde Street Pier (first Tuesday of the month)
- San Francisco Craft and Folk Art Museum (first Wednesday of the month and every Saturday between 10 a.m. and noon)
- San Francisco Museum of Modern Art (first Tuesday of the month)
- San Francisco Zoo (first Wednesday of the month)

In addition, a few worthy attractions around town are free to the public all the time. Here's the list.

- Cable Car Museum
- Fort Point National Historic Site
- Golden Gate Band Concerts (Sundays at 1 p.m., April through October)
- Golden Gate Bridge (pedestrians and bicyclists)
- Midsummer Music Festival (Stern Grove, Sloat Avenue at 19th Street, Sunday afternoons at 2 p.m., June through August)
- Museum of Money of the American West
- National Maritime Museum
- Presidio Museum
- Strybing Arboretum
- Wells Fargo History Museum

■ Great Views ■

In San Francisco, all you have to do to find a great view is walk up one of the city's 43 hills. Yet some vistas are better than others—and often worth going out of the way for. Here's our list of breathtaking views in and around San Francisco that shouldn't be missed.

1. Fort Point. Ideally, you should be blindfolded and brought to this Civil War–era fortress. You should remove the blind as you face the Marin Headlands across the Golden Gate. Overhead is the massive Golden Gate Bridge, perhaps the most beautiful suspension bridge in the world. It's a view to die for.

2. Although it's better at night, the view from Twin Peaks is good whenever the weather is clear. It's a stupendous, 360° view of San Francisco.

3. The best view of the city's skyline is from Treasure Island. To get there, take the Treasure Island exit from the Bay Bridge and drive to the parking area just outside the naval station.

4. For the best view of the waterfront, hike up Telegraph Hill to Coit Tower. Don't drive, though; parking is scarce. Either walk or take the No. 39 bus.

5. Drive across the Golden Gate Bridge, get off in Sausalito and follow signs to Mount Tamalpais, where you can drive to the 2,800-foot summit (well, almost) for a heart-stopping view of San Francisco Bay, the city, the Golden Gate and Bay Bridges, and the Pacific Ocean.

6. For a view of the bay that's almost as good as the one from Mount Tam, drive to Berkeley, go through the University of California, Berkeley campus and find Grizzly Peak Boulevard. Then drive up the winding road to the Lawrence Hall of Science. Park in the lot and enjoy the vista from the plaza of the children's science museum.

7. The view from the Golden Gate Bridge is best at sunset, when the slanting sun casts shadowy patterns on the lofty bridge towers and on the sea below—and the tour buses have left for the day. The pedestrian walkway is open until 9 p.m.

8. For an even better view of Seal Rocks than the one you get at Cliff House, walk up to Sutro Heights Park, which overlooks the Pacific from a lofty vantage point. Park in the lot just north of Cliff House (on the other side of the Great Highway).

9. Drive across the Golden Gate Bridge to Vista Point, which offers superb views of the bridge and the San Francisco skyline. It's beautiful on a sunny day, but it might be even better when the fog rolls over the hills or at night when the city glimmers beyond the Golden Gate.

10. Most people take the ferry ride to Alcatraz just to tour the famous island's prison ruins. But the view of the city is spectacular. Bring a bag lunch and savor the vista.

■ Secret Staircases ■

Scattered throughout San Francisco's many hills are pocket parks, restful benches, and many stairways—about 350 of them, mostly in residential neighborhoods and often adorned with flowers planted by neighbors. The stairways are used by residents to allow direct vertical access from one street to another, and because most streets wind around the hills, people frequently use them as shortcuts.

A walk centered around an exploration of the city's staircases is cheaper than a fitness center and frequently offers views that rival what you'll find on the Golden Gate Bridge. Put on your walking shoes, grab your camera, and explore some of the city's oldest, most scenic hidden attractions—its stairways. For a comprehensive guide to the city's stairways, pick up a copy of *Stairway Walks in San Francisco* by Adah Bakalinsky, available in bookstores or directly from the Wilderness Press (phone (510) 843-8080). Here's a sampling of some of San Francisco's best stairways.

1. The carefully landscaped stairs found near the famous Lombard Street (between Hyde and Leavenworth Streets).

2. At Broadway and Lyon Street, more than ten flights of majestic stone steps surrounded by well-kept greenery and regal views of the Palace of Fine Arts, the bay, and the Marin Headlands.

3. The Greenwich Street Steps at the base of Coit Tower on Telegraph Hill; more than three separate flights of stairs that climb through tall trees and past hillside gardens and stunning views.

4. The Fort Mason/Aquatic Park Steps overlooking Alcatraz; the small clearing at the top features tranquility and picnic tables.

5. Pemberton Stairway in the Twin Peaks neighborhood, newly renovated with terra-cotta concrete stairs and just-planted gardens.

6. Filbert Street Steps, between Sansome Street and Telegraph Hill, a 377-step climb through verdant flower gardens and charming 19th-century cottages.

San Francisco on Film

San Francisco is a favorite with Hollywood directors, who take full advantage of the city's dramatic topography, sunny beaches, swirling fog, urban decay, and high-class elegance. Thrillers, in particular, get a lot of mileage with San Francisco locations, while the city's steep streets lend themselves to the car chases Hollywood loves so much. Stumbling across a familiar location from a favorite movie is one of the pleasures of visiting San Francisco—and there's no way you'll see them all. (But if you'd like to try, pick up a copy of The San Francisco Movie Map, sold at the California Historical Society gift shop and other locations around town.) Here's a short list of movie locations used in some of the best-known movies shot (at least in part) in and around the city.

Alcatraz   The lonely prison island in San Francisco Bay is as dramatic as it gets. Films made on location include *Escape from Alcatraz* (1979), a true story starring Clint Eastwood as the leader of a trio of escapees who actually made it off the Rock. Other movies filmed here include *Murder in the First* (1995), starring Kevin Bacon; *Birdman of Alcatraz* (1962) with Burt Lancaster; and *The Rock* (1996), starring Sean Connery, Nicolas Cage, and Ed Harris.

Golden Gate Bridge   This postcard setting has been a movie favorite since it was completed in 1937. In the sci-fi classic *It Came from Beneath the Sea* (1955), a giant octopus attacks the bridge and tears it in half. Christopher Reeve in *Superman* (1978) arrives just in time to save a school bus from making the plunge as an earthquake rocks the span. More recently, Tom Cruise offers Christian Slater "the choice" in a nighttime drive across the bridge in *Interview with the Vampire* (1994).

Golden Gate Park   This is where Clint Eastwood makes an illegal arrest in *Dirty Harry* (1972) "filmed in tribute to the police officers of San Francisco who gave their lives in the line of duty." In *Star Trek IV: The Voyage Home,* a Klingon Bird of Prey warship lands in the park with the crew of the Enterprise on board to save the earth from destruction.

The Conservatory   This fanciful Victorian structure located in Golden Gate Park (now closed due to damage from a 1995 storm) can be glimpsed in several films, including *Vertigo* (1958), *Heart and Souls* (1993), and *Harold and Maude* (1972).

Hotels *What's Up, Doc?* (1972), a screwball comedy starring Barbra Streisand and Ryan O'Neal, was filmed at the San Francisco Hilton (33 O'Farrell Street), called Hotel Bristol in the film. The lobby of the Fairmont Hotel on Nob Hill was featured in the sentimental favorite *I Remember Mama* (1948), with Irene Dunne. Next door, the Mark Hopkins Inter-Continental Hotel can be seen in *Bullitt* (1968), with Steve McQueen; *Sudden Impact* (1983), starring Clint Eastwood; and *Innerspace* (1987), with Dennis Quaid.

Civic Center The classic styles of the marble edifices around City Hall can be glimpsed in many movies, including the creepy 1978 remake of *Invasion of the Body Snatchers,* starring Donald Sutherland. In Francis Ford Coppola's *Tucker: A Man and His Dream* (1988), Jeff Bridges is put on trial in City Hall. Other films that utilized the Renaissance-style building are *Jagged Edge* (1985) with Glenn Close and Jeff Bridges; and *Class Action,* starring Gene Hackman.

Union Square A key scene in *The Conversation* (1974) was filmed in this downtown park. The critically acclaimed film stars Gene Hackman and was written and directed by Francis Ford Coppola, who has lived in the Bay Area since 1968 and owns a winery in Napa Valley. (The winery features a museum with artifacts from the filmmaker's movies.)

Chinatown Much of *The Joy Luck Club* (1993), noted for its realistic depiction of Chinese Americans, was made in Chinatown. The movie was directed by Wayne Wang from a screenplay adapted from local author Amy Tan's bestseller (Tan also coscripted the screenplay).

North Beach Some of this quintessential San Francisco neighborhood's eateries have been featured in *Basic Instinct* (1992) and *Class Action.* In *Nine Months* (1995), Julianne Moore and Hugh Grant tie the knot at Saints Peter and Paul Catholic Church on Washington Square. The art-deco apartment building (1360 Montgomery Street) was where Lauren Bacall lived in the film-noir classic *Dark Passage* (1947), which also starred Humphrey Bogart. The apartment building at 1158–70 Montgomery Street was the home of Michael Douglas in *Basic Instinct.*

Vertigo It's not a place, it's a classic thriller directed by Alfred Hitchcock. The British director loved San Francisco, and he shows the town at its best in this 1958 film starring James Stewart and Kim Novak. Locations in the movie include Mission Dolores, the California Palace of the Legion of

Honor (the movie's scenes were filmed in Gallery 6), the Palace of Fine Arts, and Fort Point (where Stewart dives into San Francisco Bay to save Novak). Madeleine (Novak's character) lived in the elegant Brocklebank Apartment Building at 1000 Mason Street on Nob Hill.

Car Chases   In *Bullitt,* it seems as if Steve McQueen covers virtually every street in the city in one of the best automotive chase sequences ever filmed. Actually, much of the chase was shot on the steep streets on Russian Hill. In *What's Up, Doc?* Streisand and O'Neal are chased through a Chinatown parade and down Lombard Street. The funniest sequence, involving a pane of glass and a ladder, was shot at 23rd and Balboa Streets in the Richmond District. *The Presidio* (1988) features a nighttime car chase and a foot race through Chinatown.

North of San Francisco   The winding roads and breathtaking scenery of the Marin Headlands (on the north side of the Golden Gate Bridge) have been used in *Foul Play* (1978), starring Goldie Hawn, and *Basic Instinct.* (While Sharon Stone's character lives in Stinson Beach, the house seen in the film is actually down the coast near Carmel.) In Bodega and Bodega Bay, north of the city on the coast, Hitchcock filmed much of *The Birds* (1963), his classic horror movie starring Tippi Hedren. The Potter School-house in Bodega, built in 1873, served as the scene where the birds attack the children. Closer to the city, San Quentin State Prison was featured in the 1958 potboiler *I Want to Live* (1958), a true story starring Susan Hayward.

South of San Francisco   Thirty miles south of the city is Filoli, a beautiful estate featured in the romantic fantasy *Heaven Can Wait* (1978), starring Warren Beatty. Aerial shots of the estate were used in the opening credits of the TV series *Dynasty.* The Santa Cruz boardwalk, home of the Giant Dipper (a classic wooden roller-coaster), was used in the punk-gothic flick *The Lost Boys* (1987), starring Keifer Sutherland. *The Sting II* (1983) also features the Giant Dipper. At Mission San Juan Bautista (founded in 1797), about 100 miles south of San Francisco, Kim Novak led Jimmy Stewart up a bell tower staircase in *Vertigo.* But you won't find a bell tower here; it was an illusion created by director Hitchcock's film crew.

Day Trips in and around the Bay Area

If you've got the time or if your visit to San Francisco is a repeat trip, consider exploring some places outside the city. Northern California is spectacularly scenic and a trip to the area really isn't complete unless you take at least one day to venture beyond town limits.

From Marin County, Point Reyes, and the wine country to the north; to the East Bay cities of Oakland and Berkeley; to the villages, mountains, and coastal scenery to the south, there's plenty to see and do. A trip beyond hectic San Francisco can be a welcome respite from the heavy traffic and round-the-clock activity in the city's livelier neighborhoods. Here are a few suggestions for day trips that get beyond the city's limits.

■ Marin County ■

Sausalito and Tiburon

For folks on a tight schedule or without a car, these two bay-side villages across from San Francisco are destinations well worth visiting. And with ferry service available from Fisherman's Wharf, it's a short trip that combines a refreshing boat ride with spectacular scenery. Neither destination requires a full day; a sunny afternoon is just about perfect.

Sausalito Sausalito was once a gritty little fishing village full of bars and bordellos, but today it's decidedly more upscale. Think French Riviera, not Barbary Coast. With approximately 7,500 residents (not all of them cash-flush yuppies), the town still manages to hang on to a faintly Bohemian air, although most of its attractions are upscale boutiques and restaurants. The main drag is Bridgeway, where sleek, Lycra-clad bicyclists, rollerbladers, and joggers flash by along the waterfront.

Caledonia Street, one block inland, has a wider selection of cafés and shops. Half a mile north of town, the tourist onslaught is less evident and visitors can see the town's well-known ad-hoc community of houseboats and barges. But most folks come just to exercise their credit cards or hang out in a bar or waterfront restaurant. And that's not a bad idea: The views of the bay and the San Francisco skyline are great. Suggestions: **The No Name Bar**

(757 Bridgeway; (415) 332–1392) is a no-frills Sausalito institution. It's smoky, small, and funky, with great Irish coffee and decent martinis. **Gate Five** (305 Harbor Drive; (415) 331-5355) is a waterfront restaurant serving straight-ahead, Cape Cod–style cooking gussied up to California standards.

The **Blue & Gold Fleet** provides ferry service to Sausalito, a 20-minute boat ride from Pier 41 in Fisherman's Wharf. The cost of a round-trip is $11 for adults and $5.50 for children. For departure times and information, call (415) 773-1188. **Golden Gate Ferries** depart from the Ferry Building at the foot of Market Street. Round-trip tickets are $8.50 for adults and $6.40 for children. For schedules, call (415) 923-2000. If you're driving, take US 101 north across the Golden Gate Bridge; then take the first right, the Alexander Avenue exit. Alexander becomes Bridgeway in Sausalito.

Tiburon   Less touristy but more upscale is the best way to describe Tiburon, which is frequently compared to a New England fishing village. (Maybe so, if the New Englanders are wealthy and commute to high-rise offices by ferry every day.) Visitors can soak up this heady ambience in pricey waterfront restaurants and bars, then stroll the gorgeous promenade. Tiburon is also the most convenient stepping-off point to nearby Angel Island, where you can hike or bike on 12 miles of trails in the state park. A good lunch or dinner destination in Tiburon is **Guaymas** (5 Main Street; (415) 435-6300), with authentic Mexican cuisine and a panoramic view of San Francisco and the bay.

Ferry service to Tiburon is provided by the **Blue & White Fleet** from Pier 41 in Fisherman's Wharf; round-trip tickets are $11 for adults and $5.50 for children. For departure times and information, call (415) 773-1188. By car, take US 101 north across the Golden Gate Bridge to the Tiburon/Highway 131 exit; then follow Tiburon Boulevard all the way to downtown. It's about a 40-minute drive from San Francisco. Our advice: take the ferry.

Angel Island

Over the years Angel Island has been a prison, a notorious quarantine station for immigrants, a missile base, and a favorite site for duels. Today the largest island in San Francisco Bay is a state park; it's a terrific destination for a picnic, stroll, hike, or mountain bike ride, or simply a place to while away the time away from traffic, phones, and television.

Angel Island, located across Raccoon Straight from Tiburon, is only accessible by ferry. Visitors arrive at a small marina abutting a huge lawn area equipped with picnic tables, benches, barbecue pits, and rest rooms. There's also a small store, café, gift shop, and mountain bike rental concession. (To save money, rent a bike in San Francisco and bring it on the ferry.) Tram tours highlight the island's history. You can also rent a stable, two-person sea kayak and see the island from the water. There are 12 miles of trails on the wooded island, and cyclists and hikers can explore the spooky ruins of the former immigration center (called the "Ellis Island of the West"). Note: Tram tours and bike and kayak rentals are closed from mid-November to mid-February.

Blue & Gold Fleet ferries to Angel Island depart from Pier 41 in Fisherman's Wharf daily in the summer and on weekends in the winter. The round-trip fare is $9 for adults and $4.50 for children. For departure times and information, call (415) 773-1188. The **Angel Island–Tiburon Ferry** operates daily in summer and on weekends in winter. Round-trip fares are $6 for adults and $4 for children ages 5–11. A $1 fee is charged for bicycles. For schedule information and directions, call (415) 435-2131.

Marin Headlands

The north end of the Golden Gate Bridge is anchored by the Marin Headlands, largely undeveloped terrain dominated by 2,800-foot Mount Tamalpais. The coastline here is more rugged than on the San Francisco side of the bridge, and it's a mecca for nature lovers. Visitors are treated to great views of the city, ocean, and bay; hiking trails and rugged beaches; and the concrete remains of old forts and gun emplacements standing guard over the Golden Gate (no shots were ever fired in anger).

While physically close to San Francisco, the headlands seem a world apart. Windswept ridges, protected valleys, and beaches offer the best of nature, but they're less than an hour's drive from the hectic city. The hillsides near the Golden Gate provide magnificent views of the entrance of the bay. The **Marin Headlands Visitor Center** (phone (415) 331-1540) is open daily from 9:30 a.m. to 4:30 p.m. and offers detailed information on enjoying the rugged countryside.

The headlands offer a vast expanse of wild and open terrain; rolling hills covered with shrubs, grasses, and wildflowers; small coves, large beaches, and rocky coastal cliffs; and forested ridges and redwood valleys. The park, part of Golden Gate National Recreation Area, has abundant wildlife—hawks, deer, and seabirds are common, and bobcats and whales are sometimes sighted. Fog is heaviest in the summer in areas closer to the Golden Gate, and ocean swimming is always dangerous. Also, use caution when walking on the rocky coastline, where unwary hikers can be swept away by large waves or trapped by the incoming tide.

Major attractions include the **Point Bonita Lighthouse** (open spring through fall on weekends), Muir and Stinson Beaches, Muir Woods and Mount Tamalpais (see Zone 11, Attractions, pages 304–306), and Olema

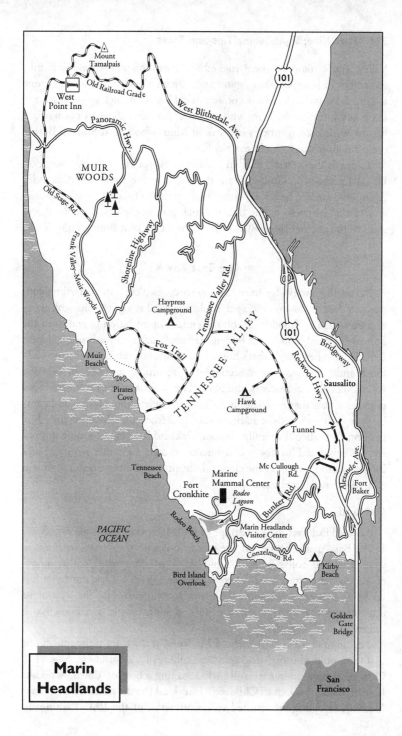

Marin Headlands

Valley. Trails, many of them rugged and steep, crisscross the headlands; remember to bring drinking water and stay off the cliffs, which are prone to landslides and covered with poison oak. Hikers can pick up detailed trail maps and information at the visitor center. And don't forget to bring your lunch: With the exceptions of cafés in Muir Woods and Stinson Beach, there are no places to eat in the headlands.

To reach the Marin Headlands and the visitor center, drive north on US 101 across the Golden Gate Bridge, take the first exit (Alexander Avenue), bear left, and follow the road up the hill. Go through the one-way tunnel (there's a traffic light), which puts you on Bunker Road and leads to the visitor center, Rodeo Beach, and the Point Bonita Lighthouse.

▪ The East Bay ▪

Across the Bay Bridge from San Francisco, two cities offer startling contrasts to the chic town on the peninsula. Oakland is a gritty, blue-collar city that earns its livelihood from shipping and transportation to and from the Port of Oakland, dominated by huge cranes. The city spreads north toward Berkeley, a college town that's home to a campus of the University of California and a fascinating cross-section of aging hippies and radicals, hustling young Republicans, students, and Nobel Prize laureates. The two towns blend together so that they're physically indistinguishable, although Oakland's low-brow reputation stands in stark contrast to Berkeley, a self-consciously hip, intellectual hotbed. Ironically, though, Oakland lays claim to some impressive historical and literary associations of its own. Gertrude Stein and Jack London both grew up in the city at about the same time, albeit at different ends of the social spectrum.

Oakland

Located just over the Bay Bridge or via BART, Oakland is the workhorse of the Bay Area, with one of the busiest ports on the West Coast. Yet in spite of its blue-collar reputation and Ms. Stein's oft-quoted, withering reference to her hometown ("There is no there there"), Oakland has a few tricks up its sleeve that make the town worth a visit. Not the least of its attributes is the weather, often mild and sunny while San Francisco is draped in chilly fog.

Leading the list is the **Oakland Museum,** really three museums in one that focus on the history, geography, and culture of California (see page 311). Other things to do in Oakland include sailing a boat on downtown Lake Merritt, taking the kids to **Children's Fairyland** (on the north shore of Lake Merritt), or ogling the restored art deco interior of the **1931 Paramount**

Theater (2025 Broadway (phone (510) 893-2300). Tours of the beautiful theater are offered on the first and third Saturdays of the month (excluding holidays), starting at 10 a.m. and lasting two hours. The cost is $1 a person and no reservations are necessary.

Jack London Square is Oakland's version of Fisherman's Wharf and shamelessly plays up the city's connection with the writer, who grew up along the city's waterfront. The complex of boutiques and eateries is just about as tacky as its cousin across the bay—and about as far from "the call of the wild" as you can get. A better eating option is **Bay Wolf** (3853 Piedmont Avenue; (510) 655-6004), the city's most venerable and revered restaurant.

To reach Oakland's Jack London Square by car, take the Bay Bridge to I-880 to Broadway, turn south, and go to the end. On BART, get off at the 12th Street station and walk south along Broadway about a half-mile (or grab the No. 51a bus to the foot of Broadway). To get to Lake Merritt, cross the Bay Bridge and follow signs to downtown Oakland and exit at Grand Avenue south. To get to the Oakland Museum, take I-580 to I-980 and exit at Jackson Street. Via BART, get off at the Lake Merritt station, a block south of the museum.

Berkeley

Probably more than any other town in the country, Berkeley conjures up images of the rebellious '60s. In this decade students of the University of California, Berkeley led the protests against the Vietnam War. At times, virtual full-scale battles were fought almost daily between protestors and cops, both on campus and in the streets of the surrounding town (most notably in People's Park, off Telegraph Avenue).

These days, things are more sedate in this college town, although admirers and detractors still refer to it as "Berserkley" and the "People's Republic of Berkeley." While student angst is down, the progressive impulse lingers and is best experienced on **Telegraph Avenue,** south of the campus. On the four blocks or so closest to the university, it's a regular street fair filled with vendors selling handmade jewelry, tie-dyed T-shirts, and bumper stickers promoting leftist causes and lifestyles. The sidewalks on both sides of Telegraph Avenue are usually jammed with students, tourists, bearded academics, homeless people, and gray-haired hippies.

Coffeehouses, restaurants, art and crafts boutiques, head shops, and excellent used book and record stores line the street; order a latte and enjoy the endless procession of interesting people who throng the street most afternoons and evenings. A good lunch option on Telegraph Avenue is **Cafe Intermezzo,** a crowded self-serve sandwich, salad, and soup place that serves great oversized sandwiches on homemade bread. Cheap, too. But the selection of restaurants is truly intimidating in Berkeley; every ethnic cuisine in the world, it seems, is represented.

The 31,000-student **University of California** campus is noted for its academic excellence and its 15 Nobel Prize winners. There are several museums on campus worth exploring, including the **Berkeley Art Museum** and, for kids, the **Lawrence Hall of Science** (easiest to reach if you've got a car; the view of San Francisco Bay from the science museum is stupendous). For more information on attractions on the campus, see Zone 12, Attractions, pages 307–310.

To reach Berkeley, about ten miles northeast of San Francisco, take the Bay Bridge, follow I-80 east to the University Avenue exit, and follow the wide street until you hit the campus. Turn right to get to Telegraph Avenue. Parking is notoriously difficult close to the campus, so try to arrive early on weekends and get a space in one of the many private parking lots located just off campus. Another option is BART, which has a Berkeley station two blocks from the campus.

■ **Point Reyes National Seashore** ■

This 85,000-acre park of sandy beach and scrubland is on a geologic "island" located about an hour's drive north of San Francisco. Windswept and ruggedly beautiful, Point Reyes is a wildlife paradise. Shorebirds, seabirds, invertebrates, and marine mammals thrive on this peninsula, which juts into the cold waters of the Pacific just west of the San Andreas fault. Folks who love scenic beauty and wildlife should put this scenic destination on their "A List" of places to go on an excursion from San Francisco.

English explorer Sir Francis Drake is said to have anchored his ship, the Golden Hind, in Drakes Bay, on the southern coast of the wing-shaped peninsula in 1579. There's evidence he careened his ship to make repairs and stayed about five weeks before sailing westward across the Pacific on his round-the-world voyage of discovery. Nearly 200 years passed before settlers arrived. After the U.S. conquest of California, the land was broken into dozens of dairy ranches, and beef and dairy cattle have roamed the brushy flatlands of Point Reyes ever since.

Touring Suggestions

The best place to begin a visit is the **Bear Valley Visitor Center** and its extensive collection of exhibits, specimens, and artifacts. The center is open from 9 a.m. to 5 p.m. on weekdays and 8 a.m. to 5 p.m. on weekends and holidays. You can pick up maps and tide tables and get advice from a ranger on places to hike, picnic, and view wildlife. Ranger-led tours are also offered on a varying schedule, and several hiking trails are accessible from the visitor center. For more information, call (415) 663-1092.

From December through March gray whales make their 10,000-mile migration between the Bering Sea and Baja California, swimming past Point Reyes. The best spot to view the whales is from **Point Reyes Lighthouse,** which has limited parking. Because of the popularity of whale-watching on weekends, the park provides shuttles to the lighthouse from Bear Valley. A better bet is to come early on a weekday to avoid the crowds. Dress warmly—it's usually cold and windy—and bring binoculars and a camera with a telephoto lens.

Nearly 500 tule elk roam Point Reyes (reintroduced following an absence of more than 100 years). The **Tule Elk Preserve** is at the northern tip of the park, and you're apt to spot some elk on a walk down the moderately difficult **Tomales Point Trail.** Other good places to view wildlife include Fivebrooks Pond (waterfowl), the wetlands of Limantour (ducks), and the promontory overlooking Chimney Rock (sea lions, harbor seals, and seabirds).

A Car Tour

Point Reyes is worth a full day or more of exploration. But if your time is limited, you can get a good sampling of what Point Reyes has to offer in about half a day—mostly through the windows of your car. From the visitor center, continue on Bear Valley Road to Sir Francis Drake Boulevard, pass through the village of Inverness and follow signs for the Point Reyes Lighthouse. For a spectacular view of the entire peninsula, turn right on Mount Vision Road, a steep and twisty paved lane that rises to almost 1,300 feet before it dead-ends.

Return to Sir Francis Drake Boulevard and turn left to continue toward the lighthouse. On the right are two beaches ripe for exploration (but not swimming; the waters are cold and dangerous) before you reach the **Lighthouse Visitor Center.** The lighthouse offers a spectacularly scenic view of the ocean and the tip of the peninsula; it's just under a half-mile walk from the parking area, followed by a 300-step descent down the cliff to the lighthouse. The visitor center is open Thursday through Monday from 10 a.m. to 5 p.m. (closed Tuesdays and Wednesdays).

After you visit the lighthouse, backtrack by car to the turn to **Chimney Rock** (a good place to view wildlife) or continue driving to the mainland. To reach the elk reserve, turn left about two miles past Mount Vision Road, and then turn left on Pierce Point Road and drive to **Pierce Point Ranch,** a renovated dairy ranch with a self-guided trail through the historic complex. Then hike down the **Tomales Point Trail,** and you may spot some elk. Wear hiking boots and be prepared for changes in the weather.

Food, Lodging, and Directions

You'll find restaurants, cafés, delicatessens, general stores, and bakeries in the nearby villages of Olema, Point Reyes Station, Inverness, and Marshall; a café is located at Drakes Beach inside the park. Bed-and-breakfasts and inns are also nearby. For more information, call the **West Marin Visitor Bureau** at (415) 669-2684.

To reach Point Reyes from San Francisco, cross the Golden Gate Bridge and stay on US 101 north. Exit at Sir Francis Drake Boulevard and head west; it's about a 20-mile drive (much of it through congested Marin County, although the scenery improves dramatically around Taylor State Park) to Route 1 at Olema. From here it's about a one-minute drive to the Bear Valley Visitor Center. A longer and more scenic route is California Route 1, reached from US 101 in Sausalito.

■ The Wine Country ■

After a few days of touring hectic San Francisco, what could be better than relaxing in a setting of pastoral splendor only an hour from Union Square? The wine country is a region of wooded hills and luxuriant valleys where tilled fields create geometric patterns across the landscape and narrow lanes wind among the hills. Quaint country inns and designer restaurants with massive wine lists are abundant and pamper the well-heeled visitors who flock to these valleys, defined by low oak- and chaparral-covered ridges.

For most folks, the visual grandeur is secondary to the lure of the fruit of the land. The wines produced in the Napa and Sonoma Valleys rival the best vintages of France—and everybody wants to see where the magic is being made. Wineries are everywhere in the two neighboring valleys, located north of San Francisco and inland of the Pacific Coast. They are so numerous that it's easy think this is the wine-making capital of California. In fact, only about 5% of the state's total production comes from the region. But far and away the best wines produced in the country come from here. The reason is the region's Mediterranean climate: Hot, dry summers and cool, wet winters result in stressed-out grapevines that produce small, thick-skinned fruit. Because most of a wine's flavor and character comes from the skin, not the pulp, the grapes that grow in these valleys result in premium vintages that impress wine snobs around the world.

Wine has been made in the valleys since the 18th century, when clerics in Spanish missions planted vineyards to produce black grapes for sacramental wines. After a series of ups and downs over the centuries, the wine business began booming in the 1960s. Wine has evolved into an increasingly pop-

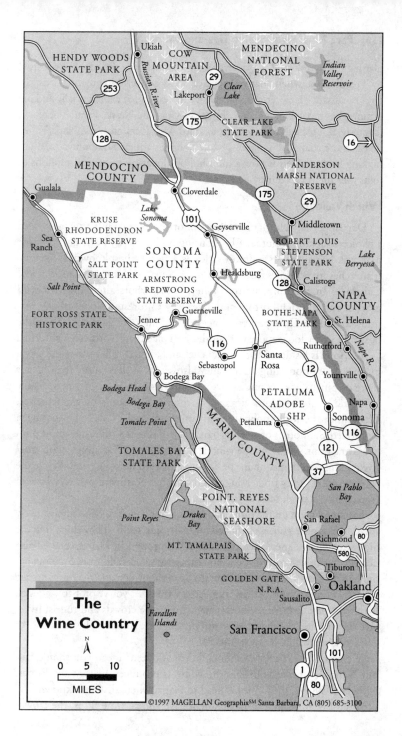

The Wine Country

N

0   5   10
MILES

©1997 MAGELLAN Geographix℠ Santa Barbara, CA (805) 685-3100

ular national drink, and the valleys have recovered from the last slump caused by Prohibition, when many vineyards were converted into orchards. Today's renaissance is extraordinary; acreage has expanded exponentially and big business has moved in, most notably Coca-Cola and Nestle. Even the French, formerly aloof, have formed partnerships with local growers. Napa Valley boasts more than 250 wineries, while Sonoma Valley has about 35. Wine-making in the valleys is now a multibillion-dollar business, and millions of folks tour the wine country each year.

Which Valley?

Daytrippers on a self-guided day tour of the wine country are faced with a choice: Napa or Sonoma? Alas, touring both valleys in one day just isn't practical. Napa, the easternmost valley, is by far the best known of the two. It stretches for 35 miles from the town of Napa north to the resort town of Calistoga. In the long, narrow valley, grape arbors alternate with wild grasses, and the rich bottomland gives way to forested slopes of the surrounding ridges. Once past the congested and unexciting town of Napa, the beautiful valley looks more like southern France than Northern California.

Yet Napa is fashionable beyond belief and attracts millionaires the way a magnet draws iron filings. The valley also seems to draw more than its fair share of pinch-faced connoisseurs who mutter in mangled French as they swirl and sniff premium vintages in the tasting rooms of the wineries. Thankfully, the wine snobs are vastly outnumbered. Napa Valley has been discovered and hordes of tourists have made it one of California's most popular attractions. Many of the wineries along Route 29 are huge, with massive parking lots that contain special areas reserved for tour buses. While the countryside is pretty (increasingly so the farther north you go), very little in Napa Valley is small scale or intimate.

Sonoma Valley, on the other hand, has fewer wineries. Most are relatively small, still family-run, and tucked away on side roads. They don't line the highway like designer discount outlets (also found in Napa). There's also notably less pretension in the wine-tasting rooms. In addition, Sonoma has more to offer than wineries, including a Spanish mission and the former estate of Jack London, one of America's greatest writers. As you've probably guessed by now, *Unofficial Guide* researchers, who loathe crowds and tourist hype, give the edge to Sonoma over its eastern neighbor. Another plus: it's closer to San Francisco (though not by much).

We prefer less-touristy Sonoma, but that doesn't mean you should rule out Napa. If one of your favorite wines is produced by, say, the Robert Mondavi Winery, by all means head to Napa, where that well-known firm provides free tours and tastings. You'll have a great time. Plus, the crowds and oversized wineries decrease the farther north you go in Napa. Calistoga, at the top of the valley, offers a lot for visitors to see and do. Another solution to the "which valley?" conundrum is make your visit an overnight affair and tour both valleys. We suggest a two-day tour on pages 244–245.

Touring Strategies

Visiting the wine country shouldn't be about following a strict itinerary and seeing how much you can do in one day of hectic touring. It's quite the opposite, a joie-de-vivre kind of thing: a celebration of the good things in life, such as wonderful scenery, great food, and good friends. These are all complimented by fine wine—thus the popularity of touring the wine country.

A rigid schedule is anathema to visiting Napa or Sonoma, but a little judicious planning can go a long way to ensuring that a visit is pleasant, even memorable. Whether you decide to visit Napa, Sonoma, or both valleys, we'll provide you with specific advice that will allow you to get the most enjoyment from a one- or two-day excursion.

Planning

Although several tour companies in San Francisco provide bus tours to the wine country, we think the best way to enjoy a visit is to rent a car, which gives you the flexibility to ensure a relaxing, fun-filled trip. If at all possible, don't go on a weekend; the best time to visit is early in the week. Plan on leaving San Francisco around 9 a.m to get past the worst of morning rush-hour traffic and into the wine country by midmorning. Be sure to eat a good breakfast before leaving; you'll appreciate it later in the morning when you've sampled your first glass or two of wine.

You'll get more from a wine-country excursion if you can give it some focus. For example, plan on visiting one or two wineries that produce wines you enjoy at home. Or structure your day around a bike ride or something else not wine-related (we provide suggestions below). Then leave some time for a spontaneous stop at one or two other wineries, a picnic in a park, a museum visit, or shopping in one of the many towns.

Don't plan on visiting more than two or three wineries in a day. Otherwise the day becomes a blur of wine-tasting rooms that run together in your memory and your palate—not to mention the problem of too much alcohol consumption. One advantage of a two-day wine-country tour is that you can trade off driving; that way, there's always someone who can taste the wine and someone who can safely navigate the car.

Many folks pack a picnic lunch, visit a winery, buy a bottle of wine, and enjoy an outdoor meal in a picnic area provided at many wineries. (Most of the picnic areas are in fabulously beautiful settings surrounded by forests and vineyards.) You can buy sandwiches or fixings at delicatessens and groceries; don't forget to bring a corkscrew. Keep in mind that the whole point of visiting the wine country is to relax and have a good time.

Winery Tours

With something like 300 wineries in and around the Napa and Sonoma Valleys, picking a few to visit can be tough. You can just wander around and stop in wineries on a whim, but we think it pays to be selective. Visit a winery that makes a wine you like or, if you need some help, consult the list of wineries below.

Virtually all of the wineries are open to the public from about 10 a.m. to 4 p.m. daily (and an hour to two later in the summer). Most only have tasting rooms and maybe a picnic area outside. While many firms offer free wine tastings, increasingly some wineries (especially in Napa) are charging a few dollars for the opportunity to sample the fruits of their vineyards.

Larger winemaking concerns, for example Mondavi in Napa and Sebastiani in Sonoma, offer free guided tours of the premises. Visitors tour in groups of about 30; the tours last a half-hour or so, ending with a visit to a tasting room. These are usually large, comfortable, and well-appointed rooms where visitors sample the wares; they can also purchase wine here or in a nearby sales room. Smaller wineries, by and large, require reservations at least a day in advance (even earlier in the summer and fall) for a tour with a smaller group that may last two hours.

So Which Tour Is Right for You?

Nonreservation Tours   If your interest in wine is casual, a nonreservation tour at one of the larger wineries should do the trick. You'll gain insight into the wine country's unusual climate, which is the main reason the area produces such good wine. You'll also get a glimpse of the winemaking process, from the huge stainless-steel vats where the grapes are fermented to the large warehouses where the new wine is stored as it ages in oak barrels. Tour guides provide a good overview of the fascinating and complex operation of a winery; tours usually depart on the hour or half-hour throughout the day. The icing on the cake, of course, is the end of the tour, when you arrive in the tasting room and sample different wines made on the premises; often you can help yourself to hors d'oeuvres as you sample different vintages.

Reservation-Only Tours   Reservation-only guided tours, also free, are longer and best appreciated by wine-savvy folks who know the basics of winemaking and want to learn more. And they will as they're led around the winery by their tour guide, often an employee who really knows and appreciates good wine. On many tours, visitors spend a lot of time in the aging rooms, which are stacked to the ceiling with oak barrels. The guide may not only discuss, say, how American versus French oak barrels affect the tannin content in red wines; he or she will also tap barrels at various stages of aging and let you taste the difference. With the exception of the actual quaffing of the grape, this can be either utterly fascinating or excruciatingly boring, depending on your level of interest.

On a reservation-only tour, you'll also get from-the-hip insights into the winemaking business (such as how much of the winery's grape production comes from leased vineyards—and why). You may also pick up some valuable tips, such as which vintages are best for particular wines. (Here's one: 1995 gets rave reviews for virtually all wines produced in the wine country; warm winds from the Central Valley swept through just before the harvest, making the grapes smaller and thickening their skins.)

Wine Tasting

The ancient Greeks had it wrong. The nectar of the gods isn't sweet ambrosia, it's wine. Yet deciding which wine is the best can be like trying to determine the one true religion. That's okay. A trip to the wine country can be the start of a lifetime enjoyment of the fermented grape as you begin an education on how to savor this mysterious beverage.

Keep in mind that there are two types of California wines: varietals, made primarily from a particular kind of grape, such as cabernet sauvignon or zinfandel, and the lower-quality generics, wines blended from several different grapes and often named for a European wine region such as Burgundy.

To learn more about wines, you need to taste them. Unfortunately, folks who are unversed in the liturgy of wine tasting can feel awfully uncomfortable as a nearby wine snob swirls and sniffs a glass of wine. Don't be intimidated. You're on vacation. Why let a self-styled connoisseur ruin your fun?

Here are some things that will provide the start to the education of your palate. First, the look or appearance is important. Wine should be clear and brilliant, not cloudy. Consider the smell, or "nose" of the vintage, which includes the aroma or scent of the grapes themselves, and the "bouquet," the smell from fermentation and aging. Finally, consider the taste. Let the wine wash around your mouth for a moment and determine if it's sweet or dry, light-bodied (watery) or full-bodied (like milk), rough or mellow. But mainly, enjoy. Chat it up with the winery employees behind the counter and you'll gain more insight (and maybe they'll pour some reserve vintages for your tasting enjoyment).

When to Go

The best time to visit the wine country is in the fall, when the harvest occurs and the air is redolent with the aroma of fermenting wine. Depending on the weather, this can be anytime in September or October. Street fairs and festivals are the norm, and it's the season of golf tournaments, wine auctions, and art and food fairs. The countryside is beautiful, with trees turning brilliant gold and red. And the weather usually cooperates, too. It can get hot, and there's not much chance of rain.

Yet there are drawbacks to visiting at harvest time: traffic clogging the major roads in both valleys and a decrease in attention from winery employees, who are justifiably consumed with getting the grapes in. If you do plan to visit the wine country in the fall, try to go during the week, not on weekends, to avoid the worst of the tourist crush. It's also a good idea to make lodging and dinner reservations weeks in advance.

Spring and summer are also prime times for visiting the wine country. And it shows—Route 29 in Napa Valley is often backed up on weekends. (You'll encounter a bit less traffic in Sonoma on spring and summer weekends.) Summer in the wine country is notoriously hot and dry, so be sure to pack a sun hat and try to get an early start. Winter, the rainy season, is a good time to visit; although the landscape isn't as colorful, there's a stark beauty to the valleys and mountains and a more laid-back atmosphere in the wineries. And the crowds are minimal.

Purchasing Wine at a Winery

Question: Can you get great deals on wine sold at wineries? The answer, by and large, is no. The sales rooms in the wineries aren't there to compete with retail liquor outlets in your hometown. As a result, the prices are pretty much what you would pay at home, give or take a couple of bucks a bottle. Of course, the selection is usually a lot better, and you'll also find special vintages only available at the winery. So while the sales rooms do a brisk business, nobody is getting great bargains.

Wine is also sold by the case at the wineries. Depending on the state you live in, you can have your purchase shipped home (you pay the shipping cost). States that allow shipments from the wineries are California, Colorado, Idaho, Illinois, Iowa, Minnesota, Missouri, Nebraska, New Mexico, Oregon, Washington, West Virginia, and Wisconsin. If you don't live in one of these states, you're not completely out of luck. Make your purchase and ship it home yourself (tax laws limit shipments by wineries to the states listed above). The cost is about $40 a case, and the folks at the winery can suggest where to take your purchase and have it shipped.

Getting There

The wine country spreads north from the top of San Francisco Bay in two parallel valleys, Napa and Sonoma; in between are the oak-covered Mayacamas Mountains. To get there by car, cross the Golden Gate Bridge on US 101 to Route 37 east. Then bear left onto Route 121; next, turn left onto Route 12 for Sonoma Valley or drive a few miles more and turn left onto Route 29, Napa Valley's main drag. In nonrush-hour traffic, it's about an hour's drive from downtown San Francisco to the southern entrances of the valleys.

■ **Napa Valley** ■

The heart of America's wine culture is found in Napa Valley, a region with roots going back to the mid-19th century. The valley is defined by two rough-hewn mountain ranges, and vestiges of its tumultuous geologic past still bubble to the surface of the earth at hot springs in Calistoga and at (the other) Old Faithful Geyser.

Compared to the natural features, the wineries in Napa Valley are recent interlopers. Virtually the entire California wine industry was killed by Prohibition; only a few wineries survived. This means most of the players in the valley today are relative newcomers—a diverse collection of wealthy doctors, lawyers, actors, filmmakers, artists, and business executives all motivated to outdo their neighbors in creating memorable vintages. The joke used to be that they were all going broke creating wine—and loving it. Today, not all of them are going broke.

Napa Valley is anchored in the south by the town of the same name, and visitors on a one-day outing should pass it by. Continue up Route 29 toward the villages of Yountville, Oakville, and Rutherford, where things start to get more interesting (and scenic). St. Helena, the next town, is considered the heart of Napa's wine-growing region, while Calistoga, a resort town for more than 100 years, is its northern anchor.

You can make a drive in the valley more interesting by heading south from Calistoga on the more scenic Silverado Trail, which creates a circuit instead of an out-and-back excursion. While not nearly as commercial, this pleasant, two-lane highway passes plenty of wineries. The crossroads between the two parallel roads are also scenic and worth exploring.

Dining in Napa is part of the whole experience. Some of the best chefs in the country now cook in this bucolic yet food-savvy region. It's a place where serious eaters spend serious bucks on serious meals. There's a wealth of fine restaurants that will satisfy dedicated diners. Making dinner reservations two or three weeks in advance of your visit is a good idea, especially in the summer and fall. Top-rated dining establishments in Napa include

Auberge du Soleil (in Rutherford; (707) 963-1211), **Domaine Chandon** (in Yountville; (707) 944-2892), **The French Laundry** (in Yountville; (707) 944-2380), **Tra Vigne** (in St. Helena; (707) 963-4444), and **Trilogy Restaurant & Bar** (in St. Helena; (707) 963-5507).

Lunches, on the other hand, can be more spontaneous. Most visitors stop at wineries between meals. Some wineries, for example Niebaum-Coppola (owned by Francis Ford Coppola of *The Godfather* fame), promote reserve tastings of their better wines. If the tasting-room staff doesn't mention anything about reserve wines, just ask. Usually the staff will pour the better stuff (and you'll pay a bit more).

Napa Valley, however, is about more than eating and drinking. The scenery is stunning, with a big blue sky from May through October (the dry season), gnarled oak trees, babbling brooks, and chaparral-covered mountain ridges. It's all enjoyable through the window of a car, on a bike, or on a stroll. Other diversions include a petrified forest, a mud bath in Calistoga, and shopping in trendy St. Helena.

Wineries

With something like 250 wineries in Napa Valley (most of which are open to the public), it's just not possible to provide a comprehensive listing. Plus, part of the fun is touring on your own without a rigid itinerary and making your own discoveries. First-time visitors will have no trouble finding wineries; both of the valley's two major routes (Route 29 and, to the east, the Silverado Trail) pass dozens of estates. To get you on your way, here's a sampling of Napa wineries well worth a visit.

Robert Mondavi Winery, on Route 29 in Oakville, is ground zero for the Napa wine industry. The winery was founded in 1966, when there were only about six wineries in the valley with national distribution. Today Mondavi offers one of the best tours in the valley, and its Spanish mission–style architecture is a knockout. A retail area sells wines, T-shirts, and books, and there is a tasting room where reserve wine is sold by the glass. Tours are offered on the hour, and it's a good idea to make reservations. Call (800) MONDAVI.

Up the road in Rutherford is the **Niebaum-Coppola Estate,** a huge operation with a fountain-enhanced plaza and a small museum highlighting the career of its owner, film director Francis Ford Coppola. The entire place is unmatched for sheer panache. The museum is free and fun; on display are old movie projectors, film props from *The Godfather* movies, a real Tucker automobile (from *Tucker: A Man and His Dream*). Of course, you'll also find a tasting room and a retail sales room. Winery tours are by appointment only; call (707) 967-3495.

Frog's Leap, also in Rutherford, was once a deserted "ghost winery." But today it sits beside 40 acres of organically grown Merlot and Sauvignon Blanc vines. Originally built in 1884, the winery features a big, red, wooden barn with period photos dotting the interior. Winery tours are by reservation only; call (800) 959-4704.

At the top of the valley in Calistoga, **Sterling Vineyards** was built with tourists in mind. An aerial tram leads to the a white cluster of Mediterranean monastic stucco buildings that rise from a bluff south of town. The 300-foot knoll features a visitor center, tasting room, self-guided winery tour, gift shop, and retail room.

Silverado Vineyards, on the Silverado Trail in Napa, has spectacular views across the valley and excellent wines. Owned by the family of the late Walt Disney, the winery has a stunning setting and an interior display of original art by American naturalist painters John James Audubon and Thomas Hill. Winery tours are by appointment only; call (707) 257-1770.

Attractions

Other things to do and see in Napa include **Bale Grist Mill State Historic Park** (north of St. Helena on Route 29), a flour mill operation that predates California statehood. Built in 1846 and restored to operating condition, the mill features a 36-foot wooden waterwheel and large millstones. On weekends, a miller grinds grain and visitors can see baking demonstrations. You can also purchase flour from the mill. For more information, call (707) 942-4575.

California's **Old Faithful Geyser,** outside of Calistoga (not to be confused with a similar geothermal phenomena at Yellowstone National Park in Wyoming), offers a spectacular show by nature as 350° water shoots 60 feet in the air for three or four minutes. The cycle repeats about every 17 to 40 minutes, and kids love it. The setting is breathtakingly scenic, with Mount Saint Helena and the craggy Palisades Mountains in the background. The cost is a pricey $6 a person, and no, you can't see this natural performance from the parking lot—tall bamboo blocks the view. For more information, call (707) 942-6463.

The **Petrified Forest,** west of Calistoga, offers a pleasant walk in the woods past 3.5-million-year-old fallen giants—fossilized redwoods, some of them eight feet in diameter. Alas, they're not upright and some of the specimens were buried and now lie in pits. It's a pleasant and scenic place to walk off that second (or third, or fourth) glass of wine. Admission is $4 a person. For more information, call (707) 942-6667.

In St. Helena there's more to do than shop. The **Silverado Museum** is dedicated to the life and works of Robert Louis Stevenson, author of classic works of literature such as *Treasure Island* and *Dr. Jekyll and Mr. Hyde.* The Scottish writer lived in the area in 1880 with his bride and regained his health in the mountain air and sunshine. The two-room museum includes memorabilia, manuscripts, childhood letters, paintings, and the desk used by the writer. Located near the public library in St. Helena (from Route 29, go east on Adams Street to Library Lane), the museum is open from noon to 4 p.m. every day except Monday and holidays; admission is free. Call (707) 963-3757 for more information.

Revisit the early days of Calistoga and Napa Valley at **The Sharpsteen Museum** in Calistoga. Built by a retired Walt Disney animator, the large, one-room museum highlights the resort's history with dioramas, old photographs, doll houses, recreations of Victorian interiors, gold-panning displays, and a horse carriage. It's an eclectic mix of historical items that's worth a peek. Admission is free; the museum is open daily (except Christmas and Thanksgiving) from 10 a.m. to 4 p.m. April through October, and from noon to 4 p.m. November through March. For more information, call (707) 942-5911.

Outdoor Fun

Napa Valley is famous for bicycling, with gentle hills, wide shoulders on the main roads, low traffic on the side roads, and great scenery. **St. Helena Cyclery** rents bikes, and the town is a good, centrally located starting point to enjoy a ride. The hourly rate is $7 for high-quality hybrid (city) bikes; included are a lock, water bottle, rear rack, and bag to carry your picnic supplies. The daily rate is $25. The shop, at 1156 Main Street in St. Helena, also provides maps and tour information. No reservations are accepted; the shop is open daily. Call (707) 963-7736 for more information.

Horseback riding in Napa Valley is scenic and fun. **Napa Valley Trail Rides** provides horses and guides at Bothe-Napa Valley State Park outside Calistoga. Rates start at $40 for a 90-minute ride; sunset and full-moon rides are also available. Reservations are required; call (707) 996-8566.

Napa's dry, southerly breezes create optimal conditions for all kinds of aerial sports. **Balloons Above the Valley,** at 5091 Solano Avenue in Napa, launches hot-air balloons with 8 to 16 passengers. Liftoff is around 6 a.m., when the cool morning air is best for ballooning (making a stay in the valley the night before almost mandatory). The flight lasts about an hour and ends with a champagne breakfast. Daily flights (weather permitting) cost $165 a person; reservations are required. Call (800) 464-6824.

Napa Valley Balloons offers daily flights; passengers meet at Washington Square in Yountville. Meeting times vary from 5:45 a.m. in summer to 7:15 a.m. in winter. Reservations are required for the flights, which last about an hour and cost $175 a person. For more information, call (800) 253-2224.

More adventurous types will want to try **Calistoga Gliders,** at 1546 Lincoln Avenue in Calistoga. In one- or two-passenger flights piloted by FAA-licensed pilots, passengers soundlessly swoop and soar past the valley's cliffs and crevices. Twenty-minute flights cost $79 for one passenger and $129 for two; a half-hour flight is $119 for one and $179 for two. For more information and reservations, call (707) 942-5000.

Shopping

Napa Premium Outlets in Napa features 50 stores specializing in discounted designer fashions and name-brand merchandise, ranging from Brooks Brothers to Tommy Hilfiger. To reach the outlet mall, take Route 29 to the First Street exit. St. Helena, generally recognized as Napa Valley's main hub, is also a mecca for shoppers. Main Street, noted for its arching sycamore trees, is lined with upscale gift shops, boutiques, clothing stores, jewelers, and wine shops.

Outside of town, **Hurd's Beeswax Candles** elevates candlemaking to an art, with candles fashioned in a myriad of shapes. At **St. Helena Premium Outlets** two miles north of town on Route 29, bargain hunters can shop till they drop at ten factory outlet and specialty stores.

In Calistoga, general-interest shops mix with more specialized retailers, including antique stores, clothing shops, and a bookstore. The historic **Calistoga Depot,** a former railway station, has been converted into a mall; the **Calistoga Wine Stop** is housed in an antique railroad car.

Health Spas

For folks who prefer their entertainment closer to the ground, Calistoga is home to about a dozen health spas featuring hot mineral springs, heated pools, mud baths, steam baths, and massages. At **Calistoga Spa Hot Springs,** guests can steep in four different mineral pools (starting at $10) or indulge in a volcanic-ash mud bath with steam rinse ($42). The spa, at 1006 Washington Street, also has 57 rooms, ranging from $85 to $130 a night. For more information, call (707) 942-6269.

Dr. Wilkinson's Hot Springs Resort, at 1507 Lincoln Avenue in Calistoga, offers a full range of soothing, invigorating treatments, including mud baths, mineral whirlpool baths, blanket wraps, therapeutic massage, facials, acupressure face-lifts, and salt glow scrubs. The Works, a two-hour spa treatment, is $85; facials start at $40. The resort is open daily, and appointments are recommended; call (707) 942-4102 for more information.

Napa Valley Wine Train

Enjoy a relaxing gourmet dining excursion on one of several restored 1915 Pullman railroad cars that run between Napa and St. Helena year-round. The **Napa Valley Wine Train** offers a three-hour, 36-mile excursion through Napa Valley. You won't stop at any wineries—in fact, you don't stop at all—but you can enjoy classic European cuisine with California overtones prepared on board. There are two seatings for lunch and dinner; passengers spend half the trip in a dining car and half in a lounge car.

Brunch ($56.50 a person) includes a glass of champagne and a choice of five entrees; lunch ($63 to $75 a person) offers four entree selections; dinner ($69.50 to $82.50 a person) offers three. Train fare and tips are included; a trip without a meal in the Deli Car, where there's an à la carte menu, costs $25. Wine, liquor, and cocktails are extra. Reservations are required; call (800) 427-4124 or (707) 253-2111.

Visitor Information

You can get more information on wineries, accommodation, dining, and attractions by contacting the **Napa Valley Conference and Visitors Bureau,** 1310 Napa Town Center, Napa, CA 94559; (707) 226-7459. Other visitor contacts in Napa Valley include the **Calistoga Chamber of Commerce** at (707) 942-6333 and the **St. Helena Chamber of Commerce** at (800) 799-6456 or (707) 963-4456.

For help finding a room, especially in the harvest season when this can be challenging, try these two free reservation services: **Napa Valley Reservations Unlimited** (phone (800) 251-6272) and **Wine Country Concierge** (phone (888) 946-3289 or (707) 252-4472). Both keep a list of available rooms at bed-and-breakfasts and other lodging. A word of advice: If your visit to Napa Valley is in the spring, summer, or fall, remember that traffic along Route 29 is relentless. Make it a point to request sleeping quarters that face the vineyards, not the highway.

▪ Sonoma Valley ▪

While Napa Valley is upscale and elegant, its next-door neighbor, Sonoma Valley, is overalls and corduroy. Instead of the sporting the eye-catching architecture in the wineries of Napa, the wineries here tend to be understated converted barns. Smaller producers whose families have grown grapes for generations still make wine in rustic buildings that are often beautiful in their simplicity. Here, family-run wineries are more apt to treat visitors like friends, and tastings are usually free.

Sonoma Valley is home to Northern California's earliest winemaking, with stunning old vineyards planted on rolling hills. The Spanish-era town of Sonoma is the cultural hub for Sonoma Valley, one of four major wine regions found in Sonoma County (the others are Alexander Valley, Russian

River Valley, and Dry Creek Valley). A charming, eight-acre plaza green in Sonoma built by General Mariano Guadalupe Vallejo in 1834 is a rural oasis surrounded by the area's best shops and restaurants.

Crescent-shaped Sonoma Valley curves between oak-covered mountain ranges and, most folks say, beats its neighbor hands-down on looks. (The scenery attracted writer Jack London, who owned a ranch in Glen Ellen; now it's a state park.) The valley presents a crisscross pattern of vineyards; unlike the nearly endless procession of megawineries lining the highway at Napa, most wineries are tucked away on winding back roads.

Wineries

About a half-dozen wineries are located a mile east of Sonoma Plaza, down East Napa Street. You could combine a visit to a few of these wineries with a tour of the Sonoma Mission, lunch on the plaza, and a side trip to an attraction outside of town. The result would be a day with a minimum amount of driving and maximum time for fun.

Wineries outside town are often located on small back roads, so get a map from the tourist office on the plaza; also, keep your eyes peeled for signposts leading to the vineyards (otherwise it's easy to miss a turn). If you get tired of running around, visit the **Wine Exchange of Sonoma,** a tasting bar open daily; you can sample wines and beers from Sonoma and the rest of California. To get you started, here's a short selection of wineries worth a visit.

For sheer convenience, **Sebastiani Winery** can't be beat. Free shuttle buses whisk visitors from Sonoma Plaza to the stone winery about a mile away. Professional guides lead tours throughout the day, and visitors learn about winemaking, see a large collection of hand-carved casks, and view a display of antique winemaking equipment.

Not as convenient to reach but a must-see is **Buena Vista Winery,** east of Sonoma. Set among towering trees and fountains, this is the birthplace of Sonoma Valley winemaking; founded in 1857, it's California's oldest premium winery. It's also drop-dead gorgeous, with huge stone buildings, a mezzanine art gallery, and historical exhibits. History tours are given at 2 p.m. daily; there's also a beautiful terraced picnic area. For more information, call (800) 926-1266.

Almost as beautiful is **Bartholomew Park Winery,** not far from Buena Vista. Surrounded by vineyards, the winery features an attractive museum that highlights winemaking, the history of the area, and the winery's previous owners. In addition, there are hiking trails, a picnic area, and a "wine garden" (a picnic area with a pavilion).

Ravenswood Winery, also east of Sonoma, is a small winery in a gorgeous hillside setting. Best known for its hearty zinfandels and it's anti-wine-snob attitude, the winery offers reservation-only tours led by knowledgeable and enthusiastic employees. To make a reservation for a winery tour (offered daily at 10:30 a.m.), call (707) 938-1960.

Head up Route 12 a few miles to reach the **Benziger Family Winery** in Glen Ellen. The winery specializes in premium estate and Sonoma County wines; they're also well known for their labels, designed by famous artists. Guided and self-guided tours are offered, and there's a picnic area where you can have lunch. For more information, call (707) 935-4046.

On Friday, Saturday, and Sunday you can enjoy a tour of caves at **Kunde Estate Winery** in Kenwood, north of Glen Ellen. A new winery and visitor center is located at the foot of a stunning mountain of grapes. The family owns 2,000 acres, with 750 acres under vine. Rustic grounds at Kenwood Vineyards complement the attractive tasting room and the winery's artistic bottle labels. Tours are by appointment only; call (707) 833-5891.

Attractions

The town of Sonoma is the site of the last and the northernmost of the 21 missions established by Spain and Mexico, called El Camino Real ("the king's highway"). Popularly called **Sonoma Mission,** El Camino Real was founded in 1823 and features a stark white facade and, inside, a small museum. Across the street is the **Sonoma Barracks,** built with Indian labor in the 1830s to house Mexican troops. It's a two-story adobe structure with sweeping balconies and a museum dedicated to California history.

Next door, the **Toscano Hotel** is furnished as it was in the 19th century, with wood-burning stoves, brocade armchairs, and gambling tables. These and other antique buildings around Sonoma Plaza are part of **Sonoma State Historic Park**; the $2 admission fee gets you into all the historic buildings. In the oak-studded plaza across the street is a monument to the Bear Flag Revolt, located on the spot where California was declared an independent republic in 1846 (and remained so for 25 days).

Traintown, a mile south of Sonoma Plaza, offers a 20-minute steam or diesel train ride through ten acres of landscaped park; it's nirvana for children. There's also a petting zoo, an antique carousel, and cabooses. Train fare is $2.50 for youngsters and $3.50 for adults; open daily June through September, and Friday through Sunday the rest of the year. For more information, call (707) 938-3912.

If Napa Valley is Robert Louis Stevenson country, then Sonoma belongs to Jack London. A world adventurer and the most famous American writer of his time (he died in 1916 at age 40), London bought a 1,400-acre ranch a few miles northwest of Glen Ellen; today it's **Jack London State Historic Park.** Attractions include a museum with memorabilia, a reconstruction of London's office, and exhibits on the fascinating life of the author of *The Call of the Wild.* There's also a continuously running video of a film made about the writer just days before his death; silent, grainy, and shaky, the short home movie is haunting.

Almost as spooky are the ruins of London's mansion, **Wolf House,** which mysteriously burned to the ground in 1913 before the author could move in. It's a half-mile stroll through gorgeous woods to the stone ruins; you can also detour to visit the writer's simple grave. For fans of American literature, the park is a real find. Admission is $5 a car. For more information, call (707) 938-5216.

Outdoor Fun

Sonoma Valley is 7 miles wide and 17 miles long, and with its rolling hills, 13,000 acres of vineyards, and forested mountains on either side, the valley offers much to do outdoors. **Goodtime Bicycle Company,** at 18503 Sonoma Highway in Sonoma, rents bikes for exploring the valley's miles of paved, low-traffic back roads. Rentals are $5 an hour and $25 a day, including a helmet, lock, cable, maps, and road service and repair during regular business hours. The shop also offers lunch rides, including food, for $55 a person. For more information, call toll-free (888) 525-0453.

The **Sonoma Cattle Company** offers organized horse rides at Jack London State Historic Park and Sugarloaf Ridge State Park. The guided tours range from general 90-minute and two-hour rides to a western barbecue ride, a sunset ride, a full-moon ride, and a gourmet boxed-lunch ride and winery tour. Reservations are required, and rates start at $40 per person for a 90-minute ride. For more information, call (707) 996-8566.

See Sonoma Valley from a hot-air balloon. **Air Flambuoyant,** based in Santa Rosa, has offered lighter-than-air excursions since 1974. The trips last about an hour, and groups of two or more can be accommodated. The cost is $175 a person and includes a gourmet champagne breakfast (balloon rides typically start at 6 a.m. in the summer). For reservations and more information, call (800) 456-4711 or (707) 838-8500.

Combine a scenic view from the air, the nostalgia of a bygone era, and the excitement of a roller coaster at **Aeroschellville Biplane and Glider Rides.** The firm offers a variety of rides in its fleet of 1940 Boeing Stearman biplanes and a North American–built, World War II Navy, SNJ-4 pilot trainer. All pilots are certified by the FAA. Twenty-minute, one-passenger rides are $70; two-passenger rides are $110. Aerobatic rides lasting 20 minutes are $80 for one passenger and $130 for two. War-plane rides start at $135 and glider rides begin at $80. For more information, call (707) 938-2444.

Shopping

The central plaza in the old Spanish town of Sonoma is where you'll find the best shops, including gourmet stores, boutiques, a designer lingerie shop, antique stores, poster galleries, and a brass shop. The **Sonoma Cheese Factory** on the square is the place to go for picnic supplies, a bottle of wine, or sandwiches for that winery picnic; you can also eat on the premises and watch cheese being made. The **Mercado,** a small shopping center just east of the plaza, houses several stores with unusual items. **Baksheesh** (14 West Spain Street) features handmade gifts crafted by third-world artisans. **Milagros** (414 First Street East) sells Mexican folk art, home furnishings, masks, and wood carvings.

Seven miles north of Sonoma off Route 12 in Glen Ellen is **Jack London Village,** located on the banks of Sonoma Creek. It's a collection of shops, art studios, craft shops, cafés, a wine shop, and a music shop in a bucolic setting. There's also the **Glen Ellen Winery** and, across the street, the **Jack London Bookstore,** an important resource center for the writer's fans.

Dining

As it is throughout the wine country, dining is serous business in Sonoma Valley. Dinner reservations should be made at least two weeks in advance in summer and fall. Probably the best restaurant around is **Babette's Restaurant and Wine Bar,** just off the plaza in Sonoma (phone (707) 939-8921). Other top-rated dining establishments include **Della Santina's** (133 East Napa Street in Sonoma; (707) 935-0576), **Kenwood Restaurant and Bar** (9900 Highway 12 in Kenwood; (707) 833-6326), **Mixx** (135 Fourth Street in Santa Rosa; (707) 573-1344), and **Willowside Cafe** (3535 Guerneville Road in Santa Rosa; (707) 523-4814).

Visitor Information

For more information on wineries, attractions, restaurants, and lodging in Sonoma Valley, call the **Sonoma Valley Visitors Center** at (707) 996-1090; ask for a free visitors' guide. You can also stop at the small visitor center located on the north side of the plaza near the Sonoma Barracks and pick up maps and brochures of the area. For help locating a room, especially in the busy summer and fall, contact **Wine Country Concierge** (phone (888) 946-3289 or (707) 252-4472), which has a list of available rooms at bed-and-breakfasts and other lodging.

■ A Two-Day Excursion in the Wine Country ■

With so much to do and see in the Napa and Sonoma Valleys—and because of their different characters—we think the ideal way for visitors to tour the wine country is to spend a night. That way you can visit both gorgeous locales, share the driving (you'll need a car), split wine-imbibing chores with a friend, and have a more relaxed trip. Here's our recommendation for an overnight trip to the wine country for first-time visitors.

If you've got a room in San Francisco and you're heading to the wine country before the end of your vacation, don't check out; the hassle of repeatedly packing and unpacking is too time consuming. (That is, unless you've scheduled your getaway at the end of your vacation and your night in the wine country is the last night.) Reserve a room at a hot-springs resort in Calistoga at the north end of the valley, grab your toothbrush and a change of underwear, and get out of town. Admittedly this is not cheap, but it's definitely hedonistic—and totally in character with this vacation within a vacation.

Here's the plan. After touring Napa Valley, head to Calistoga, where your room at one of the hot-springs resorts awaits you—say, Dr. Wilkinson's Hot Springs or Calistoga Spa Hot Springs (see above, Napa Valley, for phone numbers). Rooms range from basic motel-style and cheap (think Janet Leigh in *Psycho*) to Victorian and expensive. Then—here's the really decadent part—take a mud bath in a composition of local volcanic ash, imported peat, and naturally boiling mineral hot-springs water. Folks have been coming to Calistoga for about 150 years to experience this; now it's your turn. Your naked body will simmer at a temperature of about 104°. It's about a 90-minute experience, and your body will love you for it. A full treatment costs about $85.

The next day, drive to Sonoma Valley. Get there by either heading south through Napa Valley on the Silverado Trail to Route 121 and west to Route 12, or by taking a back road. If you go the back-road route, you can spend the second day of your wine-country visit driving south through the valley. When you get to the southern end of Sonoma Valley at the end of the day, you're less than an hour from San Francisco.

▪ South of San Francisco ▪

Coastal Highway 1 is a spectacularly scenic road that stretches south of San Francisco to Carmel, winding past cliffs and coves, pocket beaches, lighthouses, state parks, and old historic towns and villages. While that's too far for a day trip by car, visitors to San Francisco can still enjoy driving along the coast for about 75 miles to the resort town of Santa Cruz. From there, turn inland and north to return along the crest of the Santa Cruz Mountains for scenery from a higher perspective.

A Scenic Car Tour

Here's a suggested itinerary for a full day of scenic car touring. Get started around 9 a.m. and head to the Great Highway (south of Cliff

House and at the western end of Golden Gate Park) and drive south. Bring picnic supplies or plan on getting something to eat in one of the restaurants in the many towns and villages along the way. While you'll have time to get out and enjoy many of the attractions, don't linger too long if you want to get back before evening. And don't forget to bring a state highway map (in case of detours or in case you want to devise your own circuit route).

The coastline of the San Francisco Peninsula south of the city is largely undeveloped. Bluffs protect the many nudist beaches from prying eyes and make excellent launching points for hang gliders, as you can see at Fort Funston, about a mile south of the San Francisco Zoo. Skyline Boulevard follows the coast here past Daly City, a community of ticky-tacky housing that's probably the ugliest thing most folks will see on a visit to San Francisco.

But things improve after you reach Highway 1. San Pedro Beach marks the end of San Francisco's suburban sprawl and is a popular surfing beach. Continually eroding cliffs offer great scenery from the road but don't handle the presence of the highway well, and the road is washed away regularly in winter storms. Gray Whale Cove State Beach is clothing-optional and, in spite of its name, isn't an especially good place for whale-watching.

Half Moon Bay and a Scenic Side Trip

Main Street in Half Moon Bay features a gentrified shopping area with gift shops, bookstores, a saddlery, jewelry stores, cafés, bars, restaurants, and art galleries. There's also a full-size grocery store that sells sandwiches and picnic supplies. For a view of the town's eponymous bay, go to **Half Moon Bay State Beach** (turn onto Kelly Avenue from Highway 1). Parking is $5, but you can enter the park free for 15 minutes and watch the waves roll in.

For a contrast to the surf, continue south on Highway 1 and turn right onto Higgins-Purisima Creek Road. The narrow paved road winds and climbs for eight miles through ranch country before returning to Highway 1. Turn left to continue south. **Pigeon Point Light Station** is in a spectacular coastal setting, and guided lighthouse tours are offered on weekends; the half-hour tours are $2 per person.

Elephant Seals

For sightings of some unusual wildlife, stop at **Ano Nuevo State Reserve** just south of Pigeon Point. Huge northern elephant seals come ashore from early December through March to give birth and mate. Bull seals often engage in battles for breeding access to the females.

Popular guided walks to view the wildlife activity are offered by trained naturalists from December 15 through March 31 and last two hours. Advance reservations are recommended for the three-mile (round-trip) hike.

The cost is $4 a person, plus $5 for parking. Call (800) 444-7275 daily between 8 a.m. and 5 p.m. Pacific time to reserve a spot; for additional information, call (650) 879-2025. Juvenile seals are present year-round, and you can walk the trail unescorted to see them; in the winter, when 300 to 400 adults appear, visitors must be on guided tours.

Just north of Santa Cruz is **Wilder Ranch State Park,** a cultural preserve with adobe farm buildings from the Spanish mission era and buildings from the late 19th century. Docent-led tours are offered on weekends; there are also 28 miles of trails for hiking.

Mountain Scenery and Giant Redwoods

In Santa Cruz you'll have time to grab something to eat, but on a one-day outing there isn't enough to time to explore this resort city, famous for its boardwalk and roller coaster. It's a good turnaround point; you can head back to San Francisco through the mountains. Follow signs to Route 9 north, a scenic road that twists and turns through mountains, forests, and the towns of Felton and Boulder Creek, where you turn left onto Route 236.

At **Big Basin Redwoods State Park** you don't need to get out of the car to be overwhelmed by the huge trees. This forest of giant redwoods is more impressive than the stand at Muir Woods in Marin. But get out of the car anyway, even if it's just to take a few minutes to explore the park head-quarters and a small museum. Then get back in the car and continue toward San Francisco, 67 miles away. Route 236 gets narrow and twisty before returning to Route 9; turn left to continue north.

Next, turn left on Route 35 (Skyline Drive) for more incredible scenery; after a while, views open up of the Pacific on the left and San Francisco Bay on the right. There are plenty of overlooks where you can stop and enjoy the vistas. Next, take Route 92/35 (a right turn) and then turn left onto Route 35, which leads to Interstate 80, a 20-mile stretch of some of the most scenic interstate highway in the country—and, in a few minutes, San Francisco.

Beyond the Bay Area

Many outstanding destinations are too far from San Francisco for a day trip but close enough to consider for an overnight trek—or as separate destinations on a later trip. Leading the list is **Yosemite National Park,** a wilderness of evergreen forests, alpine meadows, and sheer walls of granite. Spectacular Yosemite Valley features soaring cliffs, plunging waterfalls, gigantic trees, and rugged canyons. The park is about 200 miles from San Francisco, which works out to about a five-hour drive. World-famous Yosemite attracts about 4 million visitors a year. Peak tourist season is June to August, and crowds diminish in the fall. Advance reservations are essential year-round. For more information, call (209) 372-0299.

Lake Tahoe, about 200 miles from the city, is rated one of the most beautiful bodies of water in the world. It lies in an alpine bowl on the border between Nevada and California and is surrounded by forested peaks. Tahoe features resorts, gambling, hiking trails, lakeside cabins, historic architecture, and special events such as golf tournaments. For more information, call the **Lake Tahoe Visitors Authority,** (800) 288-2463.

South of the city down the Pacific coast is **Monterey Bay,** with Santa Cruz at its northern end and Monterey at its southern end. The first capital of California, Monterey was established by the Spanish in 1770; many Spanish, Mexican, and early American buildings still stand. South of Monterey is **Carmel,** a pretty hillside town founded as an artists' colony in the early 20th century. The **Monterey Peninsula** is about a two-hour drive from San Francisco. For visitor information, call the **Monterey Peninsula Visitors and Convention Bureau** at (408) 649-1770.

North of San Francisco along the rugged coastline is **Mendocino,** a small picturesque town that was once a logging village. In the 1950s it became a haven for artists and was so well restored that the town was declared a historic monument. Inland from town are forests of giant redwood trees. The town itself is tucked away on a rocky promontory above the Pacific and retains the charm of its logging days; it's largely unspoiled by tourism. Mendocino is about 125 miles from San Francisco; a leisurely drive up the spectacular coast can take as long as ten hours one way. For visitor information, call the **Mendocino Coast Chamber of Commerce** at (707) 461-6300.

PART TEN

Attractions in San Francisco

Fisherman's Wharf and Beyond

San Francisco is a city of 43 hills on a spectacularly scenic peninsula with block after block of ornate Victorian houses. It's a shopping town, a culinary grab bag of cuisines, and a jumble of intriguing ethnic neighborhoods. At night the city is a glimmering jewel by the bay that takes your breath away.

But that's not all. Everybody's favorite city offers visitors a potpourri of attractions that show off its fascinating and often notorious past—such as Alcatraz, the country's best-known prison. Museums and galleries range from the encyclopedic de Young Museum and the Asian Art Museum to several excellent science museums, including the Exploratorium and the California Academy of Sciences. The new Museum of Modern Art and the recent restoration of the California Palace of the Legion of Honor ensure San Francisco's identity as the West Coast's center of art and culture.

The following zone descriptions provide you with a comprehensive guide to San Francisco's top attractions and list a few dogs we think you should avoid. We give you enough information so that you can choose the places you want to see based on your own interests. Each attraction includes a zone number so you can plan your visit logically, without spending valuable time crisscrossing the city.

■ A Time-Saving Chart ■

Because of the wide range of attractions in and around San Francisco— from a hall filled with sculptures by Rodin at the Legion of Honor to historic ships that visitors can explore at Hyde Street Pier in Fisherman's

Wharf—we've provided the following chart to help you prioritize your touring. In it, you'll find the zone, location, author's rating from one star (skip it) to five stars (not to be missed), and a brief description of the attraction. Some attractions, usually art galleries without permanent collections, aren't rated because exhibits change. Each attraction is individually profiled later in this section.

Attractions in San Francisco		
Attraction	**Description**	**Author's Rating**
Zone 1: Chinatown		
Cable Car Museum	History and real machinery	★★½
Zone 2: Civic Center		
Haas-Lilienthal House	Furnished Victorian mansion	★★½
Zone 4: Financial District		
Federal Reserve Bank	Currency exhibit	★
Museum of Money	History of the West	★★
SkyDeck	View from a skyscraper	★★★
Transamerica Pyramid	Virtual observatory	★
Wells Fargo Museum	Pony Express and more	★★½
Zone 5: Marina		
Alcatraz	Island prison	★★★★★
Exploratorium	Hands-on science museum	★★★½
Mexican Museum	Vibrant paintings and art	★★★½
Museum of the City of San Francisco	Local history	★★½
Palace of Fine Arts	Majestic ruin	★★★½
Ripley's Believe It or Not Museum	Museum of the odd and unusual	★
San Francisco Craft and Folk Art Museum	Small gallery	no rating
San Francisco Maritime Historical Park	19th-century ships	★★★★
San Francisco Maritime Museum	Seafaring exhibits	★★★½
UnderWater World	Commercial aquarium	★★
Wax Museum	200 wax statues	★½

Attractions in San Francisco (continued)

Attraction	Description	Author's Rating
Zone 6: North Beach		
Coit Tower	View from Telegraph Hill	★★½
Zone 7: SoMa/Mission		
Ansel Adams Center	Fine art photos	★★★
California Historical Society	History exhibits	★★
Cartoon Art Museum	Gallery of cartoons	★★★★
Jewish Museum	Jewish art and crafts	★★½
Mission Dolores	San Francisco's oldest building	★★
San Francisco Museum of Modern Art	New, huge, modern art gallery	★★★★½
Yerba Buena Gardens	Art complex and gardens	★★
Zone 8: Richmond/Avenues		
Asian Art Museum	Largest collection in West	★★★½
California Palace of the Legion of Honor	High-brow art museum	★★★★
California Academy of Sciences	Natural history for families	★★★
Cliff House	Tourist landmark on ocean	★★½
M. H. de Young Museum	American art	★★★★½
Fort Point	Old fort, great views	★★★★★
Japanese Tea Garden	Classic garden as art	★★★★
Presidio Museum	Military and San Francisco history exhibits	★½
San Francisco Zoo	Gorillas, koalas, lions, tigers . . .	★★★½
Strybing Arboretum	70 acres of gardens	★★★
Zone 11: Yonder Marin		
Mount Tamalpais	Spectacular scenery, views of the city	★★★½
Muir Woods	Giant redwood tree grove	★★★★

Attractions in San Francisco (continued)		
Attraction	**Description**	**Author's Rating**
Zone 12: Berkeley		
Berkeley Art Museum	Eclectic art on UC Berkeley campus	★★★
Lawrence Hall of Science	Hands-on science for youngsters	★
Museum of Anthropology	Native American artifacts	★½
Zone 13: Oakland		
Oakland Museum	California natural	★★★½

Zone 1: Chinatown

Cable Car Museum

Type of Attraction: A building housing the machinery that moves the city's famed cable cars; museum features photographs, old cable cars, signposts, mechanical devices, and a video explaining the system. A self-guided tour.

Location: 1201 Mason Street (at Washington Street), San Francisco, CA 94108 (Nob Hill).

Admission: Free

Hours: April through October, daily, 10 a.m. to 6 p.m.; rest of the year, daily, 10 a.m. to 5 p.m. Closed on major holidays.

Phone: (415) 474-1887

When to Go: Anytime

Special Comments: One set of stairs leads up to the mezzanine viewing area, and another set heads down to an enclosed area where you can observe the innards of the system.

Overall Appeal by Age Group:

Pre-school	Grade School	Teens	Young Adults	Over 30	Senior Citizens
★★½	★★★	★★	★★½	★★½	★★★

Author's Rating: It's fun to watch the machinery that pulls San Francisco's famed cable cars, and the price is right. ★★½

How Much Time to Allow: 30 minutes to an hour

Description and Comments When you try to envision what makes San Francisco's cable cars go, think horizontal elevator. Here you can see the machinery that moves the cables pulling the cars on the four lines of the only cable-car operation in the world. You'll also see 19th-century photos, an old cable car, some of the machinery that grip and release the cable running under the streets, and an informative video on the system. It's noisy and smells like a factory—which it is, in a way. A must for railroad buffs and most children, and a fun fill-in spot for everyone else.

Touring Tips If you're frustrated in your attempts to board the jam-packed cable cars, you can at least stop in to satisfy your curiosity about how it works. It's also a place to pick up a one-day or multiday Muni pass for unlimited rides on the city's buses, trolley, subways, and—if you're lucky or have the patience to wait in line—cable cars.

Other Things to Do Nearby Chinatown is only two blocks away. Three blocks south at California and Mason Streets is the Mark Hopkins Inter-Continental Hotel, famous for its Top O' the Mark lounge. Nob Hill, which overlooks Union Square, is home to many of the city's elite and some of its finest hotels.

Zone 2: Civic Center

Haas-Lilienthal House

Type of Attraction: The only fully furnished Victorian house in San Francisco open to the public. A guided tour.

Location: 2007 Franklin Street, San Francisco, CA 94109; near Washington Street in Pacific Heights.

Admission: $5 per person

Hours: Wednesday, noon to 4 p.m. (last tour at 3:15); Sunday, noon to 5 p.m. (last tour at 4:15).

Phone: (415) 441-3000

When to Go: Anytime

Special Comments: Two flights of stairs on the tour.

Overall Appeal by Age Group:

Pre-school	Grade School	Teens	Young Adults	Over 30	Senior Citizens
★	★★	★★	★★	★★★	★★★

Author's Rating: A fascinating glimpse into the life of an upper-middle-class San Francisco family of the late 19th century. ★★½

How Much Time to Allow: One hour

Description and Comments   This exquisite 1886 high Victorian mansion has been maintained in nearly original condition since the last descendant of the builders to live in the house died in 1972. The hour-long, docent-led tour reveals a wealth of details both on the house (one of a very few to survive the 1906 earthquake and fire) and the life of a rich (but not fabulously so) Jewish merchant family. The distinctive Queen Anne, third-floor tower is strictly decorative; the windows are nine feet above the floor, while the sliding doors on the recessed front entrance were only open when the family was receiving visitors.

Inside, the formal front parlor was used for receiving important guests, while the family parlor behind it was used for guests lower on the social scale. More fascinating details include the small dining room off the main dining room used by children and servants; what appears to be a window at the back is in fact a jib door that slides up and may have been built so that coffins could be passed in and out of the house when a family member died.

Touring Tips   Don't walk up the stairs to the main entrance; you'll get to do this later. Instead, walk to the right (as you face the house) and down the sidewalk to the tour entrance.

Other Things to Do Nearby   Two other impressive Victorian houses are nearby. You can't go in, but they're worth a look: the Edward Coleman House at Franklin and California Streets and the Bransten House at 1735 Franklin Street. Pacific Heights is home to some of the city's most expensive and dramatic real estate, with some mansions and townhouses selling for prices starting at $1 million.

Zone 4: Financial District

Federal Reserve Bank of San Francisco

Type of Attraction: The American Currency Exhibit and the World of Economics, two lobby attractions on the ground floor of the San Francisco office of America's central bank. A self-guided tour.

Location: 101 Market Street, San Francisco, CA 94105.

Admission: Free

Hours: Monday through Friday, 9 a.m. to 4:30 p.m. Closed weekends and holidays.

Phone: (415) 974-3252

When to Go: Anytime

Special Comments: All on one level. Rest rooms, public phones, and drinking water are also in the lobby.

Overall Appeal by Age Group:

Pre-school	Grade School	Teens	Young Adults	Over 30	Senior Citizens
★	★★	★	★	★	★

Author's Rating: Some interesting things (such as a $10,000 bill), but overall dry and boring. ★

How Much Time to Allow: 30 minutes to an hour

Description and Comments The lobby of the Federal Reserve Bank contains two exhibits of particular interest to serious collectors of paper currency (and we don't mean Silicon Valley fat cats) and budding capitalists. The American Currency Exhibit, a one-room display of paper money from colonial days to the present, is the most interesting. Notes from the original 13 colonies are displayed on a historical timeline with more than 400 selections from the bank's permanent collection, many of them rare and irreplaceable. Many of the designs are outstanding examples of engraving and feature images of historical events, Native American warriors, emblems, and monuments. Some of the more unusual items on display are specially marked currency printed for Hawaii (in case the Japanese invaded during World War II) and a $10,000 bill, no longer produced. The rest of the lobby is dedicated to the World of Economics, a group of elaborate displays (some interactive) that purport to explain the complexities of global currency exchange, inflation, stagflation, and supply and demand. Question: Is this any way to spend a vacation? Only if you're an aspiring capitalist.

Touring Tips   Head straight for the American Currency Exhibit, located in a small room at the south end of the lobby. A few quick glances at the towering exhibits in the World of Economics and you'll soon know if it's for you.

Other Things to Do Nearby   The Ferry Building at the foot of Market Street (you can't miss it; it's the one with the tower) is one of the few buildings to survive the 1906 earthquake and fire. Here you can board a ferry to Sausalito, Angel Island, and other San Francisco Bay destinations. The Jewish Museum is around the corner on at 121 Steuart Street; it's a small but snazzy art gallery highlighting Jewish culture.

Museum of Money of the American West

Type of Attraction: A small museum highlighting the gold rush, gold mining, and the development of money in California's history. A self-guided tour.

Location: Basement of the Bank of California, 400 California Street, San Francisco, CA 94111; in the Financial District.

Admission: Free

Hours: Monday through Thursday, 10 a.m. to 4 p.m.; Friday, 10 a.m. to 5 p.m. Closed weekends and bank holidays.

Phone: (415) 765-0400

When to Go: Anytime

Special Comments: One set of stairs to climb and descend; rest rooms are next to the museum entrance.

Overall Appeal by Age Group:

Pre-school	Grade School	Teens	Young Adults	Over 30	Senior Citizens
★	★★	★★	★★	★★	★★

Author's Rating: So that's what a gold nugget looks like. An interesting but narrow slice of California history that's worth a peek when you're in the neighborhood. ★★

How Much Time to Allow: 30 minutes

Description and Comments   California history and gold are the focus of this one-room museum in the basement of the huge Bank of California building.

On display are gold nuggets, coins, old banknotes, diagrams of the Comstock mines (the source of the fortune that founded this bank and many civic projects in San Francisco), a set of dueling pistols, and plenty of 19th-century photos of the gold rush era that put California on the map. Some interesting items on display—and it's small enough that you're not overwhelmed.

Touring Tips Check out the huge vault at the bottom of the stairs outside the entrance to the museum. You can't miss the stunning bank lobby in this colonnaded building, which was completed in 1908.

Other Things to Do Nearby The Wells Fargo History Museum is around the corner on Montgomery Street. It's only two blocks to One Embarcadero Center and the 41st-floor SkyDeck observatory. Although its 27th-floor observation deck is now closed, the Transamerica Pyramid on Montgomery Street has a lobby observatory that lets you control cameras on the roof for TV-monitor views of the city; not nearly as exciting as seeing it with your own eyes, but it's free. Transamerica Redwood Park is next to the distinctive landmark; its fountains, greenery, and whimsical sculptures make for a nice place for a brown-bag lunch.

SkyDeck at One Embarcadero Center

Type of Attraction: A panoramic 360° view of San Francisco from the top of a 41-floor skyscraper. Guided and self-guided tours.

Location: One Embarcadero Center, San Francisco, CA 94111 (at the corner of Sacramento and Battery Streets in the Financial District).

Admission: $5 for teens and adults, $3.50 for seniors and students, $3 for children ages 5–12.

Hours: Summer, daily, noon to 9:30 p.m.; winter, daily, noon to 8:30 p.m. Closed Thanksgiving, Christmas, and New Year's Day.

Phone: (800) 773-6318 for general information and directions, (415) 772-0591 for the ticket booth

When to Go: Any time the weather is good. SkyDeck offers indoor and outdoor viewing areas, so it's a good choice in cool or windy weather. The view at sunset and at night can be spectacular. On weekdays before 5 p.m., only 45-minute guided tours are offered. After 5 p.m. and on weekends, the guided tours are optional at no additional cost.

Special Comments: Because SkyDeck is sometimes rented for private functions, it's a good idea to call ahead. The ticket booth is located on the street level of One Embarcadero Center.

Overall Appeal by Age Group:

Pre-school	Grade School	Teens	Young Adults	Over 30	Senior Citizens
★★★	★★★★	★★★★	★★★	★★★	★★★

Author's Rating: Probably the best place for first-time visitors to marvel at the city's fabled view, especially in cool or windy weather. ★★★

How Much Time to Allow: One hour

Description and Comments   The view from the top of this downtown skyscraper is indisputably great—as it is from many other locations in and around San Francisco. But the advantages to paying the $5 fee are SkyDeck's enclosed viewing areas and the free use of telescopes and binoculars. In addition you'll find a few displays of artifacts uncovered when the huge Embarcadero Center complex was built, as well as computer stations offering historical and cultural information on the city. The view is the main event.

Touring Tips   45-minute guided tours are offered only before 5 p.m. Unless this is the first day of your first visit to San Francisco, the tour is too long. Come after 5 p.m. or on weekends and visit SkyDeck unescorted. The view is usually better then, anyway.

Other Things to Do Nearby   The four-building Embarcadero Center features more than 120 shops and restaurants, a five-screen movie complex, and special events throughout the year. Other attractions nearby include the Wells Fargo History Museum, the Transamerica Pyramid (which doesn't allow visitors beyond the ground floor), and the Museum of Money of the American West, located inside the Bank of California.

Transamerica Pyramid

Type of Attraction: San Francisco's tallest and most distinctive building; a virtual observatory and temporary art exhibits in the ground-floor lobby; half-acre Redwood Park, an oasis of green in the Financial District. Self-guided tour.

Location: 600 Montgomery Street, San Francisco, CA 94111.

Admission: Free

Hours: Monday through Friday, 8 a.m. to 5 p.m. Closed weekends and major holidays.

Phone: (415) 983-4000

When to Go: Anytime, but skip it if you can't see the top of the building.

Special Comments: All on one level—ironically, the ground level of the highest building in San Francisco.

Overall Appeal by Age Group:

Pre-school	Grade School	Teens	Young Adults	Over 30	Senior Citizens
★	★★	★★	★★	★★	★

Author's Rating: Enjoy the building from the distance—say, from Alcatraz. Not worth going out of the way for. ★

How Much Time to Allow: 10 to 30 minutes

Description and Comments At 48 floors and a total height of 848 feet, Transamerica Pyramid (headquarters to a huge financial services company) is the city's most distinctive high rise. The structure, completed in 1972, is topped by a spire covered with vertically louvered aluminum panels; at the tip is an aircraft warning light. Two windowless wings rise vertically from the 29th floor; the east wing contains elevators and a stairwell, and the west wing has a smoke tower. Alas, it's a shame you can't ascend San Francisco's highest building to catch the view. But all's not lost; in the lobby is the Virtual Observatory, with four stations (north, east, south, west), color TV monitors, and controls hooked to cameras on the top of the building that let you scan and zoom images of the city's skyline and environs. Is the Oakland Bay Bridge bumper to bumper? Will that bicycle messenger make it through the intersection? If it's not foggy, find out here. The lobby also features changing art exhibits.

Touring Tips Kids, who may be the most likely to get a kick out of the remote-controlled cameras, will have trouble reaching the controls and may need a lift. Voyeur alert: If it's not crowded, you can skip the wide-angle views of the bay and Mount Tamalpais and zoom in on downtown rooftops. Who knows what you might see?

Other Things to Do Nearby Redwood Park, part of the Transamerica complex, features greenery, redwood trees, whimsical sculptures, a fountain and benches, and free concerts on Fridays at lunchtime during the summer. If the Virtual Observatory doesn't satisfy your craving for a drop-dead view of San Francisco, walk over to One Embarcadero Center and zip up to its 41st-floor SkyDeck observatory (but you'll have to shell out $5).

Wells Fargo History Museum

Type of Attraction: A museum displaying artifacts and memorabilia of the American West and Wells Fargo, the banking and express firm founded in San Francisco in 1852. A self-guided tour.

Location: 420 Montgomery Street, San Francisco, CA 94163.

Admission: Free

Hours: Monday through Friday, 9 a.m. to 5 p.m. Closed weekends and bank holidays.

Phone: (415) 396-2619

When to Go: Anytime

Special Comments: One set of stairs up to the mezzanine.

Overall Appeal by Age Group:

Pre-school	Grade School	Teens	Young Adults	Over 30	Senior Citizens
★★★	★★★	★★★	★★	★★	★★

Author's Rating: Although small, this attractive museum is chock-full of authentic items that make the old West come alive. ★★½

How Much Time to Allow: 30 minutes to an hour

Description and Comments   A real, century-old stagecoach is the main attraction of this museum run by the Wells Fargo Bank, a firm famous for operating the Pony Express and a stagecoach empire throughout the western United States in the late 19th century. Other displays include mining tools, an incredibly complicated harness worn by the horses that pulled the stagecoaches, gold, money, treasure boxes, old postal envelopes, and photographs of the 1906 San Francisco earthquake and fire. It's a bright and attractive space. While not worth a special trip, it's a nice fill-in spot while you're exploring the Financial District, especially if you've got kids in tow.

Touring Tips   Don't miss the mezzanine level, where you can climb inside a stagecoach compartment and listen to a taped presentation. The real thing, on the main level below, is strictly hands-off.

Other Things to Do Nearby   It's only two blocks to One Embarcadero Center and an elevator ride to the 41st-floor SkyDeck observatory. While its 27th-floor observation deck is now closed, the Transamerica Pyramid on Montgomery Street has a lobby observatory that lets you control cameras on the roof for TV-monitor views of the city; not nearly as exciting as seeing it with your own eyes, but it's free. Transamerica Redwood Park is next to the distinctive landmark; its fountains, greenery, and whimsical sculptures make for a nice spot to enjoy a brown-bag lunch.

Zone 5: Marina

Alcatraz Island

Type of Attraction: The island in San Francisco Bay best known for its maximum-security, minimum-privilege federal penitentiary; a cellhouse tour, trails, museum exhibits, wildflowers, wildlife, and spectacular views of the San Francisco skyline. Self-guided, audio, and guided tours.

Location: In San Francisco Bay; to get there, take a 12-minute (one-way) ferry trip from Pier 41 (in Fisherman's Wharf, at the foot of Powell Street).

Admission: $13 for adults, $11.25 for seniors (ages 63 and over), and $7.75 for children ages 5–11. Tickets can be purchased without the audio tour; subtract $3.25 from the adult and senior rates, and $1.25 from the children's rate. Self-guided tour maps and guides are available on the island in English, Spanish, German, and Japanese for $1. To purchase tickets in advance by phone, call (415) 705-5555; a $2 service charge per ticket is added.

Hours: Ferries leave about every half-hour throughout the day, beginning at 9:30 a.m. Alcatraz closes at 6:30 p.m. in the summer and 4:30 p.m. the rest of the year. Closed on Christmas and New Year's Day.

Phone: (415) 705-1042

When to Go: Try to make the first ferry of the day; it's less crowded, and the weather is generally better and less windy.

Special Comments: Weather in the middle of San Francisco Bay is unpredictable; it's also frequently different from mainland weather. The best advice is to be prepared and dress in layers; shorts and T-shirts are not a good idea. You have to hike steep grades to get to the cellhouse; wear sturdy shoes. There's no food service on the island, but you can buy a snack on the ferry. Rest rooms, telephones, drinking water, and soft-drink vending machines are available on the island.

Overall Appeal by Age Group:

Pre-school	Grade School	Teens	Young Adults	Over 30	Senior Citizens
★★★★	★★★★★	★★★★★	★★★★★	★★★★★	★★★★★

Author's Rating: A San Francisco and U.S. landmark that shouldn't be missed; the audio tour of the cellhouse is outstanding. ★★★★★

How Much Time to Allow: At least two hours; bring a lunch and you can easily spend half a day on the Rock. You can catch any returning ferry back to Fisherman's Wharf; a schedule is posted at the dock.

Description and Comments One of Golden Gate National Recreation Area's most popular destinations, Alcatraz Island offers a close-up look at a federal prison long off limits to the public (and that has captured almost everyone's imagination). A couple of hours on the Rock is time well spent. Virtually no one is disappointed.

The island is best known for its sinister reputation. It was called the Rock, Hellcatraz, and Uncle Sam's Devil Island by the hardened criminals who lived there during its federal penitentiary years (1934–63). Most of the 1,545 men who did time were deemed to be escape risks and trouble-makers. Only a handful were truly notorious; the list includes Al "Scarface" Capone, Doc Barker, Alvin "Creepy" Karpis, George "Machine Gun" Kelly, and Robert Stroud, the Birdman of Alcatraz (who actually conducted his famous bird studies as a prisoner in another federal pen, Leavenworth).

On the cellhouse tour you'll see why a sentence to Alcatraz was rated hard time by prisoners. The cells are tiny (inmates were confined 23 hours a day), and extreme precautions were taken to control the prisoners, prevent escapes, and quell riots. In the dining room, considered potentially the most dangerous place in the prison, tear-gas canisters are visible in the ceiling. Some cells are also furnished as they were when Alcatraz was a working prison, with cots, personal items (such as packets of Bugler cigarette tobacco, brushes, and books), and a few pictures. A poignant note: If the wind was right on New Year's Eve, some prisoners could hear voices and music from the annual party held at a yacht club on the mainland—excruciating to men who had numbers instead of names.

In stark contrast to the deteriorating prison, Alcatraz (Spanish for "pelican") is a place of natural beauty. On trails around the island visitors can see flowers such as fuchsias, geraniums, jade trees, agave, and periwinkles, as well as outstanding views of San Francisco and Oakland. Tide pools teem with marine life, including crabs and sea stars. Alcatraz, rich in history, American iconography, and natural beauty, is an outstanding tourist attraction.

Touring Tips Make advance reservations; Alcatraz is very popular. During peak summer and holiday periods ferry rides to the island are booked as much as a week in advance. The down side to advance reservations is that no refunds are given if the weather is lousy. But Alcatraz in bad weather is better than no Alcatraz at all.

After disembarking and listening to a park ranger's introductory remarks, go inside for the 13-minute video presentation that gives a good overview of the island's history (including the takeover by Native Americans that began on November 20, 1969, and lasted 19 months). Then make note of the schedule of outdoor ranger walks offered daily. The guided walks highlight a variety of topics, including the island's military history, famous inmates, escapes, natural history, and the Indian occupation. If you arrived on the first ferry of the day (strongly recommended), make a note of the time of any ranger walks that interest you. Then take the audio cellhouse tour while it's not too crowded; go on a ranger-led tour afterward. After the video ends, walk up to the cellhouse for the 35-minute audio tour narrated by guards and inmates. Their recounting of daily life is vivid, blunt, and often scary. It's not to be missed. After the tour, don't be in a hurry to leave. Take a ranger walk or hike some of the trails to discover the natural beauty and abundant wildlife (hawks, ravens, geese, finches, and hummingbirds) that thrive on this evolving ecological preserve.

Other Things to Do Nearby   Fisherman's Wharf, where ferries to and from Alcatraz embark and arrive, is Tourist Central and has countless ways to separate you from your money. Major attractions worth your time include UnderWater World, the San Francisco Maritime Museum, and historic ships at Hyde Pier. You can also take ferries to Angel Island and Tiburon or a cruise on San Francisco Bay. Another option is to rent a bike and ride the Golden Gate Promenade to the famous bridge with the same name; it's three and a half miles one way. Restaurants, most of them not that good, abound in Fisherman's Wharf. A good, less expensive option is clam chowder in a bowl of sourdough bread (about $5) from Boudin's Bakery.

Mexican Museum

Type of Attraction: Paintings, sculptures, and other works by Mexican and Latino artists. A self-guided tour.

Location: Fort Mason Center, Building D, San Francisco, CA 94123.

Admission: $3 for adults, $2 for seniors and students, free for children ages 10 and under. Free on the first Wednesday of the month.

Hours: Wednesday through Sunday, noon to 5 p.m. Mondays and Tuesdays, closed.

Phone: (415) 441-0445

When to Go: Anytime

Special Comments: All on one level.

Overall Appeal by Age Group:

Pre-school	Grade School	Teens	Young Adults	Over 30	Senior Citizens
★★	★★	★★★	★★★	★★★	★★★

Author's Rating: A small but attractive museum filled with vibrant art.
★★★½

How Much Time to Allow: One hour

Description and Comments On display in this small, bright museum is a wide range of fantastic and colorful art, including an eight-foot Tree of Life (an incredible ceramic by Alfonso Sotano), papier mâché creatures, skeletons, drawings, paintings, watercolors, and mixed media. The Day of the Dead exhibit illustrates the Nov. 1–2 Mexican celebration, a combination of ancient meso-American traditions and the religious rites of the Catholic church. It's a reflection of the idea that life and death are inseparable—and the art is funny, colorful, vibrant, and sometimes scary. Good news: the museum is moving to larger quarters near Yerba Buena Gardens (SoMa) in 1999 or 2000.

Touring Tips Don't miss the excellent gift shop across from the museum entrance. Mexican handicrafts, unusual postcards, children's games, T-shirts, jewelry, posters, and ceramic crafts are for sale.

Other Things to Do Nearby Fort Mason Center, part of the Golden Gate Recreation Area, houses theaters, restaurants, and art galleries, including the San Francisco Craft and Folk Art Museum. Aquatic Park provides plenty of open lawns, seating, a sandy shoreline, and the Hyde Street cable-car turn-around. The San Francisco Maritime Museum features a wide array of items from San Francisco's seafaring past. The three-and-a-half-mile Golden Gate Promenade is a broad footpath and bike trail that links Fisherman's Wharf and the Golden Gate Bridge.

Museum of the City of San Francisco

Type of Attraction: Permanent and rotating exhibits showcasing the history of San Francisco from its origins as a Spanish garrison to modern times; a resource center for visitors. A self-guided tour.

Location: Third floor of the Cannery shopping complex, 2801 Leavenworth Street, San Francisco, CA 94133; across from Fisherman's Wharf.

Admission: Free

Hours: Wednesday through Sunday, 10 a.m. to 4 p.m. Mondays and Tuesdays, closed.

Phone: (415) 928-0289

When to Go: Anytime

Special Comments: Parking is available at the nearby Anchorage Garage.

Overall Appeal by Age Group:

Pre-school	Grade School	Teens	Young Adults	Over 30	Senior Citizens
★★	★★★	★★	★★★	★★★	★★★

Author's Rating: Small, but attractive and informative. ★★½

How Much Time to Allow: 30 minutes

Description and Comments   This two-room museum tucked away in the upscale Cannery shopping complex is chock-full of a wide range of historical gems. Items on display during our visit included part of a 13th-century Spanish palace purchased by media baron William Randolph Hearst, the head of the Goddess of Progress (recovered from the statue that once stood atop the San Francisco City Hall, destroyed in the 1906 earthquake), and a small exhibit dedicated to beloved newspaper columnist Herb Caen. Other memorabilia crammed into the small space are movie posters, an exhibit on the celebration of the end of World War II, memorabilia from the 1906 earthquake, and photos and exhibits from the 1989 earthquake that devastated the nearby Marina District. First-time visitors to San Francisco touring Fisherman's Wharf should make the effort to stop in this pleasant museum.

Touring Tips   Take advantage of the museum's large selection of free city maps, brochures, visitor guides, and discount coupon books.

Other Things to Do Nearby   The San Francisco Maritime Museum, another free attraction a couple of blocks to the west, is another good place to learn about San Francisco's fascinating history. Visitors can climb aboard historic ships at the Hyde Street Pier. The Hyde Street cable-car turnaround is two blocks away; if the line isn't too long, go for it. Ghirardelli Square is full of shops and restaurants, as is Fisherman's Wharf, where you can board a ferry to Alcatraz (with advance reservations) or take a cruise on San Francisco Bay. Walk or rent a bike and burn off some calories on the Golden Gate Promenade, a three-and-a-half-mile path along San Francisco Bay leading to the eponymous bridge.

Palace of Fine Arts/Exploratorium

Type of Attraction: A landmark classical Roman rotunda originally built for the Panama-Pacific Exposition of 1915; a hands-on science museum for children and adults. A self-guided tour.

Location: 3601 Lyon Street, San Francisco, CA 94123; in the Marina District just off US 101 near the Golden Gate Bridge.

Admission: Palace of Fine Arts and grounds, free. Exploratorium, $9 for adults, $7 for seniors and students, $5 for people with disabilities and children ages 6–17, and $2.50 for children ages 3–5. Free to all on the first Wednesday of the month. The Tactile Dome is $12 per person and includes admission to the museum; advance reservations are required.

Hours: Palace: Always open. Exploratorium: Memorial Day to Labor Day, Tuesday through Sunday, 10 a.m. to 6 p.m.; Wednesday, 10 a.m. to 9:30 p.m. Rest of the year, Tuesday through Sunday, 10 a.m. to 5 p.m.; Wednesday, 10 a.m to 9:30 p.m. Closed Mondays, except holidays.

Phone: Exploratorium: (415) 561-0360 (recorded information), (415) 561-0399 (recorded directions), or (415) 563-7337 (further information)

When to Go: Palace of Fine Arts: in nice weather, although the fake ruins are lovely in a light rain; just make sure you bring an umbrella. Exploratorium: avoid weekday mornings during the school year, when school field trips are scheduled. Weekends and holidays are almost always busy, but lines at exhibits are rare.

Special Comments: The Palace of Fine Arts is outdoors; dress accordingly. Ample free parking is available for both attractions.

Overall Appeal by Age Group:

Pre-school	Grade School	Teens	Young Adults	Over 30	Senior Citizens
★★★★	★★★★★	★★★★	★★★★	★★★★	★★★

Author's Rating: A restored recreation of a Roman ruin and a hands-on science museum are an odd coupling, but both succeed in their own ways. ★★★½

How Much Time to Allow: Two to four hours for the Exploratorium; 30 minutes for the Palace of Fine Arts, although it's a scenic and peaceful setting that will tempt most visitors to linger.

Description and Comments Originally built in 1915 and restored in the late 1960s, the Palace of Fine Arts is a colossal fake Roman ruin with beautifully manicured greenery, an artificial lake, and waterfowl. The gorgeous setting is a great place to stroll, eat a picnic lunch, or take a break from a hectic touring schedule. The palace was so popular that after the 1915 Panama-Pacific Exhibition (which drew more than 18 million visitors), it was retained and later completely rebuilt (after decaying into real ruins). It's a San Francisco landmark and a favorite stop for tour buses.

Inside the adjacent exhibition shed is the Exploratorium, a hands-on science museum with more than 600 exhibits dedicated to the principle that one learns by doing. Bring your thinking cap. Exhibits range from a protein production line (where you chain together metal "molecules" to form DNA in a kind of jigsaw puzzle) to gyroscopes, a pendulum, AIDS exhibits, optical illusions, and a video-enhanced bobsled run—not to be missed for the 6- to 12-year-old set. Another major attraction is the Tactile Dome, a geodesic dome that visitors explore in the dark—crawling, climbing, sliding, and exploring different textures in 13 chambers. (Some reports say private groups have experienced it in the nude.) Advanced reservations are required, and an extra fee is charged; call (415) 561-0362 weekdays between 10 a.m. and 4 p.m. Not recommended for people in casts, women in the last trimester of pregnancy, or the claustrophobic.

Touring Tips   Neither attraction lends itself to strategic touring. The palace, with its towering, curved colonnades and rotunda, is stunningly gorgeous—and otherwise empty (a great place for a brown-bag lunch). The Exploratorium is best approached with an open mind and some strong preferences for specific branches of science and technology; otherwise you run the risk of wandering until something strikes your fancy. If, say, you've always been fascinated by magnetism or acoustics, keep that in mind as you explore. Many ground-floor exhibits inside the huge, hangar-like space will appeal more to children (or stoned adults), while the upper mezzanine level contains an array of hands-on science exhibits that will keep the curious occupied for hours.

Other Things to Do Nearby   The residences of the nearby Marina District reflect the Mediterranean-revival architecture popular in the 1920s, with lots of pastel townhouses on curving streets. If you're hungry, head toward Chestnut Street to find good neighborhood restaurants and shops. The Presidio, a former army base now managed by the National Park Service, has an army museum, hiking and biking trails, and hundreds of historical buildings. On the shores of San Francisco Bay, Marina Green is often full of kite-fliers, sunbathers, joggers, and yachters. The Golden Gate Promenade, a three-and-a-half-mile path stretching between Fisherman's Wharf and the Golden Gate Bridge, offers fine views, and you're near the halfway point.

Ripley's Believe It or Not! Museum

Type of Attraction: 250 exhibits of the odd and unusual based on the comic strip by Robert Ripley, "the modern Marco Polo." A self-guided tour.

Location: 175 Jefferson Street, San Francisco, CA 94133; across from
Fisherman's Wharf.

Admission: $8.50 for ages 13 and older, $7.50 for seniors, $5.50 for
children ages 5–12.

Hours: Sunday through Thursday, 10 a.m. to 10 p.m.; Friday and
Saturday, 10 a.m. to midnight.

Phone: (415) 771-6188

When to Go: Anytime

Special Comments: Anyone nervous about earthquakes should skip the
simulated event.

Overall Appeal by Age Group:

Pre-school	Grade School	Teens	Young Adults	Over 30	Senior Citizens
★★★	★★★★	★★★★	★★	★★	★

Author's Rating: Silliness aimed at 11-year-old boys and not much on
hand that has anything to do with San Francisco. ★

How Much Time to Allow: One hour

Description and Comments   Here's where you come to gawk at displays of
human oddities such as Unicorn Man (with a 13-inch spike growing out of
the back of his head), the world's tallest man, and grainy films of restless
natives chowing down on baked crocodile. For minor titillation, a few sexy
teasers are thrown in, such as the optical illusion of the naked lady on the
beach who's not there when you walk back for a better look.

   While the overwhelming majority of exhibits have nothing to do with
San Francisco (and are repeated at other Ripley museums from Australia to
Key West), there are a couple of exceptions: the scale model of a cable car
made of matches and a simulated earthquake, along with pictures of the
1989 event. Neither is worth the price of admission.

Touring Tips   Only come in lousy weather and in the company of adoles-
cents. Better yet, send the youngsters in while you check out better options
around Fisherman's Wharf.

Other Things to Do Nearby   The Museum of the City of San Francisco is
small but worth a visit, especially for first-time visitors; it's located on the
third floor of the Cannery. The San Francisco Maritime Museum is close,
as is UnderWater World, a fish emporium that gives visitors a different perspective from the other large aquariums sprouting up around the nation. A
good and relatively cheap lunch alternative is the clam chowder in a bowl
of sourdough bread, served across the street at Boudin's Bakery.

San Francisco Craft and Folk Art Museum

Type of Attraction: Temporary exhibitions of contemporary crafts, American folk art, and traditional ethnic art. A self-guided tour.

Location: Landmark Building A North, Fort Mason Center (Laguna Street and Marina Boulevard), San Francisco, CA 94123.

Admission: $3 per person. Admission is free on Saturdays, 10 a.m. to noon, and on the first Wednesday of the month.

Hours: Thursday through Sunday, 11 a.m. to 5 p.m. Monday through Wednesday, closed.

Phone: (415) 775-0990

When to Go: Anytime

Special Comments: A steep, narrow spiral staircase leads to the upper gallery.

Overall Appeal by Age Group: Because this small gallery features constantly changing exhibits, it's not possible to rate it by age group.

Author's Rating: The museum only features temporary shows, so it's not possible to give it a rating.

How Much Time to Allow: 30 minutes to an hour

Description and Comments This small museum in the Fort Mason Center features changing exhibits of crafts and folk art. On display during our visit were contemporary works of art in silver, hammered brass, found objects (such as manual can openers), and other media. Lots of nifty stuff, in other words, in a bright and cheery setting that's also very small.

Touring Tips Because of its small size, visit the museum on a Saturday morning, when admission is free.

Other Things to Do Nearby Fort Mason Center, part of the Golden Gate Recreation Area, houses theaters, restaurants, and art galleries like the Mexican Museum. Aquatic Park provides plenty of open lawns, seating, a sandy shoreline, and the Hyde Street cable-car turnaround. The San Francisco Maritime Museum features a wide array of items from San Francisco's seafaring past. The three-and-a-half-mile Golden Gate Promenade is a broad footpath and bike trail that links Fisherman's Wharf and the Golden Gate Bridge; while usually windy, the scenery is great.

San Francisco Maritime National Historical Park— Hyde Street Pier

Type of Attraction: A collection of real 19th-century ships that visitors can board. Self-guided and guided tours.

Location: At the foot of Hyde Street in San Francisco near Fisherman's Wharf.

Admission: $4 for adults, $2 for children ages 12–17, free for seniors over age 62 and children ages 11 and under.

Hours: Mid-September through mid-May, daily, 10 a.m. to 5 p.m.; mid-May through mid-September, 10 a.m. to 6 p.m. Closed Thanksgiving, Christmas, and New Year's Day.

Phone: (415) 556-3002

When to Go: When the weather is good. Wind or rain can make for potentially perilous conditions on ship decks—and because the pier juts into San Francisco Bay, it can get cold.

Special Comments: Lots of narrow gangways, low overheads, and deck-level obstacles to negotiate. Your ticket is good for five days, so you can come back later.

Overall Appeal by Age Group:

Pre-school	Grade School	Teens	Young Adults	Over 30	Senior Citizens
★★★½	★★★★	★★★	★★★½	★★★★	★★★½

Author's Rating: Step aboard one of these great old ships and enter the long-gone world of Cape Horn passages and coastal runs under sail. Fabulous. ★★★★

How Much Time to Allow: One hour to half a day, depending on your interest

Description and Comments   While you stroll the decks and explore the passageways in these old ships, it's easy to make a mental trip back in time. On the *C.A. Thayer,* a three-masted schooner that once carried lumber and fished for cod in the Bering Sea, you can peer inside the captain's cabin and, below deck, watch a video of the ship's final voyage in 1950 narrated by her last skipper. This is nirvana for anyone who has fantasized about a sea voyage under sail.

Other ships to explore include the *Eureka,* a sidewheel ferry built in 1890 and the world's largest passenger ferry in her day. The *Alma* is the last San Francisco Bay scow schooner still afloat, and the *Balclutha* is a square-rigged Cape Horn sailing vessel launched in 1886 in Scotland. Around the corner on Pier 45 you can take an audio tour of the U.S.S. Pampanito, a restored World War II long-range submarine.

There are more ships to explore and exhibits on boat building and tools, old photographs, and detailed displays. You may also see riggers working high aloft on the masts of ships and shipwrights using traditional skills and tools. For newcomers to San Francisco, it's a pleasant surprise to discover this fascinating, high-quality national park plunked down in the dross of touristy Fisherman's Wharf.

Touring Tips   A guided tour of each ship is offered daily, based on ranger availability; stop by or call the day before for a schedule. If the weather turns bad or you get tired, come back; your ticket is good for five days.

Other Things to Do Nearby   More naval history and lore is on display in the art-deco building housing the San Francisco Maritime Museum (at the foot of Polk Street). Aquatic Park is the perfect place for a breather after the stresses of exploring Fisherman's Wharf. You can also follow the Golden Gate Promenade past the museum all the way to the Golden Gate Bridge. If the line isn't long at the cable-car stop, go for it. Almost directly across the street is Ghirardelli Square, a boutique mall where you can give your credit cards a workout. Boudin's Bakery a few blocks to the east serves clam chowder in a bowl made of sourdough bread; it's good and cheap.

San Francisco Maritime Museum

Type of Attraction: Maritime art, ship figureheads, intricate models, and thematic exhibits echoing San Francisco's maritime past. A self-guided tour.

Location: 900 Beach Street, San Francisco, CA 94109; a few blocks west of Fisherman's Wharf.

Admission: Free

Hours: Daily, 10 a.m. to 5 p.m. Closed Thanksgiving, Christmas, and New Year's Day.

Phone: (415) 556-3002

When to Go: Anytime

Special Comments: One set of stairs; rest rooms, drinking water, and telephones are available.

Overall Appeal by Age Group:

Pre-school	Grade School	Teens	Young Adults	Over 30	Senior Citizens
★★★	★★★	★★★	★★★	★★★	★★★★

Author's Rating: After exploring real ships at Hyde Street Pier, this museum is icing on the cake for folks fascinated by San Francisco's colorful seafaring past; an excellent, nontouristy destination at Fisherman's Wharf. ★★★½

How Much Time to Allow: One to two hours

Description and Comments Located in a gorgeous art-deco building at the foot of Polk Street, this small museum is jam-packed with an amazing array of maritime artifacts. While the exhibits are heavy on exquisitely detailed ship models (including the battleship U.S.S. California and a German five-masted schooner), also on hand are scrimshaw, carved nautilus shells, a ship's medicine box, a seagoing doll once owned by a sea captain's daughter (from the days when skippers took their families on long voyages), an exploding harpoon used to hunt whales, 19th-century photographs, and some small boats (not models). Not to be missed if you're fascinated by ships, nautical lore, and seafaring.

Touring Tips A great destination on a rainy day. If it's not foggy, the view of San Francisco Bay from the second-floor balcony is terrific. If looking at all those models makes you yearn for the real thing, walk a few blocks east to the Hyde Street Pier, where you can board and explore ships built in the 19th century.

Other Things to Do Nearby Aquatic Park features plenty of greenery and seating, a sandy shoreline, and great views. The Golden Gate Promenade is a scenic, usually windy, three-and-a-half-mile path to the bridge of the same name; walk or rent a bike, pack a lunch, and have a picnic at a quiet spot along the way. Aquatic Park surrounds the Hyde Street cable-car turn-around; if the line's not too long, hop on board. Ghirardelli Square and the Cannery are both only a credit card's throw away and are loaded with restaurants and shops. Walk a few blocks east to Fisherman's Wharf and the heart of the tourist hubbub, where you can rent a bike, buy a T-shirt, eat clam chowder out of a bowl made of sourdough bread (at Boudin's Bakery), take a ferry to Alcatraz (with advance reservations), or walk across the bottom of a giant fish tank (at UnderWater World).

UnderWater World

Type of Attraction: An aquarium where visitors are transported on a moving walkway through a clear tunnel to view thousands of marine animals. A self-guided audio tour.

Location: Pier 39, San Francisco, CA 94133; in Fisherman's Wharf.

Admission: $12.95 for adults, $9.95 for seniors ages 65 and over, $6.50 for children ages 3–11.

Hours: Summer, daily, 9 a.m. to 9 p.m.; fall, winter, and spring, daily, 10 a.m. to 8:30 p.m. Closed Christmas Day.

Phone: (415) 623-5300

When to Go: Anytime

Special Comments: Don't refuse the audio tour gizmo handed out before the tour begins; not much of what follows will make sense without it. Not for the claustrophobic or folks who get sweaty hands in highway tunnels.

Overall Appeal by Age Group:

Pre-school	Grade School	Teens	Young Adults	Over 30	Senior Citizens
★★★★	★★★★	★★★★	★★★★	★★★	★★★

Author's Rating: While it's neat to see a shark or ray glide overhead, this is a small attraction—and too expensive. ★★

How Much Time to Allow: 40 minutes to an hour

Description and Comments UnderWater World offers a different take on the massive fish emporiums that are sprouting like mushrooms across America's urban landscape. Instead of walking past windows and peering into large tanks, you'll find yourself transported on a moving walkway through tanks in clear tunnels where you look at fish and other marine creatures on both sides and overhead. It's a treat to see a four-foot shark pass directly over you—only inches away. The emphasis is on the marine life of northern California; the CD player hanging around your neck provides an audio commentary as you're transported (or walk—you can step off the moving sidewalk at any time) through the aquarium. After the tank tour, visitors walk through a couple of small exhibits on California nonmarine habitats and a "touch tank" for the kids. But these pale in comparison to the underwater experience and inadvertently emphasize the brevity of the tour.

Touring Tips On weekends and holidays the line for the audio tour contraption and the elevator can get long. But once under way, the line moves briskly. If a tour bus pulls in front of you and disgorges 40 hyperventilating seniors, go window-shopping on Pier 39 to kill some time until the line goes down (it won't take long).

Other Things to Do Nearby Walk on Pier 41 (where the Alcatraz ferry departs) and wave at the barking sea lions that congregate just offshore. If you bought tickets in advance, take the ferry to Alcatraz. You can also shop for overpriced tourist gewgaws on Pier 39 or eat in one of many overpriced seafood restaurants. Better bets in this tourist-crazed section of town include the San Francisco Maritime Museum and the Museum of the City of San Francisco (in the Cannery); neither of these quality establishments are trying to get their hands in your wallet. For lunch, try the clam chowder served in a bowl of sourdough bread at Boudin's Bakery just past Pier 41; it's good and cheap.

Wax Museum at Fisherman's Wharf

Type of Attraction: More than 200 wax sculptures of the famous and infamous from the past and present. A self-guided tour.

Location: 145 Jefferson Street, San Francisco, CA 94133; between Taylor and Mason Streets across from Fisherman's Wharf.

Admission: $11.95 for adults, $9.95 for children ages 11–17, $5.95 for children ages 6–12, and $8.95 for seniors.

Hours: Daily, 9 a.m. to 10 p.m.

Phone: (415) 885-4975

When to Go: Anytime

Special Comments: Lots of dimly lit stairs.

Overall Appeal by Age Group:

Pre-school	Grade School	Teens	Young Adults	Over 30	Senior Citizens
★★★	★★★	★★★	★★	★★	★★

Author's Rating: Rather quaint in this age of computer simulation and high-tech graphics. Not bad, but too expensive; a rainy-day kind of place. ★½

How Much Time to Allow: One hour

Description and Comments   It's probably easier to list who's not represented in this four-level museum of displays. But the short list of representatives include lots of presidents, Princess Diana, Sharon Stone, Paul Newman, Bogie, Brigitte Bardot, and Microsoft chair Bill Gates (a very West Coast touch). The optional Chamber of Horrors is gross enough to upset some less-jaded youngsters and offers surprisingly graphic displays of birds pecking out eyes, skeletal hands reaching out of coffins, etc. After you emerge from the dark chamber you're disconcertingly plunged into Hollywood and a display about the Wizard of Oz.

Touring Tips   Don't come here on a nice day.

Other Things to Do Nearby   Lots of schlocky tourist attractions and T-shirt shops to choose from along Jefferson Street. Better bets include the Maritime Museum, a trip to Alcatraz (advance reservations usually required), or a quick stop at the Museum of the City of San Francisco (on the third floor of the Cannery). A good, inexpensive lunch option is clam chowder served in a sourdough bread bowl at Boudin's Bakery (across the street).

Zone 6: North Beach

Coit Tower

Type of Attraction: A landmark tower with an observation deck atop Telegraph Hill. A self-guided tour.

Location: At the top of Telegraph Hill Boulevard, near North Beach in San Francisco.

Admission: The elevator ride to the top is $3 for adults, $2 for seniors, and $1 for children ages 6–12.

Hours: Daily, 10 a.m. to 7 p.m.

Phone: (415) 362-0808

When to Go: Come in the evening for a great view of the setting sun and a great photo opportunity.

Special Comments: The elevator doesn't go all the way to the top; you must negotiate a set of steep, winding stairs to the observation deck. Small children will need a lift to see the outstanding 360º view. Skip it in lousy weather.

Overall Appeal by Age Group:

Pre-school	Grade School	Teens	Young Adults	Over 30	Senior Citizens
★★★	★★★	★★★	★★★	★★★	★★★

Author's Rating: A great view, but it's almost as good from the parking lot at the base of the tower. ★★½

How Much Time to Allow: 30 minutes to an hour

Description and Comments   Built as a monument to San Francisco's volunteer firefighters with funds left by renowned eccentric Lillie Hitchcock Coit, this landmark provides a breathtaking view of the city, San Francisco Bay, the Oakland and Golden Gate bridges—the works. Some say the tower is shaped to resemble a firehose nozzle, but others disagree. There's no doubt about Ms. Coit's dedication to firefighters. Early in the gold rush, she is said to have deserted a wedding party and chased after her favorite fire engine. Lillie died in 1929 at age 86, leaving the city $125,000 to "expend in an appropriate manner . . . to the beauty of San Francisco." Coit Tower is the result. In the lobby of the tower base are 19 WPA-era murals depicting labor-union workers; admission to the murals and the ground-floor gift shop is free.

Touring Tips   Don't drive; the parking lot at the base of Coit Tower is small, and the wait for a space can be long. Walk (though the hill is very steep) or take the No. 39 Coit bus at Washington Square Park (board at Columbus Avenue and Union Street), which will take you up Telegraph Hill. Hour-long tours of the murals in the lobby are offered on Tuesday, Thursday, and Saturday at 11 a.m. for $5 a person.

Other Things to Do Nearby   Walk down steep Telegraph Hill to Washington Square and North Beach, the city's Bohemian district of bars, Italian restaurants, coffee houses, and City Lights Bookstore, the former hangout of Jack Kerouac, Allen Ginsberg, and other Beatnik greats.

Zone 7: SoMa/Mission

Ansel Adams Center for Photography

Type of Attraction: Three small galleries featuring changing exhibits of photography and contemporary art. A self-guided tour.

Location: 250 Fourth Street, San Francisco, CA 94103; in the SoMa District near Moscone Convention Center.

Admission: $5 for adults, $3 for students, $2 for seniors and children ages 13–17, free for children ages 12 and under.

Hours: Tuesday through Sunday, 11 a.m. to 5 p.m.; first Thursday of the month, 11 a.m. to 8 p.m. Closed Mondays and major holidays.

Phone: (415) 495-7000

When to Go: Anytime

Special Comments: All the rooms are located on one level, and a wheelchair ramp is available at the street level.

Overall Appeal by Age Group:

Pre-school	Grade School	Teens	Young Adults	Over 30	Senior Citizens
★	★★	★★★	★★★	★★★	★★★

Author's Rating: Small and intimate, with beautiful and provocative photo art on display. ★★★

How Much Time to Allow: One to two hours

Description and Comments Don't expect to find a full-blown exhibition of the famous landscape prints by Ansel Adams, the master photographer and advocate for the environment, at this gallery, which is dedicated to promoting creative photography as a fine art. His main collection is frequently on the road as a traveling exhibition. But you will find a wide-ranging selection of fine art photography, such as (on our visit) an exhibit of 20th-century photographs selected by Adams that included works by masters such as Margaret Bourke-White, Imogen Cunningham, and Brett Weston. You may find more than photographs on display—for example, Dominique Blain's "Missa," a multimedia installation of a hundred pairs of boots suspended from the ceiling in military formation. The work, a temporary exhibit on loan from the Montreal Museum of Fine Arts, is disturbing, provoking, and funny.

Touring Tips   Free (with admission) docent tours of the gallery are offered most Saturdays at 1:15 p.m. and 2 p.m.; call first to confirm.

Other Things to Do Nearby   Yerba Buena Gardens, a park and art gallery, are around the corner on Mission Street. The San Francisco Museum of Modern Art is on Third Street on the other side of Moscone Convention Center. The California Historical Society has a small gallery at 678 Mission Street, and the Cartoon Art Museum is located on the second floor of the Catholic Charities Building at 814 Mission Street.

California Historical Society

Type of Attraction: A gallery displaying temporary exhibitions from the society's collection of paintings, watercolors, drawings, lithographs, photographs, and artifacts. A self-guided tour.

Location: 678 Mission Street, San Francisco, CA 94103; in SoMa near Third Street.

Admission: $3 general admission, $1 for seniors and students, free for children ages 11 and under with an adult. Free to everyone on the first Tuesday of the month.

Hours: Tuesday through Saturday, 11 a.m. to 5 p.m. Closed Sundays, Mondays, and major holidays.

Phone: (415) 357-1848

When to Go: Anytime

Special Comments: The gallery is all on one level.

Overall Appeal by Age Group:

Pre-school	Grade School	Teens	Young Adults	Over 30	Senior Citizens
★	★	★★	★★	★★	★★★

Author's Rating: The airy, sky-lit central gallery is beautiful, but its small size relegates this museum to the fill-in category. ★★

How Much Time to Allow: One hour

Description and Comments   Founded in 1871, the California Historical Society moved to this new location, a block east of Yerba Buena Gardens, in 1995. Items from the society's vast collection rotate about four times a year, so what you see on your visit won't be what we saw on ours. But it's a very attractive gallery and worth a stop, especially for first-time visitors to California looking for insight into the state's fascinating history.

Touring Tips   Don't miss the storefront book store, which features books by California authors ranging from Jack London to Joan Didion. You'll also find unusual postcards and a map showing places around San Francisco used as locations in Hollywood films.

Other Things to Do Nearby   Yerba Buena Gardens is a block away, and just beyond that is the San Francisco Museum of Modern Art. Two other small galleries worth a visit are the Ansel Adams Center for Photography (on Fourth Street across from Moscone Convention Center) and the Cartoon Art Museum in the Catholic Charities Building (814 Mission Street).

Cartoon Art Museum

Type of Attraction: The only museum west of the Mississippi dedicated to the preservation, collection, and exhibition of original cartoon art. A self-guided tour.

Location: 814 Mission Street, San Francisco, CA 94103 (on the second floor of the Catholic Charities Building, near Yerba Buena Gardens in SoMa).

Admission: $4 for adults, $3 for seniors and students, $2 for children ages 6–12.

Hours: Wednesday through Friday, 11 a.m. to 5 p.m.; Saturday, 10 a.m. to 5 p.m.; Sunday, 1 to 5 p.m. Closed Mondays and Tuesdays.

Phone: (415) CAR-TOON.

When to Go: Anytime

Special Comments: While there's lots here to delight children, cartoons of an explicitly adult nature are placed in rooms restricted to ages 18 and older. Kids may need a lift to see most of the cartoons, which are displayed at adult eye level. If you're making a special trip, call ahead to make sure the museum isn't closed due to installation of a new exhibit.

Overall Appeal by Age Group:

Pre-school	Grade School	Teens	Young Adults	Over 30	Senior Citizens
★★	★★★	★★★	★★★	★★★★	★★★

Author's Rating: How can you resist a cartoon art museum? Too bad it isn't bigger. ★★★★

How Much Time to Allow: One to two hours

Description and Comments   From at least the turn of the century, the Bay Area has been home to a healthy population of professional cartoonists. (Maybe it's a combination of great vistas and San Francisco's relaxed atmosphere.) Well-known cartoonists spotlighted in this small museum over the years include Scott Adams ("Dilbert"), Bill Griffith ("Zippy the Pinhead"), Morrie Turner ("Wee Pals"), Phil Frank ("Farley"), and Paul Mavrides ("The Fabulous Furry Freak Brothers"). Many of the cartoons hail from San Francisco's underground "comix" movement of the late 1960s and early 1970s. Needless to say, most of the art is satirical, scathingly funny, and often risqué. Wonderful, in other words.

Touring Tips   Temporary exhibitions are set up in front rooms of the small (6,000 square feet) museum; there are about three major shows a year. In the back gallery you'll find cartoons from the permanent collection of 11,000 pieces of art, dating from the late 1700s to the present.

Other Things to Do Nearby   The Ansel Adams Center, an excellent museum of photography, is about two blocks down Fourth Street (toward Moscone Convention Center). Yerba Buena Gardens and Center for the Arts is a block down Mission Street, and the Museum of Modern Art is on Third Street on the other side of Yerba Buena Gardens.

Jewish Museum San Francisco

Type of Attraction: A museum dedicated to Jewish culture, arts and crafts, and history; changing exhibitions throughout the year. A self-guided tour.

Location: 121 Steuart Street, San Francisco, CA 94105 (one block from the Ferry Building at the foot of Market Street).

Admission: $5 for adults, $2.50 for seniors and students, free for children ages 11 and under. Free on the first Monday of the month.

Hours: Sunday through Wednesday, 11 a.m. to 5 p.m.; Thursday, 11 a.m. to 8 p.m. Closed Fridays, Saturdays, and Jewish and national holidays; open Christmas Day.

Phone: (415) 543-8880

When to Go: Anytime

Special Comments: Free tours are offered on Sunday at 2 p.m.

Overall Appeal by Age Group:

Pre-school	Grade School	Teens	Young Adults	Over 30	Senior Citizens
★	★★	★★	★★★	★★★	★★★

Author's Rating: On our visit the exhibition of ritual kiddush cups offered imaginative displays of more than 160 interpretations by contemporary American and Israeli artists. But the museum is small. ★★½

How Much Time to Allow: One hour

Description and Comments Basically two small galleries (one on street level and one downstairs), the Jewish Museum offers rotating exhibits throughout the year that highlight Jewish arts and crafts. The rooms are beautiful and well lit and, on our visit, featured beautiful art by mostly Jewish artists and craftspeople. The ritual cups ranged from the traditional to the bizarre and hilarious, such as one built of old clockworks and another incorporating a printed circuit board; both were laugh-out-loud funny. You'll see different art on your visit. But it's safe to say you'll find a high-quality exhibition imaginatively displayed.

Touring Tips You don't have to be Jewish to appreciate the art you'll find here. Use a visit to the museum as taste of what is to come in late 1999, when it moves to new and significantly larger quarters near the Museum of Modern Art in SoMa.

Other Things to Do Nearby Take a ferry to Angel Island or Tiburon from the Ferry Building just a block away. You'll also get a great, bottom-up view of the Oakland Bridge. The Federal Reserve Bank on Market Street has a display of paper currency from colonial times to the present and an exhibit that will tell you more than you ever wanted to know about international monetary policy. The area abounds with restaurants, bars, and cafes.

Mission Dolores

Type of Attraction: San Francisco's oldest building (1791) and the sixth of 21 missions built by Franciscan priests along El Camino Real, the Spanish road linking the missions from Mexico to Sonoma. Self-guided and audio tours.

Location: Dolores Street at 16th Street, in the Mission District, San Francisco.

Admission: $2 for teenagers and adults, $1 for children ages 5–12. The 45-minute audio tour is $3 per person.

Hours: Daily, 9 a.m. to 4 p.m.

Phone: (415) 621-8203

When to Go: Try to go when it's not raining; the cemetery, probably the most interesting part, is out in the open.

Special Comments: Rest rooms are near the cemetery entrance.

Overall Appeal by Age Group:

Pre-school	Grade School	Teens	Young Adults	Over 30	Senior Citizens
★	★★	★★	★★	★★★	★★★

Author's Rating: Surprisingly small, but worth visiting for an authentic taste of San Francisco's Spanish heritage. ★★

How Much Time to Allow: 30 minutes to an hour

Description and Comments With adobe walls four feet thick and the original redwood logs supporting the roof, Mission Dolores has survived four major earthquakes and is the only one of the original missions along the El Camino Real (the Royal Way) that has not been rebuilt. Mass is still celebrated in the building, which is 114 feet long and 22 feet wide. The repainted ceiling depicts original Ohlone Indian designs done with vegetable dyes. The decorative altar came from Mexico in 1796, as did the two side altars (in 1810).

Outside the mission, a diorama shows how it appeared in 1791. Peek inside the basilica, completed in 1918, to view beautiful stained-glass windows. The small museum displays artifacts such as lithographs of the California missions and a revolving tabernacle from the Philippines. You can also see the adobe walls, which were formed and sun-dried nearby. The highlight (for us anyway) is the cemetery—really a lush garden with headstones. Most of the markers are dated in the years following the California gold rush and many of the family names are Irish.

Touring Tips Film buffs won't find the headstone of Carlotta Valdes in the mission's cemetery. It was a prop in Alfred Hitchcock's *Vertigo,* part of which was filmed here.

Other Things to Do Nearby Walk a couple of blocks down 16th Street for a selection of ethnic restaurants. Dolores Street, planted with palm trees, is a handsome boulevard. The Mission District also has lots of restored Victorian homes, parks filled with children, and followers of alternative lifestyles. Both 16th Street and Mission Street show off the Mission District's diverse flavors, including offbeat bookstores, Asian restaurants, and interesting shops. (Good Vibrations, 1210 Valencia Street at 23rd Street, features everything you wanted to know about sex, and then some.) The Mission Cultural Center at 2868 Mission Street has a large second-floor gallery with changing art exhibitions, usually with a Hispanic flavor; it's free.

San Francisco Museum of Modern Art

Type of Attraction: Modern and contemporary art from the museum's permanent collection of 15,000 works and temporary shows. Self-guided and guided tours.

Location: 151 Third Street, San Francisco, CA 94103; south of Market Street below Union Square, between Mission and Howard Streets (adjacent to Yerba Buena Gardens and across from Moscone Convention Center).

Admission: $8 for adults, $5 for senior citizens, $4 for students, children 12 and under free (with an adult); half-price admission on Thursday, 6–9 p.m.; free to all on the first Tuesday of the month.

Hours: Friday through Tuesday, 11 a.m. to 6 p.m.; Thursday, 11 a.m. to 9 p.m. Closed Wednesdays and July Fourth, Thanksgiving, Christmas, and New Year's Day.

Phone: (415) 357-4000

When to Go: Anytime

Special Comments: Free 45-minute gallery tours are offered daily, starting at 11:30 a.m. and about every 90 minutes thereafter.

Overall Appeal by Age Group:

Pre-school	Grade School	Teens	Young Adults	Over 30	Senior Citizens
★	★★	★★★	★★★	★★★★	★★★★

Author's Rating: World-class modern art in a magnificent gallery that's a work of art itself. ★★★★½

How Much Time to Allow: Two hours to get the gist of the place, but art buffs should figure on half a day, easily.

Description and Comments   This new modern art emporium is just what you'd expect in San Francisco, an international center of the avant garde. Physically stunning and still new (it opened in 1995), the museum is designed to let the Bay Area's fabled light flood the four gallery levels. Even the floors are great; blond hardwood on a springy dance-floor base makes it easy on the feet. A central skylight bathes the piazza-inspired atrium in natural light; from above, you can watch other gallery visitors walk across a white metal bridge that spans the four levels below. Simply breathtaking.

Touring Tips   Take a free 45-minute tour; the first is offered at 11:30 a.m. and skips around to various galleries, whetting your appetite and revealing the museum's layout. It usually starts on level two, where the permanent collection features works by Henri Matisse, one of the first modern artists to use color as an expression of emotion. In other rooms you'll see works by masters such as Pablo Picasso and Georges Braque, who relied on form more than color in their paintings. After viewing the art on level two, take the elevator to level five, which features changing exhibits from artists of the 1990s. Bring an open mind and be ready to have some fun. You'll find more outrageous art on level four (walk across the white bridge and down the stairs) and a small photo gallery on level three.

The museum shop on the ground level is huge and has a great selection of postcards (none, alas, of the Golden Gate Bridge or Chinatown) and art books, among other things. Caffe Museo opens an hour before the museum and offers a good selection of reasonably priced items ($7 to $10), including salads, sandwiches, pizza, beer, and wine.

Other Things to Do Nearby   Yerba Buena Gardens, with an art gallery and attractive grounds, is across the street. Market Street, with a wide selection of restaurants, is a block and a half away. The Ansel Adams Center for Photography is on Fourth Street, on the other side of Moscone Convention Center, and the Cartoon Art Museum is a couple blocks down Mission Street on the second floor of the Catholic Charities Building.

Yerba Buena Gardens/Center for the Arts

Type of Attraction: A new cultural complex of green grass and public art, an art gallery, a theater, cafés, and a gift shop. A self-guided tour.

Location: 701 Mission Street, San Francisco, CA 94103; at Third Street south of Union Square in the SoMa District.

Admission: Gallery: $5 for adults, $3 for students and seniors. Free for students and seniors, Thursday, 11 a.m. to 3 p.m.; free for everyone on the first Thursday of the month from 6–8 p.m. Gardens are free.

Hours: Gallery: Tuesday through Sunday, 11 a.m. to 6 p.m.; first Thursday of the month, 11 a.m. to 8 p.m. Closed Mondays and major holidays. Theater: Box office is open 11 a.m. to 6 p.m. Tuesday through Sunday. Gardens are open daily, sunrise to 10 p.m.

Phone: (415) 978-2700 (administration); (415) 978-ARTS (ticket office)

When to Go: Anytime for the art gallery; in nice weather for the outdoor gardens.

Special Comments: A nice side trip—and a place to relax—after a visit to the huge San Francisco Museum of Modern Art or the Moscone Convention Center.

Overall Appeal by Age Group:

Pre-school	Grade School	Teens	Young Adults	Over 30	Senior Citizens
★★	★★	★★	★★	★★	★★★

Author's Rating: Of more interest to San Franciscans than to most visitors, who must take potluck on Yerba Buena's constantly changing schedule of exhibitions, shows, concerts, lectures, films, and videos. ★★

How Much Time to Allow: One hour for the gallery and as long as you care to linger in the five-and-a-half-acre gardens.

Description and Comments   Yerba Buena is a nonprofit arts complex that opened in 1993 in the up-and-coming SoMa neighborhood. It features two buildings (a two-level art gallery and a theater) and a park with an outdoor stage, two cafés, the Butterfly Garden, a redwood grove, sculptures, a waterfall, and a memorial to Dr. Martin Luther King Jr. The small gallery features temporary art exhibits that change about every two and a half months; on our visit there was a display of modern and avant-garde paintings and multimedia art—very San Francisco and a lot of fun.

Touring Tips   Stop in the gallery and pick up a current copy of the Center for the Arts newsletter, which gives a complete description of events at Yerba Buena. If the exhibit looks interesting, tour the gallery. Next, if it's a nice day, stroll the gardens; lunch or coffee at one of the cafés is another option. Free (with admission) walk-in gallery tours are offered on the second Saturday of the month at 1 p.m.

Other Things to Do Nearby   The San Francisco Museum of Modern Art is across Third Street, and the Ansel Adams Center for Photography is on Fourth Street. The Cartoon Art Museum is a block or so down Mission Street in the Catholic Charities Building. The area is surrounded by dozens of restaurants.

Zone 8: Richmond/Avenues

Asian Art Museum

Type of Attraction: The largest museum in the Western hemisphere devoted exclusively to Asian art. A self-guided tour.

Location: Golden Gate Park, San Francisco, CA 94118.

Admission: $7 for adults, $5 for seniors, $4 for children ages 12–17, free for children ages 11 and under. Free to everyone on the first Wednesday of the month. Admission to the adjacent de Young Museum is included.

Hours: Wednesday through Sunday, 9:30 a.m. to 4 p.m.; first Wednesday of the month, 9:30 a.m. to 8:45 p.m. Closed Mondays and Tuesdays, and July Fourth, Thanksgiving, Christmas, and New Year's Day.

Phone: (415) 379-8801

When to Go: Anytime

Special Comments: John F. Kennedy Drive is closed to traffic on Sundays; walk, ride a bike, or take public transportation.

Overall Appeal by Age Group:

Pre-school	Grade School	Teens	Young Adults	Over 30	Senior Citizens
★★	★★	★★★	★★★	★★★	★★★

Author's Rating: Fabulous and exotic art. ★★★½

How Much Time to Allow: One to two hours

Description and Comments The Asian Art Museum's collection is built around art donated by industrialist Avery Brundage. Today its holdings include more than 12,000 art objects spanning 6,000 years of history and representing more than 40 Asian countries. Because only about 15 percent of the collection can be displayed at a time, exhibits are rotated. On our visit, most of the first floor was closed because the permanent collection of Chinese and Korean art was being reinstalled after a special temporary exhibit ended. But the second floor was crammed with lavish paintings, sculptures, textiles, bronzes, jade from India, Korean ceramics, and more art from Japan, Persia, and Southeast Asia. The museum is scheduled to relocate to the Old Main Library building in Civic Center in 2001, which will more than double the space for its permanent collection.

Touring Tips   Special temporary exhibits are hosted in a gallery on the first floor. Plan on visiting the adjacent de Young Museum; admission is included in the Asian Art Museum admission fee. You'll find rest rooms and an excellent café at the de Young Museum.

Other Things to Do Nearby   At the Japanese Tea Garden next door, visitors can enjoy the formal garden and be served tea and cookies by a kimono-clad waitress. If you're not "museumed out," the California Academy of Sciences is on the other side of the Music Concourse in front of the museum. Walk across Martin Luther King Drive and turn right to reach the north entrance of Strybing Arboretum, 70 acres of gardens and tranquility. If it's a nice day, drive or walk to Stow Lake and rent an electric boat ($13 an hour), a rowboat ($9.50 an hour), or a bike (starting at $5 an hour).

California Palace of the Legion of Honor

Type of Attraction: A recently renovated museum of ancient and European art housed in a reproduction of an 18th-century French palace; a spectacularly scenic setting. A self-guided tour.

Location: In the northwest corner of San Francisco at 34th Avenue and Clement Street, in Lincoln Park.

Admission: $7 for adults, $5 for seniors, and $4 for children ages 12–17; children ages 11 and under free. A $2 discount is given to holders of Muni bus transfers. Admission is free to all on the second Wednesday of the month.

Hours: Tuesday through Sunday, 9:30 a.m. to 5 p.m.; first Saturday of the month, 9:30 a.m. to 8:45 p.m. Closed Mondays and Thanksgiving, Christmas, and New Year's Day.

Phone: (415) 863-3330 (recorded information); (415) 750-3600 (main switchboard)

When to Go: Anytime

Special Comments: Admission to the Legion of Honor also gives you free, same-day admission to the de Young Museum in Golden Gate Park; save your receipt.

Overall Appeal by Age Group:

Pre-school	Grade School	Teens	Young Adults	Over 30	Senior Citizens
★★	★★★	★★★	★★★★	★★★★	★★★★

Author's Rating: Rather highbrow in tone, but the building (reopened in 1995 after undergoing a $36 million seismic retrofitting and modernization) and much of the art and physical location are spectacular. ★★★★

How Much Time to Allow: Two hours

Description and Comments   Built in the 1920s and dedicated to the thousands of California servicemen who died in France in World War I, the California Palace of the Legion of Honor (most folks just say Legion of Honor) is visually stunning. Visitors enter through a magnificent courtyard dominated by an original cast of Auguste Rodin's "The Thinker." The building is in an eye-popping location overlooking the Golden Gate Bridge and the Marin Headlands; its design was inspired by the Palais de la Legio d'Honneur in Paris, built in 1786. If it all looks vaguely familiar, that's because you've watched *Vertigo* too many times on late-night TV; it's where Kim Novak went to gaze upon the Portrait of Carlotta (a movie prop you won't find in the museum).

Inside is an impressive collection of ancient and European art covering 4,000 years. Heavy hitters include David, Monet, Manet, Degas, Gainsborough, Reynolds, Rubens, Rembrandt, Van Gogh, Dalí, Picasso, Renoir, and Seurat. But more than paintings and sculptures are on display in sumptuous galleries, which feature soaring ceilings, blond hardwood floors, and copious natural light. You'll also find extensive collections of furniture, silver, and ceramics.

Touring Tips   Most of the art is on the main level, and ancient art and ceramics are on the lower-level terrace, where you'll also find an excellent, reasonably priced café, a gift shop, rest rooms, and phones. Probably the most popular galleries are the two dedicated to Rodin; these stunning rooms are just past the central rotunda on the main level. Galleries 1–9 (to the left as you face the entrance) feature medieval, Renaissance, and 18th-century art; galleries 11–19 (to the right) contain art from the 18th through the early 20th centuries. Special exhibits, which sometimes charge an extra admission fee, are held in Rosekrans Court, housed under a glass structure that floods the galleries with natural light.

Although parking is abundant around the museum, the convenient lot across from the entrance is small and fills quickly; leaving your car parked on a nearby side street may result in a stiff, uphill hike to the museum entrance. A good option is public transportation; from Union Square, take the No. 38 bus to 33rd and Clement Streets; transfer to the No. 18 bus (and save $2 on admission) or walk uphill to the museum.

Other Things to Do Nearby   Cliff House, a mile or so south on the coast, provides fantastic views of the Marin coast and Seal Rocks, home base for sea lions and a variety of marine birds; bring binoculars. There's also a restaurant and a visitor center. To the north are Fort Point and the Golden Gate Bridge; to the south are Ocean Beach (don't worry if you forget a swimsuit; the water is cold and dangerous anyway) and Golden Gate Park, where you can visit the de Young Museum for free (if you kept your receipt from the Legion of Honor). A couple of miles down the coast are the San Francisco Zoo and Fort Funston, with great views, easy trails, and hang gliders doing their thing on the strong ocean air currents.

California Academy of Sciences

Type of Attraction: A natural history museum, aquarium, and planetarium. A self-guided tour.

Location: Music Concourse Drive, Golden Gate Park, San Francisco, CA 94118.

Admission: $8.50 for adults, $5.50 for seniors and children ages 12–17, $2 for children ages 4–11. Free to all on the first Wednesday of the month. Tickets for 45-minute planetarium shows are an additional $2.50 for adults and $1.25 for seniors and children ages 6–17. "Laserium," a laser light show set to music in the planetarium, costs $6 for adults and $5 for seniors and children ages 6–13.

Hours: Memorial Day to Labor Day, daily, 9 a.m. to 6 p.m.; rest of the year, daily, 10 a.m. to 5 p.m.

Phone: (415) 750-7145

When to Go: To avoid boisterous school groups on school days, go in the afternoon. Penguins are fed at 11:30 a.m. and 4 p.m.; feeding in the Fish Roundabout is at 2 p.m.

Special Comments: Free one-hour tours led by museum-trained guides are offered throughout the day; inquire at the information desk near the entrance.

Overall Appeal by Age Group:

Pre-school	Grade School	Teens	Young Adults	Over 30	Senior Citizens
★★★★★	★★★★★	★★★★★	★★★★	★★★★	★★★★

Author's Rating: Kids go nuts over this place. But other than the fish in the aquarium, it's a museum full of static displays and dioramas. ★★★

How Much Time to Allow: Two hours

Description and Comments   The lobby of the West's oldest scientific institution (founded in 1853) greets visitors with a huge fossil skeleton of a *Tyrannosaurus rex;* this sets the tone for this kid-friendly science museum. Major exhibits include African Safari, which is full of wildlife dioramas and an African water-hole display where families can pose for snapshots. The action picks up in the Steinhart Aquarium, a classic fish emporium that kids love. The aquarium features 14,000 species of fish, plus reptiles and amphibians. Especially creepy are the prehistoric-looking gar fish and tanks full of piranhas. At the Fish Roundabout, visitors stroll up a ramp and peer through windows into a 100,000-gallon tank to see rays and circling sharks. The very young will like the Touch Tidepool, where they can pick up and inspect live sea urchins, hermit crabs, and starfish. Wild California has more dioramas and displays that show off the state's scenery and varied wildlife. Downstairs is Academy Cafe, which features reasonably priced family fare. The Academy Store offers books, toys, posters, and gifts for naturalists of all ages.

Touring Tips   From the main entrance, head left into African Safari and work your way counterclockwise past temporary exhibits to the aquarium (on the other side of the central courtyard). Then come back to the main entrance to view Wild California and an exhibit of gems and minerals. The Morrison Planetarium offers sky shows at 2 p.m. on weekdays and on the hour from 11 a.m. to 4 p.m. on weekends; tickets go on sale half an hour before show time at the box office in the Earth and Space Hall. Shows aren't offered on some days, so call ahead. An additional feature is "Laserium," an hour-long show in which visitors gaze at intricate light patterns cast on the planetarium dome by a krypton gas laser and listen to rock and roll. Call (415) 750-7138 for a schedule of shows on Thursday through Sunday evenings.

Other Things to Do Nearby   The de Young Museum and the Asian Art Museum are across the Music Concourse, and the Japanese Tea Garden is next to the Asian Art Museum. Behind the natural history museum is Shakespeare Garden, an oasis of quiet that could prove beneficial to adults after a hectic tour of the California Academy of Sciences. Gardeners—and just about everyone else—will enjoy Strybing Arboretum, 70 acres of plants and gardens; it's just past the Japanese Tea Garden. If it's a nice day, drive or walk to Stow Lake and rent an electric boat ($13 an hour), a rowboat ($9.50 an hour), or a bike (starting at $5 an hour). The de Young Museum has an excellent café, and you'll find a snack bar at Stow Lake.

Cliff House

Type of Attraction: A San Francisco oceanside tourist landmark with spectacular views, a restaurant, a small museum, a collection of antique mechanical amusement machines, shops and a deli, a cliffside park, the ruins of a Victorian-era resort, and a camera obscura. Self-guided tour.

Location: 1090 Point Lobos Avenue (at the Great Highway), San Francisco, CA 94121.

Admission: Free

Hours: Visitor center: daily, 10 a.m. to 5 p.m. Restaurant, daily 9 a.m. to 3:30 p.m. and 5 to 10:30 p.m. weekdays; 8:30 a.m. to 4 p.m. and 5 to 11 p.m. Friday through Sunday for breakfast, lunch, and dinner.

Phone: (415) 386-3330 (Cliff House Restaurant); (415) 556-8642 (visitor center)

When to Go: When the coast isn't socked in by fog. Cocktails at sunset in the restaurant are a San Francisco tradition.

Special Comments: Lots of stairs and climbing if you opt to explore Sutro Heights Park and the ruins of Sutro Baths. There's also a steep set of stairs down to the visitor center.

Overall Appeal by Age Group:

Pre-school	Grade School	Teens	Young Adults	Over 30	Senior Citizens
★★★★	★★★★	★★★★	★★★	★★★	★★★

Author's Rating: A bizarre blend of spectacular scenery, an overpriced seafood restaurant with a view, San Francisco history, and tourist schlock. Probably not to be missed, but it's no tragedy if you do. ★★½

How Much Time to Allow: 30 minutes to an hour (longer if you dine)

Description and Comments   A San Francisco tourist landmark for more than 100 years, Cliff House still packs them in—often by the busload. The attraction? Dining with a magnificent view of the Pacific, with Seal Rocks in the foreground just off shore. (Seal Rocks is a haven for sea lions and marine birds.) But there's more here than the opportunity to drop big bucks for an expensive lunch or dinner while you watch waves crash against the rocks. The whole place is owned by the National Park Service (it's part of the Golden Gate National Recreation Area); at the visitor center next to the restaurant you can view vintage photographs of Cliff House through its various incarnations (it was destroyed by fire twice). Next door (so to speak) are the concrete ruins of Sutro Baths, a three-acre swimming emporium that once held 1.6 million gallons of water and rented 20,000 bathing suits and 40,000 towels a day. Kids and adults will enjoy Musee Mechanique, an unworldly collection of antique penny arcade amusements that will still eat up your quarters; and the Giant Camera, a huge camera obscura you walk into to see an image of Seal Rocks magnified on a huge parabolic screen.

Touring Tips Across the Great Highway and just up the hill is Sutro Heights Park, where you walk up a short, steep path to a great view overlooking Cliff House, Seal Rocks, the ruins, and the Pacific. It's worth the effort.

Other Things to Do Nearby Drive a few miles south to Fort Funston and watch hang gliders do their thing. You can take a walk along Ocean Beach, which starts just below Cliff House, and view actual native San Franciscans. Golden Gate Park, with museums and trails, and a lake that rents rowboats, is to the south. You can't miss the entrance; look for the Dutch windmill.

M. H. de Young Memorial Museum

Type of Attraction: San Francisco's oldest art museum features American paintings, sculpture, and decorative arts from colonial times to the 20th century. A self-guided tour.

Location: Golden Gate Park, 75 Tea Garden Drive, San Francisco, CA 94188.

Admission: $7 for adults, $5 for seniors 65 and over, $4 for children ages 12–17, free for children ages 11 and under. Free for everyone on the first Wednesday of the month. Admission to the adjacent Asian Art Museum is included.

Hours: Wednesday through Sunday, 9:30 a.m. to 5 p.m.; first Wednesday of the month, 9:30 a.m. to 8:45 p.m. Closed Mondays and Tuesdays, and on July Fourth, Thanksgiving, Christmas, and New Year's Day.

Phone: (415) 863-3330

When to Go: Anytime

Special Comments: On Sundays, John F. Kennedy Drive in Golden Gate Park is closed; walk, ride a bike, or take public transportation to the museum.

Overall Appeal by Age Group:

Pre-school	Grade School	Teens	Young Adults	Over 30	Senior Citizens
★★	★★½	★★½	★★★½	★★★★	★★★★

Author's Rating: San Francisco's oldest art emporium may be its best. ★★★★½

How Much Time to Allow: Two hours

Description and Comments Big art in big rooms is one way of describing what you'll find at this venerable old museum in Golden Gate Park. While most of the collection is American art (including works by masters such as Grant Wood and Georgia O'Keeffe), you'll also find extensive collections of pre-Columbian, African, Oceanic, and textile art. Families with younger children should stop by Gallery One, a permanent exhibit featuring art, a family guide to assist parents and children in discussing themes and ideas in the museum, two computers, books, and a writing and drawing area for children.

While the building isn't in the same league as the Legion of Honor (its sister museum), the art is more diverse and not as relentlessly highbrow. San Francisco is in a turmoil over the future location of the de Young Museum. The building is externally braced from damage incurred in the 1989 earthquake, and the controversy is whether to keep it in Golden Gate Park or move it downtown (where proponents say the museum will get more visitors). Talk to any San Franciscan who loves art and you're bound to get an impassioned argument one way or the other.

Touring Tips Wednesdays and Thursdays are the least crowded, while Saturdays are usually very busy (and you must pay to park your car on nearby streets). Forget driving here on Sundays; the only way to reach the museum is by foot, bicycle, or public transportation. The small café is excellent; in nice weather you can eat al fresco near a pool and fountain and watch hummingbirds in the garden.

Other Things to Do Nearby The Asian Art Museum is located in the same building and admission is included; don't miss it. Next door is the Japanese Tea Garden, where kimono-clad waitresses will serve you tea and cookies. The California Academy of Sciences is a short walk away. Walk across Martin Luther King Drive and turn right to reach the north entrance of Strybing Arboretum, 70 acres of gardens and tranquility. If it's a nice day, drive or walk to Stow Lake and rent an electric boat ($13 an hour), a rowboat ($9.50 an hour), or a bicycle (starting at $5 an hour).

Fort Point National Historic Site

Type of Attraction: A Civil War–era brick coastal fortification beneath Golden Gate Bridge; superb vistas of San Francisco's key topographical features. Guided and self-guided tours.

Location: In the Presidio at the end of Marine Drive (at the southern end of the Golden Gate Bridge), San Francisco.

Admission: Free; donation requested

Hours: Wednesday through Sunday, 10 a.m. to 5 p.m. Closed Mondays and Tuesdays, and Thanksgiving, Christmas, and New Year's Day.

Phone: (415) 556-1693

When to Go: In July and August come before noon if you're driving; the small parking lot fills fast. A better option in these busy months (or whenever the weather is nice) is to ride a bike or walk along the Golden Gate Promenade to the fort and its dramatic setting.

Special Comments: Lots of steep, narrow stairs, tricky footing, and a scarcity of handrails in the fort. Portable rest rooms are located outside the entrance of the fort, and flush toilets are near the wharf on Marine Drive. Bring a jacket or sweater; Fort Point can be very windy and cool.

Overall Appeal by Age Group:

Pre-school	Grade School	Teens	Young Adults	Over 30	Senior Citizens
★★★	★★★★	★★★★	★★★★	★★★★★	★★★★★

Author's Rating: Come just for the view; the old fort is neat, too. Put this on your "must see" list. ★★★★★

How Much Time to Allow: One hour; longer for a guided tour and a demonstration

Description and Comments   This fort, built between 1853 and 1861 by the U.S. Army Corps of Engineers, was designed to prevent the entrance of a foreign fleet into San Francisco Bay. The setting—the Golden Gate Bridge overhead, the San Francisco skyline to the east, the rugged Marin Headlands across the straight, and the Pacific Ocean stretching to the horizon—is breathtaking. Ideally, first-time visitors to San Francisco should be blindfolded and brought to Fort Point, where the blindfold should come off; the result would leave them gasping for breath. It's that spectacular.

History buffs will enjoy exploring the fort, which symbolizes the commercial and strategic military importance of San Francisco. But most visitors will simply want to hoof it to the fourth (and highest) level for an even better view of the dramatic panorama (with Golden Gate Bridge traffic pounding overhead). The interior of the fort is bare bones, but some of the rooms on upper levels contain photo exhibits about its past. Film buffs will recognize the spot where James Stewart fished Kim Novak out of San Francisco Bay in Alfred Hitchcock's classic thriller, *Vertigo*. A final note: The fort's impressive muzzle-loading cannons (rendered obsolete by rifled cannons during the Civil War and removed by 1900) were never fired in anger.

Touring Tips   Go to the gift shop on the ground level to catch a free 17-minute video introduction to the fort. You can sign up here for a free guided tour, pick up a self-guided tour booklet, see a schedule of demonstrations (such as gun-loading by costumed personnel), and buy a postcard. You can also rent a 40-minute audio tour of the fort ($2.50 for adults, $1 for children). Be sure to walk around the sea wall to the chain-link fence for a full view of the Pacific Ocean. You may also see die-hard surfers and swimmers in wetsuits negotiating the surf and ships passing under the bridge.

Other Things to Do Nearby   At the southern end of the Golden Gate Bridge on Lincoln Boulevard is a scenic overlook, visitor center, parking lot, and starting point for a walk on the bridge or along paths overlooking the Pacific. The best bet for getting there is to drive, although you can walk up the very steep path. The Presidio, a former U.S. Army base that's now part of Golden Gate National Recreation Area, is filled with old buildings, a museum, a military cemetery, a golf course, trails, and stands of eucalyptus trees planted with military precision.

Drive south along the Pacific for more great views, magnificent private residences, the California Palace of the Legion of Honor (a classy art museum also used in *Vertigo*), Cliff House, and Ocean Beach (bring a frisbee and a dog). On the way back downtown from Fort Point are the Palace of Fine Arts and the Exploratorium (a hands-on science museum) and Fort Mason (with museums, restaurants, fishing piers, marinas, and picnic areas).

Japanese Tea Garden

Type of Attraction: A stroll-style garden with a harmonious blend of architecture, landscape, bridges, footpaths, shrines, and gates; tea house serves tea, soft drinks, juices, and cookies. A self-guided tour.

Location: In Golden Gate Park next to the Asian Art Museum.

Admission: $2.50 for adults and teenagers, $1 for seniors and children ages 6–12; children ages 5 and under free. Admission is free to all March through September, daily, 9 to 9:30 a.m. and 5:30 to 6:30 p.m.; and October through February, daily, 8:30 to 9 a.m. and 5:30 to 6 p.m. (or until sunset).

Hours: March through September, daily, 9 a.m. to 6:30 p.m.; October through February, daily, 8:30 a.m. to 6 p.m. (or until sunset). Open every day of the year.

Phone: (415) 752-4227

When to Go: In nice weather. In April the cherry trees are in bloom.

Special Comments: Some mild uphills and uneven footing.

Overall Appeal by Age Group:

Pre-school	Grade School	Teens	Young Adults	Over 30	Senior Citizens
★★	★★	★★	★★★★	★★★★	★★★★

Author's Rating: Beautiful and fascinating. ★★★★

How Much Time to Allow: One to two hours

Description and Comments   In Japan, a garden is considered one of the highest art forms, and after a visit to the Japanese Tea Garden you'll understand why. On winding paths visitors encounter carp pools, a pagoda, a bronze Buddha, dwarf trees, flowers, cherry trees, footbridges, and a Zen garden. Even when it's packed with hordes of visitors, this artfully designed garden imparts a sense of tranquility.

The garden was part of the Japanese Village exhibit of the California Midwinter International Exposition of 1894, which was held in what is now the Music Concourse in Golden Gate Park. It was built by Japanese artisans, and in the decades after the exposition closed, the garden was expanded from one acre to five acres. In that limited amount of space the garden expresses the essence of nature by the use of specially selected plants and stones arranged in harmony with the landscape. Really.

Touring Tips   Come in nice weather and don't rush the experience. The atmosphere in the garden is extremely soothing—a perfect stop on a harried touring schedule. Tea service by a kimono-clad waitress in the Tea House is $2.50. The fortune cookies were originally introduced here in 1914. (Ironically, they're called Chinese fortune cookies now.) Stop in the gift shop to see a wide array of Japanese gifts and toys, including kites and fans.

Other Things to Do Nearby   The Asian Art Museum, where you can find more Japanese art, is next door; the de Young Museum and its collection of mostly American art is included in the price of admission. The California Academy of Sciences is on the south side of the Music Concourse and is a favorite with families. Inside the Academy of Sciences you'll find the Steinhart Aquarium (a must for children) and the Morrison Planetarium (a must for space cadets). Across Martin Luther King Drive is the Strybing Arboretum, 70 acres of gardens. If it's a nice day, drive or walk to Stow Lake and rent an electric boat ($13 an hour), a rowboat ($9.50 an hour) or a bike (starting at $5 an hour).

Presidio Museum

Type of Attraction: A museum located in the Presidio's oldest surviving building showcases uniforms, weapons, photographs, dioramas, infantry field kits, and other military items. A self-guided tour.

Location: Lincoln Boulevard at Funston Avenue, in the Presidio, located in the northwest corner of San Francisco.

Admission: Free

Hours: Wednesday through Sunday, noon to 4 p.m. Closed Mondays and Tuesdays, and Thanksgiving, Christmas, and New Year's Day.

Phone: (415) 556-0856

When to Go: Anytime

Special Comments: One set of stairs from street level to the porch entrance. Until recently, the museum was called the Presidio Army Museum.

Overall Appeal by Age Group:

Pre-school	Grade School	Teens	Young Adults	Over 30	Senior Citizens
★★	★★	★★	★★	★★	★★

Author's Rating: Interesting, but not worth a special trip. ★½

How Much Time to Allow: 30 minutes to an hour

Description and Comments This old army post, occupied initially by the Spanish in 1776 and by U.S. forces since 1848, was transferred to the National Park Service in 1994. The Old Station Hospital, built in 1857, houses the Presidio Museum, a wide-ranging collection of military artifacts and historical displays highlighting the Presidio's past. (Presidio, by the way, is Spanish for "military outpost"). The first exhibit you see is a collection of 19th-century surgical tools, including sobering items such as a skull corer. Less ghoulish and fairly interesting are old photos, a diorama of San Francisco, displays on the 1906 earthquake and fire (and the army's crucial role in its aftermath), and military field kits from both world wars. All this is housed in a ramshackle building with uneven floors. Rangers on hand say long-term plans are to move the museum to new quarters on the Presidio.

Touring Tips Behind the museum building are two authentic refugee buildings left over from the 1906 disaster, when thousands of homeless San Franciscans were housed in similar small wooden buildings. One of the structures has a photo exhibit of the period; the other is decked out with period pieces such as an old bed, a woodstove for heating and cooking, a trunk, a table, and a few personal items. It's very spartan and puts a human face on the famous disaster.

Other Things to Do Nearby The Presidio, now part of the Golden Gate National Recreation Area, contains 1,480 acres, 510 historic buildings, coastal defense fortifications, a national cemetery, a historic airfield, beaches, coastal bluffs, miles of hiking and biking trails, and spectacular scenery. It's easy to spend half a day here. Visitors can explore the heart of the Presidio with a free 12-page walking tour; in addition, park rangers and docents lead programs on a variety of topics on weekends and some weekdays. The nearby Presidio Visitor Center (phone (415) 561-4323) is open daily, 9 a.m. to 5 p.m. A fast-food restaurant, snack bar, and small café are located on the main post.

San Francisco Zoo

Type of Attraction: At 66 acres and growing, the largest zoo in northern California. A self-guided tour.

Location: Sloat Boulevard at 45th Street; in southwest San Francisco near Great Highway and the Pacific Coast.

Admission: $7 for those aged 16 and older, $3.50 for children ages 12–15 and seniors, $1.50 for ages children ages 3–11. Admission to the Children's Zoo is an additional $1 per person and free for children ages 2 and under.

Hours: Daily, 10 a.m. to 5 p.m. The Children's Zoo is open Monday through Friday, 11 a.m. to 4 p.m.; Saturday and Sunday (and daily in the summer), 10:30 a.m. to 4:30 p.m.

Phone: (415) 753-7083

When to Go: In nice weather. Also, animals are more active early in the day and late in the afternoon.

Special Comments: Most animals are in unenclosed exhibits that are open to the elements; bring an umbrella if rain is expected.

Overall Appeal by Age Group:

Pre-school	Grade School	Teens	Young Adults	Over 30	Senior Citizens
★★★★★	★★★★★	★★★★	★★★★	★★★	★★★

Author's Rating: An older zoo that's nice but not spectacular. Most animals are in natural habitats behind moats, not pacing in fenced enclosures. ★★★½

How Much Time to Allow: Two hours to half a day

Description and Comments This venerable animal park, which opened in 1929, is making a comeback after the 1989 earthquake (it damaged a few exhibits). Millions of dollars have been spent on innovative exhibits such as the Primate Discovery Center; a recently passed San Francisco bond issue paves the way for more renovations and repairs—and ultimately, the management hopes, world-class status. Unlike most older zoos, the majority of the 1,000-plus animals are housed in naturalistic enclosures behind moats, and visitors can see the exotic wildlife hanging from trees, roaming through fields, and frequently snoozing in high grass.

The zoo's major exhibits include Gorilla World, one of the largest naturalistic gorilla habitats in the world; visitors can get close-up views of the huge primates from strategically placed viewing areas. This is also one of only a handful of zoos in the United States with koalas, the cuddly, eucalyptus-munching marsupials from Down Under. Penguin Island features a colony of more than 50 Magellanic penguins frolicking in a 200-foot pool (black tie required). Another recent addition is the Feline Conservation Center, a 20,000-square-foot sanctuary where rare and endangered cats such as snow, black, and Persian leopards are bred and studied. At the Children's Zoo youngsters can pet and feed barnyard animals such as goats, sheep, chickens, donkeys, and even a llama. Be careful, though: if this South American cousin of the camel starts to smile, he may be about to spit.

Touring Tips   The Zebra Train is an excellent way for first-time visitors to get a feel for the zoo. The motorized trolley ride takes about 30 minutes; you can't get off during the tour, but you can scope out the terrain and walk back later to visit whatever interests you. The cost is $2.50 for adults and $1.50 for children and seniors. The train departs near the entrance of the Children's Zoo daily at 11 a.m., noon, 1 p.m., 2 p.m., and 3:15 p.m. (in winter, on Saturdays and Sundays only), weather permitting. See the big cats get fed Tuesday through Sunday at 2 p.m. in the Lion House. Visitors can get fed at the indoor-outdoor Terrace Cafe overlooking the bear dens.

Other Things to Do Nearby   Breathe salt air and feel sand between your toes at nearby Ocean Beach, four miles long and always windy and wavy. But don't plan on a frolic in the surf; the water is always dangerous, even when it looks calm. To the south is Fort Funston ("Fort Fun" to the natives), where you'll find easy hiking trails, great views of the ocean and the seaside terrain, and hang gliders taking advantage of the area's high winds. To the north along Ocean Beach is Golden Gate Park, with some of San Francisco's best museums, trails, gardens, monuments, the Japanese Tea Garden, and a Dutch windmill. Across from the entrance to the San Francisco Zoo is the Carousel Diner, a hot-dog stand out of the 1950s; looming over the parking lot is an oversized representation of a dog clad in a chef's hat. Fans of Bill Griffith's "Zippy the Pinhead" comic strip will instantly recognize this fine example of suburban kitsch.

Strybing Arboretum and Botanical Gardens

Type of Attraction: A botanical garden featuring more than 7,500 plant species on 70 acres. Guided and self-guided tours.

Location: Ninth Avenue at Lincoln Way, Golden Gate Park, San Francisco, CA 94122.

Admission: Free

Hours: Monday through Thursday, 8 a.m. to 4:30 p.m.; Saturday, Sunday, and holidays, 10 a.m. to 5 p.m.

Phone: (415) 661-1316

When to Go: When it's not raining or extremely windy. The California Native Garden is spectacular from late March to early April.

Special Comments: Free docent tours are offered Monday through Friday at 1:30 p.m., and Saturday and Sunday at 10:30 a.m. and 1:30 p.m.; no tours on major holidays. No bicycles, roller skates, skateboards, frisbees, active sports, barbecues, or pets are allowed in the park.

Overall Appeal by Age Group:

Pre-school	Grade School	Teens	Young Adults	Over 30	Senior Citizens
★★★	★★	★★	★★★	★★★	★★★★

Author's Rating: Blissfully peaceful and beautiful; a chance to further appreciate San Francisco's Mediterranean climate. ★★★

How Much Time to Allow: One to two hours

Description and Comments Manicured grounds, paved paths, benches, ponds, and towering trees that absorb most of the nearby traffic sounds are the hallmarks of this world-class botanical garden in Golden Gate Park, which opened in 1940. San Francisco's unusual climate allows an astounding range of plant life to flourish in the gardens, including plants from Australia, South Africa, Chile, Mexico, Central America, New Zealand, and Asia. Seventeen gardens are grouped in three major collections: Mediterranean Climate, Temperate Climate, and Montane Tropic.

Touring Tips The garden has a north entrance near the Japanese Tea Garden and a main entrance on Martin Luther King Drive near Lincoln Boulevard. Unless you have a specific interest in, say, the plant life found in New World cloud forests, just wander around in a clockwise or counterclockwise direction, and eventually you'll see everything. The Strybing Bookstore offers botany and horticulture books, cards, gift items, and maps for self-guided tours of the garden and other nearby attractions (such as the Marin

Headlands). Hard-core gardeners may want to check out the Helen Crocker Russell Library of Horticulture, the largest of its kind in California; it's open daily (except major holidays), 10 a.m. to 4 p.m. The store and library are located near the main entrance.

Other Things to Do Nearby　The Japanese Tea Garden, the Asian Art Museum, and the de Young Museum are close to the north entrance of the garden. The California Academy of Sciences is across the Music Concourse from the two art museums; it's very popular with families. If it's a nice day, drive or walk to Stow Lake and rent an electric boat ($13 an hour), a rowboat ($9.50 an hour), or a bike (starting at $5 an hour). Hungry? The de Young Museum has an excellent café, and you'll find a snack bar at Stow Lake.

Zone 11: Yonder Marin

Mount Tamalpais—East Peak

Type of Attraction: A half-mile hike to the summit of Mount Tamalpais and a stunning view of San Francisco, the bay, the Golden Gate Bridge, and the Pacific Ocean. A self-guided tour.

Location: Mount Tamalpais State Park, 12 miles north of the Golden Gate Bridge in Marin County. Exit US 101 at Sausalito and follow signs to the park.

Admission: Free. Parking in the lot below the summit is $5 per car; $4 for seniors.

Hours: Daily, sunrise to sunset

Phone: (415) 388-2070

When to Go: In clear weather

Special Comments: Locals call it "Mount Tam." Wear sturdy shoes if you opt for the steep hike to the summit.

Overall Appeal by Age Group:

Pre-school	Grade School	Teens	Young Adults	Over 30	Senior Citizens
★★	★★★	★★★	★★★	★★★	★★

Author's Rating: Yet another mind-boggling view of San Francisco; this one may be the best. ★★★½

How Much Time to Allow: One hour

Description and Comments The incredible vistas you see on the drive up to the top of Tamalpais are good, but it's really worth the effort to go the distance. Until 1930, tourists rode the Mount Tamalpais and Muir Woods Railway to the top, where a tavern and dance pavilion were located near the present parking lot. From the summit, the view is spectacular—including 3,890-foot Mount Diablo to the east and, on a clear day, the snow-capped Sierras 140 miles to the east. Any soaring birds you see are probably turkey vultures. If you're not up for the half-mile, 220-foot-elevation-gain hike to the summit, you can opt for a self-guided tour around the peak or just enjoy the view from the overlook near the rest rooms.

Touring Tips   Unless you're wearing hiking boots and are used to narrow foot trails, don't take the plank trail to the summit. Although it looks easy, it quickly turns very steep, with treacherous footing. Instead, take the Verna Dunshee Trail, a self-guided tour just over half a mile long that goes counterclockwise around the peak; pick up a brochure in the gift shop. The trail starts to the right of the rest rooms. A snack bar, phones, and drinking water are available near the parking lot.

Other Things to Do Nearby   Hikers of all abilities will find plenty of scenic trails in the state park. Muir Woods National Monument is a grove of majestic coastal redwoods, the tallest trees in the world. Stinson Beach, located beneath steep hills rising to Mount Tam, offers vistas of the sea and hills, while Muir Beach, further south down Route 1, has a semicircular cove where you can relax and enjoy the scenery. To the north, Point Reyes National Seashore provides more stunning scenery, hiking trails, miles of undisturbed beaches, and, December through April, whale-watching. In Sausalito, you'll find restaurants, shopping, and yacht- and people-watching opportunities galore. Tiburon is where really wealthy San Franciscans live; stroll the path along the waterfront and shop in the town's upscale retail stores.

Muir Woods National Monument

Type of Attraction: A grove of majestic coastal redwoods, the tallest trees in the world. A self-guided tour.

Location: 12 miles north of the Golden Gate Bridge in Marin County. Exit US 101 at Sausalito and follow the signs.

Admission: $2 per person ages 17 and up

Hours: Daily, 8 a.m. to sunset; visitor center is open daily, 9 a.m. to 4:30 p.m.

Phone: (415) 388-1540

When to Go: When it's not raining. To avoid crowds, arrive before 10 a.m. or after 6 p.m.

Special Comments: Roads leading to the park are steep and winding; vehicles more than 35 feet long are prohibited. No picnicking is allowed in Muir Woods.

Overall Appeal by Age Group:

Pre-school	Grade School	Teens	Young Adults	Over 30	Senior Citizens
★★★	★★★★	★★★★	★★★★	★★★★	★★★★★

Author's Rating: These huge trees are truly awesome. ★★★★

How Much Time to Allow: 30 minutes to an hour to stroll the paved loops in Redwood Canyon; avid hikers can spend several hours or the entire day hiking unpaved trails leading to Mount Tamalpais State Park.

Description and Comments No trip to Northern California would be complete without a glimpse of these world-famous giant redwood trees, which are much like the trees that covered much of the Northern hemisphere 140 million years ago. Today, redwoods are only found in a narrow, 500-mile discontinuous strip of Pacific coast from southern Oregon to below Monterey, California. The huge specimens in the Cathedral and Bohemian Groves are the largest redwoods in Muir Woods. The tallest is 252 feet; the thickest is 14 feet across. The oldest is at least 1,000 years old, but most of the mature trees here are 500 to 800 years old. The towering trees, the fallen giants, and the canyon ferns impart awe and tranquility—even when the paved paths are clogged with visitors.

Touring Tips Take the time and the modest effort to walk the paved path to Cathedral Grove; you'll encounter fewer people, and there are more fallen trees. Try walking the paths in a figure eight by crossing footbridges over Redwood Creek. Avoid visiting on weekends and holidays; parking is usually a real hassle. The best time to come is early or late in the day; you'll encounter fewer people, and there's a better chance of seeing wildlife. The park's 560 acres include six miles of walking trails; except for the mostly level and paved main trail, the footpaths are unpaved. Wear sturdy hiking boots. The park, located in a deep canyon, is cool and shaded, so wear a jacket. If you plan to venture beyond the main trail, bring rain gear. A gift shop, snack bar, rest rooms, drinking water, and telephones are located near the main entrance.

Other Things to Do Nearby You can drive almost to the summit of Mount Tamalpais for yet another incredible view of San Francisco, the Golden Gate Bridge, and the Pacific Ocean. On a scenic drive through Marin County, stop at Stinson Beach (where you can relax and enjoy the coastal scenery) and take the white-knuckle curves along Route 1, which follows the Pacific coast. Drive north to Point Reyes National Seashore to enjoy windswept terrain, miles of undisturbed beaches, hiking trails, and whale-watching (December through April). Plenty of places to eat and drink in Mill Valley and Sausalito.

Zone 12: Berkeley

Berkeley Art Museum

Type of Attraction: One of the largest university art museums in the world. A self-guided tour.

Location: 2626 Bancroft Way, Berkeley, CA 94720 (on the University of California at Berkeley campus).

Admission: $6 for adults; $4 for seniors and children ages 12–17, non–UC Berkeley students, and disabled persons; free for children ages 11 and under. Free to everyone on Thursdays, 11 a.m. to noon, and 5 p.m. to 9 p.m.

Hours: Wednesday, Friday through Sunday, 11 a.m. to 5 p.m; Thursday, 11 a.m. to 9 p.m. Closed Mondays, Tuesdays, and major holidays.

Phone: (510) 642-0808

When to Go: Anytime

Special Comments: The museum's seven galleries are linked by carpeted ramps and stairs, and an elevator is available.

Overall Appeal by Age Group:

Pre-school	Grade School	Teens	Young Adults	Over 30	Senior Citizens
★	★★	★★★	★★★	★★★	★★★

Author's Rating: Not on par with the Legion of Honor or the de Young Museum across the bay, but still a major collection in a visually striking building. ★★★

How Much Time to Allow: One to two hours

Description and Comments　In seven linked, spiraling galleries, the Berkeley Museum of Art displays its collections of Asian art, Western art from the Renaissance to the present, and the work of 20th-century painter Hans Hofmann. The other four galleries are devoted to exhibitions that change about four times a year. The poured concrete walls, carpeted ramps, and unusual layout add to the enjoyment to the eclectic collection of art on display, although—as is the case with many state university buildings—it's a bit shabby around the edges.

Touring Tips   Parking in Berkeley is notoriously bad; if you decide to drive, arrive as early as possible to find a space in one of the many public lots in the vicinity of the campus. A better bet from San Francisco is BART; the Berkeley station is located at Center and Shattuck Streets, and it's a short walk east to the campus. The Museum Store, open during gallery hours, offers a wide range of books and periodicals on art and film, as well as posters, cards, and jewelry. Cafe Grace features better-than-average museum dining indoors or in the sculpture garden.

Other Things to Do Nearby   The Hearst Museum of Anthropology is across Bancroft Way on the ground floor of Kroeber Hall. Fossil hunters and Barney fans won't want to miss the Museum of Paleontology, which houses one of the largest and oldest collections of fossils in North America. It's open Monday through Friday, 8 a.m. to 4 p.m. , and it's located in the Valley Life Sciences Building on campus; admission is free. Youngsters will love the Lawrence Hall of Science, a hands-on science museum with an added bonus—a spectacular view of the Bay Area. Either drive or take a university Hill Service Shuttle to get there. Located in the heart of the People's Republic of Berkeley, Telegraph Avenue features an incredibly diverse selection of restaurants, gift shops, street vendors, street musicians, street people, and gray-haired hippies; it's as if the 1960s never ended.

Lawrence Hall of Science

Type of Attraction: A hands-on science museum for youngsters. A self-guided tour.

Location: Centennial Drive, Berkeley, CA 94720 (below Grizzly Peak Boulevard, overlooking the University of California, Berkeley campus).

Admission: $6 for adults; $4 for seniors, students, and children ages 7–18; $2 for children ages 3–6.

Hours: Daily, 10 a.m. to 5 p.m. Closed on major holidays.

Phone: (510) 642-5132

When to Go: When the weather is clear and you can enjoy the spectacular view.

Special Comments: Parking is very tight on this hilltop setting, so try to arrive early. In 1998 the lots became part of the university parking system, and now visitors must pay 50 cents per half-hour to park. If you're not driving, take BART to the downtown Berkeley station and catch the Local Shuttle at Center Street and Shattuck Avenue. Then transfer to the Hill Service Shuttle at the Hearst Mining Circle on campus. Call Transportation Services at (510) 643-5708 for info.

Overall Appeal by Age Group:

Pre-school	Grade School	Teens	Young Adults	Over 30	Senior Citizens
★★★★★	★★★★★	★★★	★★	★★	★★

Author's Rating: A great view but otherwise strictly for youngsters. ★

How Much Time to Allow: At least half a day for kids; you'll have to drag them away.

Description and Comments   Named after Ernest O. Lawrence, one of the University of California at Berkeley's best-known Nobel Prize laureates, this hands-on science museum enthralls tots through grade-schoolers. It's hard to list even a sampling of the many activities available, but they include a gravity wall, earthquake exhibits, play areas, and math and chemistry exhibits (where kids play scientific sleuths and use real chemical and forensic tests to solve a whodunit). Hour-long planetarium shows are offered on weekend and holiday afternoons; tickets are $2, and children ages 5 and under aren't admitted. The Lawrence Memorial Room, probably the only exhibit in the museum that's not hands-on and geared toward children, features artifacts, an explanation of how a cyclotron works, and awards given to Ernest O. Lawrence (including his Nobel Prize in physics).

Touring Tips   Outside, youngsters can clamber on Pheena—a 50-foot, 3,000-pound replica of a fin whale—and a 60-foot long, scientifically accurate model of a double-helix DNA molecule. Adults can keep one eye on the kids and the other on the drop-dead view. A cafeteria on the lower level offers school lunch–style fare and a panoramic view, while the museum store sells books, games, puzzles, and science-oriented gift items.

Other Things to Do Nearby   The university's Botanical Garden is located in Strawberry Canyon, on the winding road below the Lawrence Hall of Science and above the campus stadium; it includes a redwood grove, a large selection of native plants, plant species from around the world, and picnic tables. Fossil hunters won't want to miss the Museum of Paleontology, which houses one of the largest and oldest collections of fossils in North America. It's open Monday through Friday, 8 a.m. to 4 p.m.; it's located in the Valley Life Sciences Building on campus and admission is free. The Berkeley Art Museum, also on campus, is an excellent art museum. Telegraph Avenue is a hopping street scene with an incredibly diverse selection of restaurants, gift shops, street vendors, street musicians, street people, and gray-haired hippies.

Phoebe Hearst Museum of Anthropology

Type of Attraction: A small museum highlighting California cultural anthropology, ethnography, and archaeology. A self-guided tour.

Location: University of California at Berkeley, 103 Kroeber Hall, Berkeley, CA 94720 (Bancroft Way at College Avenue on the University of California Berkeley campus).

Admission: $2 for adults, $1 for seniors, and 50 cents for children 16 and under. Free to everyone on Thursday.

Hours: Wednesday, Friday through Sunday, 10 a.m. to 4:30 p.m.; Thursday, 10 a.m. to 9 p.m. Closed Mondays, Tuesdays, and major holidays.

Phone: (510) 643-7648

When to Go: Anytime

Special Comments: The gift shop offers a good selection of handmade crafts.

Overall Appeal by Age Group:

Pre-school	Grade School	Teens	Young Adults	Over 30	Senior Citizens
★★	★★	★★	★★	★★	★★★

Author's Rating: Ho-hum. Unless you have a strong interest in anthropology, think of this small gallery of static exhibits as a fill-in spot. ★½

How Much Time to Allow: 30 minutes

Description and Comments   In this one-room gallery you'll find tools and implements of California's Native Americans, including food preparation utensils, baskets, brushes, trays, paddles, bowls, fishing gear, and hunting tools such as slings, traps, and bows and arrows. Interesting, yes, but the exhibits don't get the adrenaline flowing.

Touring Tips   The most interesting display is about Ishi, the last Yahi Indian of Northern California who lived and worked in the museum from 1911 until his death in 1916. But it's a very small exhibit.

Other Things to Do Nearby   The Berkeley Art Museum is across the street. Fossil hunters will like the Museum of Paleontology, housing one of the largest and oldest collections of fossils in North America. It's open Monday through Friday, 8 a.m. to 4 p.m.; it's located in the Valley Life Sciences Building on campus and admission is free. Youngsters will love the Lawrence Hall of Science, a hands-on science museum with a spectacular view of the Bay Area. Drive or take a university Hill Service Shuttle to get there. Telegraph Avenue features a lively street scene with an incredibly diverse selection of restaurants, gift shops, street vendors, street musicians, street people, and gray-haired hippies.

Zone 13: Oakland

Oakland Museum of California

Type of Attraction: A museum showcasing California's ecology, history, and art. A self-guided tour.

Location: 1000 Oak Street, Oakland, CA 94607. The museum is one block from the Lake Merritt BART station. If you're driving from San Francisco, cross the Oakland Bridge and get on Interstate 880 south; exit at Jackson Street. The museum parking garage has entrances on Oak Street and 12th Street.

Admission: $5 for adults, $3 for seniors and students, free to children ages 6 and under. Free to everyone on Sunday, 4 to 7 p.m.

Hours: Wednesday through Saturday, 10 a.m. to 5 p.m.; Sunday, noon to 7 p.m. Closed Mondays and Tuesdays, and July Fourth, Thanksgiving, Christmas, and New Year's Day.

Phone: (510) 238-3401

When to Go: Anytime

Special Comments: Free tours are available on request most weekdays and at 1:30 p.m. on weekends. Check with the information desk at the entrance of each gallery.

Overall Appeal by Age Group:

Pre-school	Grade School	Teens	Young Adults	Over 30	Senior Citizens
★★★	★★★★	★★★	★★★	★★★★	★★★★

Author's Rating: Everyone should find something to like in this large, attractive, and diversified museum. ★★★½

How Much Time to Allow: Depending on your interests in things Californian, anywhere from two hours to half a day.

Description and Comments The Oakland Museum is actually three museums in one. The first level features beautiful displays and dioramas of California's various ecosystems, ranging from coastal to mountains to deserts. Level two focuses on history, culture, and technology from precolonial days through the 20th century. In the exhibits focusing on modern life, you'll find displays and artifacts that touch on Hollywood, mountain bikes, Harley-Davidson choppers, the Beat movement, surfboards, political and labor strife, and most of the things we associate with the frenetic, hedonistic California lifestyle; a confusing jumble, but fascinating. Level three is a large art gallery highlighting California artists and art ranging from huge landscapes to off-the-wall modern work. It's a gorgeous, airy, and light-filled space.

Touring Tips   Plan to linger on the second level's exhibits on history, technology, and culture. California's muticultural past is on display in all its diversity, with stories of Native American weavers and hunters, Spanish missionaries, vaqueros, gold miners, railroad builders, factory workers, union organizers, and immigrants—virtually everyone who sought the California dream. It's a big chunk of Americana. Outside—integrated with the graceful, three-tiered building erected in 1969—are seven and a half acres of gardens that give the museum the look of an old, overgrown villa. Evergreens around the perimeter provide a tall screen, while regular rows of small trees mark elevations inside the complex; flowers and fragrant plants line the walkways.

Other Things to Do Nearby   The historic Paramount Theater (at 21st Street and Broadway) is a spectacular example of art deco architecture; the old movie palace has been converted to a general entertainment complex. Oakland's waterfront Jack London Square is the city's version of Fisherman's Wharf—and just as contrived. At Lake Merritt, a beautiful outdoor wildlife sanctuary, you can rent a boat, take a lakeside stroll, and view wildlife. Kids will enjoy Children's Fairyland on the north side of the lake. Fairy tales come alive at old Gepetto's workshop and other settings from children's stories. The Oakland Museum's café serves salads, sandwiches, snacks, and desserts; for more upscale dining, the Bay Wolf (3853 Piedmont Avenue) is known for its California and Mediterranean cuisine; it's open for lunch and dinner.

PART ELEVEN

Dining in San Francisco

The voluptuous pleasures of San Francisco's table still ring with the echoes of the Barbary Coast and Baghdad by the Bay. People have been writing of memorable dining here since Mark Twain sojourned in the city and wrote of its charms in the 1860s. More than ever, people in San Francisco consider restaurants and the culinary arts one of the most important topics of discussion. And the chefs and their patrons concern themselves with both the end result and the entire process—from the origin and freshness of the ingredients, to the utensils with which they are prepared, to diners' and servers' states of mind. There's a personal quality to gastronomy in the city. Chefs adapt the lessons learned in European kitchens to the dictates of locally grown foodstuffs and further incorporate the diverse cultural influences of the region.

Perhaps unique to the city is the possibility of genuinely friendly service. The best San Francisco restaurants are not stuffy or formal and will not treat you with condescension. Most are happy to hear about unsatisfactory service or a dish that was improperly prepared. Unlike New York, San Francisco has few of the imposing, intimidating, ghastly expensive Taj Mahals of gastronomy whose raison d'être has been obscured by interests other than the table. And as for Los Angeles . . . well, San Francisco eats L.A.'s lunch!

This is the capital of the three-star restaurant. Diners want the best in food and service and the best in price. And they want no snooty waiters. Even the four- and five-star restaurants are short on pretense and long on service. The common person is king here; he (or she) just happens to have a discriminating palate.

Whence came this egalitarian gastronomy? The Old West—with its frontier meritocracy, lusty democracy, and demand for good vittles—is newest here. You still find the legacies of Spanish missionaries and ranchers, Chinese railroad workers, Italian vintners, and nouveau riche gold miners seeking to mirror European splendor. Mix in Japanese, Vietnamese, and Russian immigration. Add the organic and sustainable agriculture movement, local growers' experimentation with artisan crops such as Japanese persimmons, kiwis, habanero peppers, and heirloom varieties of fruits and vegetables; and the blossoming of boutique wineries, cheese-makers, and game farms. Put these with a skepticism of high-falutin' New York ways, and you have the makings of the culinary revolution that began in the 1970s. Creative chefs are drawn to the area because of the year-round availability of superior produce and the relative sophistication of native palates and tastes, along with diners' senses of humor and commitment to a casual brand of elegance.

There's a restaurant to suit any occasion, appetite, or budget. There's also likely to be a very good, even great place to dine within walking distance of anywhere you might be. San Francisco is known, after all, as the "walking city." A brisk walk through the cool tang of a San Francisco fog is one of the best appetizers the city has to offer. And it's free.

■ Tourist Places ■

In the restaurant profiles that make up this section, you may notice that a few well-known or highly visible restaurants are missing. This is not an oversight. The following restaurants may come to your attention, but in our opinion they're not as worthwhile as other comparable options.

Sinbad's   Seafood
Pier 2, Embarcadero Way (415) 781-2555

Scoma's   Seafood
Pier 47, Fisherman's Wharf (415) 771-4383
588 Bridgeway, Sausalito (415) 332-9551

E&O Trading Company   Southeast Asian
314 Sutter Street (415) 693-9136

Beach Chalet   American Bistro and Microbrewery
1000 Great Highway (415) 386-8439

Cliff House   Italian/American/Seafood
1090 Point Lobos (415) 386-3330

Empress of China   Pan Chinese
838 Grant Avenue (415) 434-1345

Lori's   "Fabulous 50s Diner"
500 Sutter Street (415) 981-1950
149 Powell Street (415) 677-9999
336 Mason Street (415) 392-8646

The Restaurants

■ **Our Favorite San Francisco Restaurants** ■

We have developed detailed profiles for the best and most interesting restaurants (in our opinion) in town. Each profile features an easily scanned heading that allows you, in just a second, to check out the restaurant's name, cuisine, star rating, cost, quality rating, and value rating.

Cuisine   This is actually less straightforward than it sounds. A couple of years ago, for example, "pan-Asian" restaurants were generally serving what was then generally described as "fusion" food—Asian ingredients with European techniques, or vice versa. Since then, there has been a pan-Asian explosion in the area, but nearly all specialize in what would be street food back home: noodles, skewers, dumplings, and soups. Once-general categories have become subdivided—French into bistro fare and even Provençal; "new continental" into regional American and "eclectic"—while others have broadened and fused: Middle Eastern and Provençal into Mediterranean, Spanish and South American into nuevo Latino, and so on. In these cases, we have generally used the broader terms (i.e., "French"), but sometimes added a parenthetical phrase to give a clearer idea of the fare. Again, though, experimentation and "fusion" is growing more common, so don't hold us, or the chefs, to a strict style.

Star Rating   The star rating is an overall rating that encompasses the entire dining experience, including style, service, and ambience in addition to the taste, presentation, and quality of the food. Five stars is the highest rating possible and connotes the best of everything. Four-star restaurants are exceptional and three-star restaurants are well above average. Two-star restaurants are good. One star is used to indicate an average restaurant that demonstrates an unusual capability in some area of specialization—for example, an otherwise unmemorable place that has great barbecue chicken.

Cost   To the right of the star rating is an expense description that provides a comparative sense of how much a complete meal will cost. A complete meal for our purposes consists of an entree with vegetable or side dish and choice of soup or salad. Appetizers, desserts, drinks, and tips are excluded.

Inexpensive	$14 and less per person
Moderate	$15–25 per person
Expensive	$26–40 per person
Very Expensive	Over $40 per person

Quality Rating   On the far right of each heading appears a number and a letter. The number rates the food quality on a scale of 0–100, with 100 being the best rating attainable. It is based expressly on the taste, freshness of ingredients, preparation, presentation, and creativity of food served. There is no consideration of price. If you are a person who wants the best food available, and cost is not an issue, you need look no further than the quality ratings.

Value Rating   If, on the other hand, you are looking for both quality and value, then you should check the value rating, expressed in letters. The value ratings are defined as follows:

A	Exceptional value, a real bargain
B	Good value
C	Fair value, you get exactly what you pay for
D	Somewhat overpriced
F	Significantly overpriced

Payment   We've listed the type of payment accepted at each restaurant using the following code: AMEX equals American Express (Optima), CB equals Carte Blanche, D equals Discover, DC equals Diners Club, MC equals MasterCard, and VISA is self-explanatory.

Who's Included   Restaurants in San Francisco open and close at an alarming rate. So, for the most part, we have have tried to confine our list to establishments with a proven track record over a fairly long period of time. The exceptions here are the newer offspring of the demi-gods of the culinary world—these places are destined to last, at least until our next update. Newer or changed establishments that demonstrate staying power and consistency will be profiled in subsequent editions. Also, the list is highly selective. Noninclusion of a particular place does not necessarily indicate that the restaurant is not good, but only that it was not ranked among the best in its genre. Detailed profiles of individual restaurants follow in alphabetical order at the end of this chapter.

The Best San Francisco Restaurants

Name	Star Rating	Price Rating	Quality Rating	Value Rating	Zone
Afghan					
Helmand	★★★	Inexp	85	A	6
American					
Campton Place	★★★★★	Exp	99	A	3
House of Prime Rib	★★★½	Exp	89	B+	2
LuLu	★★★½	Mod	89	B+	7
Fog City Diner	★★★	Mod	89	B+	6
Tadich Grill	★★★	Mod	89	A	4
Izzy's Steak and Chop House	★★★	Mod	85	A	5
Ruth's Chris Steak House	★★½	Mod	78	B	2
The Courtyard	★★½	Mod	77	B	5
Original Joe's	★★	Inexp	78	B	3
Perry's	★★	Inexp	75	B+	5
Tommy's Joynt	★★	Inexp	75	A	2
Hamburger Mary's	★½	Inexp	69	C	7
Bar					
Compass Rose	★★★★	Exp	99	B+	3
Bar and Grill					
Harpoon Loui's	★★	Inexp	77	B	7
Pat O'Shea's Mad Hatter	★★	Inexp	75	A	8
Cafeteria					
Salmagundi	★★	Inexp	75	B	3
California					
Moose's	★★★★	Mod	95	A–	6
Cafe Majestic	★★★½	Exp	87	B+	2
California Culinary Academy	★★½	Inexp	79	A	2
Chinese					
Tommy Toy's	★★★½	Mod	85	B+	4
China House Bistro	★★★½	Inexp/Mod	84	A	8

The Best San Francisco Restaurants (continued)

Name	Star Rating	Price Rating	Quality Rating	Value Rating	Zone
Chinese (continued)					
Hunan Village	★★★	Inexp	83	B+	1
Yuet Lee	★★½	Inexp/Mod	78	A	1
House of Bamboo	★★½	Mod	76	B	2
Yank Sing	★★	Inexp	76	B	4
Sam Woh	★½	Inexp	69	B+	1
Continental					
Bizou	★★★½	Mod	89	B	7
The Brazen Head	★★★	Mod	80	A	5
Crêperie					
Ti Couz	★★	Inexp	74	B	7
Deli/Barbecue					
Max's Opera Cafe	★½	Mod	79	B	2
Dive					
Red's Java House	★	Inexp	65	A	7
Eclectic					
Stars	★★★★½	Exp	95	B	2
Momi Toby's Revolution Cafe	★★	Inexp	78	C+	2
French					
Masa's	★★★★★	Exp	99	A	3
Alain Rondelli	★★★★★	Mod/Exp	98	A	8
Fleur de Lys	★★★★	Exp	95	B+	4
Fringale	★★★★	Mod	95	A	7
South Park Cafe	★★★½	Mod	87	A	7
Brasserie Tomo	★★★	Mod	88	A	6
Woodward's Gardens	★★★	Mod	83	B	7
Baker Street Bistro	★★½	Inexp/Mod	79	A	5
Le Trou	★★½	Mod	79	B	7
Bistro Clovis	★★	Mod	78	B	2
German					
Speckman's	★★	Inexp	75	B	7

The Best San Francisco Restaurants (continued)

Name	Star Rating	Price Rating	Quality Rating	Value Rating	Zone
Greek					
Stoyanof's	★★★	Inexp/Mod	85	B	8
Hof Brau					
Lefty O'Doul's	★★	Inexp	75	B	3
Indian					
Indian Oven	★★★½	Inexp/Mod	88	B	8
Iraqi/Mesopotamian					
YaYa Cuisine	★★★½	Mod	88	B	8
Italian					
Fior d'Italia	★★★½	Mod	85	A	6
Ristorante Ecco	★★★½	Mod	85	C	7
Buca Giovanni	★★★	Mod	89	B	6
Zuni Cafe and Grill	★★★	Mod	89	B+	2
Enrico's	★★★	Mod	88	B	6
Splendido's	★★★	Mod	88	B+	4
Washington Square Bar and Grill	★★★	Mod	88	B+	6
La Fiammetta	★★★	Mod	85	A	2
Rosmarino	★★★	Mod	84	B–	8
The Stinking Rose	★★★	Mod	80	B	6
Aromi	★★½	Exp	78	B	2
Latin American					
Cha Cha Cha	★★★½	Inexp/Mod	85	A	8
Mediterranean					
PlumpJack Cafe	★★★	Mod	83	B	5
Mexican					
Casa Aguila	★★½	Mod	79	B	8
New American					
The Dining Room at the Ritz-Carlton	★★★★★	Exp	97	B	3
The Carnelian Room	★★★★	Exp	93	B	4

The Best San Francisco Restaurants (continued)

Name	Star Rating	Price Rating	Quality Rating	Value Rating	Zone
New American (continued)					
Sheraton Palace Garden Court	★★★★	Exp	92	C–	4
Harry Denton's	★★★★	Mod	90	A	7
Town's End Restaurant and Bakery	★★★	Mod	84	B+	7
Clement Street Bar and Grill	★★	Mod	78	C+	8
Oyster Bar					
Swan Oyster Depot	★★	Inexp	78	A	2
Puerto Rican					
El Nuevo Fruitlandia	★★	Inexp	76	B+	7
Seafood					
PJ's Oyster Bed	★★★	Mod	87	B	8
Spanish					
Zarzuela	★★★½	Mod	83	A	5
Steak House					
John's Grill	★★★	Mod	80	A	3
Thai					
Dusit	★★½	Inexp	79	B+	7
Vegetarian					
Greens	★★★★	Mod	99	A	5
Millennium	★★★½	Mod	90	B+	2
Vegetarian Indian					
The Ganges	★★★	Inexp	80	A	8
Vietnamese					
Thanh Long	★★★	Inexp/Mod	86	B	8
Hung Yen	★½	Inexp	69	B+	7
Tu Lan	★½	Inexp	69	A	7

■ **More Recommendations** ■

The Best Bagels

Marin Bagel Company   1560 Fourth Street, San Rafael (415) 457-8127
Noah's New York Bagels   Bon Air Center, Greenbrae (415) 925-9971

The Best Beer Lists

Duke of Edinburgh   10801 North Wolf Road, Cupertino (408) 446-3853
Mayflower Inne   1533 Fourth Street, San Rafael (415) 456-1011
The Pelican Inn   10 Pacific Way, Muir Beach (415) 383-6000
Tommy's Joynt   1101 Geary Street (415) 775-4216

The Best Burgers

Bubba's   566 San Anselmo Avenue, San Anselmo (415) 459-6862
Flippers   482 Hayes Street, San Francisco (415) 552-8880
The Golden Nugget   2200 Fourth Street, San Rafael (415) 456-9066
Harpoon Louie's   55 Stevenson Street, San Francisco (415) 543-3540
Kirk's   1330 Sunnyvale-Saratoga Road, Sunnyvale (408) 446-2988
Pat O'Shea's Mad Hatter   3848 Geary Boulevard, San Francisco
  (415) 752-3148
Perry's   1944 Union Street, San Francisco (415) 922-9022
Rockridge Cafe   5492 College Avenue, Oakland (510) 653-1567
Spanky's   1900 Sir Francis Drake Boulevard, Fairfax (415) 455-9050

The Best Business Dining

Adriana's   999 Anderson Drive, San Rafael (415) 454-8000
Bizou   598 Fourth Street, San Francisco (415) 543-2222
California Cafe   The Village Center, Corte Madera (415) 924-2233
The Carnelian Room   555 California, San Francisco (415) 433-7500
The Duck Club   100 El Camino Real, Menlo Park (650) 322-1234
Joe LoCoco's   300 Drakes Landing Road, Greenbrae (415) 925-0808
Rue de Main   22622 Main Street, Hayward (510) 537-0812
Tadich Grill   240 California, San Francisco (415) 391-2373

The Best Coffee

Brasserie Tomo   745 Columbus Avenue, San Francisco (415) 296-7668
The Dipsea Cafe   200 Shoreline Highway, Mill Valley (415) 381-0298

The Best Desserts

Campton Place   340 Stockton Street, San Francisco (415) 781-5555
Masa's   648 Bush Street, San Francisco (415) 989-7154

The Best Dining and Dancing

Chez Luis   4170 El Camino Real, Palo Alto (650) 493-1660
Harry Denton's   169 Steuart Street, San Francisco (415) 882-1333
Horizons   558 Bridgeway, Sausalito (415) 331-3232
Jose's Caribbean Restaurant   2275 El Camino Real, Palo Alto
   (650) 326-6522

The Best Martinis

The Buckeye   15 Shoreline Highway, Mill Valley (415) 331-2600
Compass Rose   315 Powel Street, St. Francis Hotel, San Francisco
   (415) 774-0167
House of Prime Rib   1906 Van Ness, San Francisco (415) 885-4605
No Name Bar   757 Bridgeway, Sausalito (415) 332-1392
Stars   150 Redwood Alley, San Francisco (415) 861-7827

The Best Oyster Bars

LuLu   816 Folsom Street, San Francisco (415) 495-5775
PJ's Oyster Bed   737 Irving Street, San Francisco (415) 566-7775
Swan Oyster Depot   1517 Polk Street, San Francisco (415) 673-1101

The Best Pizza

Benissimo Ristorante   18 Tamalpais Drive, Corte Madera
   (415) 927-2316
Frankie Johnnie & Luigi Too   939 West El Camino Real, Mountain
   View (650) 967-5384
LoCoco's Pizzeria   638 San Anselmo Avenue, San Anselmo
   (415) 453-1238
Milano Pizza   1 Blackfield Drive, Tiburon (415) 388-9100
Mulberry Street Pizza   101 Smith Ranch Road, San Rafael
   (415) 472-7272
Salute   706 Third Street, San Rafael (415) 453-7596

The Best Seafood

The Fish Market   3150 El Camino Real, Palo Alto (650) 493-9188

Gate Five   305 Harbor Drive, Sausalito (415) 331-5355
Rooney's   38 Main Street, Tiburon (415) 435-1911
Sam's Anchor Cafe   27 Main Street, Tiburon (415) 435-4527
Tadich Grill   240 California, San Francisco (415) 391-2373

The Best Sunday Brunches

The Buckeye   15 Shoreline Highway, Mill Valley (415) 331-2600
California Cafe   The Village Center, Corte Madera (415) 924-2233
Mikayla at the Casa Madrona   801 Bridgeway, Sausalito (415) 332-0502
North Sea Village   300 Turney Street, Sausalito (415) 331-3300
Sheraton Palace Garden Court   Market at New Montgomery
   (415) 392-8600
The Station House   Main Street, Point Reyes Station (415) 663-1515

The Best Sushi Bars

Robata Grill   591 Redwood Highway, Mill Valley (415) 381-8400
Samurai   2633 Bridgeway, Sausalito (415) 332-8245
Yoshi's   510 Embarcadero West, Oakland (510) 238-9200

The Best Wee Hours Service

Marin Joe's   1585 Casa Buena Drive, Corte Madera (415) 924-2081
Max's Opera Cafe   601 Van Ness, San Francisco (415) 771-7300
Sam Woh   815 Washington Street, San Francisco (415) 982-0596
Yuet Lee   1300 Stockton Street, San Francisco (415) 982-6020

The Best Wine Bars

El Paseo   17 Throckmorton Avenue, Mill Valley (415) 388-0741
Hayes and Vine   377 Hayes Street, San Francisco (415) 626-5301
Manka's Inverness Lodge   Calendar Way at Argyle, Inverness
   (415) 669-1034
The Mountain Home Inn   810 Panoramic Highway, Mill Valley
   (415) 381-9000
Rue de Main   22622 Main Street, Hayward (510) 537-0812

ALAIN RONDELLI

French	★★★★★	Mod/Exp	**QUALITY** **98**
			VALUE **A**

126 Clement Street, San Francisco
(415) 387-0408   Zone 8 Richmond/Avenues

Reservations: Required
When to go: Sundays and weeknights
Entree range: $16–19; 6-course
  tasting menu, $55
Payment: AMEX, MC, VISA
Service rating: ★★★★
Friendliness rating: ★★★★★

Parking: Street
Bar: Full
Wine selection: Limited but good
Dress: Informal, dressy
Disabled access: Good
Customers: Locals, businesspeople,
  tourists

Dinner: Wednesday–Sunday, 5:30–10 p.m.; Monday and Tuesday, closed

Setting & atmosphere: Understated elegance in an area of Clement Street that gains cachet as the sun sets: padded banquettes, pale beamed ceilings, cream walls with glowing sconces, and a few flowers and candles. A mirrored copper bar reflects scattered Impressionist paintings and servers in bright domino waistcoats; slow, cool jazz on the sound system casts a seductive, dreamy effect.

House specialties: Stylish and original French menu changes seasonally, but it often includes a creamy artichoke and oyster soup sprinkled with pastry-wrapped oysters, artichoke hearts, and crisp sage; fresh herb salads; onion brioche tart with rosemary; lamb pot au feu with oregano, lemon, and horseradish; tripe provençal; rabbit cooked in three styles with orange-glazed carrots, green olives, and basil.

Other recommendations: Six-, nine-, or twelve-course tasting menus; warm chocolate cake with pecan praline; sweet risotto with almond tuile and warm fruit compote; orange savarin with orange cream diplomat.

Summary & comments: Among the abundantly gifted chefs in San Francisco, Alain Rondelli's genius is unique. Formerly chef at Ernie's, he opened his own venue in 1993 to ecstatic acclaim. His menus read like the offhand musings of a master: bass, cumin, and fennel acidule; sweet potato, mint, and cilantro chiffonade. But there's nothing casual about his art. Foodstuffs pass through his hands to reveal their humble, miraculous origins; their colors, scents, and textures; their essential vitality. Give yourself over to Rondelli's wizardry and you surrender to a poem of the season, celebrate its most dramatic elements, contemplate its subtle intimations. When the restaurant is packed, the interval between courses can be a bit long. Slow down. Singular art is worth savoring.

Honors & awards: *Esquire* Best New Restaurant, 1994; *Bon Appetit* Best New Restaurant, 1994.

AROMI

			QUALITY
Italian	★★½	Exp	**78**

	VALUE
	B

1507 Polk Street, San Francisco
   (415) 775-5977   Zone 2 Civic Center

Reservations: Accepted	Parking: Street
When to go: Anytime	Bar: Full
Entree range: $7.50–16.50	Wine selection: Fair and expensive
Payment: VISA, MC, AMEX	Dress: Business
Service rating: ★★	Disabled access: Yes
Friendliness rating: ★★	Customers: Locals

Dinner: Sunday–Thursday, 5–10 p.m.; Friday and Saturday, 5–10:30 p.m.

Setting & atmosphere: In a rather cacophonous part of town, Aromi is a small island of relative serenity. The wooden bar occupies a marble floor. The dining room floor is a superbly crafted wood, laid diagonally. The kitchen is set apart by a flower-decked counter. Small tables create an intimate, European setting.

House specialties: Osso bucco in an aromatic broth with white beans and greens; chicken livers in balsamic vinegar sauce; grilled salmon with pesto; roast pork with sun-dried tomatoes and red wine sauce; shellfish in a sauce of tomatoes and fennel.

Other recommendations: A peppery pasta called penne alla vodka; house-made sausage in red wine and cream.

Summary & comments: A pleasant place with a cook who originally majored in chemistry. The menu changes seasonally, and hopefully the wine list will, too; it's expensive beyond its worth. But don't stay away. Pay the $8 corkage fee and bring your own. You'll be glad you did.

BAKER STREET BISTRO

			QUALITY
French	★★½	Inexp/Mod	**79**

	VALUE
	A

2953 Baker Street, San Francisco
   (415) 931-1475   Zone 5 Marina

Reservations: Recommended; required on weekends	Payment: AMEX, MC, VISA
	Service rating: ★★
When to go: Weekdays and nights	Friendliness rating: ★★★
Entree range: Lunch, $3.50–6.25; dinner, $8–13; prix fixe, $14.50	Parking: Street
	Bar: Beer, wine

(Baker Street Bistro)

Wine selection: Limited but good
Dress: Casual, informal
Disabled access: Good but cramped

Customers: Locals, businesspeople, tourists

Breakfast: Monday–Saturday, 6:30 a.m.–noon
Lunch: Tuesday–Sunday, 11 a.m.–4 p.m.
Dinner: Tuesday–Thursday, 5–9 p.m.; Friday and Saturday, 5–10:30 p.m.

Setting & atmosphere: Bewitchingly minuscule French café and bistro occupying two small rooms with yellow walls and an open kitchen on a quiet, tree-lined street.

House specialties: Duck liver pâté; escargots forestière; mousseline of scallops; lamb stew printanier; blanquette de veau; rabbit in mustard sauce.

Other recommendations: Nightly specials; for lunch, salade niçoise; baguette sandwiches with cornichons.

Summary & comments: Baker Street Bistro would not be extraordinary on the boulevards of Paris, but it is in San Francisco, primarily for its rock-bottom pricing sauced with generous dollops of Gaelic charm. The kitchen is tiny, which makes for slow service; the food is not of a quality impressive enough to write to France about, but it is tasty and attractively served and the portions are adequate. The daytime café is tres gentil for coffee and a breakfast pastry, or a sandwich or salad lunch.

BAYWOLF				
Mediterranean	★★★★	Mod	**QUALITY**	
			90	
3853 Piedmont Avenue			**VALUE**	
(510) 655-6004 Zone 13 Oakland			**A**	

Reservations: Recommended
When to go: Any time
Entree range: $12.25–17.50
Payment: VISA, MC
Service rating: ★★★
Friendliness rating: ★★★

Parking: Street
Bar: Beer and wine
Wine selection: Excellent
Dress: Business
Disabled access: Fair
Customers: Local, business, tourist

Lunch: Monday–Friday, 11:30 a.m.–2 p.m.
Dinner: Monday–Friday, 6–9 p.m.; Saturday and Sunday, 5:30–9 p.m.

Setting & atmosphere: Two relatively small dining rooms and some nooks and alcoves give the place the intimate feeling of a lovely country inn decorated in the earlier part of this century. The sedate interior is contrasted by a more casual atmosphere on the front deck, where an almost seaside feeling prevails.

House specialties: The menu changes every two weeks. Fortnightly offerings usually feature a particular region of the Mediterranean: Spain, South of France, Italy, etc. Occasionally the menu will migrate to New Orleans or the American Southeast, but it always returns to its roots on the Middle Sea. Past offerings at dinner have included crayfish bisque with corn and chervil; buckwheat crêpes with smoked trout; sautéed soft-shell crabs; grilled duck with peach chutney; and horseradish mashed potatoes.

Other recommendations: Lunch has featured zucchini soup with pesto cream; veal and spinach salad with chickpeas; and grilled swordfish with couscous, cilantro, cucumber, and curry vinaigrette.

Summary & comments: Ask for parking secrets before arriving. In its 20 years of operation the Baywolf has earned a very loyal following of local people and regular passers-through. Many local businesspeople come here four times a week for lunch. The owners began life in literature and academe, but their devotion to the culinary arts led them along the same path as their contemporary, Alice Waters of Chez Panisse. You can still see the exactitude of the academic and the passion and imagination of the man of letters in their work, though.

BISTRO CLOVIS

French	★★	Mod	QUALITY
			78
			VALUE
1596 Market Street, San Francisco			**B**
(415) 864-0231 Zone 2 Civic Center			

Reservations: Accepted	Parking: Street
When to go: Anytime	Bar: Beer, wine
Entree range: $7.50–12.95	Wine selection: Good
Payment: MC, VISA	Dress: Casual, business
Service rating: ★★★	Disabled access: Yes
Friendliness rating: ★★★	Customers: Locals, businesspeople

Open: Monday–Thursday, 11:30 a.m.–11 p.m.; Friday, 5 p.m.–midnight; Saturday and Sunday, closed

Setting & atmosphere: Very small; nice and simple, with wood floors. Chairs and tables are restored classics; tables are set with fresh flowers. Old photos and high ceilings create the sense that you've stepped into another time.

(Bistro Clovis)

House specialties: A large blackboard displays a wide variety of daily bistro fare. Hot potato salad with herring; lamb salad with sun-dried tomatoes; smoked salmon in white wine sauce; jumbo prawns with avocado and whatever is fresh in the market that day.

Other recommendations: Beef bourguignonne, veal stew, and a delightful range of appetizers and desserts.

Summary & comments: Traditional, simply prepared, well-presented French bistro food. Come here for dinner after work; it's accessible from much of the city. Relax, enjoy a glass of good wine, and dine in peace.

BIZOU			
Continental	★★★½	Mod	QUALITY **89**
598 Fourth Street, San Francisco			VALUE **B**
(415) 543-2222 Zone 7 SoMa/Mission			

Reservations: Recommended	Parking: Street
When to go: Anytime	Bar: Full
Entree range: Lunch, $7–11; dinner,	Wine selection: Limited but good
$10.50–17.50	Dress: Informal
Payment: AMEX, MC, VISA	Disabled access: Good
Service rating: ★★★★	Customers: Locals, businesspeople,
Friendliness rating: ★★★★	tourists

Lunch: Monday–Friday, 11:30 a.m.–2:30 p.m.
Dinner: Monday–Saturday, 5:30–10:30 p.m.; Sunday, closed

Setting & atmosphere: Simple, rustic, but warm and inviting small bistro with quiet, exceedingly friendly, efficient service.

House specialties: Crisp Italian flat breads and pizzas; baked brandade of local cod; buckwheat ravioli with butternut squash; braised beef cheeks with watercress and horseradish; rosemary-braised lamb shank with creamy polenta; curried vegetable tagine; tomatoes with fresh anchovies in a sherry vinaigrette; Catalan sizzling shrimp.

Other recommendations: Delightfully presented traditional desserts, varying with the seasons. Summer berry pudding; bittersweet chocolate vacherin in crème anglaise.

Summary & comments: Jewel-box bistros have sprung up like wildflowers in this formerly industrial area of San Francisco. Attentive, efficient service—along with a quiet atmosphere and some rock-solid creativity and

(Bizou)

know-how in the kitchen—sets this one apart. Bizou's chef Loretta Keller provides a panoply of sturdy, unaffected cuisine from the provinces of France, Italy, and Spain.

BRASSERIE TOMO

French	★★★	Mod	QUALITY
			88

			VALUE
745 Columbus Avenue, San Francisco			**A**
(415) 296-7668 Zone 6 North Beach			

Reservations: Accepted	Parking: Street
When to go: Anytime	Bar: Beer, wine
Entree range: $9.95–17	Wine selection: Very good
Payment: AMEX, VISA, MC	Dress: Business
Service rating: ★★★	Disabled access: Yes
Friendliness rating: ★★★	Customers: Locals, businesspeople

Dinner: Monday–Friday, 6–10 p.m.; Saturday and Sunday, closed

Setting & atmosphere: Small, intimate French style; well-set tables covered with linen matching the decor; plentiful silver and monogrammed plates.

House specialties: There is an old Persian saying to the effect that if you can make a good soup, you can do anything well. They make a good soup here. Despite the Marx Brothers connotations, the duck soup is worth the trip. Fresh greens and salads; sauced dishes, including sweetbreads; excellent foie gras; desserts built around fresh fruits and cream.

Other recommendations: An eight-course, set menu.

Summary & comments: Chef Tomo Okuda, a French-trained Japanese practitioner, strives for perfection, not only in the kitchen but in every facet of the restaurant's operation and patrons' dining experience. Perhaps that's why the place is so small—attention to detail is easier.

THE BRAZEN HEAD

Continental	★★★	Mod	QUALITY
			80

	VALUE
	A

3166 Buchanan at Greenwich Avenue, San Francisco
  (415) 921-7600   Zone 5 Marina

Reservations: Not accepted	**Parking:** Street
When to go: Before 8 p.m. and after 10 p.m.	**Bar:** Full service
	Wine selection: Good
Entree range: $10.95–14.95	**Dress:** Casual
Payment: No credit cards; ATM nearby	**Disabled access:** None
Service rating: ★★	**Customers:** Locals, other restaurant
Friendliness rating: ★★★	workers, writers

Dinner: Daily, 5:30 p.m.–1 a.m.

Setting & atmosphere: Except for the lack of trophy animal heads, this place has the look and feel of a rich, cozy, European hunting lodge. All is deep and dark; polished hardwood and brass trim. Antique etchings and photographs cover the walls. A loyal patronage returns regularly, and one sometimes gets the feeling of being in the television bar Cheers. No credit cards or checks are accepted, but there is an ATM next to the rest rooms.

House specialties: Meat! (And fish.) As befits the hunting lodge atmosphere, grills and roasts of lamb, beef, and pork. Also pan-fried trout, sautéed prawns, chicken, burgers, and a daily pasta dish. All entrees include vegetable of the day and potato or rice.

Other recommendations: A good selection of salads and appetizers such as crab cakes, oysters, and roasted garlic; mixed greens, shrimp, and Caesar salads.

Summary & comments: Situated on a street corner not far from the Golden Gate Bridge. The cheery lights of this place beckon through the San Francisco fog like a warm cabin in a cold woods. There is often a wait for a table, but you can join the locals and regulars at the bar for a convivial drink.

BUCA GIOVANNI

			QUALITY
Italian	★★★	Mod	**89**

	VALUE
	B

800 Greenwich Avenue, San Francisco
  (415) 776-7766   Zone 6 North Beach

Reservations: Accepted	Parking: Street
When to go: Anytime	Bar: Full service
Entree range: $8.50–14.95	Wine selection: Good
Payment: AMEX, VISA, MC	Dress: Casual
Service rating: ★★★	Disabled access: Yes
Friendliness rating: ★★★	Customers: Locals, tourists

Dinner: Monday–Thursday, 5:30–10:30 p.m.; Friday and Saturday, 5:30–11 p.m.; Sunday, closed

Setting & atmosphere: The main restaurant is in the basement, where the walls are lined with wine racks and the small bar awaits the thirsty diner. You'll find friendly comfort and lots of elbow room. Being in the basement gives you an intimate, almost conspiratorial feeling. There is also dining space at street level for those who like to watch the city go by.

House specialties: Many kinds of flavorful antipasto; rich pasta dishes; game such as venison in ravioli with mushrooms; rabbit cooked with honey and vinegar. Excellent seafood, veal dishes, and lamb.

Other recommendations: Smoked salmon with herbs and sour cream; mezzaluna; cappelletti; salsa rosa, a spread of sun-dried tomatoes and spices.

Summary & comments: People from all walks of life come here, which should be no surprise since the restaurant is in the heart of North Beach. The extensive menu is reason enough to slow down and enjoy. Nothing intimidates; everything says "come hither."

CAFÉ MAJESTIC

			QUALITY
California	★★★½	Exp	**87**

	VALUE
	B+

1500 Sutter Street, San Francisco
  (415) 776-6400   Zone 2 Civic Center

Reservations: Recommended	Service rating: ★★★★
When to go: Anytime	Friendliness rating: ★★★
Entree range: $14–25	Parking: Valet
Payment: AMEX, MC, VISA	Bar: Full service

(Cafe Majestic)

Wine selection: Limited but very good
Dress: Business

Disabled access: Yes
Customers: Locals, tourists, businesspeople

Breakfast: Tuesday–Friday, 7–10:30 a.m.
Brunch: Saturday and Sunday, 8 a.m.–2 p.m.
Dinner: Monday–Friday, 5:30–9:30 p.m.

Setting & atmosphere: The place suggests an older, more elegant San Francisco, a time when long, black Cadillacs pulled up to the awning at the entrance and disgorged their tuxedoed and begowned passengers.

House specialties: Ravioli stuffed with salmon and a lemon-thyme sauce; egg rolls filled with lamb; pork medallions with apples, Calvados, and cream.

Other recommendations: The appetizer menu, which is in constant flux.

Summary & comments: Located in the hotel of the same name, this place counts as a landmark. The menu reflects the diversity of California culture and cuisine. Cooking techniques and equipment are traditional Western style, but seasonings and many ingredients have an Asian influence. Ginger, pepper, and sesame are a common baseline in the culinary tune.

CALIFORNIA CULINARY ACADEMY

California	★★½	Inexp	QUALITY 79
			VALUE A

625 Polk Street, San Francisco
(415) 771-1655   Zone 2 Civic Center

Reservations: Accepted
When to go: Anytime
Entree range: $7.50–12
Payment: Major credit cards
Service rating: ★★★
Friendliness rating: ★★★

Parking: Street
Bar: Full
Wine selection: Good
Dress: Casual to business
Disabled access: Yes
Customers: Everybody

Lunch: Monday–Friday, 11:30 a.m.–2 p.m.
Dinner: Monday–Friday, 5:30–9 p.m.; Saturday and Sunday, closed

Setting & atmosphere: Respectable without being ponderous. Bright and airy with a happy feeling.

House specialties: California cuisine prepared under the direction of European masters. Mesquite grill dishes; monster steaks; pastas in creamy sauces; freshest of fresh vegetable dishes.

(California Culinary Academy)

Other recommendations: Chile con carne; cornbread and other grain dishes. Light menu items low on cream, butter, and salt.

Summary & comments: The cooks and waiters are students, and the food they prepare and serve is their classwork. Because they're students, you get a real deal on the price. It's one of the best bargains in town. They operate three different dining rooms, each with its own menu. In the main room, the prix-fixe menu offers five courses for about $27.

CAMPTON PLACE			
American ★★★★★ Exp		QUALITY	99
		VALUE	A

340 Stockton Street, San Francisco
   (415) 781-5555   Zone 3 Union Square

Reservations: Recommended	Bar: Full service
When to go: Anytime	Wine selection: Excellent
Entree range: $24–28	Dress: Wear a tie; dressy
Payment: All credit cards	Disabled access: Yes
Service rating: ★★★★★	Customers: Businesspeople, tourists,
Friendliness rating: ★★★★	the demanding
Parking: Valet	

Breakfast: Monday–Friday, 7–11 a.m.; Saturday, 8–11 a.m.
Brunch: Sunday, 8 a.m.–2:30 p.m.
Lunch: Monday–Friday, 11:30 a.m.–2:30 p.m.
Dinner: Sunday–Thursday, 5:30–10 p.m.; Friday and Saturday, 5:30–10:30 p.m.

Setting & atmosphere: Formal but friendly. Tieless men won't be turned away, but they'll wish they'd worn a tie. Decor is modern, clean, and spare compared to most luxurious establishments. Lots of flowers. An elegant setting for a breakfast of corned beef hash and poached eggs.

House specialties: Breakfast is famous here. All of the traditional favorites, including corn muffins that are light as a cloud. Duck ravioli with summer vegetable; lobster Napoleon with crisp potatoes; roasted meats, well seasoned and juicy; variety of terrines; veal rack with pasta.

Other recommendations: Desserts, especially the fig tart.

Summary & comments: In the hotel of the same name. This is a temple to the muse of American cooking in a city famous for its foreign culinary establishments. Excellent American fare prepared to the most rigorous European standards, without the emphasis on fancy sauces. Mark Twain would have written glowingly of it. It's expensive, right down to the drinks in the bar, but nothing's overpriced. Quality is king, and you get what you pay for.

THE CARNELIAN ROOM

New American	★★★★	Exp	QUALITY
			93

			VALUE
555 California Street, San Francisco			B
(415) 433-7500 Zone 4 Financial District			

Reservations: Recommended
When to go: Sunset, brunch, or any other time
Entree range: Sunday champagne brunch, $22.50; prix-fixe dinner, $31; entrees, $19–29
Payment: All major credit cards
Service rating: ★★★½

Friendliness rating: ★★½
Parking: Pay lots and garages; street
Bar: Full service
Wine selection: Excellent
Dress: Informal, dressy
Disabled access: Good
Customers: Tourists, businesspeople, locals

Brunch: Sunday, 10 a.m.–2 p.m.
Dinner: Daily, 5:30–10 p.m.

Setting & atmosphere: High above the city on the 52nd floor of the Bank of America Building, the Carnelian Room is a private banker's club by day, and it looks it, with high ceilings, dark wood paneling, soft carpet, and upholstered chairs. But the main decorations are breathtaking wraparound views of San Francisco, the bay, the fog, and the hills beyond. The main dining room is the most formal; there's a lounge with equally stunning views and limited food service.

House specialties: Pâté of Sonoma foie gras; Dungeness crab cake with French green bean salad; fresh dill-cured salmon; escargots in phyllo; tableside Caesar salad; twice-roasted duck breast; roasted rack of lamb gremolata; braised sea scallops with Swiss chard; live Maine lobster.

Other recommendations: Prix-fixe, three-course dinner; Grand Marnier soufflé with crème anglaise.

Summary & comments: Restaurant trends may come and go, but nothing quite equals the glamor of an expensive dinner high in the sky, with a view of the surrounding world twinkling below through an evanescent veil of fog. The Bank of America's high-speed elevator has an unnerving rumble as it zooms to the top, but in the bar and dining room luxury and peace pre-

(The Carnelian Room)

vail. Service is impeccable if a bit stiff, and the food is fine, though not wildly adventuresome. The prices are, of course, a bit steep. Appetizers and drinks, or coffee and desserts in the more intimate lounge, are an excellent way to enjoy the amenities for less money, and the three-course Sunday brunch with unlimited champagne is a decent value.

Honors & awards: *Wine Spectator* Grand Award since 1982.

CASA AGUILA

Mexican	★★½	Mod	VALUE
			79

1240 Noriega Street, San Francisco	QUALITY
(415) 661-5593 Zone 8 Richmond/Avenues	**B**

Reservations: Not accepted	Parking: Street
When to go: Anytime	Bar: Beer, wine
Entree range: $8.50–14.50	Wine selection: House
Payment: AMEX, VISA, MC	Dress: Casual
Service rating: ★★	Disabled access: Yes
Friendliness rating: ★★★	Customers: Locals

Lunch: Daily, 11:30 a.m.–3:30 p.m.
Dinner: Daily, 4:30–10 p.m.

Setting & atmosphere: Bright and colorful. Orderly and well kept. Paper fruits, vegetables, and cacti hang from the walls.

House specialties: All of the usual suspects in a Mexican restaurant: tacos, burritos, enchiladas. But there's more: moles sweetened with raisins and dates; ceviche with crisp veggies; carne erlinda; puerco adobado marinated in citrus and garlic and broiled, served with vegetables and rice; roast beef.

Other recommendations: Serious seafood, mostly grilled and basted with citrus and cilantro.

Summary & comments: One of the most memorable things about Casa Aguila is the presentation. Dishes are sculpted rather than arranged on a hot plate as in most Mexican restaurants. The shapes, colors, and textures of the food are contrasted to bring out their pleasing qualities. Great attention to detail.

CHA CHA CHA

Latin American	★★★½	Inexp/Mod	QUALITY
			85
			VALUE
			A

1805 Haight Street, San Francisco
  (415) 386-7670   Zone 8 Richmond/Avenues

Reservations: Not accepted	Friendliness rating: ★★½
When to go: Lunch or early weekday dinner	Parking: Street
	Bar: Beer, wine
Entree range: Tapas, $4.50–7.75; entrees, $10.50–12.50	Wine selection: House
	Dress: Casual
Payment: Cash only	Disabled access: Limited
Service rating: ★★★	Customers: Locals, tourists

Brunch: Saturday and Sunday, 10 a.m.–4 p.m.
Lunch: Monday–Friday, 11:30 a.m.–3 p.m.
Dinner: Sunday–Thursday, 5–11 p.m.; Friday and Saturday 5–11:30 p.m.

Setting & atmosphere: Astonishingly noisy and crowded, with a funky location, nightmare parking, punk decor, and totally awesome local color.

House specialties: Sangría by the glass or pitcher. Tapas plates—really medium-sized entree portions that include the regular menu and daily specials; warm spinach salad; Cajun sautéed shrimp; saffron steamed mussels with garlic, tomatoes, and onions; barbecue pork quesadilla; Jamaican jerk chicken over rice; fried calamari with lemon garlic aïoli; flatiron steak with mashed potatoes, ancho garlic gravy, and warm roasted corn and squash salad; ceviche; fried chile pepper snapper with salsa and rice.

Summary & comments: Haight Street in the 1990s is not for the faint of heart. Neither is Cha Cha Cha, where you're practically frisked at the door, the noise level approaches the ballistic, and the line at the counter is sometimes three people deep. But pierced body parts and all, the pandemonium is engaging, the service is surprisingly efficient, and the tapas are superb, served with lots of warm French bread to soak up the piquant and savory sauces. Cha Cha Cha is for a night when you're feeling young and ready for adventure; go with a group to share the substantial portions.

CHEZ PANISSE RESTAURANT

California	★★★★½	Exp	QUALITY
			95
			VALUE
			B

1517 Shattuck Avenue
(510) 548-5525   Zone 12 Berkeley

Reservations: Recommended	Parking: Street
When to go: Any time	Bar: Beer and wine
Entree range: Fixed-price menu only	Wine selection: Excellent
Payment: VISA, MC, AMEX, DC	Dress: Business
Service rating: ★★★	Disabled access: Good
Friendliness rating: ★★★	Customers: Locals, tourists

Dinner: Monday–Saturday, first sitting 6 p.m., second sitting 8:30 p.m.

Setting & atmosphere: The restaurant is surprisingly small and, while rather formal, unpretentious considering its international reputation. The decor is soft, comfortable, trimmed in redwood, and deeply carpeted. Walls, fixtures, settings, etc., are all attractive but rather muted. Nothing to distract you from your dinner.

House specialties: The menu is set. Everybody gets the same dinner for the same price, differing only in your wine selection. A recent menu included grilled quail salad with pancetta crostini, summer savory, and pickled cherries; white corn soup with roasted chilies; Northern halibut with new potatoes, Chino ranch beans, tomatoes, and wild fennel; summer pudding.

Other recommendations: Whatever is for dinner the following night.

Summary & comments: This is where Alice Waters birthed California cuisine. It's hard to think of a restaurant, or any other human enterprise, where standards are higher or more rigorously adhered to. Only the freshest ingredients possible are used here. Over the years Chef Waters has developed her own sources of supply, which are often named in the menu. The single menu idea gives the kitchen staff the opportunity to concentrate their efforts and ensure that everything is perfect.

CHINA HOUSE BISTRO

Chinese	★★★½	Inexp/Mod	QUALITY
			84
			VALUE
			A

501 Balboa at Sixth Street, San Francisco
(415) 752-2802   Zone 8 Richmond/Avenues

Reservations: Recommended on weekends	Entree range: $6.50–32
	Payment: All major credit cards
When to go: Anytime	Service rating: ★★★★

(China House Bistro)

Friendliness rating: ★★★★
Parking: Street
Bar: Full service
Wine selection: Fair

Dress: Informal
Disabled access: Good
Customers: Locals, businesspeople, tourists

Open: Daily, 5:30–10:30 p.m.

Setting & atmosphere: 1930s Shanghai-style café with muted, provocative color scheme and lighting; ceiling fans and schoolhouse lamps; antique wood bar and bentwood chairs; white tablecloths and a mural of old Shanghai.

House specialties: Shanghai cooking, including exceptional vegetarian or pork pot stickers; sautéed pea sprouts with prawns; silver sprouts; jumping hot fish; sea bass in seaweed; Shanghai smoked pomfret; warm celery and shrimp salad; Peking spareribs; Lion's Head—huge, tender pork meatballs with gravy; hot chili fried prawns oriental; Beijing tossed noodles with minced pork or mushrooms; Shanghai crispy duck.

Other recommendations: For dessert, eight-treasure rice pudding or Yang Chow crêpes.

Summary & comments: In a setting reminiscent of the cultured café society of 1930s Shanghai, owners Joseph and Cecilia Chung have created a timeless showcase for their memorable dishes. This is a Chinese café with something extra: a glimpse into another era, complete with the welcoming host and hostess who happily expound on the particulars of their cookery and the Shanghai experience. The food is distinctive, unlike Cantonese or Szechuan, with a smoky, almost tropical quality.

CLEMENT STREET BAR AND GRILL

New American	★★	Mod	QUALITY 78
			VALUE C+

708 Clement Street, San Francisco
(415) 386-2200   Zone 8 Richmond/Avenues

Reservations: Recommended on weekends
When to go: Anytime
Entree range: Brunch, $4.95–9.50; lunch, $4.95–7.50; dinner, $8.95–14.95
Payment: All major credit cards
Service rating: ★★★

Friendliness rating: ★★★½
Parking: Street, metered during the day
Bar: Full
Wine selection: Fair
Dress: Casual
Disabled access: Good
Customers: Locals, businesspeople

(Clement Street Bar and Grill)

Brunch: Saturday and Sunday, 10:30 a.m.–3 p.m.
Lunch: Tuesday–Friday, 11:30 a.m.–3 p.m.
Dinner: Tuesday–Saturday, 5:30–10:30 p.m.; Sunday, 4:30–9:30 p.m.;
  Monday, closed

Setting & atmosphere: From the entrance, Clement Street Bar and Grill seems dim, narrow, and dominated by the bar, but there's a roomy rear dining area with an impressive brick fireplace and a ship's cabin atmosphere. It's simply furnished with dark carpet, varnished plywood benches, and captain's chairs, but the cut-glass candles and white tablecloths add a touch of ceremony; coat hooks at the entry lend a genial neighborhood mood. No smoking is allowed despite the barroom atmosphere.

House specialties: Daily specials may include roasted garlic with crostini; roasted red pepper filled with three cheeses, herbs, and pine nuts over spinach salad; wild mushroom tortellini; grilled fish specials; veal scaloppine with wild mushrooms. Vegetarian offerings include grilled portobello mushroom with warm spinach and hazelnuts; grilled and roasted vegetables; wild mushroom tortellini with roma tomatoes, garlic, herbs, and white wine.

Other recommendations: Salads, sandwiches, and burgers.

Summary & comments: This is a sociable place, the sort of comfortable neighborhood restaurant one might head for when friends drop by unexpectedly. The service combines admirable professionalism with a nice lack of pretense. The regular menu offers standards such as steaks, burgers, and a few pastas, but daily special appetizers and entrees are more interesting, generally decent, and often quite good.

COMPASS ROSE

Bar	★★★★	Exp	QUALITY
			99

			VALUE
315 Powell Street in the Saint Francis Hotel, San Francisco			**B+**

(415) 774-0167   Zone 3 Union Square

Reservations: Not accepted	Bar: Full service
When to go: Tea time	Wine selection: Limited but good
Entree range: $9–20	Dress: Business
Payment: Major credit cards	Disabled access: No
Service rating: ★★★	Customers: Businesspeople, travelers,
Friendliness rating: ★★★	correspondents, and spies
Parking: Street, garage	

(Compass Rose)

Open: Daily, 11:30 a.m.–2:30 p.m.; high tea, 3–5 p.m.

Setting & atmosphere: Art deco. Large, spacious lounge comfortably appointed with couches and easy chairs arranged around decorative coffee tables. Long, polished bar immediately adjacent to the hotel lobby.

House specialties: Caviar, smoked salmon, finger sandwiches—all served with elegance and aplomb.

Other recommendations: High tea in the afternoon.

Summary & comments: Step in and enter the 1930s. Talk discreetly with private eyes, mysterious ladies, and intriguing gentlemen while the trio plays Gershwin. Indulge your fantasies. This place is rich; better if you are, too.

THE COURTYARD

American	★★½	Mod	QUALITY 77
			VALUE B

2436 Clement Street , San Francisco
(415) 387-7616   Zone 5 Marina

Reservations: Accepted	Parking: Street
When to go: Anytime	Bar: Full service
Entree range: $6.95–16.95	Wine selection: Very good
Payment: Major credit cards	Dress: Business
Service rating: ★★★	Disabled access: Yes
Friendliness rating: ★★★	Customers: Locals and yuppies

Lunch: Daily, 11:30 a.m.–2:30 p.m.
Dinner: Sunday–Thursday, 5–9:30 p.m.; Friday and Saturday, 5–10 p.m.

Setting & atmosphere: Lots and lots of wood. Modern without being cold or impersonal; the wood keeps it warm. Full of yuppie types, but they don't bite or overbear. All are welcome at this convivial, pleasant place.

House specialties: Steak's the thing. There are a lot of other items on the menu and none are bad, but it's the steak that makes this place worth coming to. Top-quality beef is cooked to your specifications and served with mushroom and red wine sauce. Carnivores come hither.

Other recommendations: Excellent bar.

Summary & comments: This is a great restaurant for drinking. The wine list is one of the best in town, and it's reasonably priced. The bar has a wide selection of single-malt scotches, cognacs, and international beers. People come here for a good time as well as food and drink.

THE DINING ROOM AT THE RITZ-CARLTON

			QUALITY
New American	★★★★★	Exp	97
			VALUE
			B

600 Stockton Street, San Francisco
   (415) 296-7465   Zone 3 Union Square

Reservations: Recommended	Parking: Valet, street
When to go: Anytime	Bar: Full service
Entree range: Prix-fixe, 3-course dinner,	Wine selection: Excellent
$43; 4 courses, $50; 5 courses, $57	Dress: Informal, dressy, formal
Payment: All major credit cards	Disabled access: Good
Service rating: ★★★★★	Customers: Tourists, locals,
Friendliness rating: ★★★★★	businesspeople

Dinner: Tuesday–Saturday, 6–10 p.m.; Sunday and Monday, closed

Setting & atmosphere: Genteel and decorous, the Dining Room's high draped windows, cushioned chairs and couches, Asian ceramics, antique china collections, and 19th-century paintings echo the drawing rooms of an older, stodgier San Francisco. But the tone set by the staff is refreshingly down to earth and contemporary. Soft strains of a classical harp waft through the rarefied air.

House specialties: Seasonal changing menu sometimes reflecting a theme: truffles, regional wines or cuisines. Seared foie gras with caramelized onions and Fuji apples; warm quail salad with wild mushrooms, goat cheese, and pear-ginger chutney; glazed oysters with zucchini pearls and caviar; striped bass with artichoke, Meyer lemon, and fennel oil; guinea hen breast and confit of leg; sautéed veal medallion with chestnuts, apples, and wild mushrooms; squab stuffed with leeks, prosciutto, ricotta, and sage.

Other recommendations: Astonishing selection of cheeses presented at the table; caramelized pears with gingerbread and nutmeg ice cream; baked non-cholesterol Grand Marnier soufflé with raspberry sauce; trio of crème brûlées.

Summary & comments: The Ritz-Carlton's unerring taste and elegance, its solid, reassuring, neoclassical exterior, and safe, protected inner sanctum aside, the element that makes the Ritz, yep, the Ritz, is the genuinely cordial service. The top-hatted doorman; the bartender in the lounge; and the Dining Room servers treat awestruck oglers and haughty billionaires with the same friendly interest. This lack of pretension is confidence inspiring; most people feel better about spending a large amount of money when they are made to feel at ease, no matter where they are from or what they do or don't know about food and wine. Prix-fixe dinners are available in three to five courses, which may be chosen from any of the menu items. The food in

(The Dining Room at the Ritz Carlton)

the Dining Room is simply fabulous; chef Gary Danko seamlessly combines his passion for local and seasonal provender with trained international awareness and a highly evolved sense of color, texture, and flavor. A dinner in the Dining Room is a truly wonderful, memorable experience.

DUSIT			
Thai	★★½	Inexp	**QUALITY** 79
3221 Mission Street, San Francisco			**VALUE** B+
(415) 826-4639 Zone 7 SoMa/Mission			

Reservations: Accepted

When to go: Anytime

Entree range: $5.95–9.95

Payment: Major credit cards

Service rating: ★★½

Friendliness rating: ★★

Parking: Street

Bar: Beer, wine

Wine selection: House

Dress: Casual

Disabled access: No

Customers: Locals

Lunch: Monday–Friday, 11:30 a.m.–2:30 p.m.
Dinner: Daily, 5–10 p.m.

Setting & atmosphere: A small place in an ordinary neighborhood. Nothing remarkable to look at, but it's clean and well lit, and it has just a touch of class. This is a temple of Thai cuisine, and the votaries of this muse are happily at work pleasing anyone who walks in.

House specialties: Most of the items you would expect on a Thai menu, but better than usual, especially considering the price. Orchid duck boned and sautéed with ginger, mushrooms, tomatoes, pineapple, and onions; garlic prawn with black pepper and veggies; sautéed squid with bamboo, chile, and basil; chicken salad with sweet-spicy dressing.

Other recommendations: Good fried noodles. Vegetarian dinners.

Summary & comments: At lunchtime prices are somewhat lower, although the food is just as good and plentiful. But even at dinner it's downright cheap. For quality and quantity, this place is at the top of the list. It's worth a trip across town to dine well at low prices in a pleasant, undemanding environment.

EL NUEVO FRUITLANDIA

			QUALITY
Puerto Rican	★★	Inexp	**76**

VALUE
B+

3077 24th Street, San Francisco
  (415) 648-2958   Zone 7 SoMa/Mission

Reservations: Not accepted	Parking: Street
When to go: Anytime	Bar: Beer, wine
Entree range: $0.50–8.50	Wine selection: House
Payment: Cash	Dress: Casual
Service rating: ★★★	Disabled access: Yes
Friendliness rating: ★★★	Customers: Locals

Open: Daily, 11:30 a.m.–9:15 p.m.

Setting & atmosphere: Unadorned, uncomplicated, unpretentious, and small. But it's friendly and comfortable, and the staff will treat you well.

House specialties: Roast pork with rice and yucca; a variety of plantains; chicken in green sauce; shredded beef with peppers; Puerto Rican dumplings; shrimp in garlic sauce.

Other recommendations: Batidos de frutas, thick fruit shakes or smoothies.

Summary & comments: This a good place for a lunch that will stay with you the rest of the day and into the evening. If you're planning nocturnal activities and won't be able to sit down to a leisurely dinner, fortify yourself here first. Que rico!

ENRICO'S

			QUALITY
Italian	★★★	Mod	**88**

VALUE
B

504 Broadway, San Francisco
  (415) 982-6223   Zone 6 North Beach

Reservations: Accepted	Parking: Street
When to go: Anytime	Bar: Full service
Entree range: $9.25–16.95	Wine selection: Very good
Payment: Major credit cards	Dress: Casual, business
Service rating: ★★★	Disabled access: Yes
Friendliness rating: ★★	Customers: Eclectic

Open: Daily, noon–1 a.m

Setting & atmosphere: A social gathering place as much as an eatery. Booths line the walls; woodwork and plants throughout. One of the more

(Enrico's)

popular bars in North Beach. Between the entry and the sidewalk is an out-door dining and lounge area. Excellent for people-watching.

House specialties: Pizza, pasta, grilled seafood, and steak; casseroles and stews; Spanish-style paella; duck breast gumbo; market steak with white truffle oil.

Other recommendations: Pizza with wild mushrooms.

Summary & comments: A San Francisco landmark and tradition. Many local writers have used it as their writing studio or general hangout. The young man or woman studiously scribbling away while quaffing black coffee may be someone whose work you'll be reading soon. Enrico's devotees will argue to the death that Irish coffee was invented here. Every night patrons ensconce themselves in the outdoor lounge and fend off the San Francisco fog with this warm and cheering draught. Who cares where it was invented? This is the place to drink it.

FIOR D'ITALIA			
Italian	★★★½	Mod	**QUALITY** 85
601 Union Street, San Francisco			**VALUE** A
(415) 986-1886 Zone 6 North Beach			

Reservations: Accepted	Parking: Valet
When to go: Anytime	Bar: Full service
Entree range: $10.75–22	Wine selection: Very good
Payment: VISA, MC, AMEX, D, DC	Dress: Business
Service rating: ★★★	Disabled access: Good
Friendliness rating: ★★	Customers: Locals, tourists

Open: Daily, 11 a.m.–10:30 p.m.

Setting & atmosphere: Old North Beach. Spacious and well lit; starched napery; big leather booths and roomy tables. The bar is old wood, and the walls are hung with memorabilia. Quiet or boisterous, depending on the crowd. Situated at the corner of Union and Stockton Streets, the restaurant opens onto Washington Park, where it makes a beacon to the hungry on foggy nights.

House specialties: Lengthy list of Italian classics. Hot and cold antipasto; pasta, riso, and polenta; veal, chicken, beef, and fish. A separate and lengthy dessert menu features fresh fruit preparations. The regular dinner special, the "1886," is $18.86.

Other recommendations: A long list of single-malt scotches and grappas.

(Fior d'Italia)

Summary & comments: Established in 1886, this is the oldest Italian restaurant in the country. Originally where Enrico's is today, it moved to its present location in 1952. The restaurant has survived 111 years of the city's earthquakes and social upheavals, and a sedate, unflappable quality has sunk into the place, as if it knows it will be here when you are not. This breeds a justifiable confidence and a reluctance to rush.

FLEUR DE LYS

			QUALITY
French	★★★★	Exp	**95**

	VALUE
777 Sutter Street, San Francisco	**B+**
(415) 673-7779 Zone 4 Financial District	

Reservations: Accepted	Parking: Valet
When to go: Anytime	Bar: Full service
Entree range: $28–30	Wine selection: Excellent
Payment: Major credit cards	Dress: Dressy
Service rating: ★★★★	Disabled access: Yes
Friendliness rating: ★★★★	Customers: Locals, tourists

Dinner: Monday–Thursday, 6–10 p.m.; Friday and Saturday, 6–10:30 p.m.; Sunday, closed

Setting & atmosphere: The interior, designed to resemble the inside of a silken tent, recalls a movie set for the story of a sheik or a medieval joust. Lots of mirrors and cubby holes; very busy. But it's never too much. It's exotic, colorful, entertaining, yet not distracting.

House specialties: Many seafood selections: broiled bass fillet with bits of lobster wrapped in spinach and served with a sauce of beets and chives; salmon with horseradish; lobster salmi; salmon with golden caviar and chives. Also, roast lamb chops; veal with onion rings (really good onion rings); duck in spinach leaves with a juniper and pancetta sauce. A reasonably priced wine list, considering the venue.

Other recommendations: The Menu Gourmand, offering a fixed selection of appetizer, fish, entree, and desert; or the larger Menu Prestige. Both help contain costs in an expensive restaurant.

Summary & comments: One of the best, most fun restaurants in town. The service is attentive and formal, yet, like the decor, it's never too much. The food presentations are always pleasing, showcasing the natural colors and textures of the food; nothing is too sculpted or contrived.

Honors & awards: *Esquire* Restaurant of the Year, 1987.

FOG CITY DINER

American	★★★	Mod	QUALITY
			89
			VALUE
			B+

1300 Battery Street, San Francisco
   (415) 982-2000   Zone 6 North Beach

Reservations: Accepted	Parking: Street
When to go: Off hours	Bar: Full service
Entree range: $7–20	Wine selection: Good, extensive
Payment: Major credit cards	Dress: Casual
Service rating: ★★★	Disabled access: Yes
Friendliness rating: ★★★½	Customers: Locals, tourists

Open: Sunday–Thursday, 11:30 a.m.–11 p.m.; Friday and Saturday, 11:30 a.m.–midnight

Setting & atmosphere: Crowded, lively, and popular. As Fats Waller said, "The joint is jumpin'." Don't come here for a quiet, romantic dinner. The decor has elements of an old Route 66 diner and a downtown bar and grill, both from pre–World War II San Francisco.

House specialties: For big appetites try the Large Plates. Chicken on a biscuit with Virginia ham, morels, and cream gravy; rabbit with ancho chile succotash. For smaller stomachs: grilled pasilla pepper stuffed with polenta and five cheeses; garlic custard with mushrooms and walnuts; crab cakes; excellent salads.

Other recommendations: Strawberry rhubarb pie.

Summary & comments: You can come here with a huge appetite for food and merriment, and leave satisfied and not too much the poorer for it. During normal meal times, long lines snake out the front door and there's a crush at the bar. Sometimes this place is too popular for its own good.

FRINGALE

French	★★★★	Mod	QUALITY
			95
			VALUE
			A

570 Fourth Street, San Francisco
   (415) 543-0573   Zone 7 SoMa/Mission

Reservations: Highly recommended	Entree range: Lunch, $7–12.75;
When to go: Anytime, but quietest at	dinner, $9–18
late lunch on weekdays	Payment: All major credit cards

(Fringale)

Service rating: ★★★★
Friendliness rating: ★★★★
Parking: Street
Bar: Full service

Wine selection: Limited but good
Dress: Informal
Disabled access: Good
Customers: Locals, businesspeople

Lunch: Monday–Friday, 11:30 a.m.–3 p.m.
Dinner: Monday–Saturday, 5:30–10:30 p.m.; Sunday, closed

Setting & atmosphere: White wine, honey, and sunlight; rarely does a restaurant strike a chord perfectly balancing the warmth of wheat loaves and the sparkle of chilled champagne. Fringale is captivatingly simple and frequently crowded; to soak up the soul of the southwestern French provinces, go for lunch after 1 p.m. on a weekday.

House specialties: Creative interpretations of French-Basque fare: potato and goat cheese galette; sheep's milk cheese and prosciutto terrine with figs and greens; steamed mussels with garlic and parsley; roast rack of lamb with natural juices; steamed salmon with braised leeks and fried onions; New York steak with red wine butter.

Other recommendations: Pork tenderloin confit with onion and apple marmalade; fillet of tuna Basquaise; all desserts including Biarritz Rocher au chocolat; hazelnut and roasted-almond cake with chocolate sauce; iced armangnac and coffee parfait.

Summary & comments: Gerald Hirigoyan, the consummate young chef at Fringale, achieves near perfection with this disarming little bistro, where he attracts crowds with his low-priced but highly skilled, artful cooking. Casual and elegant, subtle and robust, earthy and delicate—the shadings and flavors of the culinary spectrum are eloquently embraced. The cluster of parties waiting near the door can be intimidating, so make reservations in advance. Fringale is well worth the trouble.

Honors & awards: *Esquire* Best New Restaurant, 1992.

THE GANGES

Vegetarian Indian	★★★	Inexp	QUALITY
			80
			VALUE
			A

775 Frederick Street, San Francisco
(415) 661-7290   Zone 8 Richmond/Avenues

Reservations: Recommended on weekends
When to go: Anytime

Entree range: 3-course dinner, $9.50–13.50
Payment: MC, VISA

(The Ganges)

Service rating: ★★★½
Friendliness rating: ★★★★
Parking: Street
Bar: Beer, wine

Wine selection: House
Dress: Casual
Disabled access: Good
Customers: Locals, businesspeople

Dinner: Tuesday–Saturday, 5–10 p.m.; Sunday and Monday, closed

Setting & atmosphere: Like an island of sanity in a chaotic world, the Ganges's austere setting, further becalmed on weekends by live sitar music on the red-curtained stage at the front of the room, is a surprise package. Even at peak hours, this is a restful spot.

House specialties: Light, nongreasy vegetarian Indian cooking, including ground lentil dababs; green chili fritters; steamed savory garbanzo dumplings; curries, including homemade cheese cooked with peas; garbanzo beans with onions, mushrooms, and spices; baby potatoes stuffed with fresh spices; eggplant with onions and spices; stuffed zucchini; and cauliflower with potatoes and onions.

Other recommendations: Mango lassi, a mango and yogurt drink; sheera pudding, shreekhand yogurt and sour cream dessert with rose water and saffron.

Summary & comments: With the delicacy of its cooking and the economy of its dinners, the Ganges puts most Indian restaurants to shame. Throw in the vegetarian menu, helpful staff, and gentle atmosphere, and you have a real alternative to busy city dining. The Ganges, like the jewel hidden in the lotus blossom, is a rare find.

GREENS			
Vegetarian	★★★★	Moderate	QUALITY 99
			VALUE A

Building A Fort Mason (Marina Blvd. and Buchanan), San Francisco
  (415) 771-6222   Zone 5 Marina

Reservations: Necessary
When to go: Lunch
Entree range: $10–13
Payment: Major credit cards
Service rating: ★★★
Friendliness rating: ★★★

Parking: Lot
Bar: Beer, wine
Wine selection: Very good
Dress: Business
Disabled access: Yes
Customers: All walks of life

Brunch: Sunday, 10 a.m.–2 p.m.
Lunch: Monday–Friday, 11:30 a.m.–2:15 p.m.
Dinner: Monday–Saturday, 6–9:30 p.m.

(Greens)

Setting & atmosphere: Full view of the Golden Gate Bridge bordered by the southern promontories of Marin County. Large and airy; the restaurant was formerly an enclosed pier. Polished wood floors, lovely paintings on the walls, and comfortable lounging area. Serene atmosphere.

House specialties: Mesquite grilled winter vegetables; salad of watercress and escarole, sierra beauty apples, and walnuts tossed with walnut vinaigrette; cubed winter squash baked in parchment with fresh thyme and garlic.

Other recommendations: Chocolate sabayon cake crème chantilly.

Summary & comments: No health food, no hippie food, no orange and parsley garnish, but the finest in vegetarian cuisine. This is not a PC restaurant, no one is on a crusade here. Its reason for being is the best of dining without meat.

HAMBURGER MARY'S

American	★½	Inexp	QUALITY 69
			VALUE C

1582 Folsom Street, San Francisco
(415) 626-5767 or 626-1985   Zone 7 SoMa/Mission

Reservations: Accepted; weekends,
  for parties of 5 or more only
When to go: Anytime
Entree range: Breakfast, $3.95–9.25;
  lunch or dinner, $4.50–9.50
Payment: All major credit cards
Service rating: ★★★
Friendliness rating: ★★★½

Parking: Street
Bar: Full service
Wine selection: House
Dress: Casual
Disabled access: Good
Customers: Locals, tourists,
  businesspeople

Open: Tuesday–Thursday, 11:30 a.m.–midnight; Friday, 11:30–1 a.m.; Saturday, 10–1 a.m.; Sunday, 10 a.m.–midnight; Monday, closed; specials available after 5 p.m.

Setting & atmosphere: Like the lair of a demented antique dealer: baby bottles and broken chandeliers; handpainted mirrors and headless mannequins; chromium starbursts and a life-sized cardboard Elvis; road signs, street signs, soda-pop posters, and sheet music; stained-glass windows and junkshop furniture. All jumbled together and set to driving rock and roll. There's a breakfast counter in front, a barroom to the rear, and a separate (you should pardon the expression) dining area in the corner.

(Hamburger Mary's)

House specialties: Breakfast all day. Burgers with mushrooms, chili, bacon, bleu cheese, and/or avocado, served on whole-wheat toast.

Other recommendations: Vegetarian burgers, soups, and sandwiches; salads; club, BLT, or crab salad sandwich. Chipped beef on toast.

Summary & comments: The sign at the door reads, "Seat yourself at any available table." Doing so in this 1970s relic is like wandering through the fun house: you have no idea what may appear around the next corner. The food at Hamburger Mary's is unremarkable, though. You can find better burgers with fresher accompaniments in most restaurants around town. Perhaps the best reason to go to Mary's is to eat breakfast anytime in an atmosphere that suggests you're still dreaming.

HARPOON LOUI'S			
Bar and Grill	★★	Inexp	**QUALITY** 77
			VALUE B

55 Stevenson Street, San Francisco
(415) 543-3540   Zone 7 SoMa/Mission

Reservations: Not accepted	Parking: Street
When to go: Lunch	Bar: Full service
Entree range: $4–6	Wine selection: House
Payment: VISA, MC, AMEX	Dress: Casual
Service rating: ★★	Disabled access: Yes
Friendliness rating: ★★★★	Customers: Locals, businesspeople

Lunch: Monday–Friday, 11 a.m.–3 p.m.; Saturday and Sunday, closed

Setting & atmosphere: A neighborhood tavern in an old brick building. Old photos of old stars and local sports figures and a big oil painting of a leggy nude cover the walls. Pretty much a male hangout, but ladies are welcome.

House specialties: Hamburgers and big schooners of draught beer; fried fish of the day; pasta; salads. The menu changes daily, but you can get on the mailing list and learn of advance changes if you want to be a regular. Everything is cooked to order.

Other recommendations: The Blue Plate Special. Free hot dogs at happy hour.

Summary & comments: Harpoon Loui's is a neighborhood place that considers itself part of the community. After the Loma Prieta earthquake of 1989, Loui's fed locals on the street. Service can be slow, so don't go when you're pressed for time.

HARRY DENTON'S

			QUALITY
New American	★★★★	Mod	**90**
			VALUE
			A

169 Steuart Street, San Francisco
   (415) 882-1333   Zone 7 SoMa/Richmond

Reservations: Highly recommended
When to go: Anytime
Entree range: $7.95–16.95
Payment: Major credit cards
Service rating: ★★★★
Friendliness rating: ★★★★
Parking: Valet nightly

Bar: Full service
Wine selection: Excellent
Dress: Casual, business
Disabled access: Good
Customers: Locals, tourists,
   businesspeople

Breakfast/Brunch: Monday–Friday, 7–10 a.m.; Saturday and Sunday,
   8 a.m.–3 p.m.
Lunch: Monday–Friday, 11:30 a.m.–3 p.m.
Dinner: Daily, 5:30–10 p.m.

Setting & atmosphere: Harry's has just about everything: a fashionable
location on Steuart Street (the city's new restaurant row), an adjacent boutique hotel, a smashing view of the Bay Bridge, gorgeous flowered carpets,
dark wood wainscoting and lacquered walls, a Victorian bar, red velvet, and
oodles of antiques. The mood ranges from serene to wild. On weekends the
party can approach the greatest of Gatsby proportions.

House specialties: Chicken and artichokes with white beans; pot roast with
buttermilk mashed potatoes and gravy; grilled filet mignon with cracked
pepper and cognac; Australian lamb T-bones with polenta; creamed spinach;
buttermilk onion rings.

Other recommendations: Harry's Southside Burger; oak-fired pizzas;
Nona's meat and cheeses lasagna.

Summary & comments: Harry Denton's may be the perfect all-purpose
city restaurant: sophisticated and glamorous, yet relaxed and casual; ideal for
breakfast by the bay in jeans and a T-shirt or dancing the night away in a tux
or tiara. The cuisine is big and brassy, real Barbary Coast fare; Harry encour-
ages serious partying once the music begins. "Dancing on the bar is prohibited unless accompanied by Harry." But the place can be subtle and decorous on early weeknights. Even the rest rooms have savoir faire. If it gets too
crowded, you can stroll down the avenue; there are five glittering restaurants, two hotels, and two workout gyms within two blocks.

HELMAND

			QUALITY
Afghan	★★★	Inexp	85
			VALUE
			A

430 Broadway, San Francisco
  (415) 362-0641   Zone 6 North Beach

Reservations: Accepted
When to go: Anytime
Entree range: $8.95–14.95
Payment: VISA, MC, AMEX
Service rating: ★★★★
Friendliness rating: ★★★
Parking: 468 Broadway

Bar: Full service
Wine selection: Fair
Dress: Casual
Disabled access: Yes
Customers: Locals, businesspeople,
  tourists

Lunch: Monday–Friday, 11:30 a.m.–2:30 p.m.
Dinner: Monday–Thursday, 6–10 p.m.; Friday and Saturday, 6–11 p.m.;
  Sunday, closed

Setting & atmosphere: Named for a river in Afghanistan. Rooms are decorated in classical Persian simplicity, and the tables are set with Western, though not stuffy, formality. Beautiful Persian rugs everywhere; walls are hung with Afghan portraits. Afghan strings and flutes play softly in the background.

House specialties: Afghan food is heavily influenced by neighbors India and Persia. It's based on flat breads and rice, fresh vegetables, and lamb and chicken cooked in mild spice mixtures. Tomatoes or yogurt are common bases for sauces. Dishes include rack of lamb with Persian spices; chicken sautéed with yellow split peas; potatoes and garbanzo beans in vinaigrette with cilantro; meat pies flavored with onion; leek-filled ravioli.

Other recommendations: A good number of meatless dishes and salads.

Summary & comments: This is a good family restaurant, and as such it's a bellwether for the changing neighborhood, which was once the heart of the city's topless district. The low prices and the generous portions make this one of the best restaurant deals in town. And it's the only Afghan restaurant in town. You'll find it crowded on weekends.

HOUSE OF BAMBOO

Chinese	★★½	Mod	QUALITY
			76
			VALUE
			B

601 Van Ness Avenue, San Francisco
   (415) 928-0889   Zone 2 Civic Center

Reservations: Accepted	Parking: Validated
When to go: Pretheater	Bar: Full service
Entree range: $9.95–19.95	Wine selection: Fair
Payment: Major credit cards	Dress: Casual
Service rating: ★★★	Disabled access: Yes
Friendliness rating: ★★	Customers: Locals, tourists

Lunch: Sunday–Friday, 11 a.m.–4:30 p.m.
Dinner: Sunday–Thursday, 4:30–10 p.m.; Friday and Saturday, 4:30–11 p.m.

Setting & atmosphere: Comfortable and cheery blend of Chinese and California designs. At center, black marble tables are flanked by red chairs on a jade carpet; other sections have comfortable booths.

House specialties: This restaurant matches Chinese and southeast Asian with California cookery. Ma-por pork and green onion tortilla is an adaptation of ma-po dofu, a spicy, hot mix of bean curd and minced pork; pan-fried black fillet with black beans and sun-dried tomatoes.

Other recommendations: Nam yee roasted chicken with oyster mushrooms.

Summary & comments: Casual atmosphere; waiters in blue jeans serve generous portions at affordable prices. Close to ballet, opera, and symphony.

HOUSE OF PRIME RIB

American	★★★½	Exp	QUALITY
			89
			VALUE
			B+

1906 Van Ness Avenue, San Francisco
   (415) 885-4605   Zone 2 Civic Center

Reservations: Necessary	Bar: Full service
When to go: Dinner only	Wine selection: Good
Entree range: $19.75–23.65	Dress: Business, dressy
Payment: Major credit cards	Disabled access: Yes
Service rating: ★★★	Customers: Locals, businesspeople,
Friendliness rating: ★★★½	tourists
Parking: Valet	

(House of Prime Rib)

Dinner: Monday–Thursday, 5:30–10 p.m.; Friday, 5–10 p.m.; Saturday, 4:30–10 p.m.; Sunday, 4–10 p.m.

Setting & atmosphere: Plush. Large, comfortable rooms with booths and alcoves; tables set with heavy napery. A mirrored bar with hardwood floor and fireplace in the lounge. Wall adorned with murals and heavy draperies.

House specialties: Prime rib, of course. You can have it thick cut or "English cut"—several thinner slices that some people say brings out more flavor. The jury is out on this, but either taste is accommodated here. Baked or mashed potato; creamed spinach; generous tossed salad.

Other recommendations: Fresh catch of the day for the occasional patron who prefers not to have red meat.

Summary & comments: One of the older restaurants in town and a temple to red meat. It would be hard to find more civilized surroundings for indulging in that most primitive of appetites. The meat is wheeled to your table on a silver steam cart, and the great haunch is displayed to you in all its glory. "Thick cut, madam? English cut, sir?" It can make you proud to be a carnivore.

HUNAN VILLAGE

Chinese	★★★	Inexp	QUALITY 83
			VALUE B+

839 Kearny Street, San Francisco
   (415) 956-7868   Zone 1 Chinatown

Reservations: Recommended on weekends	**Parking:** Street, public pay lots
When to go: Anytime	**Bar:** Beer, wine
Entree range: $6.50–20	**Wine selection:** House
Payment: AMEX, MC, VISA	**Dress:** Casual
Service rating: ★★★½	**Disabled access:** Good
Friendliness rating: ★★★½	**Customers:** Locals, businesspeople, tourists

Open: Daily, 11:30 a.m.–9 p.m.

Setting & atmosphere: Not fancy, but cheerful and welcoming; painted in shades of peach, green, and burnt orange, with murals depicting the misty landscapes of the Hunan province of China. Carpeting helps keep this busy restaurant quiet during peak hours.

House specialties: Spicy dishes from Hunan, many of which have been incorporated into standard Chinese menus: Hunan crab; Kung Pao shrimp,

(Hunan Village)

chicken, or squid; cashew prawns; tea-smoked duck or chicken; Hunan smoked pork; Hunan Village beef. Black mushrooms with greens; shrimp and tofu special hot pot; moo shu entrees; honey-glazed walnut prawns; Peking duck.

Summary & comments: Once you're seated in Hunan Village's hideous orange vinyl chairs, you will be handed a surprisingly classy menu recounting the legend of the crane and the pepper, an explanation of the use of fiery spices in Hunan cuisine. The rice-paper pages offer extensive calligraphied listings of moderately priced dishes, all of which are prepared with a confident hand, assertively seasoned, and sauced to sparkling perfection. In the bewildering maze of restaurants that inhabit Chinatown, Hunan Village is an excellent choice.

HUNG YEN				
Vietnamese	★½	Inexp	**QUALITY** 69	
3100 18th Street, San Francisco			**VALUE** B+	
(415) 621-8531 Zone 7 SoMa/Mission				

Reservations: Not accepted	Parking: Lot
When to go: Lunch	Bar: Beer, wine
Entree range: $3.75–7.50	Wine selection: House
Payment: Cash	Dress: Casual
Service rating: ★★	Disabled access: Limited
Friendliness rating: ★★	Customers: Locals

Open: Monday–Friday, 9 a.m.–9 p.m.; Saturday, 10 a.m.–9 p.m.; Sunday, closed

Setting & atmosphere: You can tell that it used to be a Mexican restaurant, but don't let it distract you. At the corner of Harrison Street and across from the PG&E, this is an ideal place to meet for a fine Vietnamese lunch.

House specialties: Hung Yen is best know for its spicy beef noodle soup: a broth scented with lemon grass and chiles, beef sliced so thin that the broth cooks it, noodles, onions, and fresh mint or basil. At $3.75, it's one of the best lunch bargains you'll find in the city.

Other recommendations: A full range of Vietnamese fare: fried noodle or rice dishes; combination plates; excellent vegetarian dishes. Soups and stir-fries are the most common preparations. Deep-fried imperial rolls; lemon beef salad; prawn curry; fried pineapple.

(Hung Yen)

Summary & comments: According to the extensive menu, "Hung Yen does party. Up to sixty people." It also lists "ten dishes to die for." In good weather diners often avail themselves of the covered patio (which has even more Mexican ambience than the interior). Despite the confused decor, if you can concentrate on the dishes in front of you, you might think you're in Saigon.

INDIAN OVEN			
Indian	★★★½	Inexp/Mod	**QUALITY** 88
233 Fillmore Street, San Francisco			**VALUE** B
(415) 626-1628 Zone 8 Richmond/Avenues			

Reservations: Recommended on
  weekends
When to go: Anytime
Entree range: Lunch buffet, $5.95;
  dinner, $6.95–14.95
Payment: AMEX, MC, VISA
Service rating: ★★★½
Friendliness rating: ★★★

Parking: Street
Bar: Beer, wine
Wine selection: House
Dress: Informal
Disabled access: Good
Customers: Locals, businesspeople,
  tourists

Lunch: Monday–Friday, 11:30 a.m.–2:30 p.m.
Dinner: Daily, 5–11 p.m.

Setting & atmosphere: Recently remodeled, the Indian Oven looks lovely, with faux-marbled walls, white napery, candles, flowers, and sparkling wine glasses on each table. The soft Indian music completes an impression of subtle opulence.

House specialties: Tandoori lamb, prawns, and chicken; chicken curry with tomatoes; boneless lamb with spiced cream spinach; green peas with homemade cheese cubes; bengan bhartha, roasted eggplant with chopped onions, garlic, and ginger.

Other recommendations: Combination dinners; mixed bread basket of stuffed Indian breads; mango ice cream.

Summary & comments: Quiet and romantic dining.

IZZY'S STEAK AND CHOP HOUSE

American   ★★★   Mod

QUALITY
85

VALUE
A

3345 Steiner Street, San Francisco
  (415) 563-0487   Zone 5   Marina

Reservations: Accepted	Bar: Full service
When to go: Anytime	Wine selection: Good
Entree range: $6.95–19.95	Dress: Casual
Payment: Major credit cards	Disabled access: Yes
Service rating: ★★★	Customers: Locals, businesspeople,
Friendliness rating: ★★★	tourists
Parking: Street	

Dinner: Monday–Saturday, 5:30–11 p.m.; Sunday, 5–10 p.m.

Setting & atmosphere: A modernized version of an old-time steak house. Sometimes fills to overflowing with locals who come for beef, booze, and merriment. You'll see a lot of back slapping, glad handing, laughing, and carrying on here. In the bar, where patrons are in no particular hurry, the generations mix as the big drinks flow.

House specialties: Aged Black Angus beef served in he-man portions: New York steak; pepper steak; Cajun-style blackened steak; untampered with, unalloyed steak.

Other recommendations: Creamed spinach. Huge and tasty desserts.

Summary & comments: Many of the patrons are regulars who live in the neighborhood and know each other. When they meet here it's party time. Don't come for quiet, and don't come overdressed. Come hungry and happy.

JOHN'S GRILL

Steak House   ★★★   Mod

QUALITY
80

VALUE
A

63 Ellis Street, San Francisco
  (415) 986-DASH   Zone 3   Union Square

Reservations: Accepted	Bar: Full service
When to go: Anytime	Wine selection: Good
Entree range: $13.95–39.95	Dress: Casual, Business
Payment: AMEX, MC, VISA	Disabled access: No
Service rating: ★★★	Customers: Locals, businesspeople,
Friendliness rating: ★★★	tourists
Parking: Street	

(John's Grill)

Open: Monday–Saturday, 11 a.m.–10 p.m.; Sunday, 5–10 p.m.

Setting & atmosphere: Dark wood and brass trim; the 1930s at their best. You're transported to another (many would say better) San Francisco. Sepia photographs of celebs and local potentates cover the west wall. Deep and narrow with booths and small tables; the general feeling is one of cozy intimacy.

House specialties: Steaks, chops, and seafood. Dungeness crab cakes (a must at any historic place in the city); fried oysters; sand dabs; Sam Spade's lamb chops; pork chops with apple sauce; a giant porterhouse steak; broiled calves liver; chicken Jerusalem.

Other recommendations: Variety of salads; clam chowder; oysters Wellington.

Summary & comments: "Spade went to John's Grill, asked the waiter to hurry his order of chops, baked potato, sliced tomatoes . . . and was smoking a cigarette with his coffee when . . ." Open since 1908, this landmark restaurant was the setting for Dashiell Hammett's novel *The Maltese Falcon*. To dine or drink martinis here is to imbibe the history and literature of the city.

LA FIAMMETTA

Italian	★★★	Mod	QUALITY
			85
1701 Octavia Street, San Francisco			VALUE
(415) 474-5077 Zone 2 Civic Center			A

Reservations: Accepted	Parking: Valet
When to go: Anytime	Bar: Beer, wine
Entree range: $9–10	Wine selection: Good
Payment: VISA, MC	Dress: Business
Service rating: ★★★½	Disabled access: Yes
Friendliness rating: ★★★	Customers: Locals, businesspeople

Dinner: Tuesday–Thursday, 6–10 p.m.; Friday and Saturday, 6–10:30 p.m.; Sunday and Monday, closed

Setting & atmosphere: On a corner in a quiet, tree-filled neighborhood, this restaurant promises gentility without snobbery. Inside, the white tablecloths and wall fixtures create simple elegance.

House specialties: A standard menu of two dozen items supplemented by daily specials, particularly fish. Radicchio wrapped in pancetta; antipasto plate; seafood risotto; house-made cheese-filled ravioli with a light tomato sauce; gnocchi with a variety of sauces.

(La Fiammetta)

Other recommendations: Pressed chicken grilled with herbs; flavorful casserole of duck, sausage, and beans; veal chop in mushroom sauce; rabbit in olive sauce.

Summary & comments: This is a rather small place with small prices, bent on attracting many customers who keep coming back. Everything is the best quality and affordably priced. This place is an act of love.

LE TROU			
French	★★½	Mod	**QUALITY** 79
			VALUE B

1007 Guerrero Street, San Francisco
(415) 550-8169   Zone 7 SoMa/Mission

Reservations: Accepted	Parking: Street
When to go: Anytime	Bar: Beer, wine
Entree range: $11.95–18.95	Wine selection: Limited but good
Payment: Cash	Dress: Casual, business
Service rating: ★★★	Disabled access: Yes
Friendliness rating: ★★★	Customers: Locals, businesspeople

Dinner: Tuesday–Saturday, 6–9 p.m.; Sunday and Monday, closed

Setting & atmosphere: A little neighborhood restaurant. Almost homey in its unpretentious, comfy decor. Earthenware knickknacks on shelves and doodads on the walls; nice china, although it doesn't all match. "Le Trou" means "the cave"—in this case a very cozy one.

House specialties: The menu changes seasonally. Menus are focused on a particular region of France, so whatever your table orders will be a surer match than the china. Selections may include Choucroute garni; simply fried fish with lime and capers deglazing; zucchini flan with herbs; rich, thick soups; chicken with walnuts and cream.

Other recommendations: Strawberries with red wine and honey; sweet dessert wines.

Summary & comments: Le Trou is operated by a local cooking teacher; his lessons are put to practical use here. The emphasis is on the food and maintaining its high quality. The small staff dedicates their efforts to that. Anything else is gravy.

LEFTY O'DOUL'S

			QUALITY
Hof Brau	★★	Inexp	**75**

	VALUE
	B

333 Geary Boulevard, San Francisco
  (415) 982-8900   Zone 3 Union Square

Reservations: Not accepted	Parking: Street
When to go: Anytime	Bar: Full service
Entree range: $0.50–7.75	Wine selection: House
Payment: Cash	Dress: Casual
Service rating: ★★	Disabled access: Yes
Friendliness rating: ★★★	Customers: Locals, businesspeople

Open: Daily, 7 a.m.–midnight

Setting & atmosphere: A rather gritty sports bar with a steam table and a baby grand piano. Directly across the street from the elegant Compass Rose in the Saint Francis Hotel, Lefty's seems to have been put there deliberately to add counterpoint to the high-toned hostelry and its expensive watering hole.

House specialties: All the usual roasts: beef, turkey, ham. Dinner plates, hot open-faced sandwiches. Polish sausage, lasagna, soup, salad, and daily specials.

Summary & comments: Named for the baseball player, this is a neighborhood institution full of regulars and hungry shoppers. It's big and cavernous, yet it maintains an air of cozy familiarity. It's also considered neutral ground by warring factions. When the San Francisco 49ers won their first Super Bowl there was pandemonium in the streets and a huge police presence. The celebrations went on long into the night, exhausting cops, revelers, and paddy-wagon drivers. Between skirmishes, both sides could be seen recuperating at adjacent tables in Lefty's.

LULU

			QUALITY
American	★★★½	Mod	**89**

	VALUE
	B+

816 Folsom Street, San Francisco
  (415) 495-5775   Zone 7 SoMa/Mission

Reservations: Required except in café	Bar: Full service
When to go: Anytime	Wine selection: Excellent
Entree range: $8.50–17.50	Dress: Casual, informal
Payment: AMEX, DISC, MC, VISA	Disabled access: Good
Service rating: ★½	Customers: Locals, businesspeople,
Friendliness rating: ★	tourists
Parking: Valet, metered and public	

(Lulu)

Lunch: Daily, 11:30 a.m.–2:30 p.m.
Dinner: Daily, 5:30–10:30 p.m.

Setting & atmosphere: Capacious warehouse redux with painted concrete floors, splashy pottery and prints, a behemoth open rotisserie, and a perpetual party pace. This is definitely where it's happening; if you don't believe it, just ask the staff, whose condescending attitude can be a shock. LuLu hosts a pulsating bar scene and a small café next door for drop-in business.

House specialties: Highly eclectic menu, incorporating Mediterranean and Southwest influences: whole wood oven–roasted portobello mushroom with polenta; grilled chèvre wrapped in grape leaves; duck cannelloni; pork loin with fennel and garlic mashed potatoes; calamari pizza with basil and aïoli; mixed seafood grill with salsa; lamb daube with artichokes.

Other recommendations: Rabbit fricasee provençal; pork, sage, and hazelnut sausage with crispy polenta.

Summary & comments: Once the food arrives, you'll probably forgive the attitude, since the dishes are vibrant and distinctive and the party is one of the best in town. Everything's brought to table on bright, painted platters in ample proportion, and the family-style service provides easy sharing. You can have a grand meal here without spending a fortune. Great oyster selection; desserts are good, too.

MASA'S			
French	★★★★★	Exp	**QUALITY** 99
648 Bush Street, San Francisco			**VALUE** A
(415) 989-7154 Zone 3 Union Square			

Reservations: Recommended	Parking: Valet
When to go: Anytime	Bar: Full service
Entree range: $15 and up	Wine selection: Excellent
Payment: Major credit cards	Dress: Dressy
Service rating: ★★★★★	Disabled access: Yes
Friendliness rating: ★★★★	Customers: Locals, tourists

Dinner: Tuesday–Saturday, 6–9:30 p.m.; Sunday and Monday, closed

Setting & atmosphere: It ain't cheap, and it don't look it. But it's never intimidating. How a place can be so grand and yet not be stuffy, pretentious, or snobby is hard to fathom, but there you have it. The staff are not

(Masa's)

concerned with impressing or looking down at their patrons, but with seeing that they get the superb gastronomic experience they pay so dearly for.

House specialties: A unique blend of French and California turned out in an elegant fashion that no other restaurant could imitate even if it tried. It's the result of the Japanese founder's 30 years in French kitchens, honing his style and making his mark. The rather short menu may begin with seafood sausage in beurre blanc or house-made foie gras with spinach. Entrees include roasted partridge with cabbage and thyme; veal or beef with marrow and truffles; grilled fish with caviar or herb confit; grilled lobster with quenelles.

Other recommendations: Desserts are worth the trip if you have a sweet tooth. Pineapple in dark caramel sauce; frozen mousses with crushed filberts.

Summary & comments: This is often said to be a New York restaurant located in San Francisco. That might be saying a little too much for New York. It is without a doubt one of the best restaurants in the city and, indeed, in the state. It could also be the most expensive, especially if you have wine with your meal. And the corkage fee is $20! But if you're swimming in money or content to eat humble fare for a week or two after, it's worth a blow-out splurge.

MAX'S OPERA CAFÉ				
Deli/Barbecue	★½	Mod	**QUALITY** 79	
601 Van Ness Avenue, San Francisco			**VALUE** B	
(415) 771-7300 Zone 2 Civic Center				

Reservations: Not accepted
When to go: Before or after the show
Entree range: $11.95–14.95
Payment: Major credit cards
Service rating: ★★½
Friendliness rating: ★★★
Parking: Street

Bar: Full service
Wine selection: Limited but good
Dress: Casual to dressy
Disabled access: Yes
Customers: Theatergoers, tourists, locals

Open: Monday, 11:30 a.m.–10 p.m.; Tuesday–Thursday, 11:30 a.m.–midnight; Friday and Saturday, 11:30–1 a.m.; Sunday, 11:30 a.m.–11 p.m.

Setting & atmosphere: New York deli cum piano bar and cocktail lounge with barbecue on the side. Spacious and well-lit, with high ceilings and a large window onto the streets and city hall. Though it's a broad space, it has lots of nooks, booths, and intimate corners.

(Max's Opera Café)

House specialties: Big deli sandwiches; barbecue with unique sauces, some with subtle hints of Asian spices; pasta with wild mushrooms; pastrami and corned beef (ask for it easy on the lean). Take-out orders are available.

Other recommendations: Desserts and salads.

Summary & comments: Located near the War Memorial Opera House, Herbst Theater, and Davies Symphony Hall, this is an ideal spot for a pretheater dinner. Service is generally quick and efficient with no fluff or folderol; they know you've got tickets to the show. Parking can actually be had on the street now and then.

MILLENNIUM				
Vegetarian	★★★½	Mod	**QUALITY**	
			90	
246 McAllister Street, San Francisco			**VALUE**	
(415) 487-9800 Zone 2 Civic Center			B+	

Reservations: Accepted	Parking: Street
When to go: Dinner	Bar: Beer, Wine
Entree range: $10.75–14.95	Wine selection: Well chosen
Payment: VISA, MC, AMEX	Dress: Casual
Service rating: ★★★	Disabled access: Yes
Friendliness rating: ★★★½	Customers: Locals

Dinner: Daily, 5–9:30 p.m.

Setting & atmosphere: In the ground floor and basement of the restored Abigail Hotel. Softly lit and cozy throughout, with touches of modern art. Best seat in the house is downstairs at the far end, with a picture window looking onto a tiny Japanese-style garden.

House specialties: Some of the best vegan dining to be had anywhere. The dedicated carnivore can feast sumptuously at Millennium and not even realize that he's just had a meatless, dairyless meal. A vegan diet would be a lot more popular if all the cooks came from here. The signature dish is a plantain torte; a sweet and spicy mixture of plantain is spread between layers of fresh tortilla and served over a tomato and papaya salsa. No words do it justice. It's not too sweet or spicy, and it doesn't taste Mexican despite the tortillas. If you eat nothing else in San Francisco besides the famous sourdough bread, eat this.

Other recommendations: Fresh fig and Asian pear salad; smoked portobello mushroom; morel risotto; roasted sweet onion stuffed with black bean chili.

(Millennium)

Summary & comments: An eclectic menu informed by classic cooking techniques makes Millennium one of San Francisco's treasures. Executive chef Eric Tucker makes no compromise in the pursuit of the gourmet dining experience. He labors to extract the last measure of value and character from all of the foods at his disposal, making even the simplest root or leafy green come alive on your palate. The dishes are vibrant with flavor, aroma, and varying textures and colors. A feast for all the senses.

MOMI TOBY'S REVOLUTION CAFÉ

Eclectic	★★	Inexp	**QUALITY** 78
			VALUE C+

528 Laguna Street, San Francisco
  (415) 626-1508   Zone 2 Civic Center

Reservations: Not accepted	**Parking:** Street
When to go: Anytime	**Bar:** Beer, wine
Entree range: $4.25–8	**Wine selection:** House
Payment: Cash	**Dress:** Casual
Service rating: ★★	**Disabled access:** No
Friendliness rating: ★★★	**Customers:** Neighborhood

Open: Monday–Friday, 7:30 a.m.–9:30 p.m.; Saturday and Sunday, 8:30 a.m.–10:30 p.m.

Setting & atmosphere: This renovation of a 100-year-old bakery is reminiscent of a Berlin café, right down to the lamps and the bar. Dark paneled walls and hardwood floors abound and create a comfortable atmosphere for long conversations over coffee, lunch, or dinner.

House specialties: Along with the usual coffee-shop fare try enchilada pie; meatless pesto lasagna; taquería-style burritos; Caesar salad. It seems at first glance that this is a menu that can't make up its mind, but it all hangs together nicely.

Summary & comments: This is not just a restaurant, it's a local hangout. The regulars are very regular, and people come often just to relax, linger over coffee, meet friends, and feel at home.

MOOSE'S

California	★★★★	Mod	QUALITY
			95
			VALUE
			A—

1652 Stockton Street, San Francisco
(415) 989-7800   Zone 6 North Beach

Reservations: Accepted
When to go: After the theater
Entree range: $13.75–24
Payment: Major credit cards
Service rating: ★★★★
Friendliness rating: ★★★★

Parking: Street
Bar: Full service
Wine selection: Excellent
Dress: Business
Disabled access: Good
Customers: Locals, tourists

Brunch: Sunday, 10:30 a.m.–2:30 p.m.
Lunch: Monday–Saturday, 11:30 a.m.–2:30 p.m.
Dinner: Sunday–Thursday, 5:30–10 p.m.; Friday and Saturday,
5:30–11 p.m.

Setting & atmosphere: Streamlined, stripped-down, classic San Francisco. Polished brightwork, hardwood, and marble elegance in a minimalist form. Posh without being stuffy or cloistered.

House specialties: A hard-to-pigeonhole mix of Italian, French, and California. Pizza, pasta, and Caesar salad; lamb chops and roasted chicken; smoked meats and crab cakes; mashed potatoes and gravy.

Other recommendations: An occasional special roast of pork. Diners can actually be heard moaning when they eat it.

Entertainment & amenities: String duets or trios often play in the entryway.

Summary & comments: Every dish is prepared with the utmost care and professionalism. In the open kitchen, where skillful hands are the most valuable tools in the shop, you can watch superior workers practicing their art. Service is genuinely warm and friendly, and you feel as though you have come to somebody's hearth, not a commercial enterprise.

ORIGINAL JOE'S

American	★★	Inexp	QUALITY
			78
			VALUE
			B

144 Taylor Street, San Francisco
(415) 775-4877   Zone 3 Union Square

Reservations: Accepted
When to go: Anytime
Entree range: $6.25–18

Payment: Major credit cards
Service rating: ★★
Friendliness rating: ★★★

(Original Joe's)

Parking: Lot	Dress: Casual
Bar: Full service	Disabled access: Yes
Wine selection: Fair	Customers: Locals, tourists, regulars

Open: Daily, 10:30–12:30 a.m.

Setting & atmosphere: This is the original Original Joe's. It's one of the oldest places in the neighborhood, and many will say it looks like it. Most of the staff seem to date from the same year. The menu, decor, and patrons never seem to change either. Red plastic booths and a long bar and counter overlooking the kitchen; low lights and some plants. A certain hominess prevails, perhaps borne of old familiarity.

House specialties: Italian meat and potatoes. Joe's buys whole sides of beef and then ages and cuts them in-house. From these come the monster steaks and hamburgers that the regulars eat in quantity. Also, overcooked pasta with superior sauce; thick-cut french fries; corned beef and cabbage; prime rib.

Summary & comments: The neighborhood has gone down in recent years, so you should park in the lot or nearby on the street. Unlike the OJ's in San Jose, the bar here serves up a man-sized drink in a convivial atmosphere.

PAT O'SHEA'S MAD HATTER

Bar and Grill	★★	Inexp	QUALITY
			75

			VALUE
3848 Geary Boulevard, San Francisco			A
(415) 752-3148 Zone 8 Richmond/Avenues			

Reservations: No way	Parking: Small lot, street
When to go: Anytime	Bar: Full service
Entree range: $7–12	Wine selection: House
Payment: VISA, MC	Dress: Casual
Service rating: ★★	Disabled access: Yes
Friendliness rating: ★★★	Customers: Locals, tourists

Lunch: Monday–Saturday, 11:30 a.m.–3 p.m.; Sunday, 11 a.m.–3 p.m.
Dinner: Daily, 4–10 p.m.

Setting & atmosphere: A sports bar since 1937; it's motto has always been, "We cheat tourists and drunks!" This is a proper bar with proper television sets showing proper games to proper sports drinking proper drinks. You won't find ferns or silk wall hangings among the wooden floors and pictures of sports greats. The place just happens to serve great food.

(Pat O'Shea's Mad Hatter)

House specialties: The cook is a proper chef from proper restaurants who decided he would have more fun in a bar. He produces a limited but faultless selection that leans heavily on meat and potatoes. Two-third pound burgers; carrot soup; grilled swordfish or other catch of the day; pasta with whatever is on hand; simple but excellent salads. Altogether superb pub grub. Good selection of beers and cocktails that raise mixology to the status of art.

Summary & comments: Since before World War II, serious sports people have been coming here and making it their office away from the office. Sportswriters are especially in evidence and are hailed by name by the staff. You'll see every kind of person come through here to watch a game, have a drink, hold forth in Western fashion at the bar, and tell tall tales. It's a Cheers with food.

PERRY'S				
American	★★	Inexp	**QUALITY**	75
			VALUE	B+

1944 Union Street, San Francisco
   (415) 922-9022   Zone 5 Marina

Reservations: Not accepted	**Bar:** Full service
When to go: Anytime	**Wine selection:** Fair
Entree range: $7.50–17.5	**Dress:** Casual
Payment: Major credit cards	**Disabled access:** Yes
Service rating: ★★★	**Customers:** Locals, businesspeople,
Friendliness rating: ★★★	singles
Parking: Street	

Open: Monday–Friday, 9–2 a.m.; Saturday and Sunday, 9–3 a.m.

Setting & atmosphere: Sports bar, singles meeting place, business rendezvous, bar and grill; a pleasant American bistro. Congenial long bar surrounded by checker-clothed tables on a bare wood floor. Wide windows overlook fashionable Union Street, and the back has a pleasant patio for quieter dining.

House specialties: Burgers; shoestring fries; one of the few places in town serving sautéed calves liver with bacon and onions; grilled double chicken breast; New York steak; linguine with clams.

Other recommendations: Apple Brown Betty.

(Perry's)

Summary & comments: This bar has always been a great place to meet friends or strangers. Go for a cocktail before or a cordial after dinner, or a late snack after dancing.

PJ'S OYSTER BED			
Seafood	★★★	Mod	**QUALITY** 87
737 Irving Street, San Francisco			**VALUE** B
(415) 566-7775 Zone 8 Richmond/Avenues			

Reservations: Accepted
When to go: Anytime
Entree range: $7.98–22.95
Payment: Major credit cards
Service rating: ★★★
Friendliness rating: ★★★½

Parking: Street
Bar: Beer, wine
Wine selection: Adequate
Dress: Casual
Disabled access: Yes
Customers: Locals, tourists

Lunch: Saturday and Sunday, 11 a.m.–3:30 p.m.
Lunch and Dinner: Monday–Friday, 11:30 a.m.–10 p.m.

Setting & atmosphere: Casual, comfortable atmosphere; always intriguing counter seating and table service.

House specialties: Wide selection of oyster dishes and many Cajun specialities. New Orleans–style gumbo.

Other recommendations: Try the alligator. It's good.

Summary & comments: With its "distinctive" weather, San Francisco has always been a hot-bowl-of-soup kind of town, and PJ's clam chowder fits the bill for a respite from those chilling winds and damp fogs.

Honors & awards: Voted Best Seafood Restaurant 1994 by the *Bay Guardian*.

PLUMPJACK CAFÉ

			QUALITY
Mediterranean	★★★	Mod	**83**
			VALUE
3127 Fillmore Street, San Francisco			**B**
(415) 563-4755 Zone 5 Marina			

Reservations: Accepted	Bar: Beer, wine
When to go: Anytime	Wine selection: Very good
Entree range: $16–18	Dress: Casual, business
Payment: Major credit cards	Disabled access: Yes
Service rating: ★★★	Customers: Everybody from home
Friendliness rating: ★★★	and abroad
Parking: Street	

Lunch: Monday–Friday, 11:30 a.m.–2 p.m.
Dinner: Monday–Saturday, 5:30–10 p.m.; Sunday, closed

Setting & atmosphere: The decor recalls the theater, in which the world first saw Sir John Falstaff, otherwise known as Plump Jack. But this setting is a lot cleaner and warmer than Shakespeare's Globe Theater.

House specialties: An imaginative menu based on old favorites. Bruschetta; duck confit; lemon-grass brûlée.

Other recommendations: Numerous Mediterranean specialties.

Summary & comments: PlumpJack has received plaudits from all the major food pundits in the Bay Area and some from beyond. One patron from England carried a clipping of the place for weeks before finding his way here. The excellent wine list alone makes it worth a visit.

RED'S JAVA HOUSE

			QUALITY
Dive	★	Inexp	**65**
			VALUE
Pier 30, San Francisco			**A**
No phone Zone 7 SoMa/Mission			

Reservations: No way	Parking: Street
When to go: Daytime	Bar: Beer
Entree range: $2.70–4.65	Wine selection: None
Payment: Cash	Dress: Work clothes
Service rating: ★	Disabled access: No
Friendliness rating: ★	Customers: Locals, workers

Open: Daily, 6 a.m.–5 p.m. or at the staff's discretion

(Red's Java House)

Setting & atmosphere: The chief attraction here is the view. In front you can see the East Bay and the Bat Bridge. Behind you is the bulk of the city. Red's 40-year history is documented in scores of black and white photos of people and patrons from the waterfront. All else is tacky and dirty.

House specialties: Double burgers; double hot dogs; deviled-egg sandwiches.

Other recommendations: What many will argue is a great cup of coffee.

Summary & comments: A historical gathering place for working people during the glory days of the San Francisco waterfront. Down to your last dollar? Eat here.

RISTORANTE ECCO

Italian	★★★½	Mod	QUALITY 85
101 South Park Boulevard, San Francisco (415) 495-3291 Zone 7 SoMa/Mission			VALUE C

Reservations: Recommended	Parking: Street
When to go: Anytime	Bar: Full service
Entree range: Lunch, $5.75–12.25; dinner, $10–16.50	Wine selection: Limited but good
Payment: AMEX, D, MC, VISA	Dress: Informal
Service rating: ★★★½	Disabled access: Good
Friendliness rating: ★★★★	Customers: Locals, businesspeople, tourists

Lunch: Monday–Friday, 11:30 a.m.–2:30 p.m.
Dinner: Monday–Saturday, 5:30–10 p.m.; Sunday, closed

Setting & atmosphere: Toasted brown walls and sepia prints, pungent aromas, and a peaceful hubbub; Ecco carries the old-world serenity of its South Park location indoors. Tile-floored bar with tables and a softer-edged dining room with windows onto the quiet boulevard.

House specialties: Exquisite antipasto selections; vitello tonnato; chickpea fritters with eggplant vinaigrette; roasted salmon with herb crust; pork chop with sage butter and polenta; shrimp and mussels over linguine cake in tomato curry broth.

Other recommendations: Daily risotto and seafood specials; desserts, including hazelnut chocolate ice-cream sandwich and pecan, pine nut, and hazelnut tart with orange cream.

(Ristorante Ecco)

Summary & comments: Dinner on South Park Boulevard is a stroll to a bygone era, and Ecco's streamlined service and soothing decor quietly preserve the magic of the neighborhood. The Italian menu is competently carried out, and the specials, such as tuna risotto, are unusual. This is generally forceful, highly aromatic Italian fare.

ROSMARINO

Italian	★★★	Mod	QUALITY
			84

			VALUE
3665 Sacramento Street, San Francisco			B–
(415) 931-7710 Zone 8 Richmond/Avenues			

Reservations: Recommended on
  weekends
When to go: Anytime
Entree range: Brunch, $4.50–9.50;
  lunch, $6.50–11.50; dinner,
  $11–16
Payment: AMEX, MC, VISA
Service rating: ★★★

Friendliness rating: ★★★½
Parking: Street, metered during day
Bar: Beer, wine
Wine selection: Good
Dress: Casual, informal
Disabled access: Good
Customers: Locals, businesspeople

Brunch: Sunday, 10 a.m.–2:30 p.m.
Lunch: Tuesday–Saturday, 11:30 a.m.–2 p.m.
Dinner: Tuesday–Saturday, 5:30–10 p.m.; Monday, closed

Setting & atmosphere: A small and understated but usually bustling trattoria with an outdoor heated patio, Rosmarino boasts an especially delightful location; it's hidden away behind a flower shop on a quiet block of exclusive antique shops and boutiques. The proprietors are open and welcoming.

House specialties: Pastas and risotto of the day; braised beef short ribs with roasted squash, leeks, and polenta; grilled swordfish with sauce Grabiche and artichoke confit; braised salmon with bacon and savoy cabbage. For Brunch: frittata with house-made fennel sausage and sweet bell peppers; buttermilk soufflé pancakes with fresh fruit; fried polenta with poached eggs, sautéed chard, and parmesan.

Other recommendations: Luncheon sandwiches; desserts.

Summary & comments: Rosmarino is casual and friendly and located in a lovely neighborhood; it has a good wine list. The menu is somewhat limited but not unsophisticated, and there are nightly specials. For a little night on the town, Rosmarino is a fine choice.

RUTH'S CHRIS STEAK HOUSE

American	★★½	Mod	QUALITY 78
			VALUE B

1700 California Street, San Francisco
   (415) 673-0557   Zone 2 Civic Center

Reservations: Accepted	Parking: Street
When to go: Anytime	Bar: Full service
Entree range: $17–29	Wine selection: Good
Payment: Major credit cards	Dress: Casual
Service rating: ★★★	Disabled access: Yes
Friendliness rating: ★★★	Customers: Locals, tourists

Dinner: Sunday–Thursday, 5–10 p.m.; Friday and Saturday, 5–10:30 p.m.

Setting & atmosphere: A proper-looking steak house in the best tradition. The dark wood suggests a cattle ranch, and the well-set, clean tables tell you you're in a place of serious eating. Any doubts are dispelled by the black-and-white-clad waiters, who look like real pros.

House specialties: Serious steak. It's all from the Midwest, where beef is something more than mere food. Corn-fed, aged USDA prime is what you'll get here. It makes up the top 2% of market beef; you'll taste the difference.

Other recommendations: Barbecued shrimp; pork chops; salmon; chicken; shellfish. Creamed spinach; potatoes au gratin; shoestring potatoes.

Summary & comments: The menu defines what rare means—as well as the other grades of doneness—and the cooks are good about it. You'll get what you order. Portions are big and may look daunting, but they're so good that they seem to disappear.

SALMAGUNDI

Cafeteria	★★	Inexp	QUALITY 75
			VALUE B

442 Geary Boulevard, San Francisco
   (415) 441-0894   Zone 3 Union Square

Reservations: Not accepted	Parking: Street
When to go: Pre- or posttheater	Bar: Beer, wine
Entree range: $5.95–6.95	Wine selection: House
Payment: Major credit cards	Dress: Casual
Service rating: ★★	Disabled access: Yes
Friendliness rating: ★★½	Customers: Locals, tourists

(Salmagundi)

Open: Sunday and Monday, 11 a.m.–9 p.m.; Tuesday–Saturday, 11 a.m.–11 p.m.

Setting & atmosphere: Clean, bright, white, airy, and sparkling. If it weren't for the rich aroma of soup, you might think you had walked into an ice-cream parlor.

House specialties: Soup. Five kinds of soup, and they change daily. Thirty-five soups every week. Split pea; clam chowder; vegetable; beef noodle; hot and sour; borscht. You name it. All house-made fresh daily.

Other recommendations: Sandwiches; salads; lasagna; quiche; daily specials.

Summary & comments: This might be the most famous soup kitchen in town. Its location across the street from the Geary Theater makes it ideal for a quick dinner before or a snack after the play. Service is fast and efficient, prices are low, and it's a good place to people-watch; the windows look out onto the street.

SAM WOH

Chinese	★½	Inexp	QUALITY
			69

	VALUE
	B+

815 Washington Street, San Francisco
  (415) 982-0596   Zone 1 Chinatown

Reservations: Not accepted	Parking: Street
When to go: Lunch	Bar: None
Entree range: $3.50–7.50	Wine selection: None
Payment: Cash	Dress: Casual
Service rating: ★	Disabled access: Adequate
Friendliness rating: ★	Customers: Locals, businesspeople

Open: Daily, 11–3 a.m.

Setting & atmosphere: Hole-the-wall rabbit warren. Three floors of deep, narrow rooms with a definite cramped feeling, especially during the lunchtime squeeze. Even when you're alone in the place you feel the need for elbow room. And the decor? There is no decor.

House specialties: All the usual suspects in a Chinese restaurant. Chow mein with a variety of additions; crisp fried noodles; sautéed shellfish; won ton soup; fried rice.

Other recommendations: More of the same.

Summary & comments: The motto hangs from the wall: "No credit card, no fortune cookie, just damn good food!" It's not quite a dive, but almost.

(Sam Woh)

And it's one of the most popular places in the neighborhood. Of its kind, it might be the most popular place in town. The staff are singularly intolerant, demanding, disputatious, and sometimes downright rude. "You! Move over. Somebody else gotta sit down, too." That's how you get seated when it's very crowded, as it is daily at noon. Lingering too long after lunch? "You! What-samatta you? People waiting. You go!" Somehow it's not insulting. Somehow that's just the way they say howdy. There is no wine or beer, but the package store just across the street will sell you a cold one or a bottle of jug wine and wrap it a brown paper bag for you to take into the restaurant. They know the drill, and they're quick about it. You hungry now? You go!

SHERATON PALACE GARDEN COURT

			QUALITY
New American	★★★★	Exp	**92**

	VALUE
Market Street at New Montgomery Street, San Francisco	**C−**
(415) 392-8600 Zone 4 Financial District	

Reservations: Recommended
When to go: Anytime
Entree range: Breakfast buffet, $17.50; Sunday brunch, $39; lunch, $11.50–18.25; dinner, $18.50–29
Payment: All major credit cards
Service rating: ★★★½

Friendliness rating: ★★½
Parking: Hotel garage
Bar: Full service
Wine selection: Excellent
Dress: Informal, dressy
Disabled access: Good
Customers: Tourists, businesspeople, locals

Breakfast: Monday–Saturday, 6:30–10:30 a.m.; Sunday, 6:30–9:30 a.m.
Brunch: Sunday, 10 a.m.–1:30 p.m.
Lunch: Monday–Saturday, 11 a.m.–2 p.m.
Dinner: Tuesday–Saturday, 6–10 p.m.

Setting & atmosphere: The Sheraton Garden Court may be the most gorgeously Rococo room in San Francisco, with its 40-foot atrium ceiling and copious lead crystal chandeliers dwarfing the baby grand. The room is softly carpeted, with plush sofas in the lounge. This is as grand as it gets.

House specialties: Breakfast or Sunday brunch buffet; Japanese breakfast; warm lobster salad or potato-wrapped lobster; venison scaloppine with red lentils; pan-roasted boneless quail; organic chicken with buckwheat polenta and chanterelles; rare muscovy duck breast with sun-dried plum sauce.

Other recommendations: Filet mignon; John Dory with wild mushroom ragoût; herb-encrusted monkfish with fingerling potatoes.

Summary & comments: Opulent, plush, hushed, and halcyon; if you've recently won the lottery, the Garden Court's grandeur will no doubt satisfy your need to pamper yourself. You're definitely paying for the atmosphere and deferential service; the food, while meticulously prepared and admirably presented, is among the highest priced in the city and can be equaled in quality elsewhere for considerably less. Best bet: stop in for a drink on the way to somewhere else. The afternoon teas, topping off with a champagne tea for $19.95, are a luxurious treat.

SOUTH PARK CAFE

French	★★★½	Mod	QUALITY
			87

	VALUE
108 South Park Boulevard, San Francisco	A
(415) 495-7275 Zone 7 SoMa/Mission	

Reservations: Recommended	Parking: Street
When to go: Anytime	Bar: Full service
Entree range: Lunch, $5.25–10;	Wine selection: Limited but good
dinner, $10–14.50	Dress: Casual, informal
Payment: MC, VISA	Disabled access: Good
Service rating: ★★★½	Customers: Locals, businesspeople,
Friendliness rating: ★★★½	tourists

Breakfast: Monday–Friday, 7:30 a.m. for pastries and coffee
Brunch: Saturday and Sunday, 8 a.m.–2:30 p.m.
Lunch: Tuesday–Friday, 11:30 a.m.–2:30 p.m.
Dinner: Tuesday–Thursday, 5–9 p.m.; Friday and Saturday, 5–10 p.m.

Setting & atmosphere: South Park Cafe's enchanting location on historic South Park Boulevard creates a pared-down neighborhood bistro ambience: affable clamor and bustle with relatively bright lighting. It's a very romantic street but not a romantic restaurant.

House specialties: Small tapas menu, 5–7 p.m.: grilled shrimp, sautéed mushrooms; anchoiade potatoes; steamed mussels. Dinners include grilled duck breast with wild honey and spices; boudin noir with sautéed apples; steamed mussels with saffron cream; roast rabbit with lemon confit.

Other recommendations: Nightly specials, including desserts: apple cake with geranium ice cream and Calvados crème anglaise.

(South Park Cafe)

Summary & comments: South Park's minimalist approach arrived as a fore-runner antidote to the more flamboyant and expensive dinner houses of the 1980s. Heralding the gentrification of quaint South Park Boulevard, the original affluent section of old San Francisco then down at the heels in an industrial neighborhood, South Park offered a small, well-executed bistro menu served in a simple setting for shockingly low prices. Others have followed, spiffing up the neighborhood and spawning a whole restaurant movement.

SPECKMAN'S

German	★★	Inexp	QUALITY 75
			VALUE B

1550 Church Street, San Francisco
(415) 282-6850   Zone 7 SoMa/Mission

Reservations: Accepted	Parking: Street
When to go: Anytime	Bar: Beer, wine
Entree range: $6.50–11.95	Wine selection: House
Payment: AMEX, VISA, MC	Dress: Casual
Service rating: ★★½	Disabled access: Yes
Friendliness rating: ★★★	Customers: Locals

Lunch: Monday–Friday, 11 a.m.–2 p.m.
Lunch and Dinner: Monday–Thursday, 5–9 p.m.; Friday, 5–10 p.m.; Saturday 11 a.m.–10 p.m.; Sunday, noon–9 p.m.

Setting & atmosphere: Something of a hole in the wall, but nice. Tucked around a corner in an alley where you wouldn't expect to find it. Inside, it's a little piece of Germany.

House specialties: Traditional German fare. Assorted sausages and cold plates; leek and potato soup; veal Holstein with anchovies and egg; a zesty goulash with spaetzle; stuffed beef roll; potatoes in many guises.

Other recommendations: Good selection of beers.

Summary & comments: A simple, comfortable place to really pack it in. It seems incongruous to find a German establishment deep in the Mission District, but the area is richer for it.

SPLENDIDO'S

			QUALITY
Italian	★★★	Mod	88
			VALUE
			B+

Embarcadero Center Four, San Francisco
   (415) 986-3222   Zone 4 Financial District

Reservations: Recommended   Parking: Street
When to go: Anytime   Bar: Full service
Entree range: $9.50–22   Wine selection: Very good
Payment: Major credit cards   Dress: Casual, business
Service rating: ★★★   Disabled access: Yes
Friendliness rating: ★★★   Customers: Locals, businesspeople

Lunch: Monday–Friday, 11:30 a.m.–2:30 p.m.
Dinner: Monday–Wednesday, 5:30–10 p.m.; Thursday–Saturday,
   5:30–10:30 p.m.; Sunday, closed

Setting & atmosphere: Definitely an incongruous setting: a Mediterranean-style taverna in a shopping center. And a welcome break it is, too. So many other people think so that it's hard to get in. You should make reservations a few days in advance even for lunch.

House specialties: Very creative pizza with onion confit and not-too-salty anchovy; pan-roasted chicken that's as good as any you'll get in a restaurant, served with fennel potatoes; thin-sliced dried beef with rémoulade and cheese; lamb shanks with beans and lemon.

Other recommendations: A bar menu for those who didn't come with reservations. Super desserts.

Summary & comments: The decor is an island of serenity and charm in Embarcadero Center's maelstrom of retail shopping. It makes for a perfect psychic transition from the frenzy of personal commerce to the contemplation and enjoyment of a good dinner.

STARS

			QUALITY
Eclectic	★★★★½	Exp	95
			VALUE
			B

150 Redwood Alley, San Francisco
   (415) 861-7827   Zone 2 Civic Center

Reservations: Highly recommended   Payment: Major credit cards
When to go: Anytime   Service rating: ★★★★½
Entree range: $8–30   Friendliness rating: ★★★★

(Stars)

Parking: Valet
Bar: Full service
Wine selection: Excellent
Dress: Dressy

Disabled access: Good
Customers: Locals, tourists,
   businesspeople

Lunch: Monday–Friday, 11:30 a.m.–2 p.m.
Dinner: Daily, 5:30–10:30 p.m.; late dinner until 11:30 p.m.

Setting & atmosphere: Everything about Stars is seductive: the mysterious location down an almost invisible alley, the nonchalant glamour of the decor, the air of casual and elegant ease. No longer unique, Stars set the tone for a whole generation of swank eateries—a stage for beautiful, stylish people to watch themselves enjoying life. The magic is that it works for everyone.

House specialties: Oysters Rockefeller; gravlax with peppercorn brioche and ginger cream; oven-roasted mussels with bacon and ancho chiles; lobster risotto with scallops; red pepper soup with crab and basil; sautéed halibut with tangerine vinaigrette; grilled veal loin chop with buttered greens; roast garlic rouille.

Other recommendations: Mesquite-grilled hamburgers and wood-fired pizzas; iced tuna tartare with wasabi cream and peppered mangos. Desserts.

Summary & comments: Open since 1984, Jeremiah Tower's Stars was the flagship voyager into a new constellation of fancy restaurant dining and still shines bright in the firmament. A giant mirrored bar, a star-strewn green carpet, a baby grand piano, and spiffy service make an evening at Stars one to remember.

Honors & awards: *Travel and Leisure's* Best Restaurants of San Francisco.

THE STINKING ROSE				
Italian	★★★	Mod	**QUALITY**	
			80	
325 Columbus Avenue, San Francisco			**VALUE**	
(415) 781-7673 Zone 6 North Beach			B	

Reservations: Accepted
When to go: Anytime
Entree range: $8–18
Payment: VISA, MC, AMEX, JCB
Service rating: ★★★
Friendliness rating: ★★

Parking: Street
Bar: Full service
Wine selection: Short but good
Dress: Casual
Disabled access: Yes
Customers: Locals, tourists

(The Stinking Rose)

Open: Sunday–Thursday, 11 a.m.–11 p.m.; Friday and Saturday, 11 a.m.–midnight

Setting & atmosphere: The main room is a mix of murals, a Rube Goldberg garlic factory, and toy trains. Garlic braids hang from the ceiling, photos of celebrities smile from the walls, and understatement is nowhere in sight. A recently added second room is strewn with plain wooden tables and festooned with straw-wrapped Chianti fiasci. All is exuberant without being overpowering, rather like the aroma of cooked garlic.

House specialties: "Garlic seasoned with food." The mostly Italian menu is comprised of well-made pastas and seafood laden with garlic. The garlic is usually cooked long and slow to mellow it, so you won't step out of here a bane to vampires, but people will know where you've been. Weekly specials include meat loaf with garlic mashed potatoes, paella, and salt cod.

Other recommendations: Forty-clove chicken, pork chops with sweet garlic relish and apples, braised rabbit, vegetarian dishes. Specially marked items can be made without the pungent lily on request.

Summary & comments: Stats: 1.5 tons of garlic and 12,000 mints a month! This is a fun place, one that takes itself not too seriously but not too lightly either. It's dedicated to gustatory enjoyment. The bar is a popular place to meet. Regulars will often come in just for a drink and a deep breath or two. At Candlestick Park you can buy the Stinking Rose's 40-clove chicken sandwich.

STOYANOF'S

Greek	★★★	Inexp/Mod	QUALITY
			85
1240 Ninth Avenue, San Francisco			VALUE
(415) 664-3664 Zone 8 Richmond/Avenues			B

Reservations: Recommended on weekends
When to go: Dinner
Entree range: $9.59–13.95
Payment: AMEX, MC, VISA
Service rating: ★★★
Friendliness rating: ★★★

Parking: Street
Bar: Beer, wine
Wine selection: House
Dress: Casual
Disabled access: Good
Customers: Locals, businesspeople, tourists

(Stoyanof's)

Open: Tuesday–Sunday, coffee and pastry, 10 a.m.–5 p.m.
Lunch: Tuesday–Sunday, 11 a.m.–5 p.m.
Dinner: Tuesday–Sunday, 5 p.m.–10 p.m.; Monday, closed

Setting & atmosphere: Fresh and uncluttered, with a blue ceiling, wood floors, slatted chairs, and hewn tables; Stoyanof's evokes the flavor of Greece with a few bright paintings. It's a self-serve caféteria by day with a rear garden terrace, but it converts to efficient, personable table service in the evening.

House specialties: Greek appetizers: dolmades stuffed with herbed rice; hummus and tabbouleh; tzatziki (yogurt with cucumbers) and taramasalata (red mullet roe spread); smoked eggplant with tomato, sweet peppers, and olive oil; flaky phyllo pastries with spinach, lamb, or cheese; grilled fresh salmon, cod, or sea bass; chicken breast in pastry with nutmeg, cumin, and leeks; shish kebab of beef, lamb, swordfish, or ground lamb with choice of sauces.

Other recommendations: Moussaka, both lamb and vegetarian; roast leg of lamb with herb marinade; eggplant stuffed with couscous, pine nuts, currants, and red peppers. Wonderful array of pastries.

Summary & comments: Stoyanof's open, airy ambience pours through its storefront windows and beckons to passersby. Inside, the scents and colors of Greece are as mesmerizing as ever, and the execution of traditional dishes and more innovative specials is carried off skillfully, with a lightness that does not sacrifice the assertive Greek flavors. Stoyanof's has a carefree insouciance that goes well with the comestibles, and that suits diners admirably after a day at the park nearby or the beach.

SWAN OYSTER DEPOT

Oyster Bar	★★	Inexp	QUALITY
			78

	VALUE
1517 Polk Street, San Francisco	**A**

(415) 673-1101   Zone 2 Civic Center

Reservations: Not accepted	Parking: Street
When to go: Lunch	Bar: Beer, wine
Entree range: $3.50–7	Wine selection: House
Payment: Cash	Dress: Casual
Service rating: ★★★	Disabled access: No
Friendliness rating: ★★★	Customers: Locals

Open: Daily, 11 a.m.–5:30 p.m.

(Swan Oyster Depot)

Setting & atmosphere: Really a fishmonger's, this little gem boasts a long marble bar where you sit on ancient stools feasting on the freshest seafood in town. It's an old-time San Francisco neighborhood joint.

House specialties: Raw oysters; shellfish cocktails; seafood salads.

Other recommendations: New England clam chowder with sourdough bread.

Summary & comments: Friendly family members of this Polk Street business entertain you with continuous conversation while they shuck, peel, and crack your order of shellfish. One of the few places in town that still serves old-fashioned oyster crackers.

TADICH GRILL				
American	★★★	Mod	**QUALITY**	**89**
			VALUE	**A**

240 California Street, San Francisco
  (415) 391-2373   Zone 4 Financial District

Reservations: Not accepted	Bar: Full service
When to go: Anytime	Wine selection: Good
Entree range: $7.50–15	Dress: Casual, business
Payment: Major credit cards	Disabled access: Yes
Service rating: ★★★	Customers: Locals, businesspeople,
Friendliness rating: ★★½	tourists, daytrippers
Parking: Street	

Open: Monday–Friday, 11 a.m.–9 p.m.; Saturday 11:30 a.m.–9 p.m.; Sunday, closed

Setting & atmosphere: The oldest restaurant in the city; 150 proud years in the same location. It's brightly lit, but the heavily draped tables and curtained booths give a warm ambience (if you're lucky enough to get a table or booth). Otherwise, a seat at the long marble counter affords delightful glimpses into the open kitchen.

House specialties: Seafood. Or anything else you want grilled. Tadich is a place for plain cooking, no fancy sauces or tarted-up presentations. Straightforward and honest Yankee fare.

Other recommendations: Good bar to help you through the long wait for seating.

(Tadich Grill)

Summary & comments: A culinary, cultural treasure. Quite possibly built over the sunken ships of the gold rush. Step into Tadich and partake of the city's rich gastronomic history.

THANH LONG

Vietnamese	★★★	Inexp/Mod	QUALITY
			86

			VALUE
4101 Judah at 46th Avenue, San Francisco			B
(415) 665-1146 Zone 8 Richmond/Avenues			

Reservations: Recommended on
 weekends
When to go: Weeknights
Entree range: $8.25–20.95
Payment: AMEX, DISC, MC, VISA
Service rating: ★★★
Friendliness rating: ★★★★

Parking: Street
Bar: Beer, wine
Wine selection: House
Dress: Casual, informal
Disabled access: Good
Customers: Locals, businesspeople,
 tourists

Dinner: Daily, 4:30–10 p.m.

Setting & atmosphere: Operated by the An family for more than 20 years, Thanh Long has recently renovated its dining room in shades of muted green, with one wall papered with tropical flowers. Not that anyone really notices; the food's the star here. Thanh Long is close to the beach and a neighborhood favorite, so it can get crowded on warm weather weekends.

House specialties: Whole roasted crab with garlic and lemon butter or sweet-and-sour sauce; soft rice-paper shrimp rolls; crab cheese puffs; butterfly prawns in pastry; Saigon beef broiled paper thin around green onions; squid stuffed with pork and mushrooms; lemon-grass chicken; broiled red snapper.

Summary & comments: Thanh Long's soft, green ambience provides a cool backdrop for the vibrant, flame-colored platters of whole crabs emerging from the kitchen. Crab is the main event here, and everyone orders it in one form or another; some say it's the best to be had in a town famous for its crab purveyors. The shrimp rolls are also excellent, as are the grilled pork, beef, and squid. Thanh Long is a good dinner stop after a day at the beach, but make reservations in advance to avoid a wait.

TI COUZ

Crêperie	★★	Inexp	QUALITY
			74

			VALUE
			B

3108 16th Street, San Francisco
  (415) 252-7373   Zone 7 SOMA/Mission

Reservations: Not accepted	**Parking:** Street
When to go: Before or after a movie	**Bar:** Beer, wine
Entree range: $2–6.50	**Wine selection:** Adequate
Payment: Major credit cards	**Dress:** Casual
Service rating: ★★	**Disabled access:** Yes
Friendliness rating: ★★★	**Customers:** Locals, moviegoers

Open: Monday–Friday, 11 a.m.–11 p.m.; Saturday, 10 a.m.–11 p.m.;
Sunday, 10 a.m.–10 p.m.

Setting & atmosphere: Clean, bright, polished blue and white. Simple decor befitting the simple yet good fare. Located across from the Roxie Theater, it's often peopled by a boisterous and friendly mob of film fans and bookstore denizens.

House specialties: Crêpes, crêpes, and more crêpes. Crêpes of every description and possible filling. Sweet crêpes, savory crêpes, plain and fancy crêpes. Fillings include seasonal fruits and butter or chocolate; mushrooms with sauce; seafood with sauce; cheese and crème fraîche.

Other recommendations: A pretty good selection of beers.

Summary & comments: It's quick and good, and the surroundings are undemanding of the discriminating diner. And that's meant in the nicest way. You don't have to put on the dog or your best clothes to have a good feed here.

TOMMY TOY'S

Chinese	★★★½	Mod	QUALITY
			85

			VALUE
			B+

655 Montgomery Street, San Francisco
  (415) 379-4888   Zone 4 Financial District

Reservations: Accepted	**Service rating:** ★★★★
When to go: Anytime	**Friendliness rating:** ★★★
Entree range: $6.95–18.95	**Parking:** Street
Payment: Major credit cards	**Bar:** Full service

(Tommy Toy's)

Wine selection: Good   Disabled access: Yes
Dress: Business   Customers: Locals, tourists

Lunch: Monday–Friday, 11:30 a.m.–3 p.m.
Dinner: Daily, 6–9:30 p.m.

Setting & atmosphere: It looks like you've just walked into the emperor of China's state dining room. Gilt, magnificent draperies, and carved screens and panels flank a huge collection of Chinese antiques and a flower garden.

House specialties: Sometimes called Pacific Rim, a cuisine that brings out natural flavors and presents the dishes in keeping with the magnificent decor: minced squab imperial served in lettuce cups; beef soup with scallops in a coconut shell; Peking duck with buns; Maine lobster dismembered, prepared with spices and reassembled on the plate; rich filet of beef with oyster sauce and forest mushrooms.

Other recommendations: "Chinese with just a soupçon of French." The items described this way on the menu are classical Chinese with influence from traditional French applications: crêpes filled with spicy duck; fried chicken coated with crushed almonds; sautéed lamb with spicy sauce.

Summary & comments: You can get a set piece banquet for two for $70–90 depending on season and selections, or order à la carte. Many people recommend putting yourself in the hands of the capable and friendly staff. They know all the menu items and what goes best with what, what will fill you up, and what will whet your appetite for more. Service is so attentive that you might begin to suspect that the emperor is watching. Tommy Toy and the headwaiter are, indeed, watching, though; they are likely to call on your table to welcome you and see that all is well.

TOMMY'S JOYNT

American	★★	Inexp	QUALITY 75
			VALUE A

1101 Geary Boulevard, San Francisco
   (415) 775-4216   Zone 2 Civic Center

Reservations: Not accepted   Parking: Lot
When to go: Anytime   Bar: Full service
Entree range: $3.50–8   Wine selection: Fair
Payment: Cash   Dress: Casual
Service rating: ★★   Disabled access: Poor
Friendliness rating: ★★   Customers: Everybody

(Tommy's Joynt)

Open: Daily, 10 a.m.–2 a.m.

Setting & atmosphere: Crowded, noisy, crazy place with everything conceivable on the walls and ceiling. If you've ever lost anything, you might well find it here.

House specialties: Hof brau and deli; you can also find what roams on the range: genuine buffalo stew and, as an added treat, buffalo chili. Also famous for their pastrami and corned beef. The Irish come here on St. Patrick's day.

Other recommendations: Cheesecake, innumerable beers.

Entertainment & amenities: The decor.

Summary & comments: This is one of the older places in the city to survive the earthquake of 1906. Don't come here to relax—the patrons and decor are too loud. Come for the beer, buffalo, and boisterous fun.

TOWN'S END RESTAURANT AND BAKERY

New American	★★★	Mod	QUALITY
			84
			VALUE
			B+

2 Townsend Street, Building 4, San Francisco
   (415) 512-1749   Zone 7 SoMa/Mission

Reservations: Recommended	**Parking:** Street, metered during day
When to go: Anytime	**Bar:** Beer, wine
Entree range: Breakfast or brunch,	**Wine selection:** Limited but good
$4.75–8; lunch, $6–11; dinner,	**Dress:** Casual, informal
$6.75–11.50	**Disabled access:** Good
Payment: All major credit cards	**Customers:** Locals, businesspeople,
Service rating: ★★★	tourists
Friendliness rating: ★★★½	

Breakfast: Tuesday–Friday, 7:30–11 a.m.
Brunch: Saturday and Sunday, 8 a.m.–2:30 p.m.
Lunch: Tuesday–Friday, 11:30 a.m.–2:30 p.m.
Dinner: Tuesday–Thursday, 5–9 p.m.; Friday and Saturday, 5–10 p.m.

Setting & atmosphere: Located at the breezy vanguard of the tony South Beach Marina Apartments on the Embarcadero south of the Bay Bridge, Town's End doesn't exactly command a view, but it feels as if it does, with its azure trompe l'oeil mural, glass walls, and the bridge twinkling in the distance to the north. The long, narrow dining area has an airy feel, an open kitchen, and a Zen approach to flower arrangement.

(Town's End Restaurant and Bakery)

House specialties: Baskets of house-baked breads; homemade pastas, and house-smoked red trout and salmon. Niçoise salad; grilled salmon with corn and tomatillo relish; curried lamb stew with pecan-currant couscous; grilled chicken marinated in garlic, lemon, and lime with organic greens, pears, Roquefort, and walnuts. Lemon meringue pie with raspberry sauce; white chocolate Napoleon; raspberry brown butter tartlet.

Other recommendations: Brunch: fritatta scamorza with smoked mozzarella; wild mushrooms, sun-dried tomatoes and fresh herbs; Dungeness crab cakes with red peppers and green onions; Swedish oatmeal pancakes with pears and almonds.

Summary & comments: Town's End is another SoMa venue with moderate prices and a tasty, freshly prepared menu. The fresh breads, pastries, and pastas are outstanding, but the salads and grilled offerings are good, too. Town's End's sauces are its major failing; they frequently do not equal the expertise of the pastas. Still, the unusual waterfront location, with neighboring gardens and park, offers an idyll away from but still within the boundaries of city life. All wines on the small list are offered by the glass. The bakery section, with a few small tables, is open all day for coffee and pastry.

TU LAN			
			QUALITY
Vietnamese	★½	Inexp	**69**
			VALUE
8 Sixth Street, San Francisco			**A**
(415) 626-0927 Zone 7 SoMa/Mission			

Reservations: Not accepted	Parking: Street
When to go: Anytime	Bar: Beer, wine
Entree range: $2.50–8	Wine selection: House
Payment: Cash	Dress: Casual
Service rating: ★★	Disabled access: No
Friendliness rating: ★★	Customers: Locals, businesspeople

Open: Monday–Saturday, 11 a.m.–9 p.m.; Sunday, closed

Setting & atmosphere: A scruffy, old, downtown diner with no friends. Old wooden floors, a long Formica counter, and rickety wooden tables and chairs, none which have four legs of the same length.

House specialties: Some really outstanding Vietnamese fare considering the price. Hot and spicy soup dotted with pineapple bits; pounded shrimp wrapped on sugarcane sticks and broiled; spring rolls; imperial rolls; ginger fish or chicken; pork shish kebab; lemon beef salad.

Other recommendations: Curry potatoes.

Summary & comments: You can't miss Tu Lan. It's the tacky place on the corner with all the newspaper and magazine reviews taped on the window. There is only one reason to come here: to get what is, for the money, one of the best Vietnamese meals you can find outside of Saigon. It's located in what has been for a long time a tough and seedy neighborhood. The local denizens will likely be hanging out along your route, but if you walk by quickly they won't bite.

WASHINGTON SQUARE BAR AND GRILL

Italian	★★★	Mod	QUALITY 88
			VALUE B+

1707 Powell Street, San Francisco
  (415) 982-8123   Zone 6 North Beach

Reservations: Accepted	Bar: Full service
When to go: Anytime	Wine selection: Good
Entree range: $9.50–18.95	Dress: Casual
Payment: Major credit cards	Disabled access: No
Service rating: ★★★	Customers: Eclectic, locals,
Friendliness rating: ★★★½	celebrities
Parking: Validated	

Lunch: Monday–Saturday, noon–3 p.m.; Sunday, 2–4 p.m.
Dinner: Monday–Thursday, 5:30–10:30 p.m.; Friday and Saturday, 5:30–11:30 p.m.; Sunday, 5–10 p.m.

Setting & atmosphere: Wood, brass, and white tablecloths. Nothing too much or too little. A very cordial, clubby atmosphere where anybody can feel like a member. People like their tipple here, and they like their food. They like them both abundantly. Affectionately known by its acronym: the Washbag.

House specialties: If you're lucky, cioppino. It's an Italian-inspired, tomato-based fish stew that takes the diner to unmatched heights of gustatory experience. Food writer Roy Andreis De Groot called it the best recipe in America. It can only be made with the best ingredients and a lot of time, love, and care, so it's only occasionally available. If you're not lucky, console yourself with a big steak; roast chicken with garlic; crab Louis; or a burger.

(Washington Square Bar and Grill)

Summary & comments: It's not quite accurate to call the Washbag an Italian kitchen. It has a number of items on its menu that you would find in eateries all over the country, but it's the Italian muse that inspires the cook. Many local celebs hang out here, but they come just to be, and of course to eat and drink. Political rivals leave their differences at the door (for the most part) and hobnob with local artists and writers and ordinary folk. The front windows look onto Washington Square, where kids are often playing or on their way to or from school. Gives the place a neighborhood feel.

WOODWARD'S GARDENS				
French	★★★	Mod	**QUALITY** 83	
1700 Mission Street, San Francisco			**VALUE** B	
(415) 621-7122　Zone 7　SoMa/Mission				

Reservations: Required	Bar: Beer, wine
When to go: Anytime	Wine selection: Fair
Entree range: $13.50–15.50	Dress: Casual, informal
Payment: Cash only	Disabled access: Limited
Service rating: ★★★	Customers: Locals, businesspeople,
Friendliness rating: ★★★	tourists
Parking: Street	

Dinner: Wednesday–Sunday, seatings at 6, 6:30, 8, and 8:30 p.m.; Monday and Tuesday, closed

Setting & atmosphere: Dwarfed and nearly invisible in its dreadful location under the freeway, Woodward's Gardens has an interior that replicates a miniature Parisian bistro, with lace curtains veiling the traffic outside its L-shaped dining area, open kitchen, banquettes upholstered in a flowery woven print, and velvet counter stools. This is real togetherness; there's infinitesimal space between the tables, and the clamor and smoke from the kitchen can be overpowering.

House specialties: Weekly changing menu with bounteous portions, possibly including garden salad with mango, grapefruit, kumquat, pecans, and goat cheese; warm white beans with grilled mussels, scallops, clams, cured salmon, and Meyer lemon aïoli; braised lamb ravioli with tomatoes, fresh oregano, and feta; roast salmon with garlic mashed potatoes, asparagus, and fennel oil; gumbo of prawns, duck breast, and andouille sausage over basmati rice; roasted chicken with cucumbers, ricotta salatta, tomatoes, olives, arugula, and frisée; New York steak with five-onion marmalade.

(Woodward's Gardens)

Other recommendations: Desserts, which may include strawberry tartlet with tangerine cream; raspberry crème brûlée; chocolate torte.

Summary & comments: There's something slightly heartbreaking about Woodward's Gardens, like watching Cinderella toiling away in a smoking scullery when she deserves to be at the ball. This diamond buried in the asphalt should be popped into a pumpkin coach and whisked to the palace. Chefs Dana Tomassino and Margie Conard bring forth an astonishing array of sprightly, original cookery in magnanimous portions with a minuscule kitchen and bare-bones crew. Beguiling little bistros are popping up in unlikely locations all over San Francisco, but the corner of Mission and Duboce Streets, while not actually dangerous, is visually grim, and the interior charm is all but overcome by the din. One can only hope that Woodward's current rousing success will lead to bigger things and a better location.

YANK SING				
Chinese	★★	Inexp	**QUALITY**	76
427 Battery Street, San Francisco			**VALUE**	B
(415) 362-1640 Zone 4 Financial District				

Reservations: Accepted	Parking: Street
When to go: Lunch	Bar: Beer, wine
Entree range: $4–6	Wine selection: House
Payment: Major credit cards	Dress: Casual
Service rating: ★★½	Disabled access: Yes
Friendliness rating: ★★	Customers: Locals, businesspeople

Open: Monday–Friday, 11 a.m.–3 p.m.; Saturday and Sunday, 10 a.m.–4 p.m.

Setting & atmosphere: A modernly furnished restaurant; white tablecloths and impeccable service make it a step above the usual dim sum house. A class act for simple fare.

House specialties: Dim sum and yet more dim sum constantly issuing forth fresh from the kitchen. Choose barbecued pork buns; shrimp moons; and silver wrapped chicken wheeled out on trollies.

Other recommendations: Small portions of Peking duck. A wide variety of vegetarian dim sum, including pea leaves; sautéed eggplant and mustard greens. Chrysanthemum blossom tea.

(Yank Sing)

Summary & comments: Selections are cooked with less fat than usual. Yuppies love it here; they can stuff themselves without having to spend any extra time at the gym.

YAYA CUISINE

Iraqi/Mesopotamian	★★★½	Mod	QUALITY 88
1220 Ninth Avenue, San Francisco (415) 566-6966 Zone 8 Richmond/Avenues			VALUE B

Reservations: Recommended on weekends	Parking: Street
	Bar: Beer, wine
When to go: Anytime	Wine selection: Fair
Entree range: Lunch, $7–9.50; dinner, $10.50–14	Dress: Casual, informal
	Disabled access: Good
Payment: All major credit cards	Customers: Locals, businesspeople, tourists
Service rating: ★★★½	
Friendliness rating: ★★★½	

Lunch: Tuesday–Friday, 11:30 a.m.–2 p.m.
Dinner: Tuesday–Sunday, 5:30–10 p.m.; Monday, closed

Setting & atmosphere: Sand-washed walls and deepest blue mosaic arches; Persian carpets and Mesopotamian murals; cobalt halogen lamps and a private dining area with woven cushions and floor seating. YaYa is a Middle Eastern restaurant with no small sense of style; located just across Lincoln Way at the Ninth Avenue entrance to Golden Gate Park.

House specialties: Armenian flat bread dipped into olive oil flavored with sesame, thyme, and sumac; grilled Japanese eggplant with coriander cucumber relish; date-filled ravioli with cardamom, cinnamon, and walnuts; grilled quail with hummus and tahini; grilled salmon with saffron sumac sauce; baby chicken stuffed with rice, golden raisins, cashews, and cumin with apricot sauce; eggplant stuffed with lamb, coriander, and pine nuts with tamarind tomato sauce; beef and rice with almonds, onion, raisins, and sun-dried lime.

Other recommendations: Vegetarian specialties: sorrel, spinach, feta, and shiitake mushrooms in phyllo with red bell pepper coulis; grilled vegetables with rice, almonds, and cardamom in phyllo with berry sauce; swiss chard, caramelized onions, tomato, eggplant, and cabbage over rice.

Summary & comments: Yahya Salih, who cooked with Jeremiah Tower at Balboa Café, brings a designer's sensitivities to the use of ingredients traditional to his homeland near Ninevah. Salih is an exuberant, inquisitive host, interested in comments from his guests and recommendations for his changing wine list; he's ready with information regarding the intriguing murals gracing his establishment. His is inventive, unusual cooking with sweet and sour notes, crisp clouds of pastry, and pungent pools of sauces. Portions are enormous and artistically presented. YaYa's is a worthwhile and interesting journey, particularly in a time when the American consciousness is estranged from Iraqi culture.

YUET LEE

Chinese	★★½	Inexp/Mod	QUALITY 78
			VALUE A

1300 Stockton Street, San Francisco
  (415) 982-6020   Zone 1 Chinatown

Reservations: Not accepted	Bar: Beer, wine
When to go: Anytime	Wine selection: House
Entree range: $3.50–16	Dress: Casual
Payment: Cash only	Disabled access: Good
Service rating: ★★★	Customers: Locals, businesspeople,
Friendliness rating: ★★★	tourists
Parking: Street, public pay lots	

Open: Daily, 11–3 a.m.

Setting & atmosphere: Nondescript, clangorous, Formica-tabled seafood and noodle shop on a busy corner in north Chinatown; fresh seafood tanks, chartreuse-framed windows, and an open kitchen with flying cleavers.

House specialties: Fresh seafood specialties: seasonal lobster; pepper and salt prawns; crab with ginger and onion; fresh boiled geoduck or razor clams; steelhead fillet with greens; sautéed fresh and dried squid. Clay pots: salted fish with diced chicken and bean cake; roast pork, bean cake, and shrimp sauce; oyster and roast pork with ginger and onion. Roast squab; braised chicken with abalone; fresh New Zealand mussels with black bean sauce; steamed live rock cod with ham and shredded black mushrooms. Also, a vast assortment of noodles and noodle soups: wontons and dumplings; braised noodles with beef stew; Amoy- or Singapore-style rice sticks.

Other recommendations: Rice soups or plates; roast duck.

Summary & comments: There are basically two kinds of people in the world: those who believe salvation can be found in a bowl of Chinese noodles and those who do not. If you are among the former, you will not care about Yuet Lee's fluorescent lighting, linoleum floors, and slam-bang service. You will forsake soft music and cloth napkins and candlelight. You will know that each vessel of glistening dumplings swimming in broth perfumed by star anise and ginger and scattered with emerald scallions contains all the mysteries of the universe. You will want to taste every item on the menu; stay until closing time at 3 a.m. just to watch the fragrant platters come steaming from the kitchen, yea, verily, to become one with the noodles and the fish.

ZARZUELA

Spanish	★★★½	Mod	QUALITY
			83

	VALUE
	A

2000 Hyde Street, San Francisco
   (415) 346-0800   Zone 5 Marina

Reservations: Recommended	Parking: Street
When to go: Anytime	Bar: Beer, wine
Entree range: Tapas, $2.75–5.25;	Wine selection: Limited but good
entrees, $8.50–13.95	Dress: Casual
Payment: MC, VISA	Disabled access: Good
Service rating: ★★★★	Customers: Locals, tourists,
Friendliness rating: ★★★★	businesspeople

Lunch: Monday–Saturday, 11:30 a.m.–3 p.m.
Dinner: Monday–Saturday, 5:30–10 p.m.; Sunday, closed

Setting & atmosphere: Disarming warmth beckons as piquant aromas of garlic and seafood waft over the sidewalk. Modest appointment inside; tawny walls and tile floors, beamed ceilings and arched windows, hand-painted dishes on the walls, and the music of soft guitars. The nuances of Spanish culture and charm softly beguile.

House specialties: Thirty-eight types of tapas. Mussels or clams with white wine and garlic; grilled shrimp; poached octopus with potatoes and paprika; snails baked on croutons; grilled scallops and chard with red pepper sauce; Spanish sausage with wine; cold roast veal with olives; grilled vegetables; rolled eggplant with goat cheese. Entrees include Zarzuela, a Catalan seafood stew; pork tenderloin in raisin and pine-nut sauce; paella; loin of lamb in thyme and red wine.

Other recommendations: Sangría; gazpacho; romaine salad with roasted garlic; caramel flan; Alicante Muscatel dessert wine.

(Zarzuela)

Summary & comments: Oranges and olives, garlic and olives, red wine and sherries; Spanish cuisine presents a provocative departure from French and Italian in its colorful little tapas plates and the substantial offerings issuing forth from Zarzuela's kitchen. Dishes are as refined as they are close to the earth. Prices are as soothing as the ambience, and a small group of diners can sample a wide assortment of dishes without having to run to the ATM. Darkly sweet and spicy sangría is poured into large goblets. The small selection of sherries is being widened. Zarzuela is a quintessential neighborhood restaurant: low key, low priced, and welcoming.

ZUNI CAFÉ AND GRILL

Italian	★★★	Mod	QUALITY
			89

	VALUE
	B+

1658 Market Street, San Francisco
  (415) 552-2522   Zone 2 Civic Center

Reservations: Accepted	Bar: Full service
When to go: Anytime	Wine selection: Superior
Entree range: $9–28	Dress: Casual, business
Payment: Major credit cards	Disabled access: Yes
Service rating: ★★★	Customers: Locals, businesspeople,
Friendliness rating: ★★★	tourists
Parking: Street	

Open: Daily, 7:30 a.m.–midnight

Setting & atmosphere: Lots of bustle. A happy and exuberant place full of people coming and going, eating and enjoying at all hours of the day and into the night. There's a long copper bar just right for bellying up and holding forth to all who will listen and an excellent view of busy Market Street.

House specialties: The menu changes daily, and only the best stuff is purchased for Zuni. Rib-eye steak (a recurring item); roast chicken; grilled tuna; braised cod; pasta dishes simply but expertly prepared; any soup; vegetable fritters.

Other recommendations: Regularly available hamburgers and pizza.

Summary & comments: This place concentrates on perfecting the simple. The kitchen team—and it is a team—will mine a single ingredient or recipe for the most it can give while still retaining its essential character. An example is the use of Meyer lemons. They are grown almost exclusively in the backyards of East Bay homes and are sweeter and more aromatic than other lemons. The Meyer is to lemons what the truffle is to mushrooms.

Hotel	Room Rating	Zone	Street Address
The Abigail Hotel	★★★	2	246 McAllister St. San Francisco, CA 94102
ANA Hotel San Francisco	★★★★½	7	50 Third St. San Francisco, CA 94103
Andrews Hotel	★★★	3	624 Post St. San Francisco, CA 94109
The Archbishop's Mansion	★★★★½	2	1000 Fulton St. San Francisco, CA 94117
Auberge du Soleil	★★★★★	WC	180 Rutherford Hill Rd. Rutherford, CA 94573
Beresford Arms	★★★½	3	701 Post St. San Francisco, CA 94109
Berkeley Marina Marriott	★★★★	12	200 Marina Blvd. Berkeley, CA 94710
Best Western Canterbury Hotel	★★½	3	750 Sutter St. San Francisco, CA 94109
Best Western Grosvenor Hotel	★★★	SFIA	380 S. Airport Blvd. South San Francisco, CA 94080
Best Western Miyako Inn	★★½	2	1800 Sutter St. San Francisco, CA 94115
Best Western Sonoma Valley Inn	★★★	WC	520 Second St. West Sonoma, CA 95476
Buena Vista Motor Inn	★★½	5	1599 Lombard St. San Francisco, CA 94123
Campton Place Hotel	★★★★½	3	340 Stockton St. San Francisco, CA 94108
Capri Motel	★★	5	2015 Greenwich St. San Francisco, CA 94123
The Carlton	★★★	2	1075 Sutter Street San Francisco, CA 94109
Cartwright Hotel	★★★	3	524 Sutter St. San Francisco, CA 94103
Casa Madrona	★★★★½	9	801 Bridgeway Sausalito, CA 94965
Cedar Gables Inn	★★★★½	WC	486 Coombs St. Napa, CA 94559

Local Phone	Guest Fax	Toll-Free Res. Line	Rack Rate	Discounts Available	No. of Rooms
(415) 861-9728	(415) 861-5848	(800) 243-6510	$$+	Government	61
(415) 974-6400	(415) 543-8268	(800) ANA-HOTEL	$$$ $$$–	AAA, AARP	667
(415) 563-6877	(415) 928-6919	(800) 926-3739	$$+	AAA, Gov., Senior	48
(415) 563-7872	(415) 885-3193	(800) 543-5820	$$$$$+		15
(707) 963-1211	(707) 963-8764	(800) 348-5406	$$$$$ $$$$–		52
(415) 673-2600	(415) 474-0449	(800) 533-6533	$$$+	AAA, AARP	114
(510) 548-7920	(510) 548-7944	(800) 243-0625	$$$+	AAA, AARP	375
(415) 474-6464	(415) 474-5856	(800) 227-4788	$$$+	AAA, AARP	254
(650) 873-3200	(650) 589-3945	(800) 722-7141	$$$–	Government	206
(415) 921-1400	(415) 923-1064	(800) 528-1234	$$+	Senior, Government	125
(707) 938-9200	(707) 938-0935	(800) 334-5784	$$$$–	AAA, AARP	71
(415) 923-9600	(415) 441-4775	(800) 335-4980	$$$–	AAA	50
(415) 781-5555	(415) 955-5536	(800) 235-4300	$$$$ $$$+	AAA	117
(415) 346-4667	(415) 346-3256	na	$$	AAA	46
(415) 673-0242	(415) 673-4904	(800) 227-4496	$$$$–	AAA, AARP	165
(415) 421-2865	(415) 983-6244	(800) 227-3844	$$$+	AAA, AARP	114
(415) 332-0502	(415) 332-2537	(800) 567-9524	$$$+		38
(707) 224-7969	(707) 224-4838	(800) 309-7969	$$$+	AAA, AARP	6

Hotel	On-site Dining	Room Service	Bar	Parking Per Day	Meeting Facilities
The Abigail Hotel	✔			$13	
ANA Hotel San Francisco	✔	✔	✔	$25	✔
Andrews Hotel	✔	✔	✔	$15	
The Archbishop's Mansion				Free	
Auberge du Soleil	✔	✔	✔	Free	✔
Beresford Arms	✔		✔	$15	
Berkeley Marina Marriott	✔	✔	✔	Free	✔
Best Western Canterbury Hotel	✔	✔	✔	$22	✔
Best Western Grosvenor Hotel	✔	✔	✔	Free	
Best Western Miyako Inn	✔		✔	$10	✔
Best Western Sonoma Valley Inn				Free	✔
Buena Vista Motor Inn				Free	
Campton Place Hotel	✔	✔	✔	$25	✔
Capri Motel				Free	
The Carlton	✔			$20	✔
Cartwright Hotel				$20	✔
Casa Madrona	✔	✔		$7	✔
Cedar Gables Inn				Free	✔

Extra Amenities	Business Amenities	Decor	Pool/ Sauna	Exercise Facilities
Free breakfast, massage avail.		European boutique		Privileges
	Dataport, 2-line phone	Art deco	Sauna	✔
Free breakfast, free wine	Dataport	Queen Anne/ Victorian		
Free breakfast, free wine hour	Dataport	French chateau		
Spa services,	Dataport tennis, salon	Modern/ southwestern	Pool, steam room, whirlpool	✔
Free breakfast, satellite TV	Dataport	Victorian		
Marina	Dataport	Contemporary	Pool, sauna, whirlpool	✔
	Dataport	Old English		Privileges
Free breakfast, video games			Pool	
Asian-style guest rooms	Dataport	Asian meets Western		
Free breakfast, wine in room	Dataport	Modern/ Spanish	Pool, whirlpool	✔
	Dataport, 2 line phone	European		Privileges
Wine bar evenings		Early San Francisco Estate		
Free breakfast, wine & tea hour	Dataport	Boutique		Privileges
Free breakfast, spa		Each room different	By reservation	
Breakfast, wine, non-smoking		English country manor		

Hotel	Room Rating	Zone	Street Address
Chateau Hotel	★★½	WC	4195 Solano Ave. Napa, CA 94558
Claremont Resort	★★★★½	12	41 Tunnel Rd. Berkeley, CA 94705
Clarion Bedford Hotel	★★½	3	761 Post St. San Francisco, CA 94109
The Clift Hotel	★★★★	3	495 Geary St. San Francisco, CA 94102
Comfort Inn by the Bay	★★½	5	2775 Van Ness Ave. San Francisco, CA 94109
Commodore International Hotel	★★½	3	825 Sutter St. San Francisco, CA 94109
Cow Hollow Motor Inn and Suites	★★★	5	2190 Lombard St. San Francisco, CA 94123
Crowne Plaza	★★★½	SFIA	600 Airport Blvd. Burlingame, CA 94010
Crowne Plaza Union Square	★★★½	3	480 Sutter St. San Francisco, CA 94108
Days Inn at the Beach	★★½	8	2600 Sloat Blvd. San Francisco, CA 94116
Days Inn Fisherman's Wharf	★★½	5	2358 Lombard St. San Francisco, CA 94123
The Donatello	★★★★	3	501 Post St. San Francisco, CA 94102
Doubletree Hotel San Francisco Airport	★★★½	SFIA	835 Airport Blvd. Burlingame, CA 94010
Dr. Wilkinson's Hot Springs	★★½	WC	1507 Lincoln Ave. Calistoga, CA 94515
Edward II Inn	★★★	5	3155 Scott St. San Francisco, CA 94123
El Bonita Motel	★★★	WC	195 Main St. St. Helena, CA 94574
El Dorado Hotel	★★★★	WC	405 First St. West Sonoma, CA 95476
El Peublo Inn	★★★	WC	896 W. Napa Sonoma, CA 95476

* Some rooms share baths.

Local Phone	Guest Fax	Toll-Free Res. Line	Rack Rate	Discounts Available	No. of Rooms
(707) 253-9300	(707) 253-0906	(800) 253-6272	$$$	AAA, AARP, Government	115
(510) 843-3000	(510) 848-6208	(800) 551-7266	$$$$$–	AAA, AARP	279
(415) 673-6040	(415) 563-6739	(800) 227-5642	$$$$–	AAA, AARP	144
(415) 775-4700	(415) 441-8759	(800) 65-CLIFT	$$$$ $$$–	AAA	326
(415) 928-5000	(415) 441-3390	(800) 228-5150	$$$$$–	AAA, AARP	137
(415) 923-6800	(415) 923-6804	(800) 338-6848	$$+	AAA, Gov., Senior	113
(415) 921-5800	(415) 922-8515	na	$$+		129
(650) 340-8500	(650) 343-1546	(800) 827-0880	$$$$–	AAA, AARP, Government	404
(415) 398-8900	(415) 989-8823	(800) 243-1135	$$$$$+	AAA, AARP, Government	400
(415) 665-9000	(415) 665-5440	(800) 325-2525	$$+	AAA, AARP	33
(415) 922-2010	na	(800) DAYS-INN	$$$–	AAA, AARP	22
(415) 441-7100	(415) 885-8842	(800) 227-3184	$$$$$–	AAA, AARP	93
(650) 344-5500	(650) 340-8851	(800) 222-TREE	$$$$–	AAA, AARP	291
(707) 942-4102	na	na	$$+	AAA, AARP	42
(415) 922-3000	(415) 931-5784	(800) 473-2846	$$+	AAA	28*
(707) 963-3216	(707) 963-8838	(800) 541-3284	$$$$–	AAA, AARP	26
(707) 996-3030	(707) 996-3148	(800) 289-3031	$$$$		26
(707) 996-3651	(707) 935-5988	(800) 900-8844	$$$–	AAA, AARP	38

Hotel	On-site Dining	Room Service	Bar	Parking Per Day	Meeting Facilities
Chateau Hotel	✔	✔	✔	Free	✔
Claremont Resort	✔	✔	✔	$8	✔
Clarion Bedford Hotel	✔	✔	✔	$20	✔
The Clift Hotel	✔	✔	✔	$25	✔
Comfort Inn by the Bay				$12	
Commodore International Hotel	✔		✔	$15	✔
Cow Hollow Motor Inn and Suites	✔			Free	
Crowne Plaza	✔	✔	✔	Free	✔
Crowne Plaza Union Square	✔	✔	✔	$21	✔
Days Inn at the Beach				Free	
Days Inn Fisherman's Wharf				Free	
The Donatello	✔	✔	✔	$23	✔
Doubletree Hotel San Francisco Airport	✔	✔	✔	Free	✔
Dr. Wilkinson's Hot Springs				Free	✔
Edward II Inn			✔	$9	
El Bonita Motel				Free	
El Dorado Hotel	✔		✔	Free	
El Peublo Inn				Free	

Extra Amenities	Business Amenities	Decor	Pool/ Sauna	Exercise Facilities
			Pool, whirlpool	
Full spa, tennis courts		Traditional	Pool, sauna, whirlpool	✔
Free wine evenings	Dataport	Boutique		
	Dataport, fax, 2-line phone	European		✔
Free breakfast				
	Dataport	Neo-deco		Privileges
	Dataport	Traditional	Pool, sauna, whirlpool	✔
Flower shop	Dataport			✔
Free breakfast				
Free breakfast				
Music in lounge, spa services	Dataport	European boutique	Sauna, whirlpool	✔
Free airport shuttle	Dataport			✔
Spa			Pool, whirlpool	
Evening sherry		English country		
		1950's	Whirlpool	
Free breakfast	Dataport	Old world	Pool	
		Early California	Pool, whirlpool	

Hotel	Room Rating	Zone	Street Address
Embassy Suites Hotel	★★★★	10	101 McInnis Pkwy. San Rafael, CA 94903
Embassy Suites SFO	★★★★	SFIA	150 Anza Blvd. Burlingame, CA 94010
Fairmont Hotel	★★★★½	1	950 Mason St. San Francisco, CA 94108
The Fitzgerald	★★	3	620 Post St. San Francisco, CA 94109
Fountaingrove Inn	★★★½	WC	101 Fountaingrove Pkwy. Santa Rosa, CA 95401
Galleria Park Hotel	★★★★	3	191 Sutter St. San Francisco, CA 94104
Grand Hyatt San Francisco	★★★★	3	345 Stockton St. San Francisco, CA 94108
Grant Plaza	★★½	3	465 Grant Ave. San Francisco, CA 94108
Hampton Inn Oakland Airport	★★½	OIA	8465 Enterprise Way Oakland, CA 94621
The Handlery Union Square Hotel	★★★	3	351 Geary St. San Francisco, CA 94102
Harbor Court Hotel	★★★½	7	165 Steuart St. San Francisco, CA 94105
Harvest Inn	★★★½	WC	1 Main St. St. Helena, CA 94574
Holiday Inn Financial District	★★★½	1	750 Kearny St. San Francisco, CA 94108
Holiday Inn Fisherman's Wharf	★★★½	6	1300 Columbus Ave. San Francisco, CA 94133
Holiday Lodge	★★½	2	1901 Van Ness Ave. San Francisco, CA 94109
Hotel Beresford	★★½	3	635 Sutter St. San Francisco, CA 94102
Hotel Bijou	★★★½	3	111 Mason St. San Francisco, CA 94102
Hotel Diva	★★★½	3	440 Geary St. San Francisco, CA 94102

Local Phone	Guest Fax	Toll-Free Res. Line	Rack Rate	Discounts Available	No. of Rooms
(415) 499-9222	(415) 499-9268	(800) EMBASSY	$$$$$–	AAA, AARP, Government	235
(650) 342-4600	(650) 343-8137	(800) EMBASSY	$$$$$+	AAA, Senior	340
(415) 772-5000	(415) 837-0587	(800) 527-4727	$$$$ $$$+	AAA, AARP, Government	596
(415) 775-8100	(415) 775-1278	(800) 334-6835	$$$–	AAA, AARP	47
(707) 578-6101	(707) 544-3126	(800) 822-6101	$$$$–	AAA, AARP	126
(415) 781-3060	(415) 433-4409	(800) 792-9639	$$$ $$$+	AAA, AARP	177
(415) 398-1234	(415) 391-1780	(800) 233-1234	$$$$ $$$+	AAA, Senior	685
(415) 434-3883	(415) 434-3886	(800) 472-6899	$$–	AAA, AARP, Government	72
(510) 632-8900	(510) 632-4713	(800) HAMPTON	$$$–	AAA, AARP, Government	152
(415) 781-7800	(415) 781-0216	(800) 843-4343	$$$$–	AAA, AARP	377
(415) 882-1300	(415) 882-1313	(800) 346-0555	$$$ $$$+	AAA, AARP	131
(707) 963-9463	(707) 963-4402	(800) 950-8466	$$$$$+	AAA, AARP	54
(415) 433-6600	(415) 785-7891	(800) 243-1135	$$$$–	AAA, AARP	566
(415) 771-9000	(415) 771-7006	(800) 243-1135	$$$$$	AAA, AARP, Government	585
(415) 776-4469	(415) 474-7046	(800) 367-8504	$$$–	AAA, Senior, Government	77
(415) 673-9900	(415) 474-0449	(800) 533-6533	$$$–	AAA, AARP	114
(415) 771-1200	(415) 346-3196	(800) 771-1022	$$+	AAA, AARP, Government	65
(415) 885-0200	(415) 346-6613	(800) 553-1900	$$$$–		111

Hotel	On-site Dining	Room Service	Bar	Parking Per Day	Meeting Facilities
Embassy Suites Hotel	✔	✔	✔	Free	✔
Embassy Suites SFO	✔	✔	✔	Free	✔
Fairmont Hotel	✔	✔	✔	$27	✔
The Fitzgerald				$15	
Fountaingrove Inn	✔	✔	✔	Free	✔
Galleria Park Hotel	✔	✔	✔	$20	✔
Grand Hyatt San Francisco	✔	✔	✔	$24	✔
Grant Plaza				$12	
Hampton Inn Oakland Airport				Free	
The Handlery Union Square Hotel	✔	✔	✔	$20	✔
Harbor Court Hotel	✔		✔	$20	
Harvest Inn			✔	Free	✔
Holiday Inn Financial District	✔	✔	✔	$20	✔
Holiday Inn Fisherman's Wharf	✔	✔	✔	$13	✔
Holiday Lodge				Free	✔
Hotel Beresford	✔		✔	$15	
Hotel Bijou				$14	
Hotel Diva	✔	✔		$17	✔

Extra Amenities	Business Amenities	Decor	Pool/ Sauna	Exercise Facilities
Evening reception			Pool, whirlpool	✔
Free breakfast, p.m. reception	Dataport, 2-line phone	Atrium hotel	Pool, sauna, whirlpool	✔
Rich history	Dataport, 2-line phone	Grand hotel	Sauna, whirlpool	✔
Free breakfast	Dataport, 2-line phone	European	Privileges	Privileges
Piano bar, free breakfast	Dataport	Equestrian	Pool	
Wine tasting evenings	Dataports, 2-line phone	Art nouveau		✔
Hair salon	2-line phone	European with Oriental accents		✔
Free b'fast, free airport shuttle			Pool, whirlpool	Privileges
Hair salon, video games	Dataport	Traditional European	Pool, sauna	
Wine tasting, video games	2-line phone, fax machines	1907 landmark building	Pool	Privileges
VCR rental		English Tudor	Pool, whirlpool	
	2-line phone	Chinese	Pool	✔
			Pool	✔
Massage available		Renovated 1950's courtyard hotel	Pool	
Free breakfast, satellite TV	Dataport	Victorian		
B'fast, theater, film tours, casting calls		San Francisco cinema		
Free breakfast, video rental	Dataport	Modern Italian		✔

Hotel	Room Rating	Zone	Street Address
Hotel Durant	★★★	12	2600 Durant Ave. Berkeley, CA 94704
Hotel Juliana	★★★½	3	590 Bush St. San Francisco, CA 94108
Hotel Majestic	★★★★½	2	1500 Sutter St. San Francisco, CA 94109
Hotel Milano	★★★½	7	55 Fifth St. San Francisco, CA 94103
Hotel Monaco	★★★★½	3	501 Geary St. San Francisco, CA 94102
Hotel Nikko San Francisco	★★★★½	3	222 Mason St. San Francisco, CA 94102
Hotel Rex	★★★½	3	562 Sutter St. San Francisco, CA 94102
Hotel St. Helena	★★★	WC	1309 Main St. St. Helena, CA 94574
Hotel Triton	★★★★	3	342 Grant Ave. San Francisco, CA 94108
Hotel Vintage Court	★★★	3	650 Bush St. San Francisco, CA 94108
Howard Johnson Hotel Fish. Wharf	★★★½	6	580 Beach St. San Francisco, CA 94133
The Huntington Hotel	★★★½	1	1075 California St. San Francisco, CA 94108
Hyatt Fisherman's Wharf	★★★★	6	555 North Point St. San Francisco, CA 94133
Hyatt Regency San Francisco	★★★★	4	5 Embarcadero Center San Francisco, CA 94111
Hyatt Regency San Francisco Airport	★★★★	SFIA	1333 Bayshore Hwy. Burlingame, CA 94010
Inn Above the Tide	★★★★½	9	30 El Portal Sausalito, CA 94965
The Inn at Southbridge	★★★★½	WC	1020 Main St. St. Helena, CA 95474
Inn at the Opera	★★★★	2	333 Fulton St. San Francisco, CA 94102

* Some rooms share baths.

Local Phone	Guest Fax	Toll-Free Res. Line	Rack Rate	Discounts Available	No. of Rooms
(510) 845-8981	(510) 486-8336	(800) 2-DURANT	$$$+	AAA, AARP, Government	140
(415) 392-2540	(415) 391-8447	(800) 328-3880	$$$$$–	AAA, AARP	106
(415) 441-1100	(415) 673-7331	(800) 869-8966	$$$$–	AARP	58
(415) 543-8555	(415) 543-5885	(800) 398-7555	$$$$+	AAA	108
(415) 292-0100	(415) 292-0111	(800) 214-4220	$$$ $$$+	AAA, AARP	201
(415) 394-1111	(415) 394-1106	(800) NIKKO-US	$$$$ $$$$–		523
(415) 433-4434	(415) 433-3695	(800) 433-4434	$$$ $$$–	AAA, AARP	94
(707) 963-4388	(707) 963-5402	(888) 478-4355	$$$$$–		18*
(415) 394-0500	(415) 394-0555	(800) 433-6611	$$$$$+	AAA, AARP	140
(415) 392-4666	(415) 433-4065	(800) 654-1100	$$$$+	AAA, AARP	107
(415) 775-3800	(415) 441-7307	(800) 645-9258	$$$+	AAA, AARP, Government	128
(415) 474-5400	(415) 474-6227	(800) 227-4683	$$$ $$$+		139
(415) 563-1234	(415) 749-6122	(800) 233-1234	$$$ $$$–	AAA, Senior	313
(415) 788-1234	(415) 398-2567	(800) 233-1234	$$$$ $$$$–	AAA, Senior	805
(650) 347-1234	(650) 347-5948	(800) 233-1234	$$$$$+	AAA, AARP, Government	793
(415) 332-9535	(415) 332-6714	(800) 893-8433	$$$$$–		28
(707) 967-9400	(707) 967-9486	(800) 520-6800	$$$$ $$$$+	AARP	21
(415) 863-8400	(415) 861-0821	(800) 325-2708	$$$$–	AAA, Gov.	47

Hotel	On-site Dining	Room Service	Bar	Parking Per Day	Meeting Facilities
Hotel Durant	✔	✔	✔	$5	✔
Hotel Juliana				$20	✔
Hotel Majestic	✔	✔	✔	$18	
Hotel Milano	✔	✔	✔	$19	
Hotel Monaco				$20	
Hotel Nikko San Francisco	✔	✔	✔	$27	✔
Hotel Rex	✔	✔	✔	$25	✔
Hotel St. Helena				Free	
Hotel Triton	✔			$20	✔
Hotel Vintage Court	✔		✔	$18	✔
Howard Johnson Hotel Fish. Wharf				$5	
The Huntington Hotel	✔	✔	✔	$20	✔
Hyatt Fisherman's Wharf	✔	✔	✔	$20	✔
Hyatt Regency San Francisco	✔	✔	✔	$25	✔
Hyatt Regency San Francisco Airport	✔	✔	✔	Free	✔
Inn Above the Tide				$8	
The Inn at Southbridge	✔	✔		Free	✔
Inn at the Opera	✔	✔	✔	$19	

Extra Amenities	Business Amenities	Decor	Pool/ Sauna	Exercise Facilities
		Old Europe		Privileges
Wine reception, breakfast available		European boutique		Privileges
Afternoon sherry	Dataport	Victorian boutique	Privileges	Privileges
	Dataport	Comtemporary Italian		✔
		Beaux arts/ modern eclectic		
Hair salon	Dataport, 2-line phone	Contemporary	Pool, whirlpool	✔
Free wine bar	Dataport, 2-line phone	1920's–1940's literary salon		
Free breakfast		Victorian		
Wine reception		Ultra modern		✔
Wine reception		European boutique		Privileges
Breakfast available				
Chauffered limo, sherry		European	Privileges	Privileges
Video games		Wharf/ Victorian	Pool	✔
		Modern atrium high-rise		✔
	Dataport	Modern	Pool, whirlpool	✔
Free breakfast, wine evenings	Dataport	Nautical		Privileges
Full spa, wine bar, free breakfast	Dataport, 2-line phone	European	Pool, steam room, whirlpool	✔
Free breakfast		Classic European		

Hotel	Room Rating	Zone	Street Address
The Inn at Union Square	★★★	3	440 Post St. San Francisco, CA 94102
John Muir Inn	★★★	WC	1998 Trower Ave. Napa, CA 94558
Kensington Park Hotel	★★★½	3	450 Post St. San Francisco, CA 94102
King George Hotel	★★★	3	334 Mason St. San Francisco, CA 94102
Laurel Motor Inn	★★½	8	444 Presidio Ave. San Francisco, CA 94115
Mandarin Oriental	★★★★★	4	222 Sansome St. San Francisco, CA 94104
The Mansions	★★★½	2	2220 Sacramento St. San Francisco, CA 94115
Marina Motel	★★½	5	2576 Lombard San Francisco, CA 94123
Mark Hopkins Inter-Continental	★★★★	3	1 Nob Hill San Francisco, CA 94108
Marriott Fisherman's Wharf	★★★½	6	1250 Columbus Ave. San Francisco, CA 94133
Marriott Hotel Napa Valley	★★★★	WC	3425 Solano Ave. Napa, CA 94558
Maxwell Hotel	★★★	3	386 Geary St. San Francisco, CA 94102
Monticello Inn	★★★½	3	127 Ellis St. San Francisco, CA 94102
Mount View Hotel	★★★½	WC	1457 Lincoln Ave. Calistoga, CA 94515
Napa Valley Lodge	★★★★½	WC	2230 Madison St. Yountville, CA 94599
Napa Valley Railway Inn	★★★½	WC	6503 Washington St. Yountville, CA 94599
Nob Hill Lambourne	★★★★½	3	725 Pine St. San Francisco, CA 94108
Oakland Airport Hilton	★★★½	OIA	1 Hegenberger Rd. Oakland, CA 94621

Local Phone	Guest Fax	Toll-Free Res. Line	Rack Rate	Discounts Available	No. of Rooms
(415) 397-3510	(415) 989-0529	(800) 288-4346	$$$$–	Senior	23
(707) 257-7220	(707) 258-0943	(800) 522-8999	$$$–	AAA, Gov.	59
(415) 788-6400	(415) 399-9484	(800) 553-1900	$$$+		87
(415) 781-5050	(415) 391-6976	(800) 288-6005	$$$$–	AAA, AARP, Government	143
(415) 567-8467	(415) 928-1866	(800) 552-8735	$$$–	AAA, Senior	49
(415) 885-0999	(415) 433-0289	(800) 622-0404	$$$$$ $$$$$–		158
(415) 929-9444	(415) 567-9391	(800) 826-9398	$$$$–	Gov., more	21
(415) 921-9406	(415) 921-0364	(800) 346-6118	$$+		38
(415) 392-3434	(415) 421-3302	(800) 327-0200	$$$$ $$$–		391
(415) 775-7555	(415) 474-2099	(800) 525-0956	$$$$$–	AARP, Gov.	285
(707) 253-7433	(707) 258-1320	(800) 228-9290	$$$$–	AAA, AARP	191
(415) 986-2000	(415) 397-2447	(800) 821-5343	$$$$–	AAA, AARP	152
(415) 392-8800	(415) 398-2650	(800) 669-7777	$$$$–	AAA, AARP	91
(707) 942-6877	(707) 942-6904	(800) 816-6877	$$$$–	AAA	32
(707) 944-2468	(707) 944-9362	(800) 368-2468	$$$$–	AAA, AARP	55
(707) 944-2000	na	na	$$$+	AAA, AARP, Military	10
(415) 433-2287	(415) 433-0975	(800) 274-8466	$$$$+	AAA, AARP	20
(510) 635-5000	(510) 635-0244	(800) HILTONS	$$$$$–	AAA, AARP	363

Hotel	On-site Dining	Room Service	Bar	Parking Per Day	Meeting Facilities
The Inn at Union Square		✔	✔	$22	
John Muir Inn				Free	✔
Kensington Park Hotel	✔			$17	✔
King George Hotel	✔	✔		$17	✔
Laurel Motor Inn				Free	
Mandarin Oriental	✔	✔	✔	$25	✔
The Mansions	✔	✔		$15	✔
Marina Motel				Free	
Mark Hopkins Inter-Continental	✔	✔	✔	$25	✔
Marriott Fisherman's Wharf	✔	✔	✔	$18	✔
Marriott Hotel Napa Valley	✔	✔	✔	Free	✔
Maxwell Hotel	✔	✔	✔	$17	✔
Monticello Inn				$16	
Mount View Hotel				Free	
Napa Valley Lodge				Free	✔
Napa Valley Railway Inn				Free	
Nob Hill Lambourne				$22	
Oakland Airport Hilton	✔	✔	✔	Free	✔

Extra Amenities	Business Amenities	Decor	Pool/ Sauna	Exercise Facilities
Completely non-smoking	Dataport, 2-line phone	Boutique		Privileges
VCR rental	Dataport		Pool, whirlpool	
Free breakfast, afternoon sherry	Dataport	Queen Anne		✔
	Dataport	English boutique	Privileges	Privileges
Free breakfast, kitchenettes				Privileges
Many in-room	Dataport, 2-line phone	Modern		✔
Breakfast, magic show, museum		Magic mansion		
Kitchenettes, breakfast coupons				
Live music in lounge	2-line phone	Grand hotel		✔
		Contemporary	Sauna	✔
Basketball & tennis courts	Dataport	Contemporary	Pool, whirlpool	✔
	Dataport, 2-line phone	Art deco		
Free breakfast, wine tasting	Dataport	Contemporary Colonial		
Free breakfast, full spa		California spa	Whirlpool	
Free breakfast, wine tasting	Dataports	California hacienda	Pool, sauna	✔
No telephones		Rooms in antique train cars		
B'fast, wine bar, kitchenettes, spa	Dataport, fax, 2-line phone	Business & wellness boutique		
	Dataport	Modern	Pool	✔

Hotel	Room Rating	Zone	Street Address
Oakland Marriott City Center	★★★½	13	1001 Broadway Oakland, CA 94607
Pacific Heights Inn	★★	5	1555 Union St. San Francisco, CA 94123
Pacific Motor Inn	★★½	5	2599 Lombard St. San Francisco, CA 94123
The Pan Pacific Hotel	★★★★★	3	500 Post St. San Francisco, CA 94102
Parc Fifty Five	★★★★	3	55 Cyril Magnin St. San Francisco, CA 94102
Park Plaza	★★★	3	1177 Airport Blvd. Burlingame, CA 94010
Park Plaza Hotel	★★★	OIA	150 Hegenberger Rd. Oakland, CA 94621
Petite Auberge	★★★	3	863 Bush St. San Francisco, CA 94108
The Phoenix Inn	★★★	2	601 Eddy St. San Francisco, CA 94109
The Prescott Hotel	★★★★½	3	545 Post St. San Francisco, CA 94102
Queen Anne Hotel	★★★	2	1590 Sutter St. San Francisco, CA 94109
Radisson Miyako Hotel	★★★½	2	1625 Post St. San Francisco, CA 94115
Ramada Limited Golden Gate	★★½	5	1940 Lombard St. San Francisco, CA 94123
Ramada Plaza Fisherman's Wharf	★★★	6	590 Bay St. San Francisco, CA 94133
Ramada San Francisco Airport	★★½	SFIA	1250 Old Bayshore Hwy. Burlingame, CA 94010
Rancho Caymus	★★★★	WC	1140 Rutherford Rd. Rutherford, CA 94573
Red Roof Inn	★★½	SFIA	777 Airport Blvd. Burlingame, CA 94010
Renaissance Stanford Court Hotel	★★★★½	1	905 California St. San Francisco, CA 94108

Local Phone	Guest Fax	Toll-Free Res. Line	Rack Rate	Discounts Available	No. of Rooms
(510) 451-4000	(510) 835-3466	(800) 228-9290	$$$+	AARP, Gov.	483
(415) 776-3310	(415) 776-8176	(800) 523-1801	$$$	AAA, AARP	40
(415) 346-4664	(415) 346-4665	(800) 536-8446	$$$$–		42
(415) 771-8600	(415) 398-0267	(800) 533-6465	$$$$ $$$+	AAA, AARP, Government	330
(415) 392-8000	(415) 403-6602	(800) 650-7272	$$$ $$$–	AAA, AARP	1,008
(650) 342-9200	(650) 342-1655	(800) 411-7275	$$$+	Government	301
(510) 635-5300	(510) 635-9661	(800) 635-5301	$$$+	AAA, Gov.	187
(415) 928-6000	(415) 775-5717	(800) 365-3004	$$$+		26
(415) 776-1380	(415) 885-3109	(800) 248-9466	$$$–	AAA, Gov.	44
(415) 563-0303	(415) 563-6831	(800) 283-7322	$$$$$+	AAA, AARP	165
(415) 441-2828	(415) 775-5212	(800) 227-3970	$$$$–	AAA, AARP, Gov., locals	48
(415) 922-3200	(415) 921-0417	(800) 333-3333	$$$$+	AAA, AARP, Government	200
(415) 775-8116	(415) 775-9937	(800) 2-RAMADA	$$+	AAA, AARP, Government	37
(415) 885-4700	(415) 771-8945	(800) 228-8408	$$$ $$$–	AAA, AARP, Government	232
(650) 347-2381	(650) 348-8838	(800) 2-RAMADA	$$$+	AAA,AARP, Government	146
(707) 963-1777	(707) 963-5387	(800) 845-1777	$$$$+	AAA, AARP	26
(415) 342-7772	(415) 342-2635	(800) THE-ROOF	$$$–	AAA	200
(415) 989-3500	(415) 391-0513	(800) 228-9290	$$$$ $$$+	AAA, AARP, Government	393

Hotel	On-site Dining	Room Service	Bar	Parking Per Day	Meeting Facilities
Oakland Marriott City Center	✔	✔	✔	$11	✔
Pacific Heights Inn				Free	
Pacific Motor Inn				Free	
The Pan Pacific Hotel	✔	✔	✔	$25	✔
Parc Fifty Five	✔	✔	✔	$25	✔
Park Plaza	✔	✔	✔	Free	✔
Park Plaza Hotel	✔	✔	✔	Free	✔
Petite Auberge				$20	
The Phoenix Inn	✔		✔	Free	
The Prescott Hotel	✔	✔	✔	$20	✔
Queen Anne Hotel				$12	✔
Radisson Miyako Hotel	✔	✔	✔	$15	✔
Ramada Limited Golden Gate				Free	
Ramada Plaza Fisherman's Wharf	✔	✔	✔	$10	✔
Ramada San Francisco Airport	✔	✔	✔	Free	✔
Rancho Caymus	✔	✔	✔	Free	
Red Roof Inn				Free	
Renaissance Stanford Court Hotel	✔	✔	✔	$24	✔

Extra Amenities	Business Amenities	Decor	Pool/ Sauna	Exercise Facilities
	Dataport, 2-line phone	Contemporary	Pool, whirlpool	✔
Free breakfast				
Free breakfast				
Limo service	Dataport, fax machine	Modern	Privileges	✔
		Modern	Sauna, steam rm., whirlpool	✔
24-hour airport shuttle, piano bar		Contemporary	Pool, whirlpool	✔
Airport shuttle			Pool, sauna, whirlpool	✔
Free breakfast, afternoon tea		French country inn		
Massage available		Artsy 1950's courtyard hotel	Pool	
Wine reception, Nintendo	Dataport, fax	Early California		
Free breakfast, a.m. limo, sherry		Victorian		Privileges
Japanese rooms available	Dataport, 2-line phone	Contemporary Japanese	Privileges	Privileges
Free breakfast				
Running track				
	Dataport		Pool	✔
Free breakfast		California mission		
			Pool	Privileges
				Privileges

Hotel	Room Rating	Zone	Street Address
The Ritz-Carlton	★★★★★	1	600 Stockton St. San Francisco, CA 94108
San Francisco Airport Marriott	★★★★	SFIA	1800 Old Bayshore Hwy. Burlingame, CA 94010
San Francisco Hilton and Towers	★★★★	3	333 O'Farrell St. San Francisco, CA 94102
San Francisco Marriott	★★★★	7	55 Fourth St. San Francisco, CA 94103
Savoy Hotel	★★★	3	580 Geary St. San Francisco, 94102
Seal Rock Inn	★★½	8	545 Point Lobos Ave. San Francisco, CA 94121
Shannon Court Hotel	★★★½	3	550 Geary St. San Francisco, CA 94102
Sheraton at Fisherman's Wharf	★★★★	6	2500 Mason St. San Francisco, CA 94133
Sheraton Palace Hotel	★★★★½	7	2 New Montgomery St. San Francisco, CA 94105
The Sherman House	★★★★½	5	2160 Green St. San Francisco, CA 94123
Silverado Country Club and Resort	★★★★	WC	1600 Atlas Peak Rd. Napa, CA 94558
Sir Francis Drake Hotel	★★★	3	450 Powell St. San Francisco, CA 94102
Sonoma County Hilton Santa Rosa	★★★★	WC	3555 Round Barn Blvd. Santa Rosa, CA 95403
Sonoma Hotel	★★★½	WC	110 W. Spain St. Sonoma, CA 95476
Sonoma Mission Inn and Spa	★★★½	WC	18140 California Boyes Hot Springs, CA 95476
Stanyan Park Hotel	★★★	8	750 Stanyon San Francisco, CA 94117
Star Motel	★★	5	1727 Lombard St. San Francisco, CA 94123
Super 8 Motel	★★½	5	2440 Lombard St. San Francisco, CA 94123

* Some rooms share baths.

Local Phone	Guest Fax	Toll-Free Res. Line	Rack Rate	Discounts Available	No. of Rooms
(415) 296-7465	(415) 291-0288	(800) 241-3333	$$$$ $$$$+		336
(650) 692-9100	(650) 692-8016	(800) 228-9290	$$$$$–	AAA, AARP, Government	686
(415) 771-1400	(415) 771-6807	(800) 445-8667	$$$$$+	AAA, AARP, Government	1,894
(415) 896-1600	(415) 896-6176	(800) 228-9290	$$$ $$$+	AAA, AARP, Government	1,498
(415) 441-2700	(415) 441-0124	(800) 227-4223	$$$$–	Government	83
(415) 752-8000	(415) 752-6034	na	$$$–		27
(415) 775-5000	(415) 775-9388	(800) 228-8830	$$$–	Government	172
(415) 362-5500	(415) 956-5275	(800) 325-3535	$$$$+	AAA, Gov.	524
(415) 512-1111	(415) 543-0671	(800) 325-3535	$$$$ $$$$	Government	551
(415) 563-3600	(415) 563-1882	(800) 424-5777	$$$$ $$$$+		14
(707) 257-0200	(707) 257-2867	(800) 532-0500	$$$$–	AAA, AARP	281
(415) 392-7755	(415) 391-8719	(800) 227-5480	$$$$+	AAA, AARP	417
(707) 523-7555	(707) 569-5550	(800) HILTONS	$$$+		252
(707) 996-2996	(707) 996-7014	(800) 468-6016	$$$–		17*
(707) 938-9000	(707) 939-2731	(800) 862-4945	$$$ $$$+	AARP	170
(415) 751-1000	(415) 668-5454	na	$$$–		36
(415) 346-8250	(415) 441-4469	(800) 835-8143	$$+	AAA, AARP, Government	52
(415) 922-0244	(415) 922-8887	(800) 800-8000	$$$–	AAA, AARP, Government	32

Hotel	On-site Dining	Room Service	Bar	Parking Per Day	Meeting Facilities
The Ritz-Carlton	✔	✔	✔	$29	✔
San Francisco Airport Marriott	✔	✔	✔	Free	✔
San Francisco Hilton and Towers	✔	✔	✔	$27	✔
San Francisco Marriott	✔	✔	✔	$25	✔
Savoy Hotel	✔			$18	✔
Seal Rock Inn	✔			Free	
Shannon Court Hotel	✔			$18	✔
Sheraton at Fisherman's Wharf	✔	✔	✔	$14	✔
Sheraton Palace Hotel	✔	✔	✔	$22	✔
The Sherman House	✔	✔	✔	$16	
Silverado Country Club and Resort	✔	✔	✔	Free	✔
Sir Francis Drake Hotel	✔	✔	✔	$20	✔
Sonoma County Hilton Santa Rosa	✔	✔	✔	Free	✔
Sonoma Hotel				Free free breakfast	
Sonoma Mission Inn and Spa	✔	✔	✔	Free	✔
Stanyan Park Hotel				$5	
Star Motel				Free	
Super 8 Motel				Free	

Extra Amenities	Business Amenities	Decor	Pool/ Sauna	Exercise Facilities
Massage available	Dataport	Traditional	Pool, sauna, whirlpool	✔
Video games	Dataport	Traditional	Pool, whirlpool	✔
Massage available		Modern	pool, whirlpool	✔
Hydrotherapy		Modern	Pool, whirlpool	✔
Sherry, video games	Dataport, 2-line phone	European boutique		
Kitchenettes			Pool	
Cookies, video games	Dataport	Traditional European		
Video games		Contemporary	Pool	Privileges
	Dataport	Grand hotel	Pool, sauna whirlpool	✔
		Eclectic antique		
2 18-hole golf courses	Dataport	Contemporary	Pool, whirlpool	
		California Colonial		✔
	Dataport	Modern	Pool whirlpool	✔
No phone or TV,		Victorian		
Full spa, tennis courts		Mission	Pool, sauna, steam room	✔
Free breakfast, evening cookies	Dataport	Victorian		
Free breakfast				

Hotel	Room Rating	Zone	Street Address
Town House Motel	★★	5	1650 Lombard St. San Francisco, CA 94123
Travelodge Bel Aire	★★½	5	3201 Steiner San Francisco, CA 94123
Travelodge by the Bay	★★½	5	1450 Lombard St. San Francisco, CA 94123
Travelodge Golden Gate	★★	5	2230 Lombard St. San Francisco, CA 94123
Travelodge on Columbus	★★	6	250 Beach St. San Francisco, CA 94133
Travelodge San Francisco Airport North	★★½	SFIA	326 S. Airport Blvd. South San Francisco, CA 94080
Union Street Inn	★★★½	5	2229 Union St. San Francisco, CA 94123
Vagabond Inn Airport	★★½	SFIA	1640 Bayshore Hwy. Burlingame, CA 94010
Villa Florence	★★★	3	225 Powell St. San Francisco, CA 94102
Villa Inn	★★½	10	1600 Lincoln Ave. San Rafael, CA 94901
Vintage Inn	★★★★½	WC	6541 Washington St. Yountville, CA 94599
Vintner's Inn	★★★★	WC	4350 Barnes Rd. Santa Rosa, CA 95403
Warwick Regis Hotel	★★★★	3	490 Geary St. San Francisco, CA 94102
Waterfront Plaza Hotel	★★★½	13	10 Washington St. Oakland, CA 94607
Westin Hotel San Francisco Airport	★★★★	SFIA	1 Old Bayshore Hwy. Millbrae, CA 94030
The Westin St. Francis	★★★★½	3	335 Powell St. San Francisco, CA 94102
White Swan Inn	★★★★½	3	845 Bush St. San Francisco, CA 94108
Wyndham Garden Hotel	★★★★	10	1010 Northgate Dr. San Rafael, CA 94903

Local Phone	Guest Fax	Toll-Free Res. Line	Rack Rate	Discounts Available	No. of Rooms
(415) 885-5163	(415) 771-9889	(800) 255-1516	$$+	AARP	24
(415) 921-5162	(415) 921-3602	(800) 578-7878	$$+	AAA, AARP, Government	32
(415) 673-0691	(415) 673-3232	(800) 578-7878	$$$–	AAA, AARP, Government	73
(415) 922-3900	(415) 921-4795	(800) 578-7878	$$+	Government	29
(415) 392-6700	(415) 986-7853	(800) 578-7878	$$$–	AAA, AARP, Government	250
(650) 583-9600	(650) 873-9392	(800) 578-7878	$$+	Government	197
(415) 346-0424	(415) 922-8046	na	$$$$$–		6
(415) 692-4040	(415) 692-5314	(800) 522-1555	$$+	AAA, AARP, Government	89
(415) 397-7700	(415) 397-1006	(800) 553-4411	$$$$$+	AAA, AARP	183
(415) 456-4975	(415) 456-1520	(888) 845-5246	$$+	AAA, AARP, Government	60
(707) 944-1112	(707) 944-1617	(800) 351-1133	$$$ $$$–	AAA, AARP	192
(707) 575-7350	(707) 575-1426	(800) 421-2584	$$$$+	AARP	44
(415) 928-7900	(415) 441-8788	(800) 827-3447	$$$$–	AAA, AARP, Government	80
(510) 836-3800	(510) 832-5695	(800) 729-3638	$$$$+	AAA, AARP	144
(650) 692-3500	(650) 872-8111	(800) 228-3000	$$$$+	AAA, Gov., Senior	393
(415) 397-7000	(415) 774-0124	(800) 228-3000	$$$$ $$$	AAA, AARP, Government	1,192
(415) 775-1755	(415) 775-5717	(800) 999-9570	$$$$+		26
(415) 479-8800	(415) 479-2342	(800) 996-3426	$$$–	Government	224

Hotel	On-site Dining	Room Service	Bar	Parking Per Day	Meeting Facilities
Town House Motel				Free	
Travelodge Bel Aire				Free	
Travelodge by the Bay				$5	
Travelodge Golden Gate				Free	
Travelodge on Columbus				$6	
Travelodge San Francisco Airport North	✔			Free	
Union Street Inn				$12	
Vagabond Inn Airport				Free	
Villa Florence	✔		✔	$20	✔
Villa Inn	✔			Free	
Vintage Inn			✔	Free	✔
Vintner's Inn	✔	✔	✔	Free	✔
Warwick Regis Hotel	✔	✔	✔	$23	✔
Waterfront Plaza Hotel	✔	✔	✔	$10	✔
Westin Hotel San Francisco Airport	✔	✔	✔	$5	✔
The Westin St. Francis	✔	✔	✔	$26	✔
White Swan Inn				$20	✔
Wyndham Garden Hotel	✔	✔	✔	Free	✔

Extra Amenities	Business Amenities	Decor	Pool/ Sauna	Exercise Facilities
Free breakfast				
Bay views			Pool	
Airport shuttle			Pool	
Full breakfast, wine hour		Victorian		
Free breakfast				
Wine evenings, Nintendo	Dataport	Italian Renaissance		
Free breakfast			Pool, whirlpool	
Wine in room, spa, free breakfast		California	Pool, whirlpool	Privileges
Free breakfast	Dataport, 2-line phone	European	Whirlpool	
Free breakfast		European boutique		
Ferry to San Francisco	Dataport	Nautical	Pool, sauna	✔
Airport shuttle, jogging trail	Dataport		Pool, whirlpool	✔
	Dataport, cordless phone	Grand Hotel		✔
Free breakfast	Dataport	English garden inn		
	Dataport, 2-line phone	Contemporary	Pool, whirlpool	✔

INDEX

1998 *Unofficial Guide* Reader Survey

If you would like to express your opinion about San Francisco or this guidebook, complete the following survey and mail it to:

> 1998 *Unofficial Guide* Reader Survey
> PO Box 43059
> Birmingham AL 35243

Inclusive dates of your visit: _____

Members of your party: | Person 1 | Person 2 | Person 3 | Person 4 | Person 5

Gender: M F   M F   M F   M F   M F

Age: _____

How many times have you been to San Francisco? _____
On your most recent trip, where did you stay? _____

Concerning your accommodations, on a scale of 100 as best and 0 as worst, how would you rate:

The quality of your room? _____ The value of your room? _____
The quietness of your room? _____ Check-in/check-out efficiency? _____
Shuttle service to the parks? _____ Swimming pool facilities? _____

Did you rent a car? _____ From whom? _____

Concerning your rental car, on a scale of 100 as best and 0 as worst, how would you rate:

Pick-up processing efficiency? _____ Return processing efficiency? _____
Condition of the car? _____ Cleanliness of the car? _____
Airport shuttle efficiency? _____

Concerning your dining experiences:

Including fast-food, estimate your meals in restaurants per day? _____
Approximately how much did your party spend on meals per day? _____
Favorite restaurants in San Francisco: _____

_____

Did you buy this guide before leaving? □ while on your trip? □

How did you hear about this guide? (check all that apply)

Loaned or recommended by a friend □ Radio or TV □
Newspaper or magazine □ Bookstore salesperson □
Just picked it out on my own □ Library □
Internet □

What other guidebooks did you use on this trip? _____

_____

_____

_____

On a scale of 100 as best and 0 as worst, how would you rate them?

_____

_____

_____

Using the same scale, how would you rate *The Unofficial Guide(s)?*

_____

Are *Unofficial Guides* readily available at bookstores in your area? _____

Have you used other *Unofficial Guides?* _____

Which one(s)? _____

_____

_____

_____

_____

_____

Comments about your San Francisco trip or *The Unofficial Guide(s):*

_____

_____

_____

_____

_____

_____

_____

_____

_____

_____

_____

_____

_____

_____